EDUCATION IN A COMPETITIVE AND GLOBALIZING WORLD

TEACHER TRAINING

PERSPECTIVES, IMPLEMENTATION AND CHALLENGES

EDUCATION IN A COMPETITIVE AND GLOBALIZING WORLD

Additional books and e-books in this series can be found
on Nova's website under the Series tab.

EDUCATION IN A COMPETITIVE AND GLOBALIZING WORLD

TEACHER TRAINING

PERSPECTIVES, IMPLEMENTATION AND CHALLENGES

PAULA E. MCDERMOTT
EDITOR

Copyright © 2019 by Nova Science Publishers, Inc.

All rights reserved. No part of this book may be reproduced, stored in a retrieval system or transmitted in any form or by any means: electronic, electrostatic, magnetic, tape, mechanical photocopying, recording or otherwise without the written permission of the Publisher.

We have partnered with Copyright Clearance Center to make it easy for you to obtain permissions to reuse content from this publication. Simply navigate to this publication's page on Nova's website and locate the "Get Permission" button below the title description. This button is linked directly to the title's permission page on copyright.com. Alternatively, you can visit copyright.com and search by title, ISBN, or ISSN.

For further questions about using the service on copyright.com, please contact:
Copyright Clearance Center
Phone: +1-(978) 750-8400   Fax: +1-(978) 750-4470   E-mail: info@copyright.com.

NOTICE TO THE READER

The Publisher has taken reasonable care in the preparation of this book, but makes no expressed or implied warranty of any kind and assumes no responsibility for any errors or omissions. No liability is assumed for incidental or consequential damages in connection with or arising out of information contained in this book. The Publisher shall not be liable for any special, consequential, or exemplary damages resulting, in whole or in part, from the readers' use of, or reliance upon, this material. Any parts of this book based on government reports are so indicated and copyright is claimed for those parts to the extent applicable to compilations of such works.

Independent verification should be sought for any data, advice or recommendations contained in this book. In addition, no responsibility is assumed by the Publisher for any injury and/or damage to persons or property arising from any methods, products, instructions, ideas or otherwise contained in this publication.

This publication is designed to provide accurate and authoritative information with regard to the subject matter covered herein. It is sold with the clear understanding that the Publisher is not engaged in rendering legal or any other professional services. If legal or any other expert assistance is required, the services of a competent person should be sought. FROM A DECLARATION OF PARTICIPANTS JOINTLY ADOPTED BY A COMMITTEE OF THE AMERICAN BAR ASSOCIATION AND A COMMITTEE OF PUBLISHERS.

Additional color graphics may be available in the e-book version of this book.

Library of Congress Cataloging-in-Publication Data

ISBN: 978-1-53615-633-1

Published by Nova Science Publishers, Inc. † New York

CONTENTS

Preface		**vii**
Chapter 1	Core Practices and Competencies in Teaching and Teacher Education: Definitions, Implementation, Challenges and Implications *Clodie Tal*	**1**
Chapter 2	Emergent Curriculum in the Early Childhood Education (ECE) Preparation Program in Israel- Students' Perspectives: Transformations and Challenges *Iris Levy, Michaella Kadury-Slezak, Sigal Tish, Sivan Shatil Carmon and Clodie Tal*	**75**
Chapter 3	Emergent Curriculum in the Preparation of ECE Student Teachers in Israel: Rationale, Approaches, Implementations and Children's Perspectives *Sigal Tish, Iris Levy, Michaella Kadury-Slezak, Sivan Shatil Carmon and Clodie Tal*	**101**

Chapter 4	Simulation Based on Role-Playing as a Significant Learning Tool for Training Student Teachers to Communicate with Parents	**143**
	Einat Sequerra-Ater, Orly Licht Weinish, Iris Levy, Alona Peleg, Naomi Perchik, Yael Shlesinger, Pninat Tal and Clodie Tal	
Chapter 5	The Difficulties and Challenges Facing Interns of Early Childhood Education Regarding Their Working Relations with Parents: Towards a New Model of Family-School Relations in a Culturally Diverse and Changing Society	**183**
	Alona Peleg, Naomi Perchik, Orly Licht Weinish, Iris Levy, Einat Sequerra Ater, Yael Shlesinger, Pninat Tal and Clodie Tal	
Chapter 6	"Walking on Eggshells" – Patterns of Change and Development in Student Teachers' Perceptions of Parent-Teacher Relationships in the Framework of a 'Working with Parents' Course	**239**
	Iris Levy, Yael Shlesinger, Alona Peleg, Einat Sequerra Ater, Naomi Perchik, Orly Licht Weinish, Pninat Tal and Clodie Tal	
Chapter 7	The Use of Repeated Narrative Writing by Teachers to Cope with Emotionally Loaded Incidents in the Classroom	**271**
	Clodie Tal, Aalya Kabia, Margalit Cohen and Rivka Hillel Lavian	
Chapter 8	Practical Arguments: Making Teachers' Reflections on Teaching Practices Visible	**305**
	Lea Lund	
Index		**347**
Related Nova Publications		**369**

PREFACE

Teacher Training: Perspectives, Implementation and Challenges opens with a study seeking to show how students and practicing teachers develop core professional competencies in the early childhood education department of the Levinsky College of Education in Israel. These competencies, such as relationships with children and adults, mediated learning experiences, and classroom management, are embedded in a small number of core practices that have been systematically and intensively incorporated into early childhood education studies, and sometimes integrated by the graduates into their daily practice.

The authors also introduce a study examining the transformation in perceptions of learning-teaching processes of third-year student teachers in in the early childhood education program in Levinsky College of Education while implementing emergent curriculum. A multiple case studies (Yin, 2014) approach is used to reveal learning processes and challenges.

Following this the authors show how student teachers at Levinsky College of Education implement an emergent curriculum approach (Jones, 2012; Rinaldi, 2001; Yu-le, 2004) and create bridges to diverse children's homes, focusing on the rationale of the program, its implementation and children's perspectives.

To train student teachers in the early childhood education program, a simulation center was created in which videotaped simulations are used as a critical learning tool. Subsequent analysis of the students' documented thoughts and feelings about the simulations revealed key insights regarding communication with parents.

This compilation goes on to examine how early childhood education interns interpreted communication with parents and what difficulties and challenges preoccupied them, because the identification of these central difficulties and challenges may contribute significantly to the knowledge of family-school relations in a diverse and changing society.

A subsequent study provides a careful investigation into the effects of a course on the parent-teacher relationship on student teachers' and interns' perceptions. This study was derived from the goal of preparing student teachers to cope effectively with relationships with parents.

The authors examined teachers' use of repeated narrative writing based on Pennebaker's (Pennebaker &Evans, 2014) expressive writing method to cope with emotionally loaded incidents related to behavior problems in the preschool classroom. An analysis of sixty narratives written by two Israeli teachers revealed that repeated narrative writing helped them overcome helplessness, regulate negative feelings towards people and situations involved in the incidents, and develop self-efficacy and self-determination, as well as improve their classroom management competencies.

The final chapter demonstrates an approach to elicit teachers' ideas about teaching and their reflections on teaching practices. The approach of constructing a practical argument allows for analysis of teachers' thinking in combination with their actions in the classroom.

Chapter 1 - This chapter seeks to show how students and practicing teachers develop core professional competencies in the Early Childhood Education (ECE) Department of Levinsky College of Education. These competencies, such as relationships with children and adults, mediated learning experiences, and classroom management, are embedded in a small number of core practices that have been systematically and intensively incorporated into ECE studies, and sometimes integrated by the graduates into their daily practice. The core practices employed by the Levinsky

College programs and presented in this chapter are work in small heterogeneous groups, particularly Repeated Picture Book Reading, enactment of an emergent curriculum, coping with individual children's social and behavioral problems, and work with parents. The chapter is based on the argument advanced by Ball and Forzani that practice is the core of professional preparation, and that the authors need to define and enact essential practices that novice teachers must develop in the process of becoming professionals. What are the essential, "core" competencies needed by teachers to perform these practices? Enhancing these should be one of the main focuses of professional development. Hence, this chapter presents definitions of core practices and competencies in education, and the distinctions among them, based on Ball and Forzani, Forzani, Grossman, Schneider Kavanagh, and Pupik Dean, Grossman, Hammerness, and McDonald, McDonald, Kazemi, and Schneider Kavanagh. Tal argues that the acquisition of these competencies develops throughout the teachers' professional life. Evidence is provided of improved and enacted core competencies among both student teachers and experienced teachers enrolled in graduate studies in ECE, such as mediated interactions in small groups, communication with children's parents, and forming good relationships with children, particularly challenging ones. Staff work is also perceived to be a core practice in teacher education and one that currently lacks systematic attention in the Levinsky College preparation program. The primary challenges encountered in enhancing a teacher's core competencies and practices relate to the difficulty of gaining broad acceptance of their centrality to teacher education, assuring their sustainability in the program, and having the time and effort required to accomplish this agenda. What was found to be helpful in teacher training is acceptance by the staff of the "core competency" agenda, commitment to it, relevant staff experience, and close collaboration among college staff members. The implications of acknowledging the indispensability of core competencies and practices to the professional development of teachers are presented.

Chapter 2 - In this chapter the authors introduce a study which aims to show a transformation in perceptions of learning-teaching processes of third-year student teachers in ECE program in Levinsky College of Education in Israel while implementing emergent curriculum. A multiple case studies approach is used to reveal the learning processes, difficulties, and changes in student teachers' perceptions with regards to the teaching-learning processes of young children. Results indicate that student teachers' transformation from a traditional-positivist to a social constructivist perception occurred as a sustained process, which included emotional, cognitive and epistemological components. In many cases the transformation process included intermediate stages from 'teaching as preaching' by mainly listening to the child without intervening to mediation using thoughtful guidance in the discourse. Results also suggest that student teachers' documentation, self-reflection, and support from the pedagogical and discipline mentors give them an opportunity to revisit and to interpret their learning process as part of the transformation process.

This study provides deeper understandings of student teachers' transformation process from a traditional to a constructivist approach. It also characterizes the difficulties that occur during this process. If the education system aims to adapt the 21st century learning skills then in it necessary to understand student teachers' difficulties and to construct a solid cognitive and emotional support system which support them during this meaningful process.

Chapter 3 - In this chapter the authors show how student teachers at the ECE (Early Childhood Education) department at Levinsky College of Education implement an emergent curriculum approach and create bridges to diverse children's homes. The authors will focus on the rationale of the program, its implementation and on children's perspectives. The early childhood teacher preparation program at Levinsky College of Education in Israel is based on a social constructivist perception of learning, and the student teachers do their fieldwork in public preschools as part of their training. The tasks included in the fieldwork include documentation of their practice with the children and reflection upon it in order to understand and improve their teaching practices. Within the ECE programme at Levinsky College, from the first year of study, all student teachers in their field placement are expected to lead small heterogeneous groups of children. In the third year, they are expected to engage the children in their groups in learning by employing an emergent curriculum approach. This emergent learning process of students and children is being supported by the Levinsky preparation program by two types of support systems: Face to face and Distance support. Both types of support include pedagogic as well as emotional approaches and are being provided by pedagogic and disciplinary mentors. This chapter is based on a qualitative inquiry of ten case studies of emergent curriculum programmes that were guided and documented by student teachers (in their third year of study in the ECE program at Levinsky College). The methodology used multiple case studies based on the mosaic approach. The findings revealed that using emergent curriculum principles, student teachers enabled and enhanced open discourse within small heterogeneous groups that promoted the expression of individual children's cultures. The student teachers succeeded in building collaboration among children based on the knowledge they gained of each others' families and culture. Empowering individual children was found helpful in promoting children's multicultural orientation in small heterogeneous groups.

Chapter 4 - Working with parents is one of the central challenges for teachers and should be addressed in teacher training. To that end, the Early Childhood Education program at Levinsky College of Education created a course in 2017-18 entitled "Working with Parents in the 21st Century." To train student teachers in this area, a simulation center was created in which videotaped simulations are used as a critical learning tool. In this study, 143 student teachers doing their internship in the fourth year of their program were divided into 5 classes, each class containing 5 groups. The students were asked to describe in writing a significant episode from their practicum related to work with the parents. Each group chose one episode, analyzed the different perspectives of the participants (teacher, parent, child), and role-played this episode in the simulation center. A reflective dialogue was then conducted within each class among the simulation participants, their classmates, and the lecturer regarding the teacher's performance. Students then re-enacted the simulation in which they applied the insights gained from the feedback. Subsequent analysis of the students' documented thoughts and feelings about the simulations revealed five main insights regarding communication with parents: (1) Teachers should use a personal, emotional approach and be respectful, understanding, and empathic to parents; (2) In discussing a child's difficulties, teachers should be empowering of parents and foster a sense of security and trust; (3) Dialogue with parents should be well planned and founded on facts gathered and carefully studied in advance; (4) During the dialogue, teachers should acknowledge the varied perspectives of the participants in the discourse; and (5) When necessary, teachers should be assertive with parents. The findings indicate that simulations based on role-playing in teacher education programs are an essential tool for training student teachers about how to plan and practice communication skills with parents, allowing them to experience a wide range of emotionally charged encounters within a safe environment. Simulations based on role-playing significantly contribute to improved student communication skills, self-awareness, and self-efficacy in their encounters with parents.

Chapter 5 - Communication with parents is a central aspect of the teaching profession. Significant changes in the social reality have reshaped home-school relations, requiring of the educational staff a deep understanding of the complexity of relations with parents in a diverse and changing reality, as well as effective skills and strategies for communicating with parents. However, most teacher education institutions fail to help their students develop the knowledge and tools necessary for working with parents in the 21st century. The present study examines how interns of early childhood education interpreted communication with parents, and what difficulties and challenges faced them. The study participants comprised 143 student teachers in the course "Working with Parents in the 21st Century," in the Early Childhood Education program at Levinsky College of Education. All of the student teachers, in their fourth and final year of studies, worked as practicing teachers at kindergartens and elementary schools, as part of their internship. They were asked to write accounts of social episodes describing a significant and authentic event with regard to relations with parents. The accounts of the social episodes were analyzed and coded according to qualitative, content

Preface xiii

analysis, combined with several quantitative analyses. Data analysis yielded six central themes regarding family-school relations, as reflected in the interns' social episodes. Most of the themes described difficulties, conflicts and challenges in working with parents, centering around two complementary core dimensions: (1) building trust and cultivating close and caring relations with parents; (2) setting boundaries and limits for parental behavior. In addition, two super-categories were revealed to be significant axes, expressed in all of the central themes: (1) cultural diversity and power relations between parents and teachers; (2) the parent's gender: the involvement of fathers and the communication patterns of the educational staff with fathers, in comparison to mothers. These findings show that in a reality of cultural diversity and rapid changes, the meaning and expressions of *cultivating close and caring relations with parents* have changed, requiring of the teachers new skills and strategies, such as cultural sensitivity, skills for working with minority group parents and strengthening the educational partnership with fathers. Indeed, these findings indicate an urgent need for a new model for working with parents in a culturally diverse and changing society. This model is based on a shift from "*the child at the center*" approach, to that of "*the child and his family at the center.*" Hence, school-family relations should be reformulated so that the educational system is committed to the child *and* to the parents, while redefining minority families as *families coping with special needs.* Teacher education institutions may use these insights and recommendations, as expressed in the principles of the suggested new model, to provide their student teachers with vital and relevant knowledge, skills and strategies for leading a change in school-family relations, and developing a significant partnership with parents in the 21st century.

Chapter 6 - The importance of parent-teacher relationship has been widely recognized by parents, teachers, early childhood specialists, and special education professionals. It is also acknowledged that this relationship can be perceived as challenging by both sides. Research has shown that parents' involvement in school benefits not only the child, but also the parents and teachers. Research further indicates that student teachers express concerns about parents' involvement and their ability to form a positive and effective partnership with them. Therefore, student teachers must continue to develop and expand their skills in order to maximize effective communication with parents. This study provides a careful investigation into the effects of a course on the parent-teacher relationship on student teachers' and interns' perceptions. The rationale for this study was derived out of the wish to prepare student teachers to cope effectively with the complex relationship with parents. The general approach, which the rationale of this study is based on, sees parents as partners and emphasizes fostering qualifications and strategies for working with parents during training. Psychological, sociological, and organizational perspectives were integrated throughout the course when discussing the teacher's role.

Chapter 7 - The study presented in this chapter examined teachers' use of repeated narrative writing (RNW) based on Pennebaker's expressive writing method to cope with emotionally loaded incidents related to behavior problems in the preschool classroom. An analysis of sixty narratives written by two Israeli teachers revealed that RNW helped them overcome helplessness, regulate negative feelings towards people and situations involved in the incidents, and develop self-efficacy and self-determination, as well as improve their classroom management competencies. This was manifested in more proactive leadership, a more ecological perspective of the class, improved self-regulation skills, and improved relations with children, staff, and parents.

Chapter 8 - This chapter demonstrates an approach to elicit and make visible teachers' ideas of teaching and their reflections on teaching practices. Inspired by the approach of constructing a *practical argument* allows for analysis of teachers' thinking in combination with their actions in the classroom. This approach can be viewed as a vehicle for encouraging the growth of teacher development. Drawing on an eight-month study of teachers – novice and experienced teachers – in Adult Education in Denmark this novel research approach provides the opportunity to support, stimulate and nurture critical reflection by the teachers of their own practices.

In: Teacher Training
Editor: Paula E. McDermott

ISBN: 978-1-53615-633-1
© 2019 Nova Science Publishers, Inc.

Chapter 1

CORE PRACTICES AND COMPETENCIES IN TEACHING AND TEACHER EDUCATION: DEFINITIONS, IMPLEMENTATION, CHALLENGES AND IMPLICATIONS

*Clodie Tal**
Levinsky College of Education, Tel Aviv, Israel

ABSTRACT

This chapter seeks to show how students and practicing teachers develop core professional competencies in the Early Childhood Education (ECE) Department of Levinsky College of Education. These competencies, such as relationships with children and adults, mediated learning experiences, and classroom management, are embedded in a small number of core practices that have been systematically and intensively incorporated into ECE studies, and sometimes integrated by the graduates into their daily practice. The core practices employed by the Levinsky College programs and presented in this chapter are work in small heterogeneous groups, particularly Repeated Picture Book Reading,

---

* Corresponding Author's Email: clodietal@gmail.com.

enactment of an emergent curriculum, coping with individual children's social and behavioral problems, and work with parents. The chapter is based on the argument advanced by Ball and Forzani (2009) that practice is the core of professional preparation, and that we need to define and enact essential practices that novice teachers must develop in the process of becoming professionals (Forzani, 2017). What are the essential, "core" competencies needed by teachers to perform these practices? Enhancing these should be one of the main focuses of professional development. Hence, this chapter presents definitions of core practices and competencies in education, and the distinctions among them, based on Ball and Forzani (2009), Forzani (2017), Grossman, Schneider Kavanagh, and Pupik Dean (2018), Grossman, Hammerness, and McDonald (2009), McDonald, Kazemi, and Schneider Kavanagh (2013). Tal (2016, 2018a) argues that the acquisition of these competencies develops throughout the teachers' professional life. Evidence is provided of improved and enacted core competencies among both student teachers and experienced teachers enrolled in graduate studies in ECE, such as mediated interactions in small groups, communication with children's parents, and forming good relationships with children, particularly challenging ones. Staff work is also perceived to be a core practice in teacher education and one that currently lacks systematic attention in the Levinsky College preparation program. The primary challenges encountered in enhancing a teacher's core competencies and practices relate to the difficulty of gaining broad acceptance of their centrality to teacher education, assuring their sustainability in the program, and having the time and effort required to accomplish this agenda. What was found to be helpful in teacher training is acceptance by the staff of the "core competency" agenda, commitment to it, relevant staff experience, and close collaboration among college staff members. The implications of acknowledging the indispensability of core competencies and practices to the professional development of teachers are presented.

Keywords: teacher preparation, teacher education, teacher training, core practices, core competencies, professional development

INTRODUCTION

The teacher preparation and graduate ECE programs at Levinsky College are inspired by van Manen's (1994) life-world approach and Malaguzzi's (1993) philosophy of education, which are based on relationships, communication networks, and the interaction of children in small groups. Both these approaches foster a holistic understanding of teaching situations and particularly emphasize, for example, that cognitive and social aspects are inseparable. For van Manen (1994), who helped lay the foundation of a phenomenological methodology and a relational pedagogy, "a pedagogue is an educator…who feels addressed by children, who understands children in a caring way, and who has a personal commitment and interest in children's education and their growth toward mature adulthood" (p. 138). By being "addressed by children,' van Manen means becoming acquainted with and understanding them, being interested in who they are as persons, in what they think, in what interests and bothers them. This task is particularly challenging in preschools attended by children and teachers with diverse social, economic, and cultural backgrounds.

At Levinsky College, students are encouraged to adopt a capacity-based, rather than deficit-based, orientation in their work with young children, their families, and their communities (Oyler, 2011). They are encouraged to develop growth mindsets as opposed to fixed mindsets related to human ability. A growth mindset is a belief that children's and adults' abilities as well as their success in academics and social relationships can be improved through learning, effort, training, and practice (Dweck, 2012). In addition, student teachers are encouraged to develop social sensitivity and adhere to equity pedagogy by applying teaching and classroom management approaches that are inclusive of the full range of human diversity (Oyler, 2011). Therefore, students are encouraged to become acquainted with the individual children, to form and teach small, heterogeneous groups that include children experiencing various difficulties, and to build good pedagogical relationships with them. Good relationships based on caring and acceptance, clear behavior boundaries, and the absence of efforts to manipulatively control thoughts and feelings (Barber, Stolz, & Olsen 2005) are defined as the foundation of "good" pedagogy.

Good relationships need to be formed with all children – behaviorally challenging children from socially marginalized groups, shy, withdrawn, and "regular" children alike. Furthermore, good sustained, egalitarian relationships with peers are a crucial ingredient of a child's well-being (Bukowski, Laursen, & Rubin, 2018; Hartup, 1992; Rubin, Bukowski, & Parker, 2006) and it is the teacher's role to enable these relationships or, in cases where they do not evolve on their own, to intervene to facilitate them.

However, good relationships with young children are a necessary but insufficient condition to ensure the fostering of learning in children. Constructing the conditions for inquiry and a child's active engagement in learning are other goals of the Levinsky College preparation program. We thus adopted a social cognitive approach to learning inspired by the Malaguzzi and Reggio Emilia early education system. Both our preparation of education students and the lenses through which we interpret their practice and texts (transcripts and reflections) are grounded in Vygotsky's (1978) emphasis on the social nature of knowledge construction. "Knowledge building, whether conducted alone or in the company of others, is thus always situated in a discourse in which each individual contribution both responds to what has preceded and anticipates a further response" (Wells, 2000, p. 16). These perceptions led to adoption of an emergent curriculum approach in our preparation program – one that perceives teachers and children as co-constructors of curriculum and knowledge, and that perceives the mediation of learning encounters as a core competency in education and teacher training.

Student teachers in the Early Childhood Education (ECE) program at Levinsky College typically spend one full day a week in fieldwork and two full days in coursework. An effort is made to align the fieldwork with the coursework to the extent possible. In addition, the four-year-track student teachers have a full week of intensive fieldwork each semester. Repeated picture-book reading in small heterogeneous groups is part of the experience of ECE students at Levinsky throughout their years of preparation.

TEACHING PRACTICES AND COMPETENCIES DEFINED

Teaching is about helping students of any age learn stuff (Ball & Forzani, 2009; Grossman et al., 2009). Feiman-Nemser and Buchman (1985) define teaching as helping people learn "worthwhile things." Cohen (2011) points to the deliberate nature of teaching, to the intentionality and effort involved in being simultaneously tuned to the perspective of the student, which may be different from that of the teacher, and to the knowledge teachers possess and are willing to mediate to the student. The intentional, deliberate nature of teaching makes teaching a profession. The teaching profession involves, therefore, developing practices and competencies that help enact the teachers' knowledge, that go into making the "work of teaching" (Ball & Forzani, 2009).

Practices are defined as the core tasks that teachers must execute to help students learn (Ball & Forzani, 2009, p. 497). Moreover, in adopting a moral approach to teaching, the goal of teachers is to ensure the learning "of every student in their charge" (Ball & Forzani, 2009; Lampert & Graziani, 2009). Core practices are likely to address the basic repertoire of tasks needed to enact teaching, that is, to help students learn. Collective agreement about the core practices of teaching would strengthen the field of teacher education (Feiman-Nemser, 2017, p. xxi.). Tal (2018a) adds that good practices address the whole child in the context of the group. Furthermore, good practices are those that enable the formation and maintenance of good relationships with and among children, as well as transformative learning in all children. Tal (2012) adheres to the claim of Wells (2008) that "both in childhood and in adulthood, most learning occurs in naturally-occurring, task-related apprenticeships, in which with guidance and social and emotional feedback, novices appropriate the values as well as the knowledgeable skills that enable them to persevere and achieve success" (p. 247).

Competencies are abilities acquired through training, experience, and reflection. Competencies focus on what and how the teachers must do to engage in the essential elements of teaching. The question is, what competencies are needed by teachers in order to implement effectively the core practices that will lead pupils to learning and well-being? Although there is no universally accepted definition of competency-based education (Gervais, 2016), we attempt at Levinsky College to define a few core abilities that are essential for carrying out the "job" of teaching. We permanently keep in mind that teachers need to develop abilities to help children learn while being responsible for entire classes populated by numerous children from diverse backgrounds. The core competencies in education defined by us are relationships, mediated learning experiences, and classroom management as a meta-competency.

Feiman-Nemser (2017) points to the approaches taken by different programs to the issue of enacting knowledge. The enactment of a teacher's knowledge based on core practices is currently performed by teacher-education programs using either a clinical or a practice-centered approach. Whereas clinical teacher education emphasizes guided practice integrated with coursework, practice-centered teacher education tends to design "approximations of practice in teacher education" (Grossman, 2018; Schutz, Danielson, & Cohen, in press) – simplified tasks that are analyzed and rehearsed as part of university courses with coaching and feedback before trying to enact them under real classroom conditions (Feiman-Nemser, 2017, p. xxi). At Levinsky College, we adopted a clinical approach to preparing student teachers, as core practices are performed in the students' field placements (in preschools and in first and second grades of elementary schools). The three core tasks performed by student teachers in their field placements are (1) work in small, heterogeneous groups, particularly using Repeated Picture Book Reading; (2) enactment of an emergent curriculum; and (3) planning and implementation of individualized action plans to cope with a specific child's social and behavioral problems. Also discussed in this chapter, and more fully addressed elsewhere in this book, is the practice of talking with the children's parents initiated either by the parent or the teacher, based on simulations and analysis of social episodes performed at the college, as student teachers are not allowed in their field placements to communicate directly with children's parents.

Core Practices in Teacher Education:
ECE Programs at Levinsky College of Education

This chapter presents the most central practices that student teachers are required to undertake throughout their preparation at Levinsky College – practices that the college considers indispensable in early childhood education. Therefore, they are defined as core assignments to be practiced by student teachers in the preparation program. Four such practices are discussed below: small group work and the Repeated Picture Book Reading associated with it, enactment of an emergent curriculum, planning and implementing strategies for coping with social and behavioral problems, and work with children's parents.

Small Group Work (SGW) and Repeated Picture
Book Reading (RPBR)

The small, heterogeneous learning group has been defined at Levinsky College as a core practice and, specifically, as an organizational procedure that enables learning and the formation and maintenance of relationships. In the ECE program, the learning groups are guided more often than operating autonomously. Thus, the students are required to engage in guiding small, heterogeneous groups from the very first semester of their fieldwork and subsequently each semester throughout their three years of fieldwork. Graduate students are likely to integrate small group work in teaching and research projects that they initiate.

Small group work is often referred to as cooperative or collaborative learning to emphasize the relationships and interdependence in groups that lead to the attainment of joint goals. Cooperative learning is more than just working in a group. It is organized and managed group activity in which students interact cooperatively in small groups to achieve academic as well as affective and social goals (Jacobs, Lee, & Ng, 1997). Small groups based on cooperative learning have been recognized for some four decades (Gillies & Cunnington, 2014) as a classroom method of organization and instruction that enhances learning with understanding – in schools (Bertucci, Coute, Johnson, & Johnson, 2010; Johnson & Johnson, 2002;

Shachar & Sharan, 1994; Slavin, 2013) and preschools (Malaguzzi, 1993; Sum Kim & Farr Darling, 2009; Sills, Rose, & Emerson, 2016). It was shown to benefit thinking and academic achievement in various areas of study such as mathematics, science (Lazarowitz & Karsenty, 1994; Lou, Abrami & d'Apollonia, 2001), literacy, and language (Slavin, 1996; Whitehurst et al., 1988). Participation in small, cooperative groups was also found beneficial to relationships among children and to learning strategies for conflict resolution (Emmer & Stough, 2001; Malaguzzi, 1993).

A small, heterogeneous group in terms of the participants' abilities, gender, race, and age is important, based on the assumption that discourse with peers is a central source of learning in groups. Indeed, Vygotsky asserts that collaboration with more capable children under the guidance of adults is likely to improve a child's problem-solving skill (1978). Heterogeneous rather than ability grouping is performed at Levinsky College as we believe, based on extensive evidence, that ability groups at any age are detrimental, especially for low achievers. Ability groupings bear a message of fixed ability rather than a growth mindset (Dweck, 2012) and are also likely to stigmatize those placed in the low achievement groups. Many studies found that it does not matter for high achievers whether they are placed in mixed or high achieving groups, whereas for low achievers, placement in mixed rather than homogeneous, low-achieving groups was associated with improved achievement (Alexander, 2010).

In spite of the proven contribution of SGW to children's learning and well-being, this method has not been systematically integrated into school work, particularly not in ECE. Quite often this method has been misused (Wasik, 2008). Tal (2018b) found in research focused on ECE teachers' perceptions and implementation of SGW that a majority of those studied did not use the group work to deepen learning in selected areas, but rather the groups were formed ad hoc or used by teachers to enhance individual children's skills by drilling. Thus, even when implemented, SGW was not based on discourse among children for constructing new knowledge or the development of thinking. Furthermore, in Tal's study (2018b), teachers expressed disbelief at the beginning of a graduate level course at the feasibility of performing SGW in ECE. At the end of the course, most participants reported that they now understood the importance of SGW and the possibility of implementing it. These findings underscore the need to regard small, heterogeneous group work as a foundational practice in teacher preparation and professional development.

From the very first year of studies in ECE, student teachers at Levinsky College are required to perform SGW each day of their fieldwork. Specifically, in their first year of studies, student teachers are required to perform RPBR, to teach songs and rhymes, and to perform artwork in the same heterogeneous groups. In the second year, they are expected to initially perform RPBR with each new group they are guiding and subsequently to perform with the same group a learning unit focused on number concepts, plants and animals in their nearby surroundings, and holidays. And in the third year, they are expected to plan and implement SGW throughout the academic year as part of a learning project based on emergent curriculum, which includes guidance of at least two small groups.

Repeated Picture Book Reading (RPBR) in Small Heterogeneous Groups

RPBR in small, heterogeneous groups as a core practice performed on a regular basis throughout the schoolyear in early childhood teacher education for preschools, and grades 1 and 2 in elementary schools was introduced by Tal (2004) to provide the conditions required for the children's development of language, literacy, and social competencies. A heterogeneous, small-group learning format for read-alouds is grounded in a social-cultural approach to learning (Vygotsky, 1978), which emphasizes both the social nature of knowledge construction and the importance of discourse – oral language as a carrier and improver of thought.

RPBR in the preparation program at Levinsky College was designed to enable student-teachers to become proficient and reflective small-group leaders who engage children from diverse backgrounds and competencies in vivid discussions focused on picture-book meaning-making. We instruct students, based on our understanding of the socio-cultural approach to learning, to listen to the children's interpretations of the text, encourage discourse among children about the meanings they attribute to the text, and to encourage children to offer explanations for their propositions and make inferences related to other texts and/or their life based on their interpretations of the text. As student teachers come from diverse backgrounds, we assume that their own interpretations of the procedure may vary.

RPBR during the first and second year of preparation is performed in conjunction with a Multiple Literacies course and two Children's Literature courses; thereafter, each student is advised to perform repeated storytelling every semester as a basic, routine task under the supervision of their college mentors, as a way to become acquainted with the children and learn about their dispositions and interests, as well as their language, cognitive, and socio-emotional competencies. The basic instruction of these assignments is to offer the children a few high-quality books that the students deem suitable, have the group choose one of them, read it out loud to the children multiple times, and finally think of a way to present the book to the whole class. Students are required to write an analytical review of the picture book to be read to the children. They are also required to transcribe the discourse of two of the readings, analyze them, and ponder ways to improve the guidance and mediation of the reading group based on these reflections.

As part of the RPBR procedure, we expect that, starting from their second academic year, students will include in their RPBR groups a child experiencing some type of difficulty. We do not use the more common term "special needs children," as we abstain from attributing fixed labels to children. We claim that in each class at any time, there may be children experiencing one or more difficulties (such as social withdrawal or dominance; language delay; difficulty regulating their attention or behavior; Hebrew as a second language; birth of a sibling; a health problem in the family; etc.). The task of the teacher and the student is to identify these children and find ways to make them feel safe and comfortable enough to actively cope with whatever learning or life hardships they are grappling with. We believe that through sustained, meaningful participation in intimate learning groups, these children are better able to develop language and social competencies and at the same time more likely to be perceived by their peers as equals and not as "special needs" children.

In the following section, I describe how student teachers perform and perceive the contribution of SGW in general and RPBR in particular, and difficulties encountered by them in its implementation. I then examine the contribution of RPBR in small heterogeneous groups to creating an inclusive atmosphere in groups and preschools. This is followed by the reflections of an experienced teacher who, as a graduate student, implemented RPBR as an empowerment tool for children in second grade.

Student Teachers' and Teachers' Performance and Perceptions of RPBR

To ascertain scalable and sustainable implementation of RPBR, we conducted a three-year study at Levinsky College between 2010 and 2013 that focused on the extent of implementation of RPBR and student understanding of this core practice. At the end of each semester of the three academic years, all ECE students participated in an anonymous survey about the frequency of using RPBR and of including in the group a child with difficulties. Students were also invited to add comments related to their understanding of RPBR and any factors that, in their opinion, helped or hindered its implementation. Of approximately 250 students who completed questionnaires each semester, most reported that they regularly performed RPBR: implementation in 2013 was 96% for students in the four-year academic program and 100% for those in the two-year, teacher certification program. Inclusion of children experiencing language, social, behavioral, or other difficulties in these groups was high (around 77%) from the second year of studies. Content analysis of responses to the open questions led to defining reflective categories that revealed students' conceptual understanding of RPBR. Overall, 40% of the responses in 2013 were categorized as showing either a "narrow" or "extended" understanding compared with 37% in 2012 and 20% in 2011 (Tal & Segal-

Drori, 2015). We concluded that understanding of the procedure improved and that more effort is needed to enable more students to understand the rationale of the task they are required to perform.

The following comments were added to the questionnaires by student teachers in the three-year follow-up study.

One student noted that it takes experience and reflection to learn how to guide RPBR groups so that children can fully benefit from the discourse:

At the beginning it was hard for me to use open questions that are needed to encourage discourse among children and to limit my involvement...Step by step, I learned how to ask open questions, to guide the discourse without interfering. Every new reading helped. I discovered a whole new world reflected in the book chosen for the Repeated Picture Book Reading. [third year student]

Eventually students become aware of the importance and contribution of RPBR to a child's vocabulary, literary understanding inquiry, and social skills, and to the cohesion of the group.

Repeated Picture Book Reading allows children to investigate and ponder stories in a qualitative manner so that they can understand the story from diverse perspectives. [This way of reading books] exposes children to a different way to read books than they are used to. [third year student]

The fact that there were several readings helped children understand the plot and enabled them to pay attention once again to features or details in the book. The reading aloud and the discourse help children appropriate new words, and get acquainted with and close to other children following these encounters. [third year student]

I think the read-alouds contributed to the cohesion of the [small] group and enabled quiet, less dominant children to express themselves and find focuses of interest in the reading of the book.

A second-year student underscored the importance of the discourse with and among the children as an essential element of RPBR. She indicated that more practice, reflection, and mentoring are needed to help student teachers depart from the focus on technical aspects of reading so they can be more attentive to the participation and discourse of the children in groups:

It is crucial to teach student teachers that the most important feature of RPBR is the discourse among the children and not the reading itself. That's because we, the student teachers, tend to deal with the reading itself more than with the developing discussion among the children [about the book]. My direct involvement in the encounters with preschool children led to my understanding that we must find ways to encourage children to participate and talk. [second year student]

Contribution of RPBR to the Development of an Inclusive Educational Culture

Evidence is brought in this section about how a third-year student teacher's intentional effort to help a boy moderate his behavior and be accepted by his peers enabled him to become a full participant in the group and had an impact on other children's inclusive attitude toward peers. Her attitude and work are representative of the educational approach we have been trying to promote. What follows is an excerpt from the students' field journal:

Yossi had a hard time controlling his behavior during the group encounters; he interfered, did not allow other children to complete sentences, and did not allow the discourse to unfold. The other children became restless and occasionally asked me to remove Yossi from the group. I did not give up. I felt that this was an important issue that needs to be addressed. To change things. The children learned slowly to respect and accept Yossi and not be intimidated by him. They became familiar with his strengths and the nice things he did, and they became closer to him. At the beginning they became closer to Yossi in the group. They responded to what he said and, with my help, included him in their discussion; they also responded positively to his initiatives and helped him, and some of these initiatives were presented to the whole class. He seems to be flourishing and enjoying more self-confidence; he initiated games and interactions with children he was not used to talking with; he became relaxed...He fully participated in the group discussions and revealed his opinions; shared knowledge in the group. [30 July 2017]

This student chose *Tom the Blue Cat* by Yafa Talarek in her read-alouds to help preschool children become more accepting of their peers. Her attitudes, moderation of the group discussions, and choice of the book apparently had an impact on the children's discourse. The following short excerpt from the small group discussion following repeated reading of the book demonstrates this:

> Shlomi: One should not make fun of other people who are different.
> Chen: Even if Tom didn't play the guitar and become successful, they should love him, because friends need to accept each other.

I would go with "Something else" home and the way to its home is long. I would climb the stairs by its side and put him to bed and I would sleep by its side. In the morning, we would eat breakfast together. I would play with it, with its toys, build a pool and then we would both swim and enjoy together (8.5.2013)

Above is a short narrative of a girl who participated in a series of read-alouds of picture books dealing with attitudes toward diversity. The figure shows the text dictated by the girl to the third-year student who guided the small group. The book that was read in this case was *Something Else* by Kathryn Cave (translated into Hebrew).

The text dictated by the girl shows empathy and even a full plan of how to give Something Else the feeling that it is not alone and has a companion. The read-aloud in a small group of a book that deals with inclusion enabled the girl to formulate her ideas and share them with her peers.

Integrating RPBR in the Classes Managed by Teachers Enrolled in Graduate ECE Studies at Levinsky College

Students enrolled in the ECE graduate program are typically practicing teachers in preschool, kindergarten, or first- and second-grade. One central requirement in the program is a research project focused on a pedagogical issue that is of concern or interest to them. Each year, a few graduate students who are practicing teachers perform action research aimed at integrating RPBR in their classes. The problems they encounter in integrating this core practice depend on their personal working contexts. Sometimes other staff do not cooperate, and sometimes students cite as problematic the lack of routine in the class or organizational issues, such as finding a suitable time and place for the read-alouds.

In the case described here, the graduate student identified as a difficulty the lack of participation of some children in the second-grade class she was teaching. She attributed the lack of participation to the large number of children in her class. For this reason, she initiated a research project to help her integrate small group work and RPBR as part of the "individualized hours" to which she is entitled in her school. During individualized hours, teachers are expected to work with individuals or small groups (up to five children) who need more attention either because they fell behind or because they are more advanced compared to the other children in the class. In many schools, however, individualized hours are not used optimally, but frequently employed by the school management to solve urgent problems, such as replacing sick teachers.

Yifat, the graduate student, thought that integrating RPBR into her individualized hours for the empowerment of children would be a good way to take advantage of these hours. She planned to work with heterogeneous groups including children who typically did not participate in the class and other children who display good social skills. Her goal was to support the children's language and social competencies through discourse and intimate encounters with peers in the small heterogeneous group.

One of the children in the groups she led was Idan, whose behavior and learning throughout the school year improved dramatically. The teacher attributed this improvement to Idan's participation in the small group:

> Throughout first grade and the beginning of second grade, Idan displayed aggressive behavior and experienced multiple [social and academic] difficulties. Throughout this period, I spoke regularly with his parents and with the help of the school counsellor, I developed individual intervention plans that did not work. I felt discouraged as Idan's functioning did not improve despite my efforts. I felt that I had failed. These feelings were accompanied by anger and even disgust toward Idan. Despite my skepticism that Idan's participation in a small group would help, I decided to include him in the Repeated Picture Book Reading group and to give him another chance. Throughout the Findings chapter I pointed to the beginnings of change in Idan's social and academic functioning due to his participation in the RPBR group. Idan's improvement because of his participation in the small group can be explained by Bronfenbrenner's ecological theory, which states that the child is in the center of concentric circles so that the more external circles impact the closer circles to the child. It can be stated that the small group and my mediation had an impact on Idan.

Being involved in an action research project, the teacher assumed a reflective attitude toward the change undergone by Idan.

> And indeed, looking back at the data, I conclude that I also changed through my interactions with Idan in the group. Feelings of despair, discouragement, and disgust toward Idan that I had experienced in first grade and the beginning of second grade have been replaced following

implementation of the action research by feelings of understanding, reciprocity, caring, and appreciation toward Idan and the process he went through. I think that the change that I myself underwent, which enabled me to look at Idan in a different way, to perceive him from a different perspective, enabled me to change the discourse with him in a way that helped him foster a sense of self-efficacy and build his capacity to cope with challenging tasks. This strengthens Carlebach's claim that every child needs a grown-up to believe in him. I can therefore draw the conclusion that the RPBR small group can be a teacher's essential tool that can help teachers build and improve deep relationships with pupils and thereby change the course of their [the children's] development.

Yifat testifies that her implementation of RPBR accompanied by action research led her to change her attitude and feelings toward a boy initially displaying aggressive behavior. Furthermore, the boy's participation in two cycles of RPBR (she allowed Idan to participate in two groups, thus enabling Idan to guide the new children in a second group as to how the RPBR group works) proved more beneficial than the individual intervention plans she had created. Yifat seems to have come to appreciate the power of intensive interactions in groups as a source of children's learning. It appears that the discourse in the group would have been impossible without a change in her perception of the boy and his potential to change. It also appears that the improvement in Idan's behavior and learning in the small group fueled his teacher's belief in his ability to change and helped her support him through occasional crises that he experienced throughout the school year.

To sum up, I presented above the rationale for including SGW and RPBR as core practices in ECE. I underscored that in ECE, the small groups are guided by the teacher, enabling her to support children's language, thinking, and social learning based on dialogic discourse. I also showed how SGW and RPBR have been employed and assessed at Levinsky College. The intensity and regularity of their implementation throughout the preparation years, and encouragement of inclusion in graduate research projects, reflect our view of these as core ECE practices. The effectiveness of their implementation depends, however, on the teacher's ability to form relationships with the children based on caring, and allowing the free expression of thoughts within limits set on behavior to guide interactions that lead to learning (mediated learning experiences) and to manage classroom competencies addressed in this chapter.

Planning and Implementing Projects Based on an Emergent Curriculum

One of the core practices in which students at Levinsky College are engaged is planning and implementing projects based on an emergent curriculum approach. The emergent curriculum approach is opposed to the traditional pre-determined curriculum, but is based rather on a socio-constructivist approach to learning. Emergent curriculum is not to be perceived, however, as lacking the need to plan the school work. Emergent curriculum in the context of early childhood education was formulated by Jones and Nimmo (1994), but these ideas can be also found in Doll's (1993) presentation of a post-modern perspective on curriculum, and this view of curricula can be traced back to Dewey's philosophy of education (1938).

An emergent curriculum is responsive to the children's interests and questions. Thus, teachers adopting this approach need to observe children attentively and listen to what they have to say in order to become familiar with their interests. Emergent as opposed to traditional, "pre-determined" curriculum is achieved through reflected-upon experience rather than the memorization of items of conclusive knowledge or the mechanical drilling of skills (Yu-le 2004). Following observation, teachers typically engage children in discourse leading to definitions of problems, questions, or goals of learning. All this takes into account the children's previous knowledge as well as their misconceptions. Children are partners in defining ways to conduct an inquiry and collect data related to the problem defined. Children supported by peers and the teacher systematically collect data as planned and analyze and interpret it. Inquiry and the interpretation of data often lead to new questions and problems to be studied. Thus, the emergent curriculum involves cycles of inquiry. The whole process requires documentation by both children and teachers. Documentation is used for both the inquiry itself and for the assessment of children's learning. Quite often, children guided by teachers and parents use technology in their inquiry (such as taking photos, looking up information online, using regular or electronic magnifiers).

At Levinsky College, enactment of an emergent curriculum approach by student teachers is based on their previous experience in guiding dialogic discourse in small groups, particularly those based on RPBR. However, the expectation in the third year is that students will start the process from observing the children's interest rather than relying on a book as a starting point. The main challenges include coping with uncertainty and sharing control of the learning process with the children. Employment of an emergent curriculum thus helps student teachers develop and implement a growth mindset – a belief in the human ability to change and improve through effort and experience. Students learn to value teacher's and children's mistakes and to learn from them. Dweck (2012) and Boaler (2013) emphasize the importance of learning from students' mistakes and teaching children to learn from their own mistakes as a basic practice in education.

Enactment of an emergent curriculum takes place during fieldwork and needs to be coordinated with the field mentor. The college mentors guide the entire process in the context of fieldwork inquiry (pedagogy) courses, field visits, and the use of digital blogs. The students' learning is also supported by counselors who are experts in the subject area so that discourse in small groups is based on solid knowledge.

Students are expected to engage in at least two small heterogeneous groups in cycles of inquiry and to share with the whole class their learning processes and newly acquired knowledge. In addition, at the end of each academic year, all students present their projects in an academic conference attended by students and staff of the ECE department. Sessions in this conference are chaired and monitored by students.

Another chapter in this volume written by college mentors at Levinsky College is devoted to implementation of an emergent curriculum and it documents the transformations undergone by students implementing it.

One example of this kind of project, implemented by third-year student Ly Gvili and supervised by Sigal Tish, focused on children's perceptions of families. Ly did her fieldwork in a Tel Aviv preschool whose children came from diverse families – single parents, divorced, same gender parents, and also some traditional heterosexual families. Four pairs of twins also attended this preschool. The student decided to address this diversity and chose to engage the small groups she guided in the reading of picture books related to families. She began by reading *Vanilla on his Forehead, Strawberries on his Nose* by Meir Shalev and Aviel Basil. The book recounts a close relationship between a little girl Hadas and her unconventional grandfather. The grandfather promises not to eat her ice cream while she takes a bath as required by her mom, but he can't abstain and tastes the ice cream, leaving traces on his forehead and nose. Then this unconventional grandfather promises not to play with Hadas' toys, but again he fails to keep his promise. The children in the group were genuinely shocked by the grandfather's tendency not to keep promises. They thought that they had to teach the grandfather to behave properly, but they did not know how to do that as the grandfather was a character in a book. Their discussion led them to the idea of making a film based on the book, presenting a plot similar to the one in the book, but changing the conduct of the grandfather. The grandfather in their film would keep his promises to his granddaughter. Ly listened to their idea and decided to help them produce the film. At first, they had doubts about their ability to do it. The whole process took a few months as the children had to prepare a script, cast the roles, rehearse, shoot the footage, and so on. The group turned into a supportive, cohesive team.

Maor, a shy boy, shared his gratitude for the social support he received from his peers:

> I was ashamed knowing that people will watch me [on the screen], but I got over it and the experience made me feel things. A feeling of…friendship. The film-making was embarrassing at first, but after I started to rehearse until the day we did the shooting, my friends helped me overcome my anxiety, so that I forgot I had stage fright. It was fun to

make the film. If we hadn't made it, I would still have this stage fright. You are kind and good friends.

Maor is fully aware that experiencing social support is helpful in overcoming anxieties. He seems happy that with the help of his peers he did not give in to his anxieties.

Finally, after producing the film that was shared with the whole class, children went back to discussing the book and talked about what makes a family. A short excerpt from their discussion:

> Mor: The mother decides who she wants to marry, they get married and they have a baby.
> Ori: Moran, she doesn't have to get married at all. To give birth you don't have to get married. Father can leave, and he will always be the father.
> Maor: Sometimes there's no mother in the family. I, for example, live with Father Dor and Father Ami. We are a family – isn't that right, Ly?

An authentic discourse related to what makes a group of people a family was made possible by the discussion of books and the film production, which was a successful team assignment that helped the children feel secure and belonging, allowing them to inquire about what makes a family and to what extent their own families are genuine families. The discourse is based on children's own experiences with their families and the families of peers. The inquiry emerged from their experiences and was not imposed on them. Furthermore, the student showed a great deal of cultural sensitivity and social responsiveness by guiding the process in a way that gave full voice to all the children. Implementation of the emergent curriculum supported each child's development in a different way, depending on the specific child's initial position.

Ly, the student, espoused her understanding of the project as an existing journey. Below is her exposition of her summary:

- Teacher's mediation in ECE must be based on listening, enabling each boy and girl to express him/herself, and support learning based on dialogue among peers.
- Meaningful learning processes emerge in small fixed groups that enable children to share views and express themselves. The discourse in the small group provides a secure base and exposes children to situations and views that are new to them. In this way they get acquainted with the world around them and learn to accept diversity as part of the world. They also learn about things shared by them and their peers. [June 2018]

Interventions for Coping with Social and Behavioral Problems

Young children's social and behavioral problems are prevalent; if untreated, they correlate with future adjustment and learning difficulties (Jennings & Greenberg, 2009; Kramer, Caldarella, Christensen, & Shaltzer, 2010) and are a matter of concern to parents and teachers (Campbell, 2002). Children's behavioral problems are a source of stress for teachers (Hemmeter, Santos, & Ostrovsky, 2008). Interventions focused on teaching, encouraging, and supporting prosocial behavior were shown to bring improved academic achievement and contribute to a significant reduction in young children's behavioral problems (Belsky, 2013; Durlak, Weissberg, Dymnicki, Taylor, & Schellinger, 2011; Kaiser & Rasminsky, 2017). Social and behavioral difficulties include both externalizing problems (non-compliance, disruption, aggression, bullying) and internalizing problems (withdrawal from social interactions, submission) (Conroy, Brown & Olive, 2008; Tobin & Sugai, 2005). More externalized than internalized problems are identified by teachers (Tobin & Sugai, 2005). Research shows, however, that teachers frequently implement prescribed strategies inaccurately, despite the availability of numerous intervention programs for coping with young children's behavioral issues (see Gettinger and Fischer, 2015, for a review of such programs). Although teachers know that social competence is important (Humphries, Williams, & Tanginia May, 2018), they appear to value academic performance more than social competence (Kemple, Hysmith, & Davis, 1996). Furthermore, teachers seem to attribute to parents and nature more influence on the development of children's social competence, than to teachers themselves (Kemple et al., 1996; Zinsser, Shewark, Denham, & Curby, 2014). As to teacher preparation programs, most published work includes recommendations rather than research data about how to cope with behavioral and social problems (Stough & Montague, 2015).

Regarding strategies of coping with behavioral problems, it is widely agreed that teachers must adhere to a multi-tiered approach including prevention based on warm, responsive, and trusting relationships with children together with clear expectations, enhancement of social competencies, detection of difficulties in this area, as well as individualized intervention plans, when needed, based on positive approaches including praise for prosocial behavior and efforts by the child to regulate his/her behavior, emphasizing the child's interests and strengths rather than the use of punishment and expulsion (Fox, Dunlap, & Powell, 2002; Gettinger & Fischer, 2015; Horner, Sugai, & Anderson, 2010).

As a consequence of our understanding that coping with behavioral problems is an essential part of a teacher's professional functioning, the college decided to include in its ECE preparation program a mandatory assignment on planning, implementing, and assessing social and behavioral problems. This assignment is performed in the context of coursework on social competence, and systematic coping with behavioral problems in the field placement. Students in their second year of studies were initially enrolled in a one-semester course, and subsequently in a year-long course that dealt with understanding the importance of social competence and how to prevent and cope with behavioral problems. The coursework is coordinated with the college mentors (who observe the students in the field) and students must coordinate implementation of their assignment with the field mentor and obtain parental consent to work with their child.

The goals of the course were formulated as follows:

- To enhance awareness of the student teachers and their field mentors to the importance of social competence in the children's development.

- To contribute to the inclusion of practice focused on the assessment and enhancement of social competence as a fixed component in the defined role of [preschool] ECE teachers.
- To achieve meaningful learning of social development of children from birth to 8 years with an emphasis on the preschool years (3 to 6 years of age).
- To support adoption [by preschool teachers and student teachers] of a pro-active rather than reactive approach to coping with social and behavioral problems.
- To support the student teachers' learning of observation skills and understanding of behavior that represents social competence.
- To foster the learning of intervention methods that support enhanced change of social behavior, e.g., guided small cooperative groups, direct coaching of social behavior, positive reinforcement of prosocial behavior, analysis of social episodes, role playing.
- To teach how to design and implement individualized intervention plans for children experiencing social and behavioral problems.
- To foster the ability to analyze social processes in small groups and teach how to make use of them to prevent and cope with behavioral and social difficulties.

The work in the social competence course is based on the following assumptions:

- Children can change and improve their social behavior.
- Teachers and student teachers can influence a child's social behavior (for better or worse) and it is their job to lead to improvement of a child's social competence.
- Student teachers begin the course with existing beliefs, attitudes, and knowledge as to what constitutes social competence and how it evolves; therefore, initial student teacher beliefs must be addressed.

Core Practices and Competencies in Teaching ... 25

- Children's behavior is purposeful; therefore, it is important to understand what motivates them to behave as they do.
- Children's behavior is influenced by circumstances in their surroundings; for this reason, one must observe their behavior in the natural surroundings and focus on interactions with other children and adults.
- Children need assistance in changing their social behavior and coping better with frustration and conflict. The amount of help required varies from child to child.
- Assistance must be given in the natural setting (i.e., the coaching of behavior during free play, guidance during guided small group work, and so on).

The course is comprised of discussions and lectures, as well as college and field assignments. The college assignments include a summary of a group discussion about how the student teachers define social competence, in general, and peer-related social competence. Students are asked to include social episodes in their summaries that depict high and low peer-related social competence and to justify their characterization. In addition, students must turn in a literature review focusing on social development in early childhood and processes that foster it.

Also discussed in the course are intervention practices that are compatible with a positive and ecological approach. These practices (Horner & Sugai, 2005; Malik & Furman, 1993; Tal, 2002) include a focus on establishing a good relationship with targeted children (characterized by emotional support, behavioral control, and avoiding psychological control); social skills training based on the coaching of interactions with peers during free time, placing models of positive behavior and positive reinforcement in the context of natural social encounters at school; and guiding structured learning groups. Student teachers also attempt, when needed, to improve the targeted children's reputation within the peer group in indirect ways by emphasizing the strengths of the targeted children, preparing them for learning group work, initiating attractive recess activities with the targeted children, and helping them become more attractive play partners by emphasizing during formal and informal discussions with the teacher the targeted children's successes in coping. The children's self-efficacy beliefs (Bandura, 1995) and strategies for coping with difficulties are assessed along with the social skills. Knowledge related to these intervention strategies is integrated in discussions of videotaped or written case studies raised by the students or presented by the lecturer.

The social competence course supports implementation of the field assignment. The field assignment in the first semester includes the gradual planning and implementation of an individualized intervention plan for a boy or girl displaying social or behavioral difficulties. In the second semester, student teachers are expected to continue work with this child and to design and implement an additional intervention plan focused on another child following the same steps. Identification of the boy or girl in need of support is based on the student's observations and discussions with the field mentor. Students are likely to identify children displaying externalized (aggression, bullying) or internalized (withdrawal, submission) difficulties.

After receipt of consent from the parents and the field mentor, students complete a semi-structured questionnaire focusing on how they perceive the child and their own feelings, thoughts, and interactions with that child. Finally, they are asked to conclude what in their approach toward the child was helpful and should be maintained, and what should change. Following this, students observe the child and his/her interactions in various situations (free play, guided small groups, and plenary sessions), talk to the child and the teacher, and complete, based on data, a socio-emotional characterization of the child, which includes (Tal, 2002):

1) Interests and strengths (to be used in the intervention plan).
2) Information about the child's family.
3) Characteristic ways the child copes with learning and social problems.
4) The child's usual mood, ways to express feelings and control emotions.

Core Practices and Competencies in Teaching ... 27

5) The extent the child shows initiatives – give examples.
6) A summary of social competence components: (a) how much is the child liked by peers? (b) socio-metric status – regular, popular, neglected, rejected; (c) does the child have a buddy/close friend (who are the friends)? (d) extent of empathy expressed toward peers; (e) extent of assertiveness in contacts with peers; (f) extent of offering and asking for help from others.
7) Characterization of typical interactions with adults in the preschool (teacher or assistant).
8) Observance of rules.
9) Finally, based on the detailed characterization, student teachers are asked to formulate the child's main social or behavioral difficulties in the context of his/her overall interactions in the preschool.

Students are required to base their characterizations of the child's socio-emotional functioning on data from their observations. This part of the assignment is examined by the lecturer and, following approval, student teachers design an intervention plan that includes the following elements:

A. Formulation of the main social and behavioral difficulties to be addressed.
B. The child's strengths that can be useful in improving relationships with other children and adults.
C. (1) Hypothesized factors explaining the child's difficulties; (2) Supportive factors in the environment.
D. Goals of the intervention plan.
E. Planned methods to attain the goals of the intervention in each of the following settings: (1) individual encounters with the child; (2) guided small learning groups; (3) free play; (4) plenary sessions; (5) coordination of intervention with the teacher and the other staff; and (6) informing the child's parents (by the educational staff) about the intervention.

After approval of the intervention plan by the lecturer, student teachers are asked to implement it and to document and evaluate their plans on a daily basis. Typically, students have to start documentation at the beginning of the intensive fieldwork week and to continue until the end of the semester. It is expected that reflection on the implementation written at the end of each day will impact the actions taken as part of the next day's implementation. Documentation of the implementation is structured and includes the following:

1) Date.
2) A short summary of the actions undertaken toward fulfillment of the goals of the program addressing various settings.
3) Conclusion I: What worked well in the implementation and what helped attain the goals? Conclusion II: What did not work as expected or only partially, and the revelation of any new information relevant to the child's social and emotional functioning.

Finally, toward the end of the semester, the students are asked to complete a reflective evaluation of the intervention plan based on multiple sources: (a) the child's direct and indirect input; (b) information obtained from the education staff (teacher, assistant); and (c) the student's documentation. The evaluation will include:

1) Mention of changes in the child's behavior and social functioning based on evidence.
2) An explanation of what helped and what hindered attainment of the goals.
3) A report of discussion with the teachers regarding the actions needed to maintain achieved goals that are to be taken by the education staff, particularly during the student's absence.

The preparation of students at Levinsky College to cope with behavioral and social difficulties, including a full analysis of three cases

Core Practices and Competencies in Teaching ...   29

(two in early childhood education and one in elementary school), is presented in Tal (2008). In all three cases, student teachers were engaged in systematic implementation of their intervention plans and (i) they learned that the definition of social problems must take the context into account; (ii) they understood the importance of forming a warm relationship with the children and setting clear boundaries on their behavior; (iii) they understood that maintaining warm relationships with children necessitates self-reflection and self-regulation to deal with negative feelings toward children who display emotional problems; (iv) they learned to appreciate the therapeutic power of a positive approach to the children, as opposed to an approach based on punishment and exclusion; (v) they discovered the power of beliefs, of faith in the children's ability to improve; (vi) in all three cases, students experienced crises during implementation of the intervention plan and sought the lecturer's advice; ultimately all three found ways to grow following coping with the crisis; and (vii) they implemented their intervention plans with varying degrees of cooperation of the field mentor: In one case, the teacher was supportive and asked the student to present the case in a staff meeting, encouraging staff to follow through on the student's plan; in the second case, the teacher was indifferent; and in the third case, the teacher virtually opposed the positive intervention with the disruptive boy, but did not interfere with the student's work. All three students learned that implementation based on an ecological, positive approach is possible, but that it takes planning and effort.

Below are two statements from one of the student teacher's written assignments that documents implementation of an intervention plan with a boy showing disruptive behavior that interfered with the learning in the preschool and in the small group led by the student.

I realized in the process of writing [this paper] that we tend to maintain the first impression we form of people, and this first impression serves to thwart the building of a relationship with them. During implementation of the intervention plan, I often found myself stopping and thinking about what I ought to do now since naturally [I felt] the desire to exclude him, to send him away from the group as he frequently interfered with the progress of the lesson.

The most positive thing that happened as a result of implementing the intervention plan was the change in my attitude toward the boy: [Before starting,] I tended to agree with my fieldwork mentor that Maor is hopeless, and I almost gave up on him. Today things are different.

This excerpt from the student teacher's assignment shows that she perceived relationships with disruptive children and viewed behaviors and attitudes toward children as changeable, and as the main challenge of teachers coping with children who exhibit behavioral problems. Furthermore, we learn from her account that being able to adopt a positive approach toward these children is the product of intense internal struggle to not surrender to the human tendency to exclude from groups children who display disruptive behavior.

Nevertheless, when dealing with behavioral and social problems, one must also consider the teacher's responsibility for the entire class or preschool, while coping with an individual child. Thus, we suggest including classroom management in addition to relationships and the mediation of learning experiences as recommended core competencies in teacher preparation and professional development.

Working with Children's Parents

Theory and research support what we all intuitively know: The teacher's job of supporting children's learning is affected by the quality of the relationship between the teacher and the child's parents and families. This is because a child's well-being and learning are influenced both by their direct relationships with parents, siblings, caregivers, teachers, and peers and by the indirect impact teacher-parent relationships have on teacher-child interactions and on the child's perception of his or her parents' behavior and their expectations related to the child's learning (Bronfenbrenner, 1979; Bronfenbrenner & Morris, 2006; Hoover-Dempsey et al., 2005; Walker & Hoover-Dempsey, 2015). Thus, work with children's parents ought to be viewed as a core practice in education and teacher education; being a teacher entails developing practices that lead to collaboration and cooperation with parents.

However, the education practices and teacher education related to this basic understanding are dependent on public policy and school culture (Bronfenbrenner, 1979; Walker & Hoover-Dempsey, 2015). Further, children's families throughout the world have become more culturally diverse, and teachers must adapt their work with parents to varied expectations and styles of communication. Families have also become more diverse due to changes in their composition and more fluid definitions of gender. Single-parent families and same-gender parenthood have become commonplace, and children's well-being depends on teachers' attitudes toward these changes and the communication with children's parents as a reflection of attitudes and possible biases. Furthermore, both parents and teachers are working longer hours and have access to fewer sources of "natural" support than decades ago. Technology has changed ways of communication between people in general, and also between teachers and parents.

Finally, teacher-parent relationships also depend on how teachers perceive parental involvement in preschools and schools. Addi-Raccah and Ainhoren (2009), found that an equitable balance of power between parents and teachers correlates with a teacher's positive attitudes toward the involvement of parents in school life.

Good communication with children's parents is based on reciprocity and trust, and familiarity with children and families must be established before difficulties and problems arise. Good communication is conducive to achieving coordination and agreement on issues related to both the well-being of the individual child and the learning conditions and management of the entire class.

All these factors need to be taken into account when designing preparation for fruitful work of the teacher with parents.

The understanding that work with parents ought to be a core part of education and teacher education led the ECE department at Levinsky College to design a mandatory Work with Parents course in the teacher preparation program focused on working and communicating with children's parents. The objectives of this course are to encourage student teachers to examine their knowledge, attitudes, and interactions with children's parents and to define goals of improving them in a supportive atmosphere.

Since student teachers are not directly engaged in communicating with children's parents, we decided to base the students' learning on an analysis of written accounts of critical episodes and videotaped simulations of communication between teachers and parents. Each student is required to hand in a written account of an episode involving teachers and parents. Every group of students designs and performs a simulation of an episode involving interactions between teachers and parents.

Analysis of the written accounts of critical episodes and the simulations that were recorded and transcribed help student teachers gain insight into how their messages are understood by other students playing the roles of parents, how they react to arguments put forward by parents, how they delivered sensitive information about the child, or how they explained rules that are to be kept by the children's parents. The analysis of episodes taken from the real world of communication with parents and enactment of these episodes using role-play and simulations are based on the assumption that student teachers need to learn how to deal with issues at hand (such as accepting difficulties or problems related to the development and functioning of the children) and to understand parents' perceptions and feelings related to these matters. This analysis also takes into consideration the professional role of the teacher in the communication. Understanding parents' roles, however, must also take into account the impact of sociological factors such as the division of power between various parents, based on different socioeconomic statuses. The analysis of simulations makes student teachers aware of these and other sociological issues as well as different communication styles. They have the opportunity to ponder the communication, reflect on what helps and what hinders good relationships with children's parents, and decide on aspects of communication and/or perceptions of parents that need to be improved.

Core Practices and Competencies in Teaching ...   33

Critical episodes and videotaped simulations are divided into the following key practices included in the work with parents:

1) A general meeting with the parents at the beginning of the school year, as both a get-to-know-each-other activity and as a foundation for the preschool/class-parents partnership for that year.
2) Periodic teacher-parent discussions intended to share information with parents about their child's functioning in the preschool.
3) Teacher-initiated and preplanned discussions with parents about their children's identified difficulties.
4) Teacher-initiated planned and unplanned discussions with parents focused on the parent's failure to abide by the rules.
5) Parent-initiated discussions with teachers related to their child or issues in the operation of the preschool.
6) Mutual planning and implementation of activities – birthday parties, end-of-year parties, trips, holidays (e.g., Purim, Passover).

In the 2017-18 school year, student simulations most often dealt with practices 3, 4, and 5 above, as students seemed to be apprehensive about situations related to conflicts with children's parents. Nevertheless, from the students' written accounts, they appear to have understood the need to proactively form and maintain good relationships with parents and not only to be concerned about conflicts.

In that same year, Levinsky College received a grant from the Israeli Ministry of Education that helped it coordinate syllabi and teaching among the lecturers of several groups of student teachers who took the Work with Parents course that year, to plan and evaluate teaching of this course as a team, and to collect extensive data related to students' learning of this course. This was an outstanding year, as the Work with Parents course was taught to all third- and fourth-year students (interns). Initially the course was given in the fourth year, the year of internship in Israel, as we took into account that during this year interns for the first time meet the children's parents in their responsible roles as teachers. We thought that at this stage, the course would be most appealing and relevant to students.

However, due to numerous student requests that preparation for work with parents be provided before the interns' real-life encounters with parents, we moved the compulsory course to the third year. Thus, during the 2017-18 academic year, the course was taken by about 250 students divided into eight groups and taught by six lecturers.

To assess the impact of the course on the learning of the student-teachers, the team who collaborated in planning and teaching the Work with Parents course undertook research about the materials produced throughout the course (written accounts of episodes, statements related to the importance of work with parents at the beginning and the end of the course, a short anonymous questionnaire focused on self-efficacy and satisfaction with the course, transcriptions of simulations and discussions following simulations). Three chapters in this volume address various aspects of the implementation of this course.

Work with Parents Perceived by Student Teachers and Interns as a Core Practice

The following accounts provide evidence of student understanding that work with parents is a core competency:

> The most important thing I understood throughout the course was that in order to succeed [in our work as teachers], we need to reconcile ourselves to the fact that parents are an important part of the preschool. We need to allow parental involvement along with setting clear boundaries. [fourth year student]
>
> Regarding work with parents, I believe that preschool is a continuation of the home and when a child comes to school, he comes with his parents. My approach is aligned with the Reggio approach founded on relationships, that is, parents need to be perceived as partners and be expected to be involved in what's going on in the preschool. [fourth year student]

These written accounts by student teachers show that some students (such as the writer of the second account) begin the course with a sound view that children need continuity of care and that education is about

Core Practices and Competencies in Teaching ...   35

relationships, both assumptions leading to the idea that we must view children's parents as partners. The first account shows that the student reached this understanding through the coursework.

Relationships with Parents Must Be Based on Trust, Empathy with Parents and Children, and Clear Boundary-Setting

The following accounts indicate how students perceive their professional relationship with children's parents:

> To interact well with children's parents from the very beginning, I need to build trust. Parents must feel that they can trust me and believe in my good intentions and that we both (the teacher and the parents) have common goals. [fourth year student]
> The teacher is a person with whom the parent can feel safe to talk and tell her things beyond the child's problem. The kindergarten teacher can be regarded as a "pillar of support" for the parents. When there is good communication based on respect and trust, it is easier to achieve cooperation with the parents and also easier for the teacher to find the right solution for the child and sometimes understand where the problem comes from. [third year student]
> I believe that the preschool teacher has to understand parents as she has to understand their children and that she must be patient and attentive to their needs, detect problems that arise in the preschool, and respond to their requests. Nevertheless, it is [also] important to set clear limits on the parents' involvement in a pleasant way and to remind them that rules have been set and need to be respected. It is very important that the teacher be perceived as accessible, that she give parents the feeling that teachers can be approached and are prepared to take care of issues so that the pressure diminishes, and parents feel reassured that they can trust the preschool where they leave their most precious person [the children]. [fourth year student]
> I learned about the importance of knowing and understanding the parents' perspective, but I also learned how and when to set limits. Setting limits as part of communication with children's parents is very important. [third year student]
> At the beginning of the course, my view about working with parents in preschools was that as a teacher I must be very assertive and stick to

my opinion. Through the course, as I watched various simulations, I realized that as an educator I need to show empathy toward children and parents, to display flexibility when dealing with various situations, to do everything to make children and parents feel secure. [third year student]

From the student teacher accounts, we learn that through the course the understanding emerged that a good relationship with children's parents has to be based on trust and reciprocity. Some appear to have realized that reciprocity with children's parents is not a given and needs to be attained through intentional effort. Students seem to have started the course concerned about whether they appear authoritative in the parents' eyes, but through the course they gradually realized that the relationships with parents cannot be one-sided, that they need to be based on reciprocity, being attentive to parents' perspectives, and setting and keeping clear rules for the sake of the children and adults involved.

Students Developed Proactive Thinking About How to Engage Parents in Order to Form Good Relationships Based on Trust

These student accounts bring evidence of proactive thinking in their work with parents and perceived change in their communication with parents.

First of all, I will use the observation tool, I will observe each child closely both as an individual and [as a participant] in groups, and I will also use another tool I learned this year from my field mentor, namely, assessing a child's learning profile while working in small groups. In this way, I help myself feel comfortable talking to parents about their child [to prepare herself for the semi-annual talks with the parents of all children]. [third year student]

[I understand that I have] to plan individual discussions with the parents of each child, activity that is not widely employed in preschools [in Israel], so that you don't meet the parents only when problems arise. [third year student]

The testimonies of some student teachers show signs of a proactive approach – thinking of practices that will foster good relationships with children's parents as a foundation of working with them. Student teachers show awareness that they need to center their relationships with the parents on being well acquainted with their children. They show an understanding that they must not wait for problems to arise in order to initiate talks with the parents. In one account, the field mentor is perceived as an important source of knowledge for the student.

The above discussion about working with parents as a core practice also dealt with relationships with parents as core competencies, as the two seem inseparable. The work with parents includes practices that enable the formation and maintenance of relationships with them. The very essence of working with parents is communicating with them.

Changes in Working with Parents Following a Study Performed by a Graduate Student

Research performed by a graduate student who was a second-grade teacher (Breuer & Tal, in press) focused on how parents, children, and teachers perceive their own role and the role of the other in an effort to create a successful and supportive relationship in the children's first year of school. The researchers sought to understand the perceptions and perspectives of children, parents, and teachers based on the assumption that the successful adjustment of first graders is also contingent upon good relations among the partners – children, parents, and the teaching staff.

Breuer and Tal found that the emotional climate of the school was regarded as positive by all the respondents. Although all respondents expressed a desire for more interpersonal communication with each other, the expectations of parents and teachers differed in regard to the desired frequency and setting limits on the communication between them. Another concern of the parents was related to the bus rides between their homes and the regional school. The children spoke clearly in favor of the physical presence of their parents in the school throughout the school year, not just during the adjustment period. The children, however, found ways to cope with their parents' physical absence by symbolic means and by creating meaningful relationships with their teachers. The children also expressed a desire to involve their parents in their learning and the products of their learning.

After this research was completed and following personnel changes in the school administration, Breuer initiated broad-based changes in concert with other staff members (teachers, school counselor, principal), parents, and children to address the needs that came to light in her study.

Regarding the involvement of the parents, their physical presence in the school, and communication between the parents and teaching staff, many activities were introduced in addition to what had been done prior to the research. These actions involved the entire teaching staff and parents, and included:

- Meetings of the school counselor, the principal, and the assistant principal for first and second grades with the parents in their communities during the summer vacation, or before their children graduate kindergarten in order to clarify and coordinate expectations.
- Parents who wish to talk with the school staff personally are invited to meet with them prior to the start of the school year.
- The teaching staff updates the parents about what takes place in the classroom, both in a class internet forum and personally by email or phone concerning the functioning of individual students.
- An evening roundtable is held once a year with the participation of teachers and parents to discuss subjects of concern to all (homework, educational innovations, etc.).
- Parents are invited to teach a class as experts in their fields, and to volunteer in the library on Fridays. The intent is to increase the physical presence of parents in the school in response to the needs articulated by the children.
- To increase the involvement of parents, activities were defined in diverse areas, such as taking responsibility for being in contact with the parents in the communities, inviting parents interested in

educational innovations to learn about them and help introduce them to the classroom, etc.

- These initiatives come from both the teachers and the parents. In 2016-2017, parents replaced the teachers on Teacher's Day, giving them an unusual type of morning, and this was made a permanent event by decision of the school staff and parent representatives at the beginning of the subsequent schoolyear.
- Regarding bus transportation, a task force was created to include representatives of the parents from the communities, a transport coordinator, and older students who serve as bus monitors. Bus rules were written that give special attention to the youngest students boarding first. Changes were made in the bus parking area to improve the conditions for students waiting for buses. These changes were adopted in response to the needs of the parents revealed by the research and also following requests by sixth graders in the school.

Core Competencies

The core competencies viewed as essential in teacher education and preparation are as follows: the ability to form good relationships with children, parents, and staff; the mediation of children's learning experiences; and classroom management as a meta-competency orchestrating all aspects of the teacher's functioning to facilitate well-being and learning. These competencies target essential key abilities and not segmented skills. We claim that these competencies are necessary in order to perform the core practices in which teachers are involved. Indeed, in the previous sections, relationships with children and parents were frequently mentioned by student teachers and teachers as important aspects of their small group work, RPBR, enactment of an emergent curriculum, and coping with social and behavioral problems. Relationships with children's parents dominated the discourse on working with parents. Many mentions of mediated learning experiences related to actions taken by teachers to make the physical and social world more accessible, learnable, and understandable for the children were also embedded in the discourse about RPBR and emergent curriculum. Classroom management was not cited as frequently and its relevance as a core meta-competency will be presented in this section. It should also be recognized that competencies defined in this chapter are dynamic and evolve throughout the teachers' cyclical involvement in planning, acting, and reflecting on these practices.

In this section each core competency will be succinctly defined and how each is fostered in the preparation program at Levinsky College will be described.

Relationships as a Core Competency: "No Education without Relation"

Teaching, particularly early childhood education, is inconceivable without relationships. The title of Bingham and Sidorkin's (2004) book *No Education Without Relation* encapsulates the idea that relationships must be perceived as core competencies in education. Teachers must be able to form and maintain relationships with children, parents, and staff. Life in schools and preschools and learning are based on relationships, on connections between people – between teachers and children, between teachers and parents, among children, and among staff. Wentzel (2012) based on Hinde (1997) defines relationships as "enduring connections between two individuals, uniquely characterized by degrees of continuity, shared history, and interdependent interactions across settings and activities" (p. 20). Relationships are formed on the basis of numerous interactions, and they differ from interactions because they also include individuals' representations of the relationships. Notwithstanding their relative continuity, relationships change and develop.

Good relationships are essential in teaching. However, as emphasized by Dahlberg, Moss, and Pence (2013), educational institutions are not families, hence, relationships between teachers and children are no substitute for parent-child relationships, and relationships among peers are no substitute for sibling relationships. These are professional and transient relations. Therefore, thought must be invested in creating pedagogical

Core Practices and Competencies in Teaching ... 41

modes of organization that turn schools into institutions that enable individuals and groups to form good relationships among them. The sense of security and belonging among children and adults as well as learning depend on the quality of relationships among individuals and groups in institutions of education.

In addition, since relationships connect between people, to understand them one must be aware of how situations and the relationships themselves are perceived by the partners to the relationship. As relationships include interactions, representations, and expectations, assessing relationships must include both observations and other tools such as written episodes and journals as well as discussions intended to learn about the feelings and thoughts of those involved. Relationships are dynamic and evolving. Therefore, teachers need to form good relationships with children and to continuously reflect on the ongoing interactions with them in ordinary as well as emotionally challenging situations. Reflection is needed in the continuous process of regulating interactions and feelings in order to maintain good relationships and overcome crises and problems that may occur.

The tools used in preparation for teaching to evaluate relationships and continuously regulate interactions, feelings, and thoughts associated with them include:

1) Journal and educational blog writing, including social episodes, some emotionally challenging, as reflective tools. Journal and social episode writing is based on the assumption that expressive writing about meaningful and often traumatic personal experiences help in understanding feelings and situations, regulating feelings, and freeing the mind to better grasp how personal perspectives shape one's understanding of relationships and their impact on children's well-being and learning.

2) Examination of videotaped interactions in small groups or plenary sessions enables reflection on interactions and their possible links to thoughts and feelings experienced during the interactions. Furthermore, the inspection of videotaped interactions helps focus

on concrete aspects of the interactions that hinder the formation of good relationships and learning, and thus need to be changed. Observations of videotaped interactions in the context of daily activities (such as small group work, or plenary sessions) can be useful in finding ways to change such interactions in the natural context in which they occur.

3) Discussions with children, listening to their perspectives on relationships with teachers and peers. As relationships are bi-directional, it is essential to understand children's perspectives of their interactions with adults and other children.

4) Feedback from college and field mentors following observations of planned and casual interactions between students and children. Field and college mentors engage student teachers in discussions about how they and the students view the interactions and relationships with children.

In the following sections I succinctly describe the characteristics of good teacher-children, teacher-teacher (staff), and teacher-parent relationships. Practices employed to foster relationships were presented in previous sections; below, the college courses that deal with relationships are noted.

Relationships with Children as a Core Competency

Bronfenbrenner and Morris (2006) view daily interactions that children have in the microsystem (with parents, siblings, teachers, and peers) as the proximal processes constituting the main mechanism that impacts development.

In their view, human development takes place through processes of progressively more complex reciprocal interaction between an active, evolving biopsychological human organism and the persons, objects, and symbols in its immediate external environment. To be effective, the interaction must occur on a fairly regular basis over extended periods of time. Such enduring forms of interaction in the immediate environment are referred to as proximal processes. The nature of these interactions and their impact on development are influenced by characteristics of the persons involved, the context in which they occur, and time (p. 795).

Interactions, perceived by Bronfenbrenner and Morris (2006) as the main mechanisms explaining development, are the building blocks of relationships. Therefore, relationships must be regarded as core competencies. Teachers' relationships with children, and what they do or abstain from doing to influence relationships in the peer group, have a critical impact on children's learning and well-being.

As part of the attempt to better understand teacher-children relationships as reciprocal endeavors, Wentzel (2012) suggests that relationships should be studied transactionally, in addition to the more common causal or linear model, on the assumption that teacher-child relationships affect children's learning and social participation. Indeed, the pedagogical view of relationships as bi-directional and vertical (Hinde, 1997) – in the sense that the teacher's role is to support children emotionally and, at times, to set boundaries on their behavior, but never on the expression of their thoughts and feelings (Barber, Stolz, & Olsen, 2005) – is integrated into the Developmental Systems Model of Teacher-Child Relationships (Pianta, Hamre, & Stuhlman, 2003). Pianta and colleagues suggest that teacher-child relationships are dynamic systems that include the properties of teachers and children; dyadic, bi-directional teacher-child interactions; representations of relationships of teachers and children (beliefs, expectations, emotions); and external influences (such as the number of children in class, pressures to implement policies and curricula, and so on).

Fumoto (2011) found that key factors enabling good teacher-children relationships were the teachers' "firm understanding of the context of children's development, and their awareness of the role they play in creating this context" (p. 27) as well as the teachers' organizationally enabled autonomy to create social and learning environments in which they are totally involved in supporting young children's growth. Yet it was repeatedly found that teachers tend to be less supportive of children who display challenging behavior (Brophy-Herb, Lee, Nievar, & Stollak, 2007; Sava, 2002; Spilt & Koomen, 2009). Nevertheless, studies also show that in some cases teachers are successful at regulating their negative feelings and rejection of disruptive children and subsequently their levels of sensitivity and patience were found to be associated with the children's more competent social behavior (Hamre & Pianta, 2005; Riley, Watt, Richardson, & de Alwis, 2012; Rimm-Kaufman et al., 2002).

Relationships with children are embedded in teachers' various activities: in individual, small group, and plenary encounters with children; in planned and casual encounters with children. Teachers and children enter these activities with various personal abilities to form relationships. For teachers, as suggested in this chapter, the ability to form good relationships with children should be regarded as a precondition to performing the job of teaching. Throughout these activities, relationships are formed, maintained, and changed. In this chapter we emphasize, as presented in preceding sections, the centrality of teacher-children and peer relationships in designing core practices such as small group work in heterogeneous groups and RPBR, enactment of an emergent curriculum, and implementation of intervention plans designed to cope with social and behavioral problems.

Relationships are dynamic and evolving. Therefore, teachers need to both form good relationships with children and to continuously reflect on their ongoing interactions with them in regular as well as emotionally challenging situations. Reflection is needed in the continuous process of regulating interactions and feelings in order to maintain good relationships and overcome crises and problems.

Evaluation and continuous improvement of relationships with children are addressed in depth in the Inquiry of Fieldwork Experience course. Fieldwork is always performed at Levinsky College in conjunction with an Inquiry of Fieldwork Experience course. The lecturers of these courses are usually the college mentors who visit students in their fieldwork and function as mediators between the college and the field mentors. Relationships with children are also addressed in the Social Competence course (presented in a previous section) and the Classroom Management seminar that will be presented in a next section.

The assessment of relationships focuses on the ability to express warmth and empathy in relationships with the children, as well as the ability to set clear rules of conduct and apply them consistently. Also assessed is the teacher's ability to accept children's expressions of positive as well as negative feelings and thoughts – all these in the context of individual, small group, and plenary encounters. Aware of the emotional strain experienced by teachers as a result of intensive relationships with children displaying behavioral problems, we also assess the teacher's ability to acknowledge negative feelings toward perpetrators, as well as the ability to find ways to deal with these feelings and self-regulate their expression using more positive thoughts and expectations.

In the sections focused on small groups, emergent curriculum, and coping with behavioral problems, we showed how relationships with children have been reflected upon and changed by student teachers and teachers in the process of documenting and assessing their practice.

Relationships with Staff

From an ecological perspective (Bronfenbrenner, 1979), relationships with staff are located in the mesosystem, including connections between microsystems, thus bearing an important and indirect impact on children's well-being and learning. Collaboration, the core of relationships with staff, is defined as working together toward a common goal. Therefore, collaboration among staff members to enact educational practices is critical, so that all staff members agree to work toward the attainment of common goals.

Collaboration includes communication (the exchange of knowledge and opinions to optimize the understanding of tasks by partners), cooperation (an agreed division of labor related to completing tasks), and responsiveness (active and insightful participation) (Hesse, Care, Buder, Sassenberg, & Griffin, 2015).

At Levinsky College, we found that the preparation program does not place sufficient and systematic emphasis on helping student teachers develop practices and improve competencies of communication with staff. Although students are instructed to align activities with the expectations of the field mentors and they are often placed in pairs to encourage collaboration, no specific assignment focused on staff work is compulsory. Furthermore, the preparation program does not offer a course focused on staff work. Issues related to staff work are likely to be dealt with in the Inquiry of Fieldwork Experience course, mostly in a reactive fashion, when difficulties arise. Occasionally students choose to deal with staff work in the Classroom Management seminar. Each year, two or three students in each class choose to focus on staff work. Nevertheless, this is not addressed as a core competency – an issue that our preparation program needs to address. In our graduate program, we offer action research and a mentoring course focused on an inquiry of staff work related to educational issues selected by practicing teachers.

Relationships with Parents

From an ecological perspective, teachers' relationships with parents and families are situated in the mesosystem (Bronfenbrenner, 1979), thus indirectly affecting teachers' direct interactions and relationships with children. As relationships with parents are key to working with them, these relationships were amply discussed in the section focused on the practice of working with parents.

Mediation of Children's Learning Experiences as a Core Competency

There is agreement that teaching and teacher education need to help students learn (Ball & Forzani, 2009; Cohen, 2011; Feiman-Nemser, 2017; Grossman et al., 2009). Furthermore, they must help children learn how to learn so they will be able to thrive in a fast-changing world.

Mediated learning experiences are the actions taken by teachers to make the physical and social world more accessible, learnable, and understandable for the children. Mediated learning experiences include interactions based heavily on "talk" as well as arrangement of the physical environment with and for the children. The perception of mediated learning experiences as a core competency in education and teacher education is based on the socio-constructivist assumption (Vygotsky, 1978; Feuerstein & Feuerstein, 1991) that an individual's ability to learn and the

Core Practices and Competencies in Teaching ...   47

specific learning associated with various situations and contents are critically affected by interactions with more capable and experienced members of a community (parents, teachers, peers). Also, as mentioned in previous sections, Bronfenbrenner and Morris (2006) claim that direct, intensive, bi-directional interactions between developing children and their social and physical world constitute, as proximal processes, the main mechanism that explains human development. Therefore, the effort to characterize and improve these interactions is one of the most central tasks of education and teacher education. It should be remembered that interactions are also foundational to forming interpersonal relationships.

According to Feuerstein and Feuerstein (1991), the ability to learn is modified by social and physical stimuli and phenomena. Thus, Vygotsky (1978) together with Feuerstein and Feuerstein (1991) claim that cognitive modifiability and the knowledge possessed by the child are determined by the quality of the interaction between the person and the environment. However, not every interaction can be regarded as a "mediated experience" – one that has an impact on children's learning. The key element that makes an interaction mediated is that the mediator has the intention to transcend the immediate needs or concerns of the recipient of mediation by going beyond the here and now, in space and time, to attain the recipient's reciprocity (Feuerstein & Feuerstein, 1991).

Guided mediated interactions include dialogic discourse aimed at achieving what Feuerstein, Rand, Hoffman, and Miller (1980) call cognitive modifiability; or, in Vygotskian terms, interaction aimed at the acquisition of psychological tools (mental tools that mediate cognitive action such as language, private talk, writing, maps, tables, and diagrams) and formal scientific concepts that help children become self-regulated thinkers and learners. Alexander (2008) explains the importance of this kind of mediated dialogic discourse as

> Talk [that] vitally mediates the cognitive and cultural spaces between adult and child, between teacher and learner, between society and the individual, between what the child knows and understands and what he or she has yet to know and understand. Language not only manifests

thinking but also structures it, and speech shapes the higher mental processes necessary for so much of the learning which takes place, or ought to take place, in school...It follows that one of the principal tasks of the teacher is to create interactive opportunities and encounters that directly and appropriately engineer such mediation (p. 92)

Feuerstein and Feuerstein (1991) defined Mediated Learning Experience (MLE) as a comprehensive model of adult-child interaction that is systematically related to cognitive performance (i.e., the ability to make inferences, form inner representations of phenomena, and the like). Klein (1988, 1991) empirically formulated five interaction characteristics that lead to cognitive modifiability in an MLE. She found that interactions based on these characteristics predicted a child's later cognitive development.

The five characteristics of mediated interactions, as formulated by Feuerstein (Feuerstein & Feuerstein, 1991) and Klein (1988, 1991) are as follows:

1) Intentionality and reciprocity – any purposeful act directed toward achieving a change in the partner's perception or response that results in the responsiveness of the partner. There must be a clear indication of the adult's intention to engage the child, and a child's clear behavior that indicates responsiveness. Mediated interactions are sometimes initiated by children. In this case, the child shows intentionality, an attempt to draw the adult's attention, and the adult must be sensitive and responsive to the child's attempt to initiate a new direction of action.

2) Transcendence – an adult's or child's actions directed toward broadening the partner's awareness beyond what is necessary to satisfy the immediate need that triggered the interaction; one example is asking children to hypothesize what will happen or initiating comparisons between phenomena. Transcendental discourse is embedded in questions or explanations initiated by the adult or the child.

3) Mediation of meaning relates to actions that express verbal or nonverbal appreciation or affect with respect to objects, people, feelings, or events. This may be reflected in naming objects, phenomena, or feelings (cognitive meanings), or in nonverbally expressing positive or negative feelings toward objects, people, or phenomena (affective meaning). Meaning is also embedded in questions or explanations that can be initiated by the adult or the child.

4) Mediation of feelings of competence is reflected in actions intended to enhance children's feelings of competence about their ability. These are actions of praise for the child's effort to cope with a challenge accompanied by an explanation or by changing the task to allow for the child's successful completion of it.

5) Mediation of behavior control relates to adult behavior that models, demonstrates, and/or verbally suggests to the child the need to regulate his or her behavior respective to the nature of the task. Mediation of control of behavior is embedded both in questions or verbal explanations and can be initiated by either the child or the adult.

Feuerstein and Feuerstein (1991) claimed that the combination of intentionality and reciprocity, transcendence, and mediation of meaning constitute the necessary and sufficient conditions for mediated learning experiences. One of the important contributions of the criteria defining mediated learning experiences, suggested by these theorists, is the inclusion of affectional characteristics of interactions (i.e., emotional mediation of meaning and feelings of competence) in the model of adult-child interactions explaining cognitive modifiability.

Feuerstein et al. (1991) defined and studied dyadic adult-child mediation. However, in our work at Levinsky College and in alignment with Vygotsky's and Malaguzzi's ideas, we perceive small group work as the preferred unit of learning in preschools and schools. Therefore, Tal (2004) added the following two criteria to mediated learning experiences in small, adult-guided groups: direct discourse among children uninterrupted by the teacher and a balanced distribution of turns talking among the participants. Thus, discourse in small groups leading to learning includes exchanges that are linked together into coherent and deepening lines of inquiry (Alexander, 2017).

Thus, discourse with and among the children needs to be reciprocal (what is called in the MLE intentionality and reciprocity) and it needs to be tuned to the participants' attention, interests, and feelings, mediating the meaning of physical and social phenomena and seeking to guide the children to transcend the immediate situation in their discourse (by comparing data, offering hypotheses, making inferences). Consequentially, when children are encouraged to participate and offer their insights and suggestions, the discourse becomes what Alexander (2008, 2017) calls "cumulative" (contents developed throughout the conversation based on other participants' contributions) and the "product" of the discourse becomes the newly developed knowledge of the topic at hand. In addition, formal scientific concepts and psychological tools that support self-regulation are being developed and appropriated following social interactions with more competent others.

Small heterogeneous groups and RPBR, in particular, as well as enactment of an emergent curriculum are considered at Levinsky College to be practices that facilitate mediated learning experiences, as noted in preceding sections. We recognize, however, that student teachers and teachers bring with them their characteristic modes of interaction with children. Our assumption is that at any given point in time, the typical interaction of any student teacher or teacher with children has some properties that foster, and others that hinder, children's learning. Therefore, we claim that student teachers and teachers need to engage in continuous inquiry in their education encounters into what fosters and what hinders children's learning in their interactions with children. In the light of this inquiry, teachers need to continuously set personal goals of improving their mediational interactions with children.

Mediated learning experiences with children are addressed at Levinsky College less formally in the Inquiry of Fieldwork Experience course related to their practice, and formally in courses focused on mediated learning experiences. In the preparation program, student teachers are typically required to take a one-unit course focused on mediated learning experience. The main assignment in this course concerns analysis of the transcript of a learning interaction in small groups taken from fieldwork experience, using the criteria of Feuerstein and Feuerstein (1991) and Klein (1988, 1991), and identifying characteristics that promote and hinder learning. This course was initially mandatory and subsequently classified as elective. Currently, it is again classified as a mandatory course. In addition, students can choose a seminar in their fourth year on Mediated Learning Experiences associated with either literacy, mathematics, or science. In the graduate program, we offer a seminar focused on mediation in the school environment based on ideas of Vygotsky and Feuerstein. In this seminar, students perform action research in which they seek to identify hindering characteristics in their interactions and learning environments, and then design, implement, and evaluate action plans to improve the mediated learning interactions and environments. This course is based on analyzing and interpreting interactions, reflections on interactions written immediately after the learning encounter, and photos of the learning environment relevant to the encounter under scrutiny.

Tal (2012) followed the development of mediational interactions and reflections of three student teachers who performed RPBR during their three years of fieldwork. The data related to regular assignments associated with the Inquiry of Fieldwork Experience course and not to a specific Mediated Learning Experience course. She found that all three students started out controlling the discourse with the children using primarily rigid, predetermined questions and adhering to set plans; by their third year of fieldwork, they were able to become involved in the discussion, allowing for the free exploration of books by the children as well as questions and proposals initiated by them. Early interactions tended to be discontinuous due to the students' preset questions or poor management of the children's behavior, but subsequent interactions allowed for more continuous discourse parallel with the students' emergent ability to listen to the children and encourage discussion among them that focused on the ideas, content, and illustrations of the books. Moreover, children participating in the discourse guided by these three students seemed to be able to reconstruct the stories or poems. All three showed genuine concern for the participating children's emotional well-being. Yet only one of the students showed conscious and intentional efforts to enhance the children's literary understanding of the text. Following this research, we introduced into our preparation program a group inquiry of children's books as mandatory preparation prior to the implementation of RPBR.

Moral Classroom Management as a Core Meta-Competency and a Way of Understanding Classrooms

Relationships between teachers and children, mediated learning experiences in small groups as features of emergent curriculum, and implementation of intervention plans coping with children who display social and behavioral problems take place in preschools and elementary school classes. These classes include large numbers of children and staff coming from diverse backgrounds who live and learn in given physical spaces and time. Therefore, the job of helping each student learn and thrive also depends on the teachers' ability to orchestrate the multiple factors that impact the functioning of the class as a whole.

Moral Classroom Management is about "learning to create conditions for learning and well-being for children and teachers coming from a variety of backgrounds" and is viewed as "an evolutionary process, one for which teachers need professional development, support, and dialog" (Evertson & Harris, 1999, p. 73). Thus, being a good teacher involves being a classroom manager who cares for the well-being and learning of the children, parents, and staff. Therefore, classroom management can be considered a core, emerging meta-competency in the teacher's professionalism, hence, educating for effective classroom management ought to be one of the main goals of teacher preparation.

A competent classroom manager is a teacher who assumes responsibility for the learning conditions of all the children and the functioning of the staff; who understands the class ecologically, i.e., is able to perceive all aspects of the classroom life as well as interactions or links among these aspects; who embraces a proactive mindset, adopting coping alternatives that take into account possible scenarios based on knowing the class dynamics and the characteristics of individual children; who understands that relationships are foundational to education; and who is able to set goals not only for the work of her class, but also to continually regulate her own actions as necessary to deal with situations concerning encounters with children' families and staff. The quality of the classroom management is reflected in both the *daily actions and the central decisions* taken by the teacher.

Classroom management is thus a meta-competency comprising an infinite number of daily activities of self-regulation, management of interpersonal relations, and organization of the environment – all this before and during the instruction that takes place within a timetable that ultimately creates learning conditions and a feeling of security and belonging, which provides everyone (teachers and students) with a sense of emotional well-being. In addition to the conventional measures of classroom management – involvement of all the children in learning, on-task behavior, and cooperating with the rules – we further propose a dynamic measure of effective classroom management – an operational definition that includes "*the ability to modify classroom activities in the wake of difficulties in order to facilitate the children's learning and well-being*" (Tal, 2016, p. 17).

Tal (2010, 2016) claims that this meta-competency develops gradually through the years of study of student teachers, and not just through one or another classroom management course. The complexity of the perceptions and competencies involved in classroom management requires that the preparation must link coursework with an analysis of field experience. These links between field experience and academic studies must be two-directional: On the one hand, the theoretical ideas, concepts, and principles learned in academic courses are intended to guide performance in the field; no less important, however, time and attention must be given at college – whether in the framework of the Classroom Management course or of the Inquiry of Fieldwork Experience course – to an analysis of real events in the field so that students can take the insights drawn from analysis and apply them, thereby learning to cope, and experience success in handling difficult situations. Our suggestions for teacher training are based on Flyvbjerg's (2011) and Stake's (1995) thoughtful recommendations to employ case studies as a central component in the professional preparation of teachers.

Teacher preparation that seeks to connect teachers to moral goals related to the children's well-being is important, but not a simple task. A trusting environment is not only emotionally warm, but also one in which children are treated fairly by teachers and protected from exploitation and harm by other children (Nucci, 2006, p. 717). To enhance a critical and inquisitive, but not a judgmental, approach, the analysis of case studies chosen by teachers and students in preparation and professional development may prove helpful. The use of action research, case studies, and episode analysis related to classroom management enables the development of a range of strategies to deal with often challenging and complex real-life situations. Elimination of a judgmental approach by both students and mentors, accompanied by the motivation to maximize learning from the case and a commitment to deeply understand it, are critically important (Stake, 1995).

Theoretical frameworks of classroom management provide conceptual tools to help understand the reality in the classroom and allow for self-improvement. The goal must always be self-improvement. For example, an analysis of accounts of episodes, observations, reflections, and feedback from children can be used by mentors and colleagues to assess the quality of actions and decisions initiated by student teachers and teachers. These may be pondered to assess whether they have taken into account the impact on children and staff and made good use of space and time (an ecological mindset), whether they are proactive or reactive. It is important to continually evaluate the quality of relationships with and among children and with staff before, during, and after planned and unplanned activities. Importance is placed on self-correction efforts among students during their practice teaching. In addition to providing opportunities for analyzing episodes and cases, and encouraging ongoing efforts to correct errors, educational planning should consider the reactions of diverse students, teachers, and other staff, and the effects of the physical environment on learning. In addition, in planning every educational activity, teachers as well as students should be encouraged to consider the factors that might affect the course of action and introduce these into their curricula. In teacher preparation, one should encourage every expression of initiative by the students and their active coping with difficulties more than their achievements and success. Appreciation should be expressed to the students for their efforts at self-correction – verbally and in grades. In parallel, every effort should be made to collaborate with the field mentors, who should be encouraged to adopt patterns of classroom management described in this chapter. In this way, students will have an additional channel of learning by observing experienced teachers who are effective classroom managers even under trying circumstances.

The aforementioned guidelines for teacher education training have been implemented at Levinsky College of Education. At the beginning, classroom management was taught as a one-credit course and based on analyzing a sequence of episodes dealing with a Moral Classroom Management problem identified by a student-teacher or a teacher doing in-service training (Tal, 2010). The analysis of successive episodes about a classroom management problem was introduced to reflect the belief in the emergent nature of classroom-management competencies and based on growth mindset beliefs (Dweck, 2012). In addition, in the Inquiry of Fieldwork Experience course, students discuss critical episodes with their college mentors. In their third year of studies, student teachers are expected to assume responsibility of the operation of a preschool or a class for a full day, twice a year.

For about nine years now, an empirical seminar including action research aimed at improving classroom management competencies has been offered. For a few years, this seminar was compulsory for all student teachers at Levinsky College. In recent years, it is an elective for third-year students.

In the Classroom Management seminar, students are encouraged to identify an issue related to their practice that they are concerned about. We perceive and present the research in this seminar as an opportunity for student teachers to systematically improve a specific, defined aspect of their practice and to understand the meaning of classroom management by making an in-depth inquiry into an issue of concern to them. Furthermore, we expect student teachers and teachers to adopt this systematic approach to the inquiry of practice as a "way of life" in the work of teaching. The lecturer of the seminar and student colleagues offer support and feedback throughout the planning, implementation, analysis, and evaluation of the research.

Students perform action research or work on case studies focused on the issues they choose to investigate. Action research primarily focuses on the students' attempts to improve their classroom management competencies. Case studies are employed to allow students to explore how to manage a class in diverse situations as preparation for their future practice. They collect data at their field placements throughout the entire academic year. Furthermore, students are encouraged, whenever relevant, to include in their studies episodes and observations related to their fieldwork practice from previous years.

Issues chosen by students to address in their studies during recent years include: (1) ways to improve the setting of rules and boundaries (in small groups and/or in plenary sessions) while maintaining warm relationships with children; (2) ways to improve the inclusion of children displaying a range of difficulties in their small groups; (3) managing a preschool in special circumstances such as when one of the children's parents dies or is jailed, or when there is suspicion of child abuse in the family; (4) managing a preschool or class that has one or more pairs of twins; (5) managing a preschool or class that has children with life-threatening allergies; (6) improving classroom management as related to implementing an emergent curriculum in the preschool (in an art project or in the educational garden); (7) the impact of single-gender families in managing a preschool or class; (8) improving collaboration among the teacher, her assistant, and the student teacher; (9) challenges faced by teachers in their work with parents in an era of multiple channels of communication.

Students in the classroom management seminar have the opportunity to learn about their colleagues' studies and prepare themselves for dealing with special situations in their practice, in addition to the in-depth inquiry they perform in their own studies.

A few teachers enrolled in the ECE graduate program chose topics of research related to classroom management. Several studies were focused on integrating repeated book reading in small groups in preschools and first and second grade classes. Integration of RPBR in small groups included collaborating with staff, engaging children throughout the year to participate in these groups, and cooperating with children's parents. Some research focused on instituting reforms in preschools. For example, graduate students did studies about the impact on three-year-olds of adding an assistant in their preschool. Although the addition of an assistant was meant to help, it changed the balance of power in the preschool staff and necessitated adaptations – some graduate students researched these adaptations. Another group of studies focused on various aspects of working with parents and families. A few studies dealt with developing positive strategies to deal with conflicts related to working with parents, while others focused on working with various types of families (single-parent families).

Making compulsory a course on classroom management in teacher preparation is a reflection of the view that classroom management is a core meta-competency affecting all areas of a teacher's functioning. Nevertheless, as noted in this chapter, due to personnel and policy changes at Levinsky College, the status of the course has changed over the years. In spite of its critical importance in teacher preparation, colleges and universities have not yet accepted classroom management as a pivotal issue and focus of teacher preparation.

The evolving nature of classroom management as a core meta-competency is reflected in the need to continue to study aspects related to its implementation throughout a teacher's professional life.

CONCLUSION

The conceptualization presented in this chapter concerning the central practices and competencies in teacher education has been developed through many years of engagement in teacher education and professional development. The identification of core practices and competencies and their introduction into ECE teacher preparation at Levinsky College of Education have also been a gradual process. Through the years, courses focused on competencies have been introduced into the program: Work with Parents, Social Competence and Preventing and Coping with Behavioral Problems, Mediated Learning Experiences, and finally Classroom Management. At the outset, courses were given as electives, with each lecturer designing his or her own course and coordinating efforts with respective college mentors in order to implement assignments in fieldwork.

In 2007 an opportunity arose when Israeli colleges of education and universities were required to adopt a new framework of preparation (Ariav Commission, 2006). The main goal of the commission was to establish a uniform policy at teachers colleges and universities for teacher education in Israel. The commission mandated a specific number of fieldwork hours (fewer than previously required by teacher colleges, more than had been required by universities), a specific number of education courses, a specific number of ECE courses, etc. The commission did not mention particular competencies or practices to be introduced into the new curriculum. It presented core principles such as the centrality of language in teacher education, alignment of fieldwork and coursework, and so on.

At Levinsky College, an attempt was made to design common practices and courses that link the fieldwork and practice in all departments. Efforts were also made to define agreed upon assignments for fieldwork. As the head of the ECE department and teacher preparation at the time, I was responsible for coordinating the design and implementation of the new program outlines. The gradual introduction of practices and competencies presented above formed part of the implementation of the Ariav Commission recommendations as we interpreted them. The sequence of implementation was set by year of study: The first year of preparation was the first to begin the reform and the fourth year was the last. Thus, implementation each year was handled both in general staff meetings of the ECE department and by the staff working with the year that was to begin the reform.

In the next section I summarize what helped and what hindered the sustained and coherent integration of core competencies and practices in the preparation of ECE teachers.

What Helped Integrate Practices and Competencies in ECE Teacher Preparation?

The processes that supported the sustained integration of core competencies and practices included a clear vision, discontent with some aspects of the existing preparation, involvement in the field of education and listening to teachers' and children's voices, taking advantage of opportunities, cooperation among staff members, defining and agreeing on central fieldwork and coursework assignments, systematic and sustained implementation, emotional support for the students, research focused on aspects of the implementation, conferences, and publications. In more detail:

- Integrating practices and competencies throughout the years of the preparation program depends on the vision of those involved. The staff at Levinsky College believe in children's rights, competence, agency, and the importance of relationships between people involved in teaching and teacher education. We believe in the children's ability and right to participate in the decision-making about what they learn. We also believe that children need good relationships with adults and peers in order to thrive.
- Discontent with the fragmented preparation of teachers and with teachers' frequent reactive and punitive approach toward young children displaying behavioral problems motivated our search for

practices and competencies to improve teachers' practice and preparation.

- Involvement in the field of education as teachers prior to joining the staff of Levinsky College, or as counselors in professional development, helped attain recognition with the children's teachers and parents, and understand their needs. These understandings guided the design of some practices and the identification of competencies required to meet the teachers' and children's needs.

- Some staff members of Levinsky College and its ECE department decided to view the Ariav Commission recommendations as an opportunity to improve preparation rather than a regulatory demand imposed on them. The demand to implement the recommendations helped those feeling discontent with the existing preparation, and helped convince colleagues to find ways to design assignments that improve learning and well-being (such as small group work, RPBR, and an emergent curriculum) and to build or integrate courses that support implementation of these assignments. Another opportunity that we took advantage of was a grant from the Ministry of Education that supported improvement of the Work with Parents course.

- The central assignments mediated to student teachers play a key role in their learning how to make connections between college work and fieldwork and in the formation of their professional identities as teachers. Some of the assignments helped students implement practices – those dealing with small group work, RPBR, designing and implementing individual plans to cope with children's social problems, and emergent curriculum. Other assignments guided the self-evaluation and improvement of competencies – writing and analyzing field journals and social episodes using theoretical concepts and analysis of mediated interactions.

- Design and implementation of assignments depend on the quality of the team work among the college staff. The assignments and analysis of student teachers' accounts and reports are the product of staff meetings at the level of the ECE department, specifically lecturers and field mentors teaching same year preparation students. In addition, staff initially teaching the same course worked collaboratively to formulate syllabi, assignments, and their analysis.

- The more reflected-upon practice experienced by student teachers in their preparation, the greater the chance that these practices will be implemented when they become teachers. Therefore, what helped is the repeated implementation of some practices: small group work, RPBR and the yearlong implementation of the emergent curriculum. All these are accompanied by field journal writing.

- Integration of practice and meaningful learning is facilitated by the emotional support given to student teachers by their mentors. College mentors are usually accessible to students, offer them support when they experience professional or personal difficulties, and help them identify and cope with problems.

- Finally, some staff members are constantly involved in research about our practice at the college, presenting their work in national and international conferences, and publishing about it. These academic activities are performed jointly by groups of staff members and they have an impact on the preparation. A few chapters related to various aspects of our work appear in this volume (focused on work and communication with parents, the implementation of an emergent curriculum, and coping with behavioral problems).

What Interfered with a Sustainable Integration of Practices and Competencies in ECE Teacher Preparation?

The main challenges encountered in teacher preparation focused on enhancing core competencies and practices are related to the difficulty of gaining broad acceptance of their centrality in teacher education, assuring their sustainability in the program, and the time and effort required to accomplish this agenda. Specifically:

- The quality of teacher preparation depends on the cooperation and collaboration among the departments in the college or university – in the case of Levinsky College, these departments are Education, Early Childhood Education, and Specializations (children's literature, science, arts, etc.). Initially, all departments supported the practice and competency agenda. However, shifts in policy and personnel led to changes in the emphasis of preparation. As the Classroom Management and Mediated Learning Experience courses belong to the Education Department and not the Early Childhood Education Department, they became electives rather than compulsory courses. As classroom management suffers from a bad academic reputation, it was hard to convince the heads of the Education Department to make compulsory a seminar on this core competency. Whether a course or assignment is compulsory in teacher education determines its perception as a core competency and practice.
- The sustainability of implementation is undermined by staff changes in the ECE department – heads of the programs, college mentors, lecturers in courses about core practices and competencies. The framework of practice created by the program has to be transferred to new staff. Some veteran staff members assumed responsibility for supporting the new staff in becoming part of the existing community of practice. In 2018, for example, all but one staff member responsible for integration of the emergent curriculum is a member of the original team. And yet due to staff member's belief in the work of the ECE department, and her determined and inclusive approach, all new staff implement emergent curriculum, and together develop new tools to support the learning and professional development of the students in this area.

- In spite of the enormous efforts involved in preparation, and various models of collaboration between the college and the field mentors, the work with field mentors is not optimal. In some cases, due to the initiative of field mentors or student teachers, student assignments are well integrated into the fieldwork and teachers engage in modeling and guiding of students beyond the requirements of the college. Some field mentors allow the students to influence the education work in their preschools – in these cases, the students learn best. However, in many other cases, student teachers are allowed to perform their assignments, but they perform these in isolation. They are not fully integrated into the work of the preschool. Improvement in this area may be associated with improving the preparation of student teachers with regard to teamwork.

- The workload involved in implementing the practice and competency framework constitutes a real challenge for its sustainable implementation. It is a challenge for the college staff as well as for students who become teachers. This type of preparation and practice is based on data collection documentation and frequent staff meetings. It is challenging to invest all the effort and time required to continue implementing this agenda. A strong vision and belief in the importance of early childhood education, close collaboration among staff, and mutual support keep us together.

Recommendations for Improving the ECE Program at Levinsky College of Education

To be relevant and effective, any preparation program must continuously evaluate itself and define improvement goals. Therefore, this chapter closes with some recommended directions for improving ECE preparation at Levinsky College:

- Inclusion of field assignments and a course focused on teamwork in the program, and improving collaboration with the field mentors.
- Finding organizational ways to merge the Mediated Learning Experience and Classroom Management courses with the Inquiry of Fieldwork Experience course, to ensure their status as compulsory.
- Design of a digital portfolio documenting student teachers' professional development on core competencies through the preparation years. It is suggested that this portfolio include student-selected critical episodes, transcriptions of interactions, representative photos, plans of units of learning, and plans of coping with behavioral problems. Twice a year, based on these documents, students will evaluate their relationships with children, staff, and parents (whenever possible), the characteristics of their mediational interactions with children, the characteristics of a few pivotal decisions they made, and the extent of classroom management competencies (leadership, proactive mindset, self-regulation, etc.). At the end of each year, under the guidance of field and college mentors, and supported by colleagues, students should be asked to set personal goals of competency improvement. The attainment of these goals is to be assessed at the end of the following year in parallel with setting new goals for improvement. Integration of a portfolio would be helpful in attaining more continuity between years of study, as well as supporting students' professional development.

REFERENCES

Addi-Raccah, A., & Ainhoren, R. (2009). School governance and teachers' attitudes to parents' involvement in schools. *Teaching and Teacher Education*, 25(6), 805-813.

Alexander, R. (2008). *Essays in pedagogy*. London: Routledge.

Alexander, R. (Ed.). (2010). Children, their world, their education. *Final Report and Recommendations of the Cambridge Primary Review.* London: Routledge.

Alexander, R. (2017). *Towards dialogic teaching: Rethinking classroom talk* (5th ed.). York: Dialogos.

Ariav Commission (2006). *Report of the committee for determining outlines for teacher education in higher education institutions in Israel* [Hebrew].

Ball, D., & Forzani, F. M. (2009). The work of teaching and the challenge for teacher education. *Journal of Teacher Education, 60*(5), 497-511.

Bandura, A. (1995). Exercise of personal and collective efficacy in changing societies. In A. Bandura (Ed.). *Self-efficacy in changing societies* (pp. 1-45). New York, NY: Cambridge University Press.

Barber, B. K., Stolz, H. E., & Olsen, M. (2005). Parental support, psychological control and behavioural control: Assessing relevance across time, culture and method. *Monographs of the Society for Research in Child Development, 70*(4), 1-137.

Bertucci, A., Coute, S., Johnson, D. W., & Johnson, R. T. (2010). The impact of size of cooperative group on achievement, social support and self-esteem. *Journal of General Psychology, 135*(3), 256-272.

Belsky, J. (2013). Differential susceptibility to environmental influences. *International Journal of Child Care and Education Policy, 7*(2), 15-31.

Bingham, C., & Sidorkin, A. M. (Eds.). (2004). *No education without relation.* New York, NY: Peter Lang.

Boaler, J. (2013). Ability and mathematics: The mindset revolution that is reshaping education. *Forum, 55*(1), 143-152.

Brophy-Herb, H. E., Lee, R. E., Nievar, M. A., & Stollak, G. (2007). Preschoolers' social competence: Relations to family characteristics, teacher behaviors and classroom climate. *Journal of Applied Developmental Psychology, 28*(2), 134-148.

Bronfenbrenner, U. (1979). *The ecology of human development experiments by nature and design.* Cambridge, MA and London: Harvard University Press.

Bronfenbrenner U., & Morris P. A. (2006). The bioecological model of human development. In R. M. Lerner & W. Damon (Eds.), *Theoretical models of human development*. Vol. 1 of the *Handbook of child psychology* (5th ed.) (pp. 793-828). New York, NY: John Wiley & Sons.

Breuer, M., & Tal, C. (in press). Parents', school staff's and children's perceptions of their and their partners' roles related to the transition from preschool to the first grade, In E. Tabak & Y. Gilat (Eds.), *Parents' involvement in the children's education* [Hebrew].

Bukowski, W. M., Laursen, B., & Rubin, K. H. (2018). Peer relations: Past, present and promise. In W. M. Bukowski, B. Laursen, K. H. Rubin (Eds.). *Handbook of peer interactions, relationships and groups* (pp. 3-23). New York, NY: Guilford Press.

Campbell, S. B. (2002). *Behavior problems in preschool children: Clinical and developmental issues* (2nd ed.). New York, NY: Guilford Press.

Cohen, D. K. (2011). *Teaching and its predicaments*. Cambridge, MA: Harvard University Press.

Conroy, M. A., Brown, W. H., & Olive, M. L. (2008). Social competence interventions for young children with challenging behaviors. In W. H. Brown, S. L. Odom & S. R. McConnell (Eds.), *Social competence of young children: Risk, disability, and intervention* (pp. 205-231). Baltimore, MD: Brookes.

Dahlberg, G., Moss, P., & Pence, A. (2013). *Beyond quality in early childhood education and care languages of evaluation*. New York, NY: Routledge.

Dewey, J. (1938). *Experience and education*. New York, NY: Simon and Schuster.

Doll, W. E. (1993). *A post-modern perspective on curriculum*. New York, NY: Teachers' College Press.

Durlak, J. A., Weissberg, R. P., Dymnicki, A. B., Taylor, R. D., & Schellinger, K. B. (2011). The impact of enhancing students' social and emotional learning: A meta-analysis of school-based universal interventions. *Child Development, 82*(1), 405-432.

Dweck, C. S. (2012). Mindsets and human nature: Promoting change in the Middle East, the schoolyard, the social divide, and will power. *American Psychologist*, *67*(8), 614-622.

Emmer, E. T., & Stough, L. M. (2001). Classroom management: A critical part of educational psychology with implications for teacher education. *Educational Psychologist*, *36*(2), 103-112.

Evertson, C. M., & Harris, A. (1999). Support for managing learning-centered classrooms: The classroom organization and management program. In H. J. Freiberg (Ed.), *Beyond behaviorism: Changing the classroom management paradigm* (pp. 59-74). Boston, MA: Allyn & Bacon.

Feiman-Nemser, S. (2017). Alternative approaches to teacher education: What differences make a difference? In S. Feiman-Nemser & M. Ben-Peretz (Eds.), *Getting the teachers we need. International perspectives on teacher education* (pp. xiii-xxiii). Lanham, MD: Rowman & Littlefield.

Feiman-Nemser, S. & Buchman, M. (1985). Pitfalls of experience in teacher preparation. *Teachers College Record*, *87*(1), 53-65.

Feuerstein, R. & Feuerstein, S. (1991). Mediated Learning Experience (MLE): A theoretical review. In R. Feuerstein, P. Klein & A. Tannenbaum (Eds.), *Mediated Learning Experience: Theoretical, psychosocial and learning implications* (pp. 3-51). London: Freund Publishing House.

Feuerstein, R. Klein, P., & Tannenbaum, A. (Eds.). (1991). *Mediated learning experience: Theoretical, psychosocial and learning implications*. London: Freund Publishing House.

Feuerstein, R., Rand, Y., Hoffman, M. R., & Miller, R. (1980). *Instrumental enrichment for cognitive modifiability*. Baltimore: University Park Press.

Flyvbjerg, B. (2011). Case study. In N. K. Denzin and Y. S. Lincoln (Eds.), *Sage book of qualitative research* (4th ed.) (pp. 301-316). Thousand Oaks, CA: Sage.

Forzani, F. M. (2017). Centering teacher education on high-leverage practices. In S. Feiman-Nemser. & M. Ben-Peretz (Eds.), *Getting the teachers that we need: International perspectives on teacher education* (pp. 61-71), Lanham, MD: Rowman & Littlefield.

Fox, L., Dunlap, G., & Powell, D. (2002). Young children with challenging behavior: Issues and consideration for behavior support. *Journal of Positive Behavior Interventions, 4*, 208-217.Fumoto, H. (2011). Teacher-child relationships and early childhood practice. *Early Years: An International Research Journal, 31*(1), 19-30.

Gervais, J. (2016). The operational definition of competency-based education. *Journal of Competency-Based Education, 1*(2), 98-106.

Gettinger, M., & Fischer, C. (2015). Early childhood education classroom management. In E. T. Emmer & E. J. Sabornie (Eds.), *Handbook of classroom management* (pp. 141-166). New York and London: Routledge.

Gillies, R. & Cunnington, R. (2014). Cooperative learning: The behavioral and neurological markers that help to explain its success. In *Quality and equity: What does research tell us* (pp. 38-43), Research Conference, Adelaide. Australian Council for Educational Research.

Grossman, P. (Ed.). (2018), *Teaching core practices in teacher education.* Cambridge MA: Harvard Education Press.

Grossman, P., Hammerness, K., & McDonald, M. (2009). Redefining teaching, re-imagining teacher education. *Teachers and teaching: Theory and practice, 15*(2), 273-289.

Grossman, P., Schneider Kavanagh, S., & Pupik Dean, C. G. (2018). The turn towards practice-based teacher education: Introduction to the work of the Core Practice Consortium. In P. Grossman (Ed.), *Teaching core practices in teacher education* (pp. 1-15). Cambridge. MA: Harvard Education Press.

Hamre, B. K., & Pianta, R. C. (2005). Can instructional and emotional support in the first-grade classroom make a difference for children at risk of school failure. *Child Development, 76*(5), 949-967.

Hartup, W. W. (1992). Social relationships and their developmental significance. *American Psychologist, 44*(2), 120-126.

Hemmeter, M. L., Santos, R. M., & Ostrovsky, M. (2008). Preparing early childhood educators to address young children's social-emotional development and challenging behaviors: A survey of higher education programs in nine states. *Journal of Early Intervention, 30*(4), 321-340.

Hesse, F., Care, E., Buder, J., Sassenberg, K., & Griffin, P. (2015). A framework for teachable collaborative problem-solving skills. In P. Griffin & E. Care (Eds.), *Assessment and teaching of 21st century skills: Methods and approach* (pp. 37-57). Dordrecht: Springer.

Hinde, R. (1997). *Relationships: A dialectical perspective.* Hove, East Sussex, UK: Psychological Press.

Hoover-Dempsey, K. V., Walker, J. M. T., Sandler, H. M., Whetsel, D., Green, C. L., Wilkins, A. S., & Closson, K. (2005). Why do parents become involved? Research findings and implications. *Elementary School Journal, 106*(2), 105-130.

Horner, R. H., & Sugai, G. (2005). School wide school positive support: An alternative approach to discipline in schools. In L. Bambara & L. Kern (Eds.), *Positive behavior support* (pp. 359-390). New York, NY: Guilford Press.

Horner, R. H., Sugai, G. & Anderson, C. A. (2010). Examining the evidence base for school-wide positive behavior support. *Focus on Exceptional Children, 42*(8), 1-16.

Humphries, M. L., Williams, B. V., & Tanginia May, T. (2018). Early childhood teachers' perspectives on social-emotional competence and learning in urban classrooms. *Journal of Applied School Psychology, 34*(2), 157-179.

Jacobs, G. M., Lee, C., & Ng, M. (1997, June). *Co-operative learning in the thinking classroom.* Paper presented at *the International Conference on Thinking*, Singapore. Retrieved from http://files.eric.ed. gov/fulltext/ED574147.pdf.

Jennings, P. A., & Greenberg, M. T. (2009). The prosocial classroom: Teacher social and emotional competence in relation to student and classroom outcomes. *Review of Educational Research, 79*(1), 491–525.

Johnson, D. W., & Johnson, R. T. (2002). Learning together and alone: Overview and meta-analysis. *Asia Pacific Journal of Education, 22*(1), 95-105.

Jones, E., & Nimmo, J. (1994). *Emergent curriculum*. Washington DC: National Association for the Education of Young Children.

Kaiser, B., & Rasminsky, J. S. (2017). *Challenging behavior in young children* (4th ed.). Boston: Pearson.

Kemple, K. M., Hysmith, C., & Davis, G. M. (1996). Early childhood teachers' beliefs about promoting peer competence. *Early Child Development and Care, 120*(1), 145-163.

Klein, P. (1988). Stability and change in interaction of Israeli mothers and infants. *Infant Behavior and Development, 11*(1), 55-70.

Klein, P. (1991). Moral assessment and parental intervention in infancy and early childhood: New evidence. In R. Feuerstein, P. Klein and A. Tannenbaum (Eds.), *Mediated learning experience: Theoretical, psychosocial and learning implications* (pp. 213-239). Jerusalem: International Center for Enhancement of Learning Potential.

Kramer, T. J., Caldarella, P., Christensen, L., & Shaltzer, R. H. (2010). Social and emotional learning in the kindergarten classroom: Evaluation of the "Strong Start" curriculum. *Early Childhood Education Journal, 37*(4), 303-309.

Lampert, M., & Graziani, F. (2009). Instructional activities as a tool for teachers' and teacher educators' learning. *Elementary School Journal, 109*(5), 491-509.

Lazarowitz, R., & Karsenty, G. (1994). Cooperative learning and students' academic achievement, process skills, learning environment, and self-esteem in tenth-grade biology classrooms, In S. Sharan (Ed.), *Cooperative learning: Theory and research.* (pp. 23-37). New York: Praeger.

Lou, Y., Abrami, P., & d'Apollonia, S. (2001). Small group and individual learning with technology: A meta-analysis. *Review of Educational Research, 71*(3), 449-521.

Malaguzzi, L. (1993). For an education based on relationships. *Young Children, 11*(93), 9-13.

Malik, N. M., & Furman, W. (1993). Practitioner review: Problems in children's peer relations: What can the clinicians do? *Journal of Child Psychology and Psychiatry, 34*(8), 1303-1326.

McDonald, M., Kazemi, E., & Schneider Kavanagh, S. (2013). Core practices and pedagogies of teacher education: A call for a common language and collective activities. *Journal of Teacher Education, 64*(5), 378-386.

Nucci, L. (2006). Classroom management for moral and social development. In C. M. Evertson & C. S. Weinstein (Eds.), *Handbook of classroom management: Research, practice and contemporary issues* (pp. 711-728). Mahwah, NJ: Erlbaum.

Oyler, C. (2011). Preparing teachers of young children to be social justice-oriented educators. In B. S. Fennimore and A. L. Goodwin (Eds.), *Promoting social justice for young children* (pp. 147-161). New York, NY: Springer.

Pianta, R. C., Hamre, B., & Stuhlman, M. (2003). Relationships between teachers and children. In W. Reynolds & G. Miller (Eds.), *Comprehensive Handbook of Psychology: Educational Psychology* (vol. 7, pp. 199-234). Hoboken, NJ: Wiley and Sons.

Riley, P., Watt, H. M. G., Richardson, P. W., & De Alwis, N. (2012). Relations among beginning teachers' self-reported aggression, unconscious motives, personality, role stress, self-efficacy, and burnout. In T. Wubbels, P. den Brok, J. van Tartwijk and J. Levy (Eds.), *Interpersonal relationships in education: An overview of contemporary research* (pp. 151-166). Rotterdam, Netherlands: Sense Publishers.

Rimm-Kaufman, S. E., Early, D. M., Cox, M. J., Saluja, G., Pianta, R. C., Bradley, R. H., & Payne, C. (2002). Early behavioral attributes and teachers' sensitivity as predictors of competent behavior in the kindergarten classroom. *Journal of Applied Developmental Psychology, 23*(4), 451-470.

Rubin, K. H., Bukowski, W., & Parker, J. (2006). Peer interactions, relationships and groups. In N. Eisenberg (Ed.), *Handbook of child psychology: Social, emotional, and personality development* (6th ed.) (pp. 571–645). New York, NY: Wiley.

Sava, F. A. (2002). Causes and effects of teacher conflict-inducing attitudes towards pupils: A path analysis model. *Teaching and Teacher-Education*, *18*(8), 1007-1021.

Schutz, K. M., Danielson, K. A., & Cohen, J. (in press). Approximations in English language arts: Scaffolding a shared teaching practice. *Teaching and Teacher Education*. Retrieved from https://doi.org/10.1016/j.tate.2019.01.004.

Shachar, H. & Sharan, S. (1994). Talking, relating and achieving: Effects of cooperative learning and whole-class instruction. *Cognition and Instruction*, *12*(4), 313-353.

Sills, J., Rowse, G., & Emerson, L. M. (2016). The role of collaboration in the cognitive development of young children: A systematic review. *Child: Care, Health and Development, 42*(3), 313-324.

Slavin, R. E. (1996). Research on cooperative learning and achievement. What we know, what we need to know. *Contemporary Educational Psychology*, *21*(1), 43-69.

Slavin, R. E. (2013). Classroom applications of cooperative learning. In S. Graham (Ed.), *APA handbook of educational psychology* (pp. 359-378). Washington, DC: American Psychological Association.

Spilt, J. L., & Koomen, H. M. Y. (2009). Widening the view on teacher-child relationships: Teachers' narratives concerning disruptive versus non-disruptive children. *School Psychology Review*, *38*(1), 86-101.

Stake, R. E. (1995). *The art of case study research*. Thousand Oaks, CA: Sage.

Stough, L. M., & Montague, M. L. (2015). How teachers learn to be classroom managers. In E. T. Emmer & E. J. Sabornie (Eds.), *Handbook of classroom management* (pp. 446-458). New York and London: Routledge.

Sum Kim, B., & Farr Darling, L. (2009). Monet, Malaguzzi and the constructive conversations of preschoolers in Reggio-inspired classrooms. *Early Childhood Education Journal, 37*(2), 137-145.

Tal, C. (2002). *Social competence: Development, evaluation, enhancement and coping with difficulties*. Tel Aviv: Technosdar Ltd. [Hebrew].

Tal, C. (2004). One more time. Repeated picture book reading – training kindergarten teachers. *Hed Hagan*, 4-16 [Hebrew].

Tal, C. (2008). Teacher training for developing social skills as a means of preventing violence. *Dapei Yozma*, 5, 24-46 [Hebrew].

Tal, C. (2010). Moral Classroom Management. In S.B. Thompson (Ed.), *Kindergartens: Programs, functions, and outcomes* (pp. 115-132). New York, NY: Nova Science Publishers.

Tal, C. (2012). Discourse and reflection competencies developed by student teachers through repeated children's book read-alouds: A multiple case study. *ISRN Education*, vol. 2012, Article ID 308198, 10 pages. Retrieved from https://doi.org/10.5402/2012/308198.

Tal, C. (2016). *Moral Classroom Management in early childhood education*. New York: Nova.

Tal, C. (2018a). *Core competencies in teacher education*. Retrieved from https://clodietaldan.wordpress.com/?s=%D7%9B%D7%99%D7%A9% D7%95%D7%A8%D7%99+%D7%9C%D7%99%D7%91%D7%94&s ubmit=%D7%97%D7%99%D7%A4%D7%95%D7%A9 [Hebrew].

Tal, C. (2018b). The challenge of implementing small group work (SGW) in early childhood education (ECE). *Global Education Review*, 5(2), 123-144.

Tal, C., & Segal-Drori, O. (2015). Student teachers' implementation and understanding of repeated picture-book reading in preschools. *Australian Journal of Teacher Education*, 40(1). Retrieved from http://dx.doi.org/10.14221/ajte.2015v40n1.2.

Tobin, T. J., & Sugai, G. (2005). Preventing problem behaviors: Primary, secondary, and tertiary level prevention interventions for young children. *Journal of Early and Intensive Behavior Intervention, 2*(3), 125-144. Retrieved from http://dx.doi.org/10.1037/h0100309.

van Manen, M. (1994). Pedagogy, virtue and the narrative identity in teaching. *Curriculum Inquiry, 4*(2): 135-170.

Vygotsky, L. (1978). *Mind in society: The development of higher psychological processes*. Cambridge, MA: Harvard University Press.

Walker, J. M. T., & Hoover-Dempsey, K. V. (2015). Parental engagement and classroom management. In E. T. Emmer & E. J. Sabornie (Eds.),

Handbook of classroom management (pp. 459-478). New York and London: Routledge.

Wasik, B. (2008). When fewer is more: Small groups in early childhood classrooms. *Early Childhood Education Journal, 35*(6), 515-521.

Wells, G. (2000). Dialogic inquiry in education: Building on the legacy of Vygotsky. In C.D. Lee and P. Smagorinsky (Eds.), *Vygotskian perspectives on literacy research: Constructing meaning through collaborative inquiry* (pp. 51-86). New York, NY: Cambridge University Press.

Wells, G. (2008). Dialogue, inquiry, and the construction of learning communities. In B. Lingard, J. Nixon, & S. Ranson (Eds.), *Transforming learning in schools and communities* (pp. 236–257). London, UK: Continuum.

Wentzel, K. R. (2012). Teacher-student relationships and adolescent competence at school. In T. Wubbels, P. den Brok, J. van Tartwijk & J. Levy (Eds.), *Interpersonal Relationships in education: An overview of contemporary research* (pp. 19-37). Rotterdam, Netherlands: Sense Publishers.

Whitehurst, G. J., Falco, F. L., Lonigan, C. J., Fischel, J. E., DeBaryshe, B. D., Valdez-Menchaca, M. C., & Caulfield, M. (1988). Accelerating language development through picture book reading. *Developmental Psychology, 24*(4), 552-559.

Yu-le, Z. (2004). Some thoughts on emergent curriculum. *Paper presented at the Forum for Integrated Education and Educational Reform sponsored by the Council for Global Integrative Education*, Santa Cruz, CA, October 28-30. Retrieved from http://www.edpsyc interactive.org/CGIE/yule.pdf.

Zinsser, K. M., Shewark, E. A., Denham, S. A., & Curby, T. W. (2014). A mixed-method examination of preschool teacher beliefs about social-emotional learning and relations to observed emotional support. *Infant and Child Development, 23*(5), 471-493.

In: Teacher Training
Editor: Paula E. McDermott

ISBN: 978-1-53615-633-1
© 2019 Nova Science Publishers, Inc.

Chapter 2

EMERGENT CURRICULUM IN THE EARLY CHILDHOOD EDUCATION (ECE) PREPARATION PROGRAM IN ISRAEL- STUDENTS' PERSPECTIVES: TRANSFORMATIONS AND CHALLENGES

Iris Levy, Michaella Kadury-Slezak, Sigal Tish, Sivan Shatil Carmon and Clodie Tal*

Early Childhood Education, Levinsky College of Education,
Tel-Aviv, Israel

ABSTRACT

In this chapter we introduce a study which aims to show a transformation in perceptions of learning-teaching processes of third-year student teachers in ECE program in Levinsky College of Education in

---

* Corresponding Author's E-mail: irislevi96@gmail.com.

Israel while implementing emergent curriculum. A multiple case studies (Yin, 2014) approach is used to reveal the learning processes, difficulties, and changes in student teachers' perceptions with regards to the teaching-learning processes of young children.

Results indicate that student teachers' transformation from a traditional-positivist to a social constructivist perception occurred as a sustained process, which included emotional, cognitive and epistemological components. In many cases the transformation process included intermediate stages from 'teaching as preaching' by mainly listening to the child without intervening to mediation using thoughtful guidance in the discourse.

Results also suggest that student teachers' documentation, self-reflection, and support from the pedagogical and discipline mentors give them an opportunity to revisit and to interpret their learning process as part of the transformation process.

This study provides deeper understandings of student teachers' transformation process from a traditional to a constructivist approach. It also characterizes the difficulties that occur during this process. If the education system aims to adapt the 21st century learning skills then in it necessary to understand student teachers' difficulties and to construct a solid cognitive and emotional support system which support them during this meaningful process.

Keywords: mentoring of student teachers, emergent curriculum, student teachers' preparation programs, transformative learning

INTRODUCTION

One of the challenges of teachers' education in the 21st century is to train student teachers to understand and implement constructivist approaches, as in many cases it involves transformation processes. Transformation in students' perceptions with regards to learning teaching approaches is a challenging process. Students' perceptions are shaped by former individual experiences and knowledge that meet theory and practice during their studies. This study seeks to demonstrate the transformation in Early Childhood Education (ECE) student teachers' perceptions that are related to teaching and learning processes, from a traditional approach to a socio-constructivist approach. The study also aims to pinpoint facilitators and challenges in the process of the pedagogical transformation.

Clodie Tal, the former head of the ECE program at Levinsky College of Education, described the implementation of emergent curriculum approach within the training programme (Tal, 2014). According to Tal (2014), the teacher preparation programme is inspired by van Manen's lifeworld approach (1994), which fosters a holistic understanding of teaching situations and emphasizes that cognitive and social aspects are inseparable. Students are encouraged to become acquainted with the individual children, to form and teach small, heterogeneous groups including special needs children, and to form good pedagogical relationships with them. Tal (2014) stressed that constructing conditions for inquiry and vivid learning on the part of all children is an additional goal of the programme.

Emergent Curriculum

The main goal of emergent curriculum is to respond to the children's individual needs and interests. It is an open-ended and self-directed learning process, and it lends itself to a play-based environment. Emergent curriculum depends on teachers' initiatives and intrinsic motivation (Jones, 2012). According to Yu-le, 'emergent curriculum is a constructive curriculum in which the teachers, students, teaching materials and environment interact in the context of dialogue' (Yu-le, 2004, 2).

The primary role of the teacher, in emergent curriculum, is to create a stimulating learning environment that aims to encourage children to explore and learn according to their interests. The teachers must notice children's questions and create ways to facilitate and extend them. During this process, teachers document children's activities and interactions and encourage the development of new questions (Jones, 2012). This documentation offers the children and teachers another opportunity to reflect on and interpret their learning, and to acknowledge not only the product, but also the learning processes (Rinaldi, 1998). Emergent curriculum is characterized as reflection upon practice, instead of the traditional curriculum that focuses on memorizing and on the practice of mechanical skills (Yu-le, 2004).

Implementation of Emergent Curriculum

The ECE preparation programme at Levinsky College is based on a social constructivist perception of learning. One of the main pedagogic tools in the learning process of the student teachers is documentation. The student teachers examine their practice at the preschool by documenting their practice with the children and then reflecting upon it in order to understand and improve their teaching practices (Tal, 2014). According to Rinaldi (1998), documentation is an essential process that supports the educational and the dynamic exchanges related to learning. It is interrelated with social constructivist practices and openness to change, and it enables reflective practice (Schön, 1983 & 1987). Documentation of their practices within the preschool offers the student teachers a unique opportunity to look back at the learning process – re-listen, revisit, reflect and interpret it, in order to improve and plan the continuous learning according to the children's needs and subjects of interest.

Levinsky's programme is based on a deep acquaintance of the student teachers with each individual child (Tal, 2014). This is established by working in small, heterogeneous permanent groups in preschools. Working in heterogeneous small groups is an important organizational component of classroom management, contributing to meaningful learning (Tal, 2016). Within the small groups student teachers listen to the children, mediate and promote the children's individual expression in 'hundred languages' (Rinaldi,1998). According to Rinaldi (1998), hundred languages are the endless ways that children may express their thoughts, understandings and feelings (visual, sensual, musical etc.). This approach is based on emergent curriculum method of listening to children rather than speaking (Rinaldi, 1998). The Mosaic approach (Clark and Moss, 2011) is an integrated multi-method approach for listening to children, which combines visual and verbal documentation where children and adults are acknowledged as co-constructors of meaning. Listening according to this approach is understood as a process, which is not limited to the spoken word (Clark and Moss, 2011).

Within the ECE programme, each student chooses and studies two of four disciplines in depth: Literature, Judaism, Art, and Science. In their third year of studies, the student teachers lead emergent curriculum programme in one of their chosen disciplines, together with small groups of children, During this process, the ECE programme provides the students with two types of support systems: face-to-face and distance support. This support system includes pedagogical and emotional aspects and is provided by pedagogic and disciplinary mentors.

Students' face-to-face system consists of two sources of support: (1) an academic course titled 'inquiry of practice,' which includes teaching-learning of pedagogical theories and approaches as well as students teachers sharing experiences (2) a pedagogical mentor who observes students' pedagogical work in the preschool and provides feedback.

Students' distance support system includes: individual and group WhatsApp discussions, E-mail exchanges, phone conversations, and a personal Blog that provides the student teachers with the opportunity to re-listen, revisit, reflect and interpret their learning process (Rinaldi, 1998). It also provides the student teachers with an opportunity to share their knowledge, thoughts, and indecision with their fellow students and mentors. All these ways of communication and reflection support the student teachers in their transformation preprocess.

Transformative Learning

Teaching, according to Mezirow and Taylor (2011), is based on promoting change. Educators challenge learners to critically question and assess the integrity of their deeply held assumptions about how they relate to the world around them (Mezirow and Taylor, 2011, p. XI).

80   *Iris levy, Michaella Kadury-Slezak, Sigal Tish et al.*

The importance of reflection in teaching and learning processes has been thoroughly discussed over the years (e.g., Brookfield, 1995; Dewey, 1933; Schon, 1987). Dewey (1933) called for teachers to take reflective action, which involves "active, persistent, and careful consideration of any belief or supposed form of knowledge in light of the grounds that support it and the further consequences to which it leads" (Dewey, 1933, p. 9).

Fostering transformative learning is seen as teaching for change. Critical reflection, particularly critical reflection of assumptions (CRA), is central to the understanding of how adults learn to think for themselves rather than act on the concepts, values, and feelings of others. It is how adults test their justification through rational discourse, and strive for decisions through consensus building (Mezirow, 1995; Mezirow and Associates, 2000, in Mezirow and Taylor, 2011).

Berger (2004) stresses that a transformation process is an outcome of a learning process. New knowledge transforms through exposition to new theories, which make us observe our perception with a new perspective that can cause internal conflict. In this process, according to Berger, new knowledge must take its place within the former knowledge and the teacher must reorganize it within the existing frames of knowledge (Berger, 2004).

This study seeks to demonstrate the continued conflicts that is part of the transformative learning of student teachers in ECE at Levinsky College of Education, from a traditional approach to a socio-constructivist approach. It also aims, to pinpoint facilitators and challenges in the process of the pedagogical transformation.

METHODOLOGY

The study employed a multiple case studies approach (Yin, 2014). There were 180 student teachers in their third year in the ECE programme in Levinsky College in Israel during the years 2015-2016. We focus on 14 cases and explore their transformation process. The participants were chosen due to their reflective expression abilities in both word and image modalities. The student teachers' age range was 25-30 years old. The purpose of the multiple case studies is to reveal the learning process, difficulties, and change in student teachers' perceptions with regard to teaching-learning processes of young children.

At the time of the study, student teachers were required to do fieldwork in public Israeli preschools, once a week during a period of 8 months, each year of their tenure in the programme. In addition, towards the end of each semester, student teachers worked daily in the preschools for a full week. The participating preschools consisted of 30-35 children, aged 4-6. During their practice, student teachers worked with small, heterogeneous groups of 4-6 children. Within the small group meetings, student teachers were instructed to develop emergent curriculum according to the children's interests and needs. The small group meetings were audio- and video-recorded and were reflected on by the student teachers on a weekly basis.

Tools

The main tools for collecting data in this study were:

(1) Regular posts in personal blogs (open to the pedagogic mentor only) during the learning process, which include student teachers' documentation of the weekly small group activities. Analysing photographs, audio-recordings, and graphic illustrations of the student teachers' perceptions within the learning process were an essential part of the blog posts.

(2) Face-to-face feedback and consulting meetings between the student teachers and their pedagogic mentor. These meetings were conducted five times during the ten-month period.

(3) In-depth, semi-structured interviews were conducted with the student teachers at the end of the academic year. The interviewees volunteered to take part in the research study.

Data Analysis

Data were collected throughout the years 2015-2016 and analysed, based on both the Mosaic approach (Clark & Moss, 2011) and thematic analysis (Richie & Spencer, 1994, Freeman, 1998). This multi-method approach is important to understand that listening is a process that is not limited to the spoken word (Clark & Moss, 2011). In the current study, the researchers analysed student teachers' visual and verbal documentation of their activities and interactions with the small groups of children in the preschools.

The mosaic approach enabled us to reveal how student teachers and children co-constructed meanings within the small groups, and thereby gain understandings of the students' perceptions regarding the learning-teaching processes with young children.

In the process of thematic analysis, the researcher becomes familiar with the richness, depth, and diversity of the data and begins a process of conceptualisation. In this process the researchers drawn upon a priori issues, emergent issues, or analytical themes (Richie & Spencer, 1994), and identify, name, and code key issues, concepts and themes according to which data can be explored. This process continues, with the researcher grouping and finding relationships in the data, ending with the last stage, which is a display where the researcher aims to set out the patterns and relationships among the categories. In the current study, key issues that emerged from the data were grouped and relationships were found between the different categories within the verbal and visual data. This enabled us to find connections of similarities in the learning processes of ECE students with regards to teaching-learning and to identify similar stages of transformation in their perceptions.

Ethics: All student teachers agreed to participate in the study, and their identities remained confidential by using a pseudonym. The semi-structured interviews with the volunteer student teachers were conducted at the end of the academic year, following the students' formal academic evaluation.

FINDINGS

The research findings revealed that in most cases, student teachers' transformation process included three main stages. The first stage was a traditional perception of teaching and learning (stage A). The following stage was characterized by cognitive and emotional confusion and a struggle to understand and implement the constructivist emergent curriculum approach (stage B). The last stage was characterized by expressions of transformation in student teachers' perceptions – from a traditional to a constructivist approach (stage C).

According to the data analysis, most participants went through all three stages in a continuous process. The transition from one stage to another was not precise, which means that stages may overlap. In addition, as student teachers are not homogenous groups, these stages varied in different ways, such as the length or the intensity of each stage.

In the following section we will detail the first stage in the transformation process and provide examples that illustrate this stage.

Stage (A): Traditional Perception of Teaching and Learning Processes

At the beginning of their third year in the college, most of the student teachers held traditional perceptions with regards to teaching and learning processes. Ronit, for instance, noted in a face-to-face meeting with her pedagogic mentor:

> 'At the beginning, I thought that I am the source of knowledge… that I know everything.'

Ronit's perception at the beginning of the year is that the teacher owns the knowledge, and learning is about transferring the information from the teacher to the child. This is a traditional teacher-centered approach.

Karen, another student teacher, acknowledged her life experience as a reason for her traditional perception of learning and teaching:

'We grew up in an education system that is focused on workbooks. I don't remember a teacher that when a child came to her or him with an idea that the teacher would develop it.... We grew up differently... .'

As a child learning in the Israeli education system learning Karen experienced teacher-centered, traditional learning with no focus on the children's ideas and interests. These childhood learning experiences constructed her knowledge frames with regards to teaching learning processes. Learning the new constructivist approach requires learning new theoretical approaches and also organizing this knowledge within her former knowledge about learning processes, reflecting the complexity of transformation processes.

Evidence for a traditional approach to the learning-teaching process also emerged from the graphic representations that the student teachers posted on their blogs. For instance, Debi, drew a line of children figures placed one after the other. She drew herself at the front of the line with her back facing the children. There is no interaction between her and the children or between the children. The parallel lines at the sides of the illustration may suggest that there is one way of learning. Debi placed herself, as the leader of the group with the children following her. It seems that she considers herself as the primary source of knowledge (see Figure 1).

Similarly, Rona posted a photo of her activity with the group of children at the beginning of the year on her blog. In this photograph (see Figure 2), the student teacher sits in front of the group of children while she is holding a book. The children's chairs are organized in semi-circle, which allows them to focus on the teacher but also to interact with each other. The student teacher is looking at the children and it seems that she is carefully listening to them. Here, too, Rona seems to perceive herself as the source of knowledge.

Figure 1. Debi's perception of the teaching -learning process.

Figure 2. Rona's perception of the teaching-learning process.

Although both student teachers reflect a traditional approach to the learning-teaching process, there are differences in their position within this stage. While Debi positions herself with her back to the children with no interactions between them, Rona position herself facing the children, listening to them.

As illustrated in the examples above, at the beginning of their third year, all the student teachers expressed traditional perceptions about the teaching-learning process. They view the teacher as the center and the source of knowledge. The second stage in the process of transformation is described next.

Stage (B): Confusion and Struggle

The second stage in the transformation process is characterized by confusion and a struggle to understand and implement the constructivist emergent curriculum approach. Two main aspects characterize this stage: the first is the emotional and cognitive confusion and the second is the external and objective environmental aspects.

Emotional and Cognitive Confusion

Emotional and cognitive confusion was evident in student teachers' reflections during their learning process. For example, Lona, emphasizes her fear of the unstructured planning of emergent curriculum and the lack of detailed planning of learning process:

> 'At the beginning, I came [to the process] with a lot of fear … at one stage I thought: "this is impossible ….how will I develop a program (emergent curriculum)?"

Lona uses the words 'fear' and 'impossible' to emphasize her feelings of helplessness in developing emergent curriculum. She seems to feel that she does not have the skills for developing an open curriculum.

Along similar lines, Keren describes the emotional turmoil she went through at the second stage of the transformation:

> 'I have never worked that way… It stresses me out … it is difficult for me to change my way of thinking … I don't have a list of aims, examples of past projects… I'm stepping into the unknown…'

Keren notes that this is the first time that she has worked according to emergent curriculum principles. She emphasizes the difficulty of dealing with the lack of a list of operative aims that usually assist her with planning her lessons. Keren emphasizes the emotional difficulties and the stress in the second stage of her transformation process.

The emotional difficulties in the second stage may prevent student-teachers from implementing emergent curriculum principles in the preschool. This is noted by Shir:

'In the past, I liked coming with a very organized plan ... it blocked me... .'

Shir describes how the traditional approach 'blocked' her from developing emergent curriculum. This 'block' could be due to an integration of cognitive and emotional factors.

The above examples demonstrate how some of the student teachers describe the second stage in the transformation process and how the cognitive and emotional factors may impact implementation of emergent curriculum in the preschool. Other student teachers noted environmental aspects that interfered with the implementation of emergent curriculum, as detailed below.

External and Objective Environmental Aspects

Student teachers' blogs and interviews revealed three environmental factors that interfered with implementing emergent curriculum in the preschool. The first factor was children's perceptions of teaching-learning processes.

Children in many Israeli preschools are used to traditional approaches of teaching. Ori pointed out that in the group meetings with her heterogeneous group of children, they struggled in reflecting on her open questions, asking questions, and in expressing their views in an open manner. According to the Ori, the children were confused by the wealth of opportunities that were provided to them. She emphasized her frustration and noted:

'The children did not understand what I want... .'

Sarah also points out the difficulties of the children to participate in an open conversation within the small group and to understand that they can lead the discourse:

'The children are used to a specific way of working and learning and it was difficult to change it.'

A heavy academic load and limited working time with the children in the preschool was the second aspect that the student teachers noted as interfering with implementing the curriculum. It is important to note that developing and implementing emergent curriculum is part of an academic assignment that includes an assessment. This may lead to stress for the student teachers, as is depicted by Shani.

'We work with a group of children and then you have to report on it and your work is being assessed and graded ... there is always a fear that there will not be any significant materials ... that the children will not talk about significant issues ... for writing an academic work. It was also limited in time.'

Shani stresses that the children's active involvement in the learning process is the main factor in the students' assessment, as emergent curriculum should be developed according to the children's interests and views. However, the children's learning processes which are, to a great extent, unpredictable, lead to fear and stress for the student teachers.

The third environmental factor that the student teachers noted was limited learning time and space within the preschool. The learning environment within the Israeli preschools usually does not support emergent curriculum learning, as there is a low child-staff ratio. There are approximately 35 children working with two staff members. Additionally, the preschool is generally a small space in relation to the number of children. The lack of space was noted by Roni as complicating the implementation of emergent curriculum:

Emergent Curriculum in the Early Childhood Education (ECE) ... 89

'There is no space which is separate... where I can quietly sit with a group of children and listen to them.'

The crowding and lack of space for small-group interactions In the Israeli preschools is a common problem that the student teachers face in implementing emergent curriculum in the preschool.

Many student teachers also mentioned that the fieldwork in the preschool is only once a week and the learning process that they lead are not continuous enough. As Ela notes:

'I feel that... umm... because I met them once a week it's hard for me to develop continuous learning process and it's hard for me to help the children to remember the ideas and thoughts that were mentioned and discussed in the previous meeting.'

While other students focus on their own struggle to implement emergent curriculum, Ela focuses on the children's difficulties to relate and develop emergent curriculum due to the time gaps between the group meetings. Development of emergent curriculum is based on children's ideas and thoughts that are developed in cooperation during the group discourse (Tal, 2014, 2018). According to Ela, the gap between the group meetings interferes in constructing the group's new knowledge.

All the above examples illustrate the confusion facing the student teachers and their struggle with the process of transformation. In the following section we will focus on the third stage, which illustrates expressions of transformation to a constructivist approach to learning and teaching.

Stage (C): Transformation to Emergent Curriculum Approach

Despite the internal and external difficulties in understanding and implementing the constructivist approach described by the student teachers in stage B, we nonetheless found expressions of transformation in student teachers perceptions, the third stage in the process. In this stage, the student teachers realize that the learning process should be based on an open discourse lead by the children. They have realized that this is a shared learning process in which they and the children participate in a dialogue.

For example, Dana emphasizes the importance of the cooperative learning during the meeting in the preschool and her personal learning process:

> 'I went through a personal process, I learned about myself. I learned from the children: language, imagination, responsibility ... I learned how not to interfere with the learning process so it would be theirs.'

In this account Dana positions herself as a learner not as the teacher. Dana also reported that she learned 'not to interfere with the learning process,' which indicates her perceptions with regards to her position as an educator within the learning process. This perception matches the constructivist approach, where the role of children is to talk and express their thoughts and opinions and the role of the educator is to listen.

Ori also describes the transformation she went through in the ways she works with the children:

> 'I wanted to teach the children about values, knowledge... and suddenly a whole world opened ... I learned a lot about myself. I discovered a world where the children are the inventors, the leaders. To listen to them – it's magic ... they always surprise you... .'

Ori shifts from the position of teaching to the position of learning – 'I wanted to teach... I learned'. She notes that she learned about herself, however, it seems that she also learned about teaching-learning processes. She discovered that teaching is a process where the educator can let the children lead the learning process according to their own personal interests. Ori uses the word "magic" to describe this kind of learning process. It seems that in the past Ori thought that this kind of learning is impossible – this may indicate the transformation in Ori's perceptions with relation to teaching-learning processes.

Sarah also describes her present perceptions with regards to teaching-learning processes:

'I learned that it (the learning process) belongs to the children, not to take it from them. It is totally theirs... the hard work is to let go... .'

Sarah states that the learning process 'belongs to the children'. This perception matches the constructivist approach to the teaching–learning process where children lead the learning process. Sarah notes her difficulties during the transformation process to differently construct her position and role as an educator, to 'let go'.

Yonit, another student teacher, reflected on her learning at the ECE program at Levinsky College, and noted several pedagogical practices that she employs when working in small groups; these practices match the constructivist approach:

'I learned how to listen to the children, to let them lead, to let them make assumptions, to express their thoughts, I learned how to ask questions.'

According to Yonit's description it is clear that she provide the children opportunities within the group work to express their interests.

Several student teachers described the transformation process using graphic illustrations. For instance, Hadas illustrated the steps that she went through in the process. She showed how the difficulties turned into a motivating force for development and change (Figure 3).

Hadas demonstrated how she coped with the difficulties of implementing emergent curriculum. Then she illustrated how these difficulties created new thinking that lead her to act (doing). This produced the turning point in her perceptions with regards to teaching-learning processes and implementing emergent curriculum. Hadas summarized her learning process: 'I learned to grow with difficulties'.

Figure 3. Illustration of implementing emergent curriculum - Hadas.

Debi's graphic illustration also shows the transformation in her perceptions from a traditional approach to emergent curriculum approach (Figure 4).

Figure 4. Debi's illustration of implementing emergent curriculum.

Emergent Curriculum in the Early Childhood Education (ECE) ... 93

Earlier in this paper we provided Debi's illustration of her perception at the beginning of her learning process (Figure 1). As described, the student teacher was situated at the front and the children were positioned behind her. In her illustration of present practices Debi demonstrates stage C. In Figure 4, the student teacher is positioned in the middle of the illustration and the children are positioned around her, mainly in front of her. In this illustration, Debi used rounded arrows to demonstrate the creativity and the openness of the learning process. The learning is no longer pre-planned and led by the student but rather, emerges and develops all through the process. Debi reflected on the process:

> 'I felt that I was privileged to experience and be exposed to the children's deep, original thoughts and to learn so much from them while taking part in the learning processes.'

Rona presents the transformation in her perceptions of learning processes using two photos of her with the group of children and by self-written reflection in her personal blog. The first photo (Figure 2) represents stage A and was discussed previously. At the end of the year Rona's photo represents stage C (Figure 5). In this photo Rona is positioned as part of the group, she is at the same height as the children, listening and investigating with them. This photo represents the emergent curriculum process where the learning subject (the ants) emerged from the children's shared investigation and discourse.

In her self-written reflection at stage A, Rona writes about herself and about the children separately. She refers to the children as "they" and to herself as 'I':

> 'I read the story to the children from the beginning to the end. They were very excited. During the reading, they expressed amazement from the course of events in the story... when I finished reading, they asked many questions. They looked again in different sections of the book and talked about the events.'

Figure 5. Rona's implementing emergent curriculum.

At the end of the learning process (stage C), Rona no longer separates herself from the children, rather she becomes part of the learning group using the pronoun "we", that demonstrates the equal participation of the children and herself in the learning process:

> 'With one group, we finished reading the story about the ladybug. With the other group, we continued reading the book about the stone soup. We started from the beginning and deepened our understandings of the story's meanings. We talked about happiness, what it means and what makes us happy.... We tried to understand how a soup of stones can make a whole village happy.'

From all the examples described above it is clear that not only we, the researchers, could see the transformation, but that the students themselves were aware of the transformation process they went through.

CONCLUSION

The present study examined the transformation process that student teachers underwent, from a traditional-positivist perception to a social constructivist perception of the teaching-learning process using meta-cognitive strategies. These Meta –cognitive strategies include thoughts and activities that assist learners to reevaluate their learning process and to make plan for learning for better outcome (Oxford, 1990; Chamot & O' Malley, 1990).

Results revealed that at the beginning of the process (Stage A), the student teachers positioned themselves as the leaders of the learning process, the 'source of knowledge' (Ronit, student-teacher, 2016). Stage B was characterized by a lot of confusion and emotional stress, as described: 'it comes with a lot of fear' (Lona, Student-teacher, 2015), 'now what?', (Shani, student teacher, 2015),'it stresses me out' (Keren, Student teacher, 2015) 'It blocks me' (Shir, student teacher, 2015). In Stage C, we observed the beginning of the transformation process from the traditional perception where the student teacher leads the learning process to the constructivist perception and the student teacher becomes part of the learning process:' I discovered a world where the children are the inventors, the leaders' (Ori, Student teacher, 2015), 'I felt that I was privileged to experience and be exposed to the children's deep, original thoughts' (Debi, Student teacher, 2015). The findings reveal that all the student teachers went through all three stages A, b and C. We also found that all student teachers went through emotional and cognitive difficulties during the transformation process. Furthermore, we found differences between student teachers in the implementation of emergent curriculum principles.

The goal of the ECE program in Levinsky College of Education is to expose the students to constructivist theories and methods of teaching and learning. This study reveals that most of the preschool student teachers come from a traditional school system, which becomes part of their perception of the teaching-learning process. In accordance with findings of previous studies (Pintrich et al., 1993), we found that the transformation process included cognitive and emotional conflicts and difficulties, with the conflicts at the heart of the transformation process. Our results demonstrate how transforming these traditional, well-established perceptions become a great challenge for the pedagogical and discipline mentors in the College. Despite the challenges, the emotional and cognitive support system of the ECE pedagogical and disciplinary mentors were one of three factors that we found supported student teachers through their transformation process. These mentors provided the students with the opportunity to share their emotions with them and with their peers and to reflect upon them (Mezirow and Taylor, 2011). This supports previous research emphasizing the complexity of the pedagogical mentor role (Bar-Ziv, 2009).

A second factor that supported student teachers through their transformation process was self-reflection. Our results suggest that student teachers' documentation provided them with an opportunity to listen again, revisit, reflect and interpret their learning process (Rinaldi, 1998; Mezirow and Taylor, 2011). The student's learning of constructivist theories via their academic studies together with their self-reflections on their practices emphasize Mezirow and Taylor's (2011) insight about critical self-perception of the student teachers regarding the learning process. According to the scholar, critical reflection and particularly critical reflection of assumptions, is central to the understanding of how adults learn to think for themselves rather than act on concepts, values, and feelings of others, (Mezirow, 1995; Mezirow & Associates, 2000, in Mezirow and Taylor, 2011). Our results also stressed the importance of exposure to new theories and ideas as which supported the students to transform their perception to the newly acquired knowledge (Berger, 2004).

The last factor that supported the student teachers' transformation was the face-to-face and distance support systems that included pedagogical and emotional aspects. This support system was provided to the students by the pedagogic and disciplinary mentors as we mention at the beginning of this chapter. Face to face support also included sharing of experiences and thoughts with the pedagogical mentor and other students. Working in collaboration is one of the essential skills of the 21st century (21st Century Partnership, 2009). Our results reveal this element as a meaningful component of the student teachers' transformation process. Sharing experiences with each other includes inquiry and reflection of the students' community-based activities that some of them are part of the students'

Emergent Curriculum in the Early Childhood Education (ECE) ... 97

tasks and other are the result of the environment that allows and promotes sharing of experience and thoughts (McLaughlin & Talbert, 2006).

Study Limitations: Data collection for this study was part of the student teachers' academic work that illustrates students' professional development. We take into consideration that this may have influenced student teachers' responses and representations when discussing their learning processes with their pedagogic and discipline mentors.

IMPLICATIONS

This study highlights that most of the student teachers possess a traditional perception of learning at the beginning of their studies. Understanding this may assist the pedagogical and discipline mentors to adopt a curriculum that matches the student teachers' developing perceptions with regards to teaching-learning processes.

In addition, we learned that the transformation is a complicated process that needs time to assimilate the principles of emergent curriculum. It also needs repeated experience, documentation, reflection, face-to-face meeting and cooperative learning that help to implement emergent curriculum methods. It consists of emotional and cognitive aspects that are essential to the perception change. Therefore, the role of the pedagogical mentor is to know the student teacher and to find a unique way to help her in the transformation process.

We found that the documentation and reflection by the student teacher during the transformation process helps them to understand their perceptions and support transformation processes. In addition it assists the pedagogic mentors to characterize the difficulties in the learning process and to find ways to support the student teacher. We consider students' documentation and reflection a primary tool in learning and transformation processes.

Our research is a continuation of research begun by Tal (2014). She represented student teachers' direct ways of working with children as part of implementing emergent curriculum. This study reveals student teachers' inner mental and cognitive processes. These processes were part of the transformation of perceptions of teaching- learning processes from a socio-positivistic perception to a socio- constructivist approach.

REFERENCES

Bar-Ziv. I. (2009). The Pedagogical Mentor Perception of his Role in Relation to the Styles of Existence. In *Styles of Existence: Theoretical, Scientific and Implementing Aspects*, edited by D. Shkolnik and I. Rand, 224-279. Tel Aviv: Mofet Institute.

Berger, P. L. and Luckmann, T. (1989). *The Social Construction of Reality: A Treatise in the Sociology of Knowledge.* Garden City, NY: Anchor Books.

Berger, R. (2004). Perceptions and Attitudes of Teachers of Literature Regarding the Integration of the Kobovi Method in Teaching Literature. In *Discourse in Education: Researching Educational Events,* edited by I. Kupferberg and E. Olshtain, 156-185. Tel Aviv: Mofet Institute.

Copple, C. and Bredekamp, S. (2009). *Developmentally Appropriate Practice in Early Childhood Programs Serving Children from Birth through Age 8.* 3rd ed. Washington, DC: National Association for the Education of Young Children.

Dewey, J. (1933). *How We Think: A Restatement of the Relation of Reflective Thinking to the Educative Process.* Boston, MA: D.C. Heath & Co Publishers.

Feiman-Nemser, S. 2001. From Preparation to Practice: Designing a Continuum to Strengthen and Sustain Teaching. *Teachers College Record* 103 (6): 1013-1055.

Franklin, M. B. and Biber, B. (1977). Psychological Perspectives and Early Childhood Education: Some Relations between Theory and Practice. In *Current Topics in Early Childhood Education,* Vol. 1, edited by L. Katz, 1–32. Norwood, NJ: Ablex.

Gandini, L. and Kaminsky, J. A. (2004). Reflections on the Relationship between Documentation and Assessment in the American Context: An Interview with Brenda Fyfe. *Innovations in Early Education: The International Reggio Exchange*, 11(1): 5-17.

Jones, E. 2012. The Emergence of Emergent Curriculum. *Young Children*, 67 (2): 66-68.

Jones, E. and Nimmo, J. (1994). *Emergent Curriculum*. Washington, DC: NAEYC.

Jones, E. and Reynolds, G. (2011). *The Play's the Thing: Teachers' Roles in Children's Play*. 2nd ed. New York: Teachers College Press.

McLaughlin, M. W. and Talbert, J. E. (2006). *Building School-Based Teacher Learning Communities: Professional Strategies to Improve Student Achievement*. New York: Teachers College Press.

Norman, P. J. and Feiman-Nemser, S. (2005). Mind activity in teaching and mentoring. *Teaching and Teacher Education* 21 (6): 679–697.

O'Malley, J. M. and Chamot, A. U. (1990). *Learning strategies in second language acquisition.* Cambridge: Cambridge University Press.

Oxford, R. L. (1990). *Language Learning Strategies: What Every Teacher Should Know*. Boston, MA: Heinle and Heinle.

Pintrich, P. R., Marx, R. W. and Boyle, R. A. (1993). Beyond cold conceptual change: The role of motivational beliefs and classroom contextual factors in the process of conceptual change. *Review of Educational Research* 63: 167-199.

Rinaldi, C. 2001. The Pedagogy of Listening: The Listening Perspective from the Reggio Emilia. *Innovations in Early Education: The International Reggio Exchange* 8 (4): 1–4.

Schön A. D. 1983. *The Reflective Practitioner: How Professionals Think in Action.* New York: Basic Books.

Schön, A. D. 1987. *Educating the Reflective Practitioner: Toward a new design for teaching and learning in the professions.* San Francisco: Jossey-Bass Publishers.

Tal, C. 2014. Introduction of an emergent curriculum and an inclusive pedagogy in a traditional setting in Israel: a case study. *International Journal of Early Years Education,* 22 (2): 141-155.

Tal, C. 2018. The Challenge of Implementing Small Group Work in Early Childhood Education. *Global Education Review* 5 (2): 123-144.

Van Manen, M. (1994). Pedagogy, Virtue and the Narrative Identity in Teaching. *Curriculum Inquiry* 4 (Summer): 135–170.

Vygotsky, L. (1978). *Mind in Society: The Development of Higher Psychological Processes.* Cambridge, MA: Harvard University Press.

Yu-le, Z. (2004). Some Thoughts on Emergent Curriculum. Paper presented at the *Forum for Integrated Education and Educational Reform sponsored by the Council for Global Integrative Education,* Santa Cruz, CA, October 28-30.

In: Teacher Training
Editor: Paula E. McDermott

ISBN: 978-1-53615-633-1
© 2019 Nova Science Publishers, Inc.

Chapter 3

EMERGENT CURRICULUM IN THE PREPARATION OF ECE STUDENT TEACHERS IN ISRAEL: RATIONALE, APPROACHES, IMPLEMENTATIONS AND CHILDREN'S PERSPECTIVES

Sigal Tish, Iris Levy, Michaella Kadury-Slezak, Sivan Shatil Carmon and Clodie Tal

Early Childhood Education, Levinsky College of Education,
Tel-Aviv, Israel

ABSTRACT

In this chapter we show how student teachers at the ECE (Early Childhood Education) department at Levinsky College of Education implement an emergent curriculum approach (Jones, 2012; Rinaldi, 2001; Yu-le, 2004) and create bridges to diverse children's homes. We will focus on the rationale of the program, its implementation and on children's perspectives. The early childhood teacher preparation program at Levinsky College of Education in Israel is based on a social constructivist perception of learning, and the student teachers do their fieldwork in public preschools as part of their training (Tal, 2014). The tasks included in the fieldwork include documentation of their practice with the children and reflection upon it in order to understand and improve their teaching practices.

Within the ECE programme at Levinsky College, from the first year of study, all student teachers in their field placement are expected to lead small heterogeneous groups of children. In the third year, they are expected to engage the children in their groups in learning by employing an emergent curriculum approach. This emergent learning process of students and children is being supported by the Levinsky preparation program by two types of support systems: Face to face and Distance support. Both types of support include pedagogic as well as emotional approaches and are being provided by pedagogic and disciplinary mentors. This chapter is based on a qualitative inquiry of ten case studies of emergent curriculum programmes that were guided and documented by student teachers (in their third year of study in the ECE program at Levinsky College). The methodology used multiple case studies (Yin, 2014) based on the mosaic approach (Clark, 2010). The findings revealed that using emergent curriculum principles, student teachers enabled and enhanced open discourse within small heterogeneous groups that promoted the expression of individual children's cultures. The student teachers succeeded in building collaboration among children based on the knowledge they gained of each others' families and culture. Empowering individual children was found helpful in promoting children's multicultural orientation in small heterogeneous groups.

Keywords: ECE preparation programme, diversity, emergent curriculum, small groups, multicultural education

INTRODUCTION

The Early Childhood Education (ECE) teacher preparation programme at Levinsky College of Education in Israel is committed to instilling a socially inclusive pedagogical approach in the student teachers that is based on a social constructivist perception of learning. These principles are translated into an inquiry approach to practice and an emergent curriculum (Tal, 2014). Alongside other disciplinary courses within the ECE programme, the programme's foundation is constructed of four pillars that interact and support each other: (a) the importance of a deep acquaintance with every individual child; (b) working in small groups; (c) multicultural education; and, (d) an emergent curriculum. In the following section, we will review each of these elements and describe the ways they are constructed within the programme.

Acquaintance with Every Individual Child

The ECE teacher preparation programme at Levinsky College promotes a holistic understanding of teaching situations and emphasises that cognitive and social aspects are inseparable (Tal, 2014). This approach stems from Van Manen's (1994) life-world approach, which views a pedagogue as an educator "who understands children in a caring way, and who has a personal commitment and interest in children's education and their growth towards mature adulthood" (p. 138). This means knowing the children within their social and cultural ecological system (Bronfen-Brenner, 1979) and understanding the values and the characters of the world that surrounds them (Berger & Luckmann, 1989). At Levinsky, from their first year, students are required to focus on an individual child – to get acquainted with all the children and understand them, to be interested in who they are as individuals, in what they think, in what interests and bothers them (Tal, 2014). In the second and third year, the students focus on the individual child within small, sustained, heterogeneous groups (in the second year they get acquainted with four children and in the third year with eight). The students are required to observe and listen to the child and use several pedagogical tools in order to gain knowledge about the children and to be able to develop a responsive curriculum that emerges from the children's interests, needs, and abilities and promotes them. In their work with young children, their families and their communities, the students are required to adopt a capacity orientation rather than a deficit orientation (Oyler, 2011).

Within the ECE programme, the students, from their first year, are required to gain knowledge about the children's socio-cultural context by listening to them and collecting information from the preschool teacher. The student teachers do not create connections with the children's parents. In addition, they learn how to use different observational tools such as the COR- Child Observation Record (2003), an assessment tool that they use to observe, record, and analyse the children's achievements. They also learn how to use the MABATIM (Hebrew) - Observing Children in their Natural Environment (2016) observational tool, which has been adopted by the Israeli Department of Education. They need to use this knowledge in constructing and developing the learning program that relates to each individual child in the small group.

Working in Small Groups

Working in small, sustained, heterogeneous groups is another key element and requirement in Levinsky's ECE programme. In the first and second year, students work with one group and in the third year with two groups. Within these groups, the students are required to get acquainted with all children and to construct an emergent curriculum according to the children's needs and subjects of interest.

Our program is informed by Vygotsky's (1978) sociocultural theory, which emphasises that children learn and develop through social interaction with others. According to Vygotsky's Zone of Proximal Development (ZPD) theory, not only adults but also peers who are more competent, play a critical role in advancing children's development and learning. Within the small group, the student teachers foster the principles of the emergent curriculum and encourage the children to interact with one another, and develop meaningful, open discourse, which shapes the group's curriculum.

Previous research (e.g., Dickinson & Porche, 2011; Justice, Skibbe, McGinty, Piasta & Petrill, 2011) emphasises the importance of scaffolding practices in helping children reach their academic and social potential.

Working in small, sustained groups provides the teacher with a closer look at what each child may be struggling with and at the skills that the children have already begun to develop (Abu Al-Rub, 2017). According to research, working in small group arrangements in early childhood settings increases the efficiency of instruction, offering opportunities for incidental observational learning (Ledford, Lane, Elam, & Wolery, 2012), and for programmed social exchanges between peers (Wolery, Ault, Doyle, Gast, & Griffen, 1992). According to Katz (1999), the data on children's learning suggests that preschool and preschool experiences and an intellectually oriented approach in small groups provide them with the opportunity to make sense of their own experience.

Multicultural Education

In the twenty-first century – an era of globalisation and mass technology, multi-culturalism, the dynamic demographic reality of the diversity of people, cultures, and lifestyles is "manifested in various forms and increasing rapidly" (Grant, 2018, p. 328). Multicultural education emerged from the Civil Rights Movement of the 1960's, which aimed to eliminate discrimination in different dimensions of social life, including education. Multicultural education as a concept, an educational reform, and a process aims to provide all students with an equal chance to experience school success with no connection to their gender, social class, and ethnic, racial, or cultural characteristics (Banks, 2010). Due to these characteristics, some students have a better chance to succeed at school as it is currently structured (Banks, 2010). Heath (1983) argued that "unless boundaries between classrooms and communities can be broken, and the flow of cultural patterns between them encouraged, the schools will continue to legitimate and reproduce" (p. 369) dominant cultures, customs and ways of thinking. Similarly,

French sociologist Pierre Bourdieu (1986) criticised the assumption that the unequal achievement of children from different social classes or cultural heritage is a result of differences in their 'natural' ability. He argued that educational action is part of the "contribution which the educational system makes to the reproduction" of the specific social structure by approving transmission of specific materials, behaviours, and skills (Bourdieu, 1986, p. 244). The "pedagogic action", according to Bourdieu, reflects the interests of the dominant groups of the specific society.

Multicultural education refers to a wide range of practices and programs that involve changes in the school's educational environment. Banks (2010) focuses on five dimensions that promote multiculturalism within the educational system:

1. Knowledge construction: Teachers must help students understand, investigate and determine how implicit cultural assumptions and perspectives within a discipline may influence the ways in which knowledge is constructed.
2. Prejudice reduction: This dimension focuses on the characteristics of students' racial attitudes and how they can be modified by teaching methods and materials.
3. Content integration: This deals with the extent to which teachers use examples and content from a variety of cultures in their teaching.
4. Equity pedagogy: This occurs when teachers modify their teaching in ways that will facilitate the academic achievement of students from diverse racial, cultural, gender, [special needs], and social class groups.
5. Empowering school culture: School's agenda and practices and the interaction of the staff and the students across ethnic and racial lines must be examined to create a school culture that empowers students from diverse groups (Banks, 2010).

Chen and Starosta (2000), emphasise that multicultural competence consists of cultural sensitivity and awareness. Multicultural sensitivity "includes an agreement between one's own culture and of others, gender and class issues and minority rights... and eliminates cultural prejudice, as well as fosters an interest in learning about and experiencing dissimilar cultures" (Huh, Choi, & Jun, 2015, p. 111). Multicultural sensitivity begins with the teachers' self-perceptions on diversity that impact their behaviours within the preschool. Therefore, teachers must always be aware of their own emotions, knowledge, and attitude of others (Seefelt, 2001). This means that teacher educators must develop student teachers' reflective ability, which requires deep acquaintance with all children (based on observation tools, engagement with the children and sincere interest in their world), their families, and their socio-cultural background, in order to develop a curriculum that is meaningful and equal to all children. Within the ECE program in Levinsky, the student teachers are required to work in small, heterogeneous groups to expose the children to texts, pictures and media that represent diverse cultures, to promote attentiveness to diverse cultures and religions, and to ask questions that encourage participation of all children and promote values of acceptance of the other.

Since its establishment in 1948, Israel's demographics have shifted dramatically due to large waves of immigrants. Reflecting this, Israel is the 2nd on the OECD foreign-born population scale (OECD, 2011). According to the OECD data, 26.5% of the population in Israel is not born in Israel, well above the OECD average of 11.7%. Israeli Jews constitute 75% of the total officially registered population, 4.3% are non-Jews, and 20.7% are Arabs (Aderet, 2014). Migrant workers, who are not officially registered, constitute 2% of the total population in Israel (Central Bureau of Statistics, 2014).

The educational system is structurally separated into Jewish and Arab divisions (Gibton, 2011). Israel's approach to the various cultural groups is determined by its Zionist ideology and by democratic values. Thus, there is a different form of legal integration for each cultural group (Kalekin-Fishman & Eden, 2003).

Following its independence in 1948, Israel enacted the Mandatory Schooling Law, 5709 -1949, acknowledging the importance of education for all (Israeli Mandatory Schooling Law, 1953). This was one of the first laws enacted by the Israeli parliament. The law emphasises the prohibition of discrimination on the basis of a sector, prohibits punishing students for actions or inaction by parents, and assures free schooling from the first day of preschool up until the last day of high school (Feldman, 2009). Twenty years later, in 1988, the Special Education law 5758-1988 (The Special Education Law), was legislated in Israel to ensure education to all individuals with disabilities between the ages of 3 to 21 (Israeli Special Education Law, 1998). In 2002, the Special Education Law was amended to the 'Inclusion Law' (the 7th Amendment to the Special Education Law) aiming to ensure the priority of inclusion (over exclusion) and integration of students with disabilities in the mainstream education. In 2007, a public committee – the Dorner committee – was appointed to examine the special education system in Israel. According to the Dorner committee recommendations, which were submitted in 2009, the state will budget the services of special education children within the mainstream education system. In 2018, the reform of the special education law was implemented, where the parents of children with special needs were given, as much as possible, the right to choose the educational setting that their children attend.

Emergent Curriculum

An emergent curriculum is based on social constructivist views of learning (Vygotsky, 1978), and is focused on educators' responsiveness to children's needs and subjects of interest. An emergent, as opposed to a traditional, 'pre-determined' curriculum, is achieved via investigations and reflections upon experience rather than the memorisation of items of conclusive knowledge or the mechanical drilling of skills (Yu-le, 2004).

The implementation of an emergent curriculum is based upon the adults' attentive listening to the children's diversity and the encouragement of an open discourse with and among the children (Forman & Fyfe, 1998; Rinaldi, 2001) in order to create a meaningful and equal curriculum for all children. The curriculum is built on the interaction between the educational environment, the children, and the student teacher. The role of the educator is to be a facilitator of the children's learning, to extend and to provoke the children's learning and to provide them with opportunities and incentives to construct their learning (Fosnot, 1996). The educator allows and encourages children to "raise their own questions, generate their own hypotheses and models of possibilities, and test them for viability" (Fosnot, 1996, p. 29). Listening carefully to children's words and thoughts, and searching for the themes and struggles in their discussions (Ballenger, 2009), leads to the construction of the emergent curriculum.

Loris Malaguzzi (1993), the founder of the Reggio Emilia approach, a social constructivist pedagogy, which utilizes the emergent curriculum, termed the idea of "one hundred languages," which represents the many different ways that a child expresses his or her learning. In implementing an emergent curriculum, educators must use different types of documentation in order to extend and deepen the ways of listening to the children's expressions. Clark (2010) argues that it is crucial to understand that listening is a process that is not limited to the spoken word. Clark introduces the mosaic approach as an integrated approach that combines the visual with the verbal (Clark, 2010). According to this approach, for example, educators record children's conversations and use photography as part of the documentation process—these techniques provide the educators with time to reflect and build on the children's ideas. Children's dialogues can foster many insights into their thinking, and the role of the teacher is to use documentation to further develop the curriculum. Documentation is an essential process that supports the educational exchanges related to learning (Rinaldi, 1998). It is interrelated with social constructivist practices and openness to change, and it enables reflective practice (Schön, 1983, 1987). Dutton (2012) highlighted the power of documentation and reflection in understanding children's learning and in improving teaching.

As described above, in the ECE program, the student teachers dedicate the first weeks in the preschool to get acquainted with the children using professional tools such as the COR (Child Observation Record, 2003). This acquaintance is developed during the group meetings and shapes the emergent curriculum. The curriculum is not pre-planned and emerges from children's needs and subjects of interests and develops from one group meeting to another. It is also based on pedagogical, long-term goals. These goals include social-emotional goals such as listening to and among the children, inclusion and tolerance in order to create an intimate, safe space for the children. Other goals include exposure to quality texts, children's expression in 'one hundred languages' (a metaphor for the endless ways children can express their thoughts and ideas) and development of higher-order thinking skills/metacognitive skills and concepts, critical thinking and developing disciplinary vocabulary.

Student Teachers' Support System in the ECE Preparation Programme at Levinsky College

ECE programmes and services aim to address children's developmental (physical, emotional, nutritional, educational) needs. As noted above, the ECE preparation programme at Levinsky College aims to introduce and implement a socially inclusive pedagogical approach that is based on a social constructivist perception of learning teaching processes (Tal, 2014). Unlike students of other disciplines, education students have "inside knowledge" when they begin their studies as they have been students within the education system (Pajares, 1992).

Most of Levinsky's students grew up and learned in a constructivist educational system, which requires deep transformation processes. Therefore, student teachers' support system is a crucial component in the implementation of constructivist principles in students' practices. Students in their third year of study are required to work with two heterogeneous groups within the Israeli preschools, and to construct an emergent curriculum. Children are perceived as "rich in potential, strong, powerful, competent, and most of all connected to adults and other children" (Malaguzzi, 1993, p.10), as well as active participants in groups, classes, communities, and cultures (Rogoff 2003). The role of the student teachers is to facilitate group discourse, to mediate between the world and the children, to coordinate efforts made by different children, and to contribute to the organisation of discourse in order to enable the emergence of newly agreed upon understandings and ideas (Tal, 2014).

Emergent Curriculum in the Preparation ... 111

From the first year of their academic studies in the ECE program, the students focus on two main disciplines out of the following four: literature, Bible, art, and science. The emergent curriculum that the students lead with the small groups must be based on one of these disciplines. The ECE program provides the students with a support system that consists of face-to-face support and distance support. This includes the pedagogical mentors, the discipline mentors, the preschool teachers, and fellow students (see Figure 1).

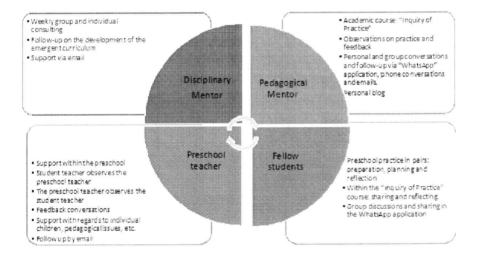

Figure 1. ECE student teachers' support system.

The support of the pedagogical mentors includes an academic course, titled "inquiry of practice." This course focuses on pedagogical theories and approaches and sharing and analysing student teachers' experiences within the course group. Sharing within the group also enables students to reflect, respond, and learn from one another's experiences. In addition, the pedagogical mentor observes the student teachers in action in the preschools where they practice and conducts a feedback and assessment conversation. Within this conversation, the other student teachers who practice in the preschool also participate, reflect and respond.

There is also a distance support system available for the students that includes: personal and group conversations via the 'WhatsApp' application, phone conversations, and emails that enable the students to share or consult with the pedagogical mentor on a daily basis. In addition, the student teachers are required to write in their personal blogs, which are open to the pedagogic mentors and enable the student teachers to share or reflect upon the learning process.

The disciplinary mentors meet with the student teachers in a weekly group meeting or personal consulting sessions. In these meetings, the mentors stress the disciplinary principles, concepts, and approaches, and discuss the ways to implement these within the emergent curriculum.

Preschool teachers meet with the students within the preschool, however, the students also contact the teachers via email, phone calls, and the WhatsApp application.

At all levels the students' support system includes two aspects: the cognitive aspect that refers to pedagogical knowledge and to content knowledge, and the emotional aspect that includes emotional support in coping with stress, confusion, and concerns.

METHODOLOGY

The methodology used is multiple case studies (Yin, 2009) based on the mosaic approach (Clark, 2010). Participants in this study were ten student teachers (23-30 years old) in their third year of the ECE programme at Levinsky College of Education in Israel, who studied in the years 2016-2018. These student teachers represent diverse ways of developing an emergent curriculum based on multicultural education principles (Banks, 2010). The student teachers have practised in preschools of the Israeli public education system, once a week for ten months. The participating preschools consisted of 30-35 children, aged 4-6-years-old. During their practice, the student teachers worked with small heterogeneous groups of 4-6 children on a weekly basis. Within these meetings, student teachers were instructed to develop an emergent program according to the children's backgrounds, experiences, diverse needs, and subjects of interest.

Emergent Curriculum in the Preparation ... 113

The small group meetings were audio and video documented and were reflected on by the student teachers. The student teachers uploaded these documentations, reflections, and photographs into a personal blog on a weekly basis. This data was analysed using aspects and practices of thematic analysis (Freeman, 1998; Richie & Spencer, 1994).

The student teachers practised in the following Israeli preschools:

- Preschool 1: The preschool is located in the city of Jaffa in the center of Israel and includes children between 4-6-years-old coming from a variety of cultures including Jews, Christians (Orthodox, Catholics and Armenians), Muslims, and new Jewish immigrants from Ethiopia and Russia. The children are from diverse socio-economic status (SES) and there are wide economic gaps between the children.
- Preschool 2: The preschool is located in the city of Ramla in the center of Israel and includes children between 5-6-years-old coming from a variety of cultures, including Jews, Christians (Orthodox, Catholics and Armenians), Muslims and new Jewish immigrants from Ethiopia, Peru, Russia, Colombia, and more. The children are coming from diverse SES and there are wide economic gaps between the children.
- Preschool 3: The preschool is located in the city of Rehovot in the center of Israel and includes children between 5-6-years-old coming from socially diverse Jewish families such as Jewish religious families, secular Jewish families, divorced parents, and single-parent families.

FINDINGS

In all cases, the student teachers worked with the children in small, sustained heterogeneous groups. In all cases, the group's curriculum emerged from the children's interests and it was based on the individuals' and groups' social, cognitive, and emotional characteristics. The student teachers aimed to work with the children on quality texts and images that matched children's needs and development, however, these choices were subjective and were influenced by the student teachers' personality and life experience. During the development of the emergent curriculum, the student teachers went through a self-learning process, which included transformation from the traditional approach to constructivist approach. This learning process was based on self-reflection, peer learning and was guided by the pedagogical and disciplinary mentors. In the following section, we will discuss five cases each case and the ways the emergent curriculum principles were implemented.

Case A: From Diverse Languages to the Creation of One Shared Language

Phahimma is a 23-year-old student who practices in preschool 1. She comes from a Muslim family and lives in Jaffa. Phahimma's first language is Arabic. She is a religious woman and wears a traditional Hijab in her everyday life. She is one of a few Muslim students within Levinsky and her attire represents her different cultural heritage. In the first face-to-face meeting with her pedagogical mentor, Phahimma explained her pedagogical perception and related it to her personal experience as a Muslim student within the college:

> It is important to show the difference… that every child is different. They [the children] learn that everyone has a different language and culture – but we are all together! It was hard for me as well (pointing her clothes- Hijab)- I know the feeling, it was important for me to be accepted. It is something personal (11.2016).

Phahimma stresses the importance of highlighting the uniqueness of each individual child, and at the same time of creating a sense of belonging to the group. This perception seems to derive from her personal experience as a minority Muslim student within the majority of Jewish students within the college as she noted, "I know the feeling." Based on this perception, Phahimma developed an emergent curriculum that is created from a deep cultural sensitivity and fosters group collaboration.

One of the main activities in the curriculum was creating routines that foster inclusion and cooperation among the children within the group. For example:

> I open every group meeting in a conversation where everyone tells us something... whatever they like- the aim is an acquaintance of each others' world. Everyone participates. They love it. They cannot wait for their turn to tell, even the shy girl in the group tells us something (12.2016).

In this example, Phahimma created an inclusive, safe, environment for the children where they could share their inner world, their everyday experiences, and freely express their feelings and thoughts. Within this environment, the children told their stories, and Phahimma and the other children were keen listeners and were sincerely interested in the stories they told. Also, within the group discourse, the children could receive responses from their peers who reflected upon their stories from their own perspective. The children (who come from diverse cultures) were thus exposed to diverse stories and points of view. This experience expands the children's world knowledge and develops social values and skills such as tolerance and acceptance of the uniqueness of every individual. Studies show that utilising small groups in early childhood education settings can foster the social exchanges between peers (Oyler, 2011; Wolery et al., 1992). Phahimma's methods and strategies encouraged reducing prejudiced views and also created equity pedagogy (Banks, 2013), by providing every child with an equal opportunity to express oneself and share one's personal experience.

Children's Literature Promotes Group Discourse

Following Phahimma's acquaintance with the children as individuals and as a group, she chose to read to them the book "Little Beauty" by

Anthony Browne (2010). Browne's story fosters the values of acceptance of the other and empowers the uniqueness of each individual. The story is about a gorilla who lives in a civilized environment with three therapists, with whom he communicates in sign language. However, the gorilla was sad and asked for a friend. The therapists decided to bring him a kitten. Despite their differences, the gorilla and the kitten became good friends. After reading the story a discussion emerged within the group:

> Rachel: I speak Amharic
> Alex: If I will speak Russian will you understand?
> Helen: I speak Arabic?
> Ali (referring to Helen): سة‏Do you understand?
> Roni: I speak only Hebrew!

This exchange illustrates the diversity of the children's cultures and the moment they discover and realize the differences in their mother tongues. This discourse allowed construction of knowledge of the different languages. This can lead to prejudice reduction and equity pedagogy as the language of every child was presented in the exchange (Banks, 2013). It is important to highlight the position of the child who speaks Hebrew. The child stresses: "I speak only Hebrew!" The use of the word 'only' emphasizes the child's acknowledgment that all the children in the groups speak other languages in addition to Hebrew and he speaks only Hebrew. Although Hebrew is the official language of Israel, knowing the Hebrew language did not put the child in a higher position than the children who speak it as a second language. The child also acknowledged in this discourse that Hebrew is only one of the languages that are spoken within the group and not the main one. This highlights the equity pedagogy constructed by Phahimma within the group (Banks, 2013).

From Group Discourse about Languages to the Language of Art: Expanding the Students' Knowledge

Student teachers are required to seek creative ways to develop an emergent curriculum that is constructed from the interactions within the group between the children and the student teachers. These interactions are between individuals who are part of their communities (Rinaldi, 1998) and their ecological systems (Bronfenbrenner, 1979). According to the emergent curriculum approach, the position of the children and the educator are equal in the construction of the curriculum. In this case, Phahimma developed a curriculum that emerged from sociocultural aspects such as self-identity, along with the children's and her own interests and preferences.

Another requirement of the ECE program is that the student teachers' emergent curriculum will be based on one of their main chosen disciplines. Phahimma's main chosen discipline was art, and in the guidance of the art discipline mentor, she chose to expand her knowledge about different calligraphy artists whose main interest is to investigate the graphic representation of the written word. This included Annette Messenger, David Reeb, Shirin Neshat, and Anisa Ashkar. We chose to elaborate here about one of the artists that Phahimma chose- the Arabic tattoo artist- Anisa Ashkar.

Ashkar is an Arabic Israeli citizen who was born in Acre, an Arab-Jewish-Druze mixed city, in 1979. In her teens, Ashkar understood her life experiences as being different and became curious about the world and its relation to the other. She began to create art performances and presented a series of photographs that were inspired by mythology and deal with major themes that she could relate to in her biography (Husni al-Khatib Shehada, 2012). Ashkar explained her way of creating:

> In my work I also raise questions related to the essence of art itself and the boundaries between the work and the artist, using my body and my face as a canvas that I decorate in Arabic calligraphy as a symbol of religious, popular and social customs in the Arab tradition (Israeli artist's website- Anisa Ashkar, 2016).

It seems that Phahimma chose to focus on Anisa Ashkar, a strong Arabic woman with whom she can identify. Banks (2013) stresses that in order to construct cultural tolerance and equity we have to expose children and adults to a culture with which they can identify. Levinsky encourages the students to relate to their own identity, self-interests and cultural heritage in their learning process. This process expands and constructs Pahimma's knowledge about language representations in art, its meanings and implication on the viewer.

From the Language of Art and Back to Group Discourse

Following Phahimma's research about language and art as a response to the children's subject of interest (languages), she planned to present to the children different representations of calligraphy of the different languages they have mentioned within the group discourse. However, the preschool teacher did not approve the idea. The teacher claimed that the children's exposure to different written languages might confuse them as they are in a stage where they are beginning the process of learning to read and write in Hebrew. When Phahimma realized that she cannot pursue her original plan she consulted with her pedagogic mentor as part of the students' support system. The pedagogic mentor guided her to ask the children what they want to do with their subject of interest – languages.

Student teachers at Levinsky are encouraged to position themselves and the children equally in constructing the emergent curriculum (Rinaldi, 1998; Tal, 2014). This process is represented in Phahimma's reflection that emphasises the children's impact on the learning program: "From the productive discourse… the children reached the understanding that there is a need for a common language to be able to communicate – they decided that they want to make up their own language" (Phahimma, 6.2016). Within the group discourse, the children negotiated the characteristics of 'their own language'- they discussed symbols that will represent different words, but after few sentences, one of the children stopped the discussion and suggested:

Ali: Maybe we will do the symbols with our hands...
Alex: Yes, we can do the same kind of signs that we do during the circle time with our fingers when we need to go to the toilet.

Roni: We can make up other signs...
Helen: True! We can make up our own sign language
Phahimma: Ok so let's start ..."

Consequent to the children's meaningful learning process in the small group, they created their own sign language. This sign language emerged from the children's interests and in consideration with the preschool teacher's request to find a language that is not formal or written. This illustrates how limitations, obstacles and difficulties during the learning process contribute to developing creative and flexible thinking.

In Phahimma's reflection, she stressed the importance of working in sustained small heterogeneous groups (Tal, 2014) as a place to develop multicultural sensitivity (Banks, 2010):

> In a multicultural preschool, it is important to work in small groups and to make children feel connected to one another; to provide an opportunity for self-expression and to believe in the children's ability to work as a group. The discourse about language led the children to important understandings about culture and social values. (Phahimma, 2016)

Phahimma explains that within the small group she created a culturally sensitive environment where all children in the group can connect with one another. She also related to the place of the individual within the group and activated equity pedagogy (Banks, 2010), constructed from an understanding and acceptance of the children's needs and points of view.

Phahimma's ability to reflect upon her perceptions (Seefelt, 2001) and personal connection to the Arabic language, art, and the artist Anisa Ashkar, led her to a deep understanding of the role of language and the children's points of view. This understanding helped her construct with the children, despite all the difficulties, a new language that suits the ecological environment of the preschool.

Case B: Art and Literature as a Mirror of Diverse Families

Sarah, a 23 years old Jewish student, practised in preschool 2, in the city of Rehovot, which is located in the center of Israel. Sarah lost her father a few weeks prior to the beginning of the year. All the children in this preschool come from socially diverse Jewish families, most of them from a high SES. Sarah chose to read the book Father Orange and his Daughter Clementine (Savir, 2002) to the children. Ariela Savir is an Israeli children's author, poet, and composer. The story is about a father and his daughter who travel together but during their trip, the daughter gets lost. The story tells about the ways that she is looking for her family.

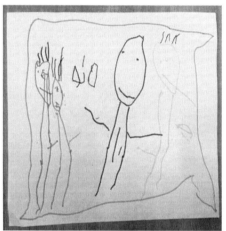 

Tom (3.4): "(This is) Mum, I am the small one and Gal is the big one."

Yuli (4): "Me by myself on Shabbat, Mum is next to me and dad is at home."

Figure 2. Two children's drawings of their family.

Sarah read this story to the group of children. After reading the story, the children asked to draw their own families. Sarah encouraged them to draw and then asked them to explain their drawing to the other children in the group.

Within the group discourse, the children responded to one another:

Emergent Curriculum in the Preparation ... 121

    Ella (3.2): But Yuli what do you do alone all day on Shabbat?
    Tom (3.4): Don't you have anybody to play with? Are you sad?
    Ohr (3): Why are you alone? Where are your brothers?

Following this discourse, Sarah asked the children to bring photographs of their Shabbat activities with their families. The children presented the photographs within the group, and they commented on each other's photos.

Yuli:"me and my mum sit and eat the chocolate cake that we have made"

Yuli: "When I stay at mum's house we make chocolate cake together with chocolate chips"

Figure 3. Example of a child's drawing and sculpture/

    Or (3): I didn't bring a photo because we (me and my family) don't take pictures on Shabbat. We stay at home and have Kiddush (Jewish traditional Friday night ceremony) at Grandma's house.
    Yuli (4): My mum and my dad do not do Kiddush.
    Tom (3.4): At my house, we also do Kiddush, but not all the time.

Within this discourse, the children expressed themselves and shared their own experiences with the other children in the group. They were also exposed to the cultural diversity of the children's families with regards to traditional Jewish customs. This discourse, where children get acquainted with diverse customs and perspectives, reduces prejudiced views about diverse families and promotes equity pedagogy (Banks, 2013).

As the learning process developed, the children asked to represent their Shabbat stories in sculpture. For example, Yuli, a 4 years old child:

Yuli's parents are divorced and he described Shabbat at his mother's house. When Yuli shared his Shabbat story, not only were the children exposed to cultural diversity, in the different ways of celebrating Shabbat, but also to the social diversity in their peers' family structures. In this case, as in the case of Phahimma (Case A), the small, sustained group became a secure and inclusive space where children from diverse sociocultural backgrounds feel a sense of belonging and are able to express their diversity. This activity represents the implementation of Banks' (2010) five dimensions of multicultural education.

Case C: Art and Literature as a Mirror of Families' Country of Origin

Jane, a 26-year-old Jewish student, practiced in preschool 2. She is married and lives in the city of Ramla. Jane began the learning process in reading the book: "My Father Always Embarrasses Me" (Shalev, 1988) to the children. The story is about a child whose mother is a news reporter and whose father does all the housework. One day the teacher organized a cake competition and the child feels embarrassed when his father stands with his odd looking cake together with all the mothers and their beautiful cakes. But then his father's cake turns out to be a big surprise, which makes the child proud. While reading the story, the children shared their home cultural cooking and expressed their willingness to prepare unique dishes for their families. The dishes that the children suggested were culturally related. For example:

Liam: I will make ice cream for my mum because she always eats ice cream.
Sapir: I will make chocolate balls for my mum.
Noam: I want to make MAHAGI, which is Indian food.
Tomer: I will make a pot of OSHPELO [Uzbekistan food].

Following this discourse, the student teacher offered the children to represent their thoughts using clay. This pedagogical decision is based on the emergent curriculum principles where the educator enables the children to express themselves in "one hundred languages" (Rinaldi, 2001).

The children worked with clay and sculpted the kind of food they want to make for their families. They also included other materials of their choice to represent their thoughts. At the end of the learning process, Jane reflected on the process and wrote:

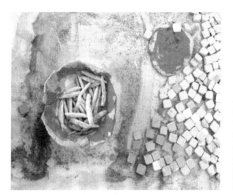

Tomer: "My gift is Oshpelo dish" Noam: "My gift is Mahaji dish and a red heart".

Figure 4. Examples of the children's clay representations.

    Listening to the children was an inseparable part of the project. By listening, I learnt about them… I learnt about their interests and their inner world, and I learnt that the family is their whole world and this is an inseparable part of them. Among other things during the project, the children developed social skills and became a group, based on help, respect, and listening to one other. (Jane, 6.2016)

In this reflection, Jane acknowledged that listening to children is a key principle in developing a meaningful learning process. In this process, the educator becomes the listener and the children the speakers (Rinaldi, 2001). She reflected on the development of the children's social skills in the construction of the learning process within the small group. Within the small group, Jane described the ways she learnt about each one of the participating children. She learnt about the critical position of the family in the children's ecological system and constructed the emergent curriculum accordingly.

To conclude, Jane created an environment where all the children in the group were able to express themselves within an open discourse. Their knowledge was relevant and was equally appreciated within the group discourse. In this activity, Banks' (2010) dimensions of multicultural education were implemented.

Case D: Jewish Studies and Art: Creating a Multicultural Celebration Table

Maya practised in preschool 3 in the city of Rehovot. All the children in this preschool come from Jewish families, primarily from a high SES. Maya's emergent curriculum started from a discourse about the Genesis creation narrative. The children shared their experiences from Shabbat (Saturday), a day that they do not meet in the preschool, but spend with their families and communities. Maya reported: "We developed a discourse about the Shabbat day that is different from the rest of the week, and I asked the children what do they like to do on Shabbat?"

> Dan: To go to grandma with my mum and my dog.
> Talia: To go to the beach and to travel.
> Yael: To watch TV all day.
> Ron: To be with all my family at home and with my sister.

Emergent Curriculum in the Preparation ... 125

This discourse also arose regarding the children's experiences from Shabbat dinner and other family gatherings and special events that include a special meal such as holidays and birthdays. The children shared their knowledge about special meals:

Yael: There should be a white tablecloth and a cup of wine
Ron: You dress in new clothing
Dan: The dishes are made of gold
Tala: We invite guests

Following this discourse, the children were asked to draw their own special dinner tables. Figure 5 represents one of the children's works of the Novigod celebration (Russian Jewish celebration of the New Year).

Figure 5. Picture of the Novigod celebration

In the center of the drawing, the child drew a big table. On both sides, he drew two smiling people and two Christmas trees. On the table, the child drew different dishes and a candle in the centre of the table. In the upper part of the drawing, the child drew three hearts, one of which carries the child's name. This drawing represents harmony and joy that the child expresses about a special dinner celebration. This activity provides the child with an opportunity to express himself in another way and expose his thoughts and ideas within the group. In Maya's reflection she pointed out, "The discourse allowed me to learn more about the children and their different cultural habits. I wasn't aware of the Novigod customs, I learnt from the children."

This case highlights the position of the child as a capable and active agent and the position of the educator as a listener in the development of the learning process (Rinaldi, 2001). It also illustrates the importance of the "hundred languages" to the expansion of knowledge in the small group. In this case, the language of art enabled the children to express detailed information about the holiday as they celebrate it in their homes not only via words, but also using images and colours. In this way, they could elaborate and include more details. The use of the language of art enabled the children in the group and the student teacher to construct more extensive knowledge about the different dimensions of the holiday and foster multicultural perceptions.

Case E: Children's Songs - Learning the Hebrew Language

Rachel worked in preschool 2, a socio-culturally mixed preschool in a city in the center of Israel. The learning process she developed stemmed from the reflection written in her personal blog. In the blog she described her difficulties in conducting a discourse in a group where the children come from diverse cultures and possess different mother tongues: Amharic, Arabic and Hebrew:

> Within the first meeting with the group I noticed that the native language of all children, except Omri, is not Hebrew, therefore there is a gap in their linguistic capabilities: speaking, writing etc. I also noticed that in music lessons the children were flourishing and cooperating. Therefore, I decided that instead of reading a book during the group

meeting, we could work on short songs. I decided to choose the poet, Yehonatan Geffen, and to read songs from his book "The Sixteenth Sheep". (Rachel, 11.2016).

Yehonatan Geffen is an Israeli author, poet, songwriter, journalist, and playwright. Most of his poems for children are personal and reflect the landscape of his childhood (Barzilai, 1984). Rachel chose Yehonatan Geffen's children's songs aiming to provide a platform for developing the discourse in the heterogeneous group as it provides access to the Hebrew language via short quality texts.

Learning Through the Language of Art

The first song that Rachel chose for learning in the group was 'I Love' by Yehonatan Geffen (Geffen, 1978). The song focuses on the author's perception of children's favourite things, such as food, special days like birthdays, celestial bodies, seasons, first love, family members and their preschool teacher. The intensity of love reaches its peak in the child's encounter with himself. Following the reading of the song's lyrics in the small group, the children shared a variety of foods that they like to eat:

Racheli: Popsicle
Tomer: Strawberries
Ofek: Chocolate
Adva: Cakes

The children's use of one-word sentences supports Rachel's arguments about her difficulties in developing an open and rich discourse within the group. Therefore, she decided to use another language for the children's expression - the arts (Rinaldi, 2001), and she offered the children the opportunity to draw their favorite foods. When the children completed their drawings, Rachel asked them to tell their friends about their work. Here, the children used a whole sentence to describe their drawing. For example:

Abraham: Abraham likes cakes
Tedi: I like ice cream in different flavours

These examples represent the ways children expand their discourse by using the language of art. The children expressed themselves in longer sentences compared with the former discourse. This emphasizes how the use of "one hundred languages" (Rinaldi, 2001) contributes to the development of the children's discourse within the small group as part of the emergent curriculum.

Figure 6. Artwork by Abraham (left) and Teddy (right).

The Language of Movement

After this discourse, Rachel decided to read to the children another song by Geffen (Geffen, 1978) titled, "How a Song is Born." The song describes the process of writing a song. Geffen writes: "It begins from within" - which describes the moment of the artist's inspiration. Geffen continues: "How was a song born? Like laughter," describing the pleasure in the creative process. Then he writes, "The song is born like a baby," where he parallels the process of writing a song to the birth of a baby. Geffen completes the song with the idea that when a song is published "everyone is happy." The song emphasizes the process of writing as a personal creative act, which then becomes part of the public domain.

The children loved the song; they spoke about it, laughed and tried to understand all the different phrases using movement. Then they decided to dramatize the song using movements that they decided on in an open, shared, equal discourse. For instance: with regards to the sentence "It starts from the inside," the children decided to touch both hands in the stomach (Image 1). For the phrase "rolled out," the children spread their hands forward (Image 2). Also, for the sentence 'How was a song born? Like a baby', they joined their hands and moved them from side to side (Figure 1). It seems that the children chose to express their shared interpretation of the song lyrics in the language of motion. They listened to each other and negotiated the suitable movements. The children were very proud of the movements they made and wanted to show it to the rest of the children in the preschool. They decided that they need some rehearsals and then they presented the dramatized song to the whole preschool group during circle time and taught them the song lyrics and the movements.

The learning process surrounding the song "How a Song is Born" expresses the principles of the emergent curriculum approach, which enables participation of all children and expression in "one hundred languages" (Rinaldi, 2001). In this case, the language of motion emerged as a result of listening to and understanding the children's abilities and needs. The children were active participants in the learning process: they led, designed, and executed the song's performance using the language of movement.

Fostering Discourse on Multiculturalism

The last song that Rachel chose to read to the children in the small group was 'The Most Beautiful Girl in the Preschool' (Geffen, 1978). The song is written from the perspective of a girl who watches another girl in her preschool, who in her eyes is 'the most beautiful in the garden'. The girl describes in detail the beauty of the other girl and claims that she does not understand how a girl who is so beautiful can be sad. This song raises the issue that external appearance does not indicate the person's inner world and personality. After reading the song lyrics to the children and opening the discourse among the children about the song, Rachel asked, "What is more important- being pretty on the inside or the outside"?

Teddy: On the outside, so that people could see the beauty
Avraham: On the inside, you can't see anything
Tomer: On the inside! It is important to be good
Ofek: Both inside and outside
Adva: It is important to behave and listen to the preschool teacher

Within this discourse, Teddy related to the outside appearance. Avraham continued Teddy's answer and extended the argument saying that one cannot make the 'inside' of the other person visible. Tomer explained the concept "inside" as the inner character, the ability to be good. Ofek summarized the discourse: "both inside and outside". She included all the answers and suggested a solution in which everyone is 'correct'. Adva put this discourse in the context of the kindergarten and stressed: "It is important to behave and listen to the preschool teacher."

The discourse analysis suggests that although the student teacher asked a closed question (What is more important- being pretty on the inside or the outside?), a discourse developed in the group as all children participated in the discourse, elaborating their perceptions, listening to one another, and constructing their new knowledge. The student teacher was in the position of the listener and did not interrupt the discourse. Based on this discourse and the children's knowledge construction, they continued to connect the abstract concepts of inner and outer beauty to their friends in the group:

Ofek: Avraham and Adva are different because Avraham is white and Adva is black, but they are friends.
Adva: Me and Ofek are the same because we are both Ethiopians.
Tomer: I am friend with all the kids because I love them due to their behaviour

Emergent Curriculum in the Preparation ...   131

In this exchange, Ofek pointed out the differences in the skin colour of two of his friends but mentioned that this difference does not prevent them from being friends. Adva constructed her answer on the word "different" that Ofek used and stressed the similar outside characteristic between her and Ofek - the skin colour. She broadened the word "black" Ofek used and connected it to their ethnic origin - Ethiopian. Tomer's answer is related to the primary question about 'inside and outside' characteristics as he stresses that he cares about the inside - the children's behaviours and not their appearance. His answer demonstrates the development of the open discourse and the ways it circulates and develops according to the children's experiences, understandings, and perceptions and the ways they gain an understanding of these abstract concepts.

Rachel, the student teacher, added another provocative question to the discourse: "Can different people be friends?"

> Teddi: I am friends with Arabs, and even Muslims and even Ethiopians.
>
> Tomer: He is a Christian and I am Jewish, he eats pork, and I am also Bukhari, and he is a Muslim and I am friends with everyone.
>
> Abraham: I am not a friend of Nehorai, he annoys me, and I am an Arab and he is a Jew.
>
> Adva: I am different from Tomer because he is older than me and I am his friend.

In this discourse, Teddi interpreted the question of differences regarding religion and ethnic diversity while Tomer pointed out the religion (Christian, Jewish, Muslim) and ethnic origin (Bukhari) of the children and related to differences in customs (eats pork) of each group. Tomer is aware of the differences between the children in the group, and he perceives them all as his friends. It seems that this diversity is part of the child's ecological system. Abraham stresses his point of view on the behavior of his friends and the impact of it on his preference. He concludes his argument by pointing out that they are from different religious groups, but this is not the reason for not being friends. Adva looked at the diversity of the group from a new perspective and stressed the age difference between the children. The discourse that developed within the small, sustained group gave Rachel a closer look at the children's perceptions of diversity (Abu Al Rub, 2017) and allowed her to gain an understanding of the children's perceptions and their social and cultural ecological system (Bronfenbrenner, 1979).

The discourse programmed social exchanges between peers (Wolery et al., 1992) and demonstrates equity pedagogy (Banks, 2013) where all children's knowledge is relevant and all children's voices, perceptions, and views are heard and part of the construction of the new knowledge. All the children point out the differences between them but perceive these differences as normal. In her reflection Rachel concluded her insights from the learning process:

> Listening to the children and letting the discourse emerge from their own world contributes to the development of meaningful discourse and the development of the children's self-expression. The best way to learn is via active participation and enjoyment, peer learning and an emergent curriculum. Children express themselves in a hundred languages, and the educator's role is to listen and mediate. (Rachel, 6.2016)

To conclude, the emergent curriculum and the use of "one hundred languages" for expression enabled the children to express themselves on various issues that are connected to diversity. This process promoted attitudes and values of inclusion and equity among the children. Rachel's decision to position herself as a listener of the children's thoughts and perceptions and the use of "one hundred languages" as a method, enabled them to express themselves in a more detailed way. The use of an emergent curriculum constructed a meaningful learning process that promoted the children's learning as individuals and as a group.

DISCUSSION

This chapter focuses on five cases of ECE student teachers' emergent curriculum development (See table 1). In all cases, the student teachers worked with the children in small, sustained, heterogeneous groups. The student teachers were required to develop a curriculum based on the emergent curriculum principles (Jones, 2012; Rinaldi, 2001; Yu-le, 2004). The curricula emerged from the children's interests and were based on the individuals' and groups' social, cognitive, and emotional characteristics. The student teachers aimed to work with the children on quality texts and images that match the children's needs and development, however, it is unavoidable that these choices were subjective and were influenced by the student teachers' personality and life experience. All the student teachers encouraged the children to "raise their own questions, generate their own hypotheses and models of possibilities, and test them for viability" (Fosnot, 1996, p. 29). This learning process was based on self-reflection, peer learning, and was guided by the pedagogic and disciplinary mentors. The student teachers implemented the emergent curriculum approach, creating bridges to children from diverse homes.

Table 1. Five Cases of ECE Student Teachers' Emergent Curriculum Development

Student teacher	Preschool	Case
Phahimma	Preschool 1 (Jaffa)	Case A: From diverse languages to the creation of one shared language
Sarah	Preschool 3	Case B: Art and literature as a mirror of diverse families
Jane	Preschool 2	Case C: Art and literature as a mirror of families' country of origin
Maya	Preschool 3	Case D: Jewish Studies and art: Creating a multicultural celebration table
Rachel	Preschool 2	Case E: Children's songs: Learning the Hebrew language

In all cases, the children's voices were heard and shaped the group's emergent curriculum. Two out of the five cases (Phahimma- Case A, Rachel-Case E) focused on the spoken language. As some of the children in the group were from cultural minorities and their home language was not Hebrew, the subject that emerged in the group was language.

Phahimma (Case A) constructed an emergent curriculum that integrated the discourse that emerged from the children's needs and subjects of interests and her personal cultural background, perceptions, and preferences. Phahimma's interest in art and the children's interest in languages led her to search for artists who focus on the appearance of the language's written form. In the group discourse, the children decided to create a new language (in movement) with no cultural characteristics.

Rachel (Case E), on the other hand, encountered difficulties in implementing an emergent curriculum. It was challenging for her to create an open, meaningful discourse within the group due to the differences in the children's home language. Rachel's decision was to expose the children to short songs by Yehonatan Geffen, and this was a starting point for the learning process. Whereas Phahimma co-constructed with the children, Rachel's starting point was constructed as a response to the children's needs. The end of the process revealed the children's involvement and influence on the construction of the curriculum by creating a shared language of movement to provide a new interpretation to the song lyrics.

Both learning processes (cases A and E) illustrate the ways the student teachers empowered all children and created equal opportunities for learning (Banks, 2010). In both cases, the children's voices were heard, and their knowledge and views were valued and considered in the construction of the learning process. Both student teachers implemented the main principles of the emergent curriculum approach (Jones, 2012; Rinaldi, 2001; Yu-le, 2004) such as: listening to the children, documenting and constructing curriculum according to the children's needs and subjects of interest. With the lack of a shared, equal language to all children, they created a new language with no cultural characteristics. The student teachers started from different perspectives and considerations; however, both focused on creating a new language as this was the children's need.

Sarah's (Case B), Jane's (Case C), and Maya's (Case D) learning processes reflected the children's diverse families. In these cases the student teachers reached the children's families and communities (Bronfenbrenner, 1979) via meaningful, open discourse, listening to the children, and allowing expression in "one hundred languages" (Rinaldi, 2001). Sarah's (Case B) and Maya's (Case D) learning processes highlighted the diversity of the children's family structure (such as single parenting, single-gender families, traditional family) and the diversity of the families' leisure time. Jane's case (Case C) illustrated the families' country of origin via sharing, discussing, and creating their home cultural habits in "one hundred languages."

CONCLUSION

This chapter depicts the policy of the ECE program at Levinsky College of Education, which promotes working with small, heterogeneous, sustained groups in order to foster inclusion and equity pedagogy (Gillies & Cunnington, 2014; Sills, Rowse, & Emerson, 2016; Tal, 2014, 2018). It also reveals the great richness and diversity of the ECE student teachers' emergent curricula within the preschools. Although all students study in the same college and practice in Israeli public preschools, the curricula they constructed were diverse as these were based on the children's and student teachers' ecological context (Bronfenbrenner, 1979).

Data analysis revealed two major aspects related to all student teachers' work in the preschool. First, the student teachers implemented an inclusive and equity pedagogy based on Banks' (2010) dimensions of multicultural education. Learning in small groups fostered the equal participation of all children, peer learning, and the development of a meaningful emergent curriculum. The discourse allowed the children to be exposed to a variety of perceptions, habits, family structures, and cultural customs of their peers. The learning process led the student teachers and the children to create a unique, tailor-made curriculum and exposed the children to diverse texts and images that reflected the children's and student teachers' diversity.

All the student teachers' sustained groups became a secure and inclusive space where children from diverse socio-cultural backgrounds felt a sense of belonging and were able to express their diversity. Within this discourse, the children expressed themselves and shared their own experiences with the other children in the group. They were also exposed to the cultural diversity of their peers' families with regards to traditional Jewish customs, and different families' languages, ethnic foods, and leisure activities. This helps to reduce prejudiced views about diverse families and promotes equity pedagogy (Banks, 2013). The student teachers managed to cross boundaries between the preschool and the children's communities, facilitated a flow of cultural knowledge (Heath, 1983), and enabled all children to equally express experiences and knowledge that they carry in their "virtual schoolbags" (Thomson, 2003). This process allowed the children to compare and contrast new shared knowledge.

Second, the student teachers constructed an emergent curriculum that developed from listening to the children's needs and subjects of interest, using "one hundred languages" of expression (Rinaldi, 2001). These varied types of expression enriched the group discourse as it raised children's perspectives, thoughts, and ideas that the children are not always able to express in their spoken language or that they do not count as unique or important issues. Sharing children's photographs, drawings and the like in the group's open discourse, encouraged the children to elaborate upon their explanations for the different objects. This in turn, helps the group construct new knowledge.

In a group of five children, five different stories were heard. The group discourse demonstrated the heterogeneity of the group. In addition to the individual child's empowering of the self, family, and community, this process broadens and deepens their world knowledge and promotes social skills and values of tolerance and acceptance of the other.

The student teachers implemented the emergent curriculum principles by listening closely to each unique child and managed to create an original, unique, and relevant curriculum that reflects all the children's voices. The student teachers were positioned as facilitators of the children's learning, extended and provoked their learning and provided them with opportunities and incentives to construct their learning (Fosnot, 1996).

In sum, the five cases illustrate five different stories of connections between student teachers and children's life experiences, ecologies and personalities. These connections influenced the construction of unique, tailor-made curricula.

IMPLICATIONS

This study illustrates the importance of considering and listening to diversity in all levels of the educational system. Institutions of education must consider social and cultural diversity as a critical factor in the training program for student teachers. It is critical for student teachers and children to be considered competent, influential, and active partners in the learning process. Listening to their diverse backgrounds, perceptions, thoughts, ideas, and knowledge should be at the heart of the learning process in order to construct reflective and equal education. Working in small, sustained heterogeneous groups is a key factor in fostering an equal, meaningful, relevant curriculum in preschools. Only small, sustained groups allow real listening to each individual child. Additionally, empowering individual children helped promote children's multicultural orientation in the small heterogeneous groups. In order to construct an equal curriculum for all children, student teachers must be attentive to the children's personal stories. This also illustrates to the student teachers that there are multiple pathways to construct a meaningful curriculum.

REFERENCES

Abu Al Rub. M. (2017). The Impact of small group instruction on preschool literacy skills. *Journal of Educational and Psychological Studies, 11*, 794-802. Web.

Ballenger, C. (2009). *Puzzling moments, teachable moments: Practicing teacher research in urban classrooms*. New York: Teachers College Press.

Banks, J. A. (2010). Multicultural education: Characteristics and goals. In J. A. Banks & C. A. M. Banks (Eds.), *Multicultural education: Issues and perspectives*, 7th edition, (pp. 1-32). Hoboken, NJ: Wiley.

Banks, J. A. (2013). The construction and historical development of multicultural education, 1962–2012. *Theory into Practice* 52, (1). Available from: https://www.researchgate.net/publication/317367781_Multicultural_Education_in_the_US_Current_Issues_and_Suggestions_for_Practical_Implementations [accessed Sep 14 2018].

Barzilai, A. (1984). Formal measures in the poetry of Yehonatan Gefen. *Literature for Children and Youth, 10*, 53-54.

Berger, P. L., & Luckmann, T. (1989). *The social construction of reality: A treatise in the sociology of knowledge*. Garden City, NY: Anchor Books.

Bourdieu, P. (1986). The forms of capital. In J. G. Richardson (Ed.), *Handbook of theory and research for the sociology of education* (pp. 241–258). New York: Greenwood Press.

Bronfenbrenner. U. (1979). *The ecology of human development*. Cambridge, MA: Harvard University Press.

Browne. A. (2010). *Little Beauty*. Candlewick Press.

Chen G., & Starosta, W. J. (2000). *The development and validation of the intercultural sensitivity scale*. Paper presented at the 86th annual meeting of the National Communication Association, Seattle, WA.

Clark, A. (2010). *Transforming children's spaces: Children's and adults' participation in designing learning environments*. London, UK: Routledge.

COR- Child Observation Record (2003). *High scope educational research foundation press*. Third ed. Retrieved from https://www.research connections.org/childcare/resources/22440.

Dickinson, D. K., & Porche, M. V. (2011). Relation between language experiences in preschool classrooms and children's kindergarten and fourth-grade language and reading abilities. *Child Development, 82*(3), 870-886.

Dutton, A. S. (2012). Discovering my role in an emergent curriculum preschool. *Voices of Practitioners, 7*(1), 3-17.

Feldman, D. (2009). Human rights of children with disabilities in Israel: The vision and the reality. *Disability Studies Quarterly, 29*(1).

Forman, G., & Fyfe, B. (1998). Negotiated learning through design, documentation, and discourse. In C. Edwards, L. Gandini, & G. Forman (Eds.), *The hundred languages of children: The Reggio Emilia approach to early childhood education* (2nd edition) (pp. 239-251). Greenwich, CT: Ablex Publishing.

Fosnot, C.T. (1996) *Constructivism: Theory, perspectives, and practice.* New York: Teachers College Press.

Freeman, D. (1998). Collecting and analysing data. In D. Freeman (Ed.), *Doing teacher-research: From inquiry to understanding* (pp. 86–120). Pacific Grove, CA: Heinle Cengage Learning.

Geffen Yehonatan (1978). *The sixteen sheep - songs and stories for children.* Dvir Publication.

Gibton, D. (2011). Post-2000 law-based educational governance in Israel: From equality to diversity? *Educational Management Administration & Leadership,* 39(4), 434-454.

Gillies, R., & Cunnington, R. (2014). Cooperative learning: The behavioural and neurological markers that help to explain its success. *Quality and Equity,* 38-43.

Grant, C. A. (2018). A better multicultural society: Woke citizenship and multicultural activism. *Multicultural Education Review, 10*(4), 327-333

Heath, S. B., (1983). *Ways with words: Language, life and work in communities and classrooms.* Cambridge, MA: Cambridge University Press.

Huh, H. K., Choi, S. W., & Jun, J. (2015). Relationships among multicultural Sensitivity, multicultural education awareness, and level of multicultural education practice of South Korean teachers. KEDI *Journal of Educational Policy, 12*(1), 107-126.

Husni al-Khatib Shehada (2012). 'And Acre will stay in this consciousness forever': Anisa Ashkar and the search language after the subjective, critical reading in the artist's work: 'Rubbish and other installations',

140   *Sigal Tish, Iris Levy, Michaella Kadury-Slezak et al.*

in *Anisa Ashkar – 'Rubbish' (catalog)*. Tel Aviv, Ashkar and Nelly Aman.

Israeli artist's website– Anita Ashkar. (2016). Retrieved from http://www.israeliartists.co.il/m/%D7%90%D7%A0%D7%99%D7%A1%D7%94_%D7%90%D7%A9%D7%A7%D7%A8_Anisa_Ashkar.

Israeli Central Bureau of Statistics. (2019). *Demographic Characteristic.* Retrieved from https://www.cbs.gov.il/he/mediarelease/pages/2018/%D7%90%D7%95%D7%9B%D7%9C%D7%95%D7%A1%D7%99%D7%99%D7%AA-%D7%99%D7%A9%D7%A8%D7%90%D7%9C-%D7%91%D7%A4%D7%AA%D7%97%D7%94-%D7%A9%D7%9C-%D7%A9%D7%A0%D7%AA-2019-2018-19.aspx.

Israeli Mandatory Schooling Law. (1953). Retrieved from https://www.nevo.co.il/law_html/Law01/152_024.htm.

Israeli Special Education law. (1998). Retrieved from http://cms.education.gov.il/EducationCMS/Units/Zchuyot/ChukimVeamanot/Chukim/HockKhinuhMeuhad.htm.

Jones, E. (2012). The emergence of emergent curriculum. *Young Children, 67*(2), 66-68.

Justice L. M., Skibbe L. E., McGinty A. S., Piasta S. B., & Petrill S. (2011). Feasibility, efficacy, and social validity of home-based storybook reading intervention for children with language impairment. *Journal of Speech, Language, and Hearing Research, 54,* 523–538.

Kalekin-Fishman, D., & Eden, D. (Eds.). (2003). *Multiculturalism: Living it, talking about it, doing it: Intervention and research in a university setting.* Haifa, Israel: University of Haifa.

Katz. L. G. (1999). *Curriculum disputes in early childhood education. ERIC Digest.* ERIC Clearinghouse on Elementary and Early Childhood Education Champaign IL. 1-7.

Ledford, J. R., Lane, J. D., Elam, K. L., & Wolery, M. (2012). Using response-prompting procedures during small-group direct instruction: Outcomes and procedural variations. *American Journal on Intellectual and Developmental Disabilities, 117*(5), 413-434.

MABATIM (Hebrew) - *Observing Children in their Natural Environment* (2016). Israeli Ministry of Education. Retrieved from http://meyda.education.gov.il/files/PreSchool/mabatim16.pdf.

Malaguzzi, L. (1993). For an education based on relationships. *Young Children, 49*(1), 9-12.

Organisation for Economic Co-operation and Development (OECD) (2011). *Foreign-born population (indicator)*. Retrieved from https://data.oecd.org/migration/foreign-born-population.htm.

Oyler, C. (2011). Preparing teachers of young children to be social justice-oriented educators. In B. S. Fennimore & A. L. Goodwin (Eds.), *Promoting social justice for young children*, (pp. 147–161). New York: Springer.

Pajares, M. F. (1992). Teachers' beliefs and educational research: Cleaning up a messy construct. *Review of Educational Research, 62*(3), 307-332.

Richie, J., & Spencer, L. (1994). Qualitative data analysis for applied policy research. In A. Bryman, R. G. Burgess (Eds.) *Analysis of qualitative data* (pp. 173-194). London: Routledge.

Rinaldi, C. (2001). The pedagogy of listening: The listening perspective from the Reggio Emilia. *Innovations in early education: The international Reggio exchange, 8*(4), 1–4.

Rinaldi, C. (2006). *In dialogue with Reggio Emilia: Listening, researching and learning*. London, UK: Routledge.

Rogoff. B. (2003). *The cultural nature of human development*. New York: Oxford University Press.

Savir, A. (2002). *Father Orange and his daughter Clementine*. Rishon Lezion: Viziart Press.

Schön A. D. (1983). *The Reflective practitioner: How professionals think in action*. New York: Basic Books.

Schön, A. D. (1987). *Educating the reflective pPractitioner: Toward a new design for teaching and learning in the professions*. San Francisco: Jossey-Bass Publishers.

Seefelt, C. (2001). *Social studies for the pre-school-primary child* (6th ed.). Upper Saddle River, NJ: Prentice-Hall.

Sills, J., Rowse, G., & Emerson, L. (2016). The role of collaboration in the cognitive development of young children: A systematic review. *Child: Care, Health, and Development, 42*(2), 313-324.

Tal, C. (2014). Introduction of an emergent curriculum and an inclusive pedagogy in a traditional setting in Israel: A case study. *International Journal of Early Years Education, 22*(2), 141-155.

Tal, C. (2018). The challenge of implementing small group work in early childhood education. *Global Education Review, 5*(2),123-144.

Thomson, P. (2003). *Schooling the rustbelt kids: Making the difference in changing times.* Crow's Nest, NSW: Allen & Unwin.

Van Manen, M. (1994). Pedagogy, virtue, and narrative identity in teaching. *Curriculum Inquiry, 24*(2), 135-170.

Vygotsky, L. S. (1978). *Mind in society: The development of higher mental process.* Cambridge, MA: Harvard University Press.

Wolery, M., Ault, M. J., Doyle, P. M., Gast, D. L., & Griffen, A. K. (1992). Choral and individual responding during small group instruction: Identification of interactional effects. *Education and Treatment of Children*, 289-309.

Yin. R. K. (1989). *Case study research: Design and methods*, 4th ed. Thousand Oaks, CA: Sage.

Yu-le, Z. (2004). Some thoughts on emergent curriculum. Paper presented at the *Forum for Integrated Education and Educational Reform sponsored by the Council for Global Integrative Education*, Santa Cruz: CA October 28-30. Retrieved from http://www. edpsycinteractive.org/CGIE/yule.pdf.

In: Teacher Training
Editor: Paula E. McDermott

ISBN: 978-1-53615-633-1
© 2019 Nova Science Publishers, Inc.

Chapter 4

SIMULATION BASED ON ROLE-PLAYING AS A SIGNIFICANT LEARNING TOOL FOR TRAINING STUDENT TEACHERS TO COMMUNICATE WITH PARENTS

Einat Sequerra-Ater, Orly Licht Weinish, Iris Levy, Alona Peleg, Naomi Perchik, Yael Shlesinger, Pninat Tal and Clodie Tal*
Early Childhood Education, Levinsky College of Education,
Tel Aviv, Israel

ABSTRACT

Working with parents is one of the central challenges for teachers and should be addressed in teacher training. To that end, the Early Childhood Education program at Levinsky College of Education created a course in 2017-18 entitled "Working with Parents in the 21st Century." To train student teachers in this area, a simulation center was created in

---

* Corresponding Author's E-mail: einatse@gmail.com.

which videotaped simulations are used as a critical learning tool. In this study, 143 student teachers doing their internship in the fourth year of their program were divided into 5 classes, each class containing 5 groups. The students were asked to describe in writing a significant episode from their practicum related to work with the parents. Each group chose one episode, analyzed the different perspectives of the participants (teacher, parent, child), and role-played this episode in the simulation center. A reflective dialogue was then conducted within each class among the simulation participants, their classmates, and the lecturer regarding the teacher's performance. Students then re-enacted the simulation in which they applied the insights gained from the feedback. Subsequent analysis of the students' documented thoughts and feelings about the simulations revealed five main insights regarding communication with parents: (1) Teachers should use a personal, emotional approach and be respectful, understanding, and empathic to parents; (2) In discussing a child's difficulties, teachers should be empowering of parents and foster a sense of security and trust; (3) Dialogue with parents should be well planned and founded on facts gathered and carefully studied in advance; (4) During the dialogue, teachers should acknowledge the varied perspectives of the participants in the discourse; and (5) When necessary, teachers should be assertive with parents. The findings indicate that simulations based on role-playing in teacher education programs are an essential tool for training student teachers about how to plan and practice communication skills with parents, allowing them to experience a wide range of emotionally charged encounters within a safe environment. Simulations based on role-playing significantly contribute to improved student communication skills, self-awareness, and self-efficacy in their encounters with parents.

INTRODUCTION

The Complexity of Working with Parents in the 21st Century

The partnership of parents and teachers has been associated with enhanced academic achievement, proper behavior, well developed social skills, and a high level of student adjustment to school (Henderson, 2007) as well as a positive school climate and parental support of the teachers' work (Epstein, 2018). Effective communication between teachers and parents enables both sides to have a deeper understanding of the mutual expectations regarding children's needs (Epstein, 2018; Epstein & Sanders, 2006; Wandersman et al., 2002) and fosters greater parental involvement in school (Evans, 2004; Graham-Gray, 2002). Despite the significant contribution of parent-teacher partnership to child development, communication between teachers and parents is considered a complex and challenging issue. Teachers and parents are all interested in seeing the child advance, but discrepancies in their perceptions of the child's needs and functioning often become a source of tension and conflict (Lake & Billingsley, 2000). Teachers are interested in parental support of the children's learning processes, and parents want teachers to address their children's specific needs, but the two sides often stumble in finding common ways to promote these goals (Auerbach, 2012; Wanat, 2010).

The difficulty in forming a partnership between the education system and parents stems from possible psychological, technological, linguistic, or cultural barriers on the part of all three involved parties: *the parents* (who may have a passive or uninvolved approach to school life, lack trust in or appreciation of the teacher, or lack time, knowledge, or confidence in their ability to assist their child); *the teachers* (who may fear excessive parental intervention in the teacher's professional decisions, hesitate to incur disagreement with the parents, or differ with the parents in assessing the child's performance and needs); and *the school* (which may be blocking parental attempts at school involvement, maintain contact with the parents only regarding a child's difficulties, or use communication channels that are not accessible to or regarded as suitable by the parents) (Colombo, 2004; Christenson, 2004; Hoover-Dempsey, Walker, Jones, & Reed, 2002; Lasater, 2016; Ozmen, Akuzum, Zincirli, & Selcuk, 2016; Semke & Sheriden, 2012; Terek, Glušac, Nikolic, Tasic, & Gligorovic, 2015; Wanat, 2010; Zieger & Tan; 2012). These barriers can engender frustration and suspicion between the school system and the parent. They can intensify feelings of confusion, resistance, lack of understanding, anger, and helplessness on both sides, and undermine positive communication between them. Specifically, the barriers may create a limited, partial, or fully conflictual discourse between the teacher and parents regarding their mutual expectations, the child's functioning, and the schools' role and approach.

The Importance of Training Students to Work with Parents in the Framework of Teacher Training

De Bruïne et al. (2014) examined teacher training programs in the United States, the Netherlands, and Belgium and found that, despite the importance these programs ascribe to parental involvement in education, the subject of parental involvement is not structured into specialized courses in teacher training programs. The development of effective communication skills between teachers and parents should be an essential component of teacher training, as it can help students cultivate an attentive, open, and fruitful dialogue with parents, one that respects their difficulties, needs, and perspectives, and establishes appropriate linguistic, cultural, and technological channels to work together for the well-being of the child. Communication skills between teachers and parents can be enhanced during teacher training by combining the study of theoretical models that construct effective dialogue with parents and engaging the students in diverse dialogues with parents using methods such as case studies, simulations, and discussions. In this chapter, we focus on simulation as a pedagogical and reflective learning tool for cultivating optimal communication with parents in the framework of teacher training.

Simulation Based on Role-Playing as a Learning Tool in Professional Training

Simulation has been defined as the "ongoing representation of certain features of a real situation to achieve some specific training objective" (Morris & Thomas, 1976, as cited in Davies, 2013, p. 66) or as an attempt at "reproduc[ing] the real-world phenomena as closely as possible to ensure simulation is a valid representation of these phenomena" (Hays &

Singer, 1988, as cited in Davies, 2013, p. 15). Simulations are a learning tool that enables participants to practice their skills in diverse contexts that resemble real-world situations and acquire relevant professional skills while training in a safe environment (Davies, 2013).

The professional literature on simulations as an academic learning tool refers to a broad and diverse array of learning methods, such as role-playing, case studies, class discussions, and technical simulations. Simulation based on role-playing involves the representation of a realistic situation, often within a given scenario in which participants act out roles following a set of rules. The purpose of using simulation based on role-playing is to practice skills relevant to a specific field of learning and to become aware of and thoughtful about these skills (Lean, Moizer, Towler, & Abbey, 2006; Van Ments, 1999). The use of role-playing simulation is common in many academic fields such as economics (Sandford & Bradbury, 1971), history (Beidatsch & Broomhall, 2010; Duveen & Solomon, 1994), geography (Maddrell, 2007), languages (Magos & Politi, 2008), and particularly fields requiring practical vocational training, such as medicine (Bosse et al., 2010; Chan, 2012; Finlay, Stott, & Kinnersky, 1995; Nestel & Tierney, 2007, Wayne et al., 2005), engineering (Cobo, Conde, & Quintela, 2011; Mitri, Cole, & Atkins, 2017), psychotherapy (Remer, 1990); management (Abdullah, Hanafiah, & Hashim, 2013; Shen, Nicholson, & Nicholson, 2015; Westrup & Planander, 2013) and teaching (Bender, 2005; Flaitz, 1986; Kilgour, Reynaud, Northcote, & Shields, 2015; Sharma, 2015).

Simulation based on role-playing has many advantages as a learning tool. Engaging in such simulations increases the participation and involvement of learners, encourages active learning processes, develops interpersonal communication skills, and deepens the learner's critical thinking ability. It has been found that simulation based on role-playing expands participants' perspectives regarding the simulated event (Agboola Sogunro, 2004), raises their awareness of how they performed (Daly, Grove, Dorsch & Fisk, 2009), enhances problem-solving skills (Alkin & Christie, 2002), and increases professional confidence, communication skills, and empathy toward the other participants in the simulation (Gough,

Frydenberg, Donath, & Marks, 2009). This is made possible by creating a learning environment in which participants experience complex, relevant, and credible situations adapted to their professional developmental stage within a safe space (Ward, Williams, & Hancock 2006). The use of simulation based on role-playing helps learners integrate the theoretical knowledge they acquired with its application in real-life situations, expands their openness and flexibility in ambiguous or conflictual situations, and provides constructive, multi-perspective feedback about their functioning (Cobo, Conde, & Quintela, 2011; Jeffries 2005).

Simulation based on role-playing was found to be a particularly effective learning tool for deepening the student teachers' attitudes and perceptions about themselves and relevant aspects of the given learning situation. For example, Kilgour et al. (2015) found that students who practiced role playing (of teaching methods, interviews, and conversations with parents) while studying history, intercultural education, mathematics, and leadership reported a change in attitude toward the field, increased openness to other points of view, and greater self-awareness about emotions, thoughts, and attitudes that affect their performance. Similarly, Zamboanga, Ham, Tomaso, Audley, and Pole (2016) found that role-playing contributed to students' understanding of the complexity of acculturation and increased their sensitivity and empathy toward those undergoing this process.

In view of the uniqueness of simulation based on role-playing to deepen a student's awareness of feelings and thoughts about him/herself and others in complex life situations, this method is particularly useful in professions that require interpersonal training for dealing with conflicts and problem solving. Role playing allows the student to practice functioning in complex situations that simulate real life, while receiving feedback about the motivations, attitudes, thoughts, feelings, and behavior of participants in these simulations. Thus, learners are encouraged to rethink and reconstruct their assumptions, attitudes, and behavior while performing in challenging professional contexts (Zamboanga et al., 2016; DeNeve & Heppner, 1997; Kilgour et al. 2015; Rao & Stupans, 2012).

Simulation Based on Role-Playing as a Tool for Developing Reflective Thinking in Teacher-Training

Reflection is a process of profound observation and examination of a given situation and of one's thoughts, emotions, attitudes, and behavior with the aim of becoming aware of these responses and acting to maintain or change them, if necessary. Reflective practice is a "challenging, focused, and critical assessment of one's own behavior as a means towards developing one's own craftsmanship" (Osterman, 1990, p. 134). Reflective thinking is one of the most important learning skills, especially in professions that involve complex interpersonal processes, because it enables an individual to observe thoughts, feelings, and behavior and to adapt them dynamically in order to best cope with the challenges arising from conflict in working with others.

In recent decades, teacher training programs have increasingly sought to develop students' critical and reflective thinking about their attitudes, beliefs, and behavior in relation to their work (Kilgour et al. 2015; Sharma, 2015; Tabachnick & Zeichner, 1991). Focusing on honing the skill of reflective thinking during teacher training is based on the assumption that teachers face challenges that arise not only from possible differences between their initial values and beliefs and those acquired in the training (Korthagen, 1992), but also from possible differences between the values and beliefs acquired in training and their ability to implement them in the field (Smyth, 1989). The development of reflective thinking during one's training helps integrate professional-scientific knowledge with the values, beliefs, and experiences related to actual performance (Dana & Westcott, 1995), allowing student teachers to change, adapt, and expand their attitudes and behaviors dynamically in accordance with the situation in the field (Osterman, 1990).

One model that emerged from attempts to develop reflective thinking in teacher training was created by Brockbank and McGill (1998) based on Schön's definitions (1987) of the reflection that takes place in learning. According to Schön, "propositional knowledge" comprises our theoretical knowledge of a particular subject area, "knowledge-in-action" concerns our practical knowledge of it, while "reflection-in-action" includes our reflections about that practical knowledge. Reflection-in-action occurs in the application of our practical knowledge, and arises when we need a way of coping that is not within the automatic set of our practical knowledge of a situation. Based on Schön, Brockbank and McGill developed a model of a reflective learning process that includes five stages: (1) *action* – a description that includes reference to the event, to the participants, and to how the learner functions in the situation; (2) *reflection-in-action* – the learner's observation of the situation and his/her functioning within it, while relating to the behavior, thoughts, and feelings that arose; (3) *description of the reflection-in-action* – observation and feedback of the learner, the fellow learners, and the mentor including their thoughts and feelings about how the learner has coped with the situation; (4) *reflection on the description of the reflection-in-action (reflection-on-action)*– the learner's and the colleagues' renewed observation of the situation and behavior after the previous reflective stage, while understanding, applying, and re-adapting the theoretical models and the group feedback; and (5) *reflection on the reflection-on-action* – group observation guided by the lecturer of the group's learning process, integration, and reasoning on principles learned in situations similar to those that arose during this session.

The reflective practice described in the Brockbank and McGill model enables students to expand their understanding and awareness of various aspects of their professional functioning in their work with others, such as their understanding of the motivations for their response, the effectiveness of their functioning, and their ability to relate to different perspectives in the given situation. Thus, the students expand their range of coping options in a conscious and flexible manner, and are better able to adapt the theoretical models acquired in class to the appropriate professional response required. Through the practice of reflective thinking, students can better understand their own learning processes.

The Brockbank and McGill model (1998) can serve as a basis for the development and practice of reflective thinking in the context of learning communication skills between teachers and parents by simulating dialogue between teachers and parents and conducting personal and group reflections on the simulations. Experimenting with different simulations of parent-teacher dialogue while reflecting on their feelings, thoughts, and functioning in the simulations together with feedback from their peers can cognitively and emotionally deepen the student's understanding of how to cope with parents. Learning through such simulations may enhance planning and preparation for conversing with the parent, deepen the teacher's awareness of the parent's experience and perspectives, improve communication skills with parents, and enhance the teacher's sense of self-efficacy in establishing effective communication with parents.

The Importance of Simulation Based on Role-Playing in Teaching Students to Work with Parents

Despite the critical importance of developing effective communication skills with parents, and despite the demonstrated effectiveness of simulation based on role-playing in diverse professional training courses, role-playing that engages the student in a range of parent-teacher communications is not a common learning tool in teacher training programs (Grossman, Hammerness, & McDonald 2009).

One of the few parent-teacher communication simulations that is sometimes offered in teacher training programs is the parent-teacher conference simulation. Walker and Legg (2018) proposed criteria for constructing parent-teacher conference simulations as part of a teacher training program designed to assess the professional knowledge and planning ability of the students and to improve their communication skills with parents. They developed two parent-teacher conference simulations in which the practicing student received information about a child and had to analyze and communicate the information to the parent through role-playing. At the end of the simulation, the student received feedback from classmates and the lecturer, and was asked reflective questions about his or her perceived performance in the simulation. The student was also asked what could be improved in a revised simulation and what insights and inputs emerged from the experience. Based on their research, Walker and Legg proposed criteria for evaluating the student's performance in the simulation: planning of the meeting, openness to dialogue with the parent, information gathered and shared about the child, interest expressed in the parents' perspective of the child and in maintaining contact with the parents, attentiveness to and empathy expressed with the parents, and maintaining focus on discourse beneficial to the child. Studies that examined the use of parent-teacher conference simulations in teacher training programs found that participation in the simulation increased the level of social responsiveness of the student teachers and enhanced their awareness of the emotional and social dynamic in parent-teacher interactions (Dotger, 2010; Dotger, Harris, Maher, & Hansel, 2011).

Parent-teacher encounters in the 21st century differ from formal parent-teacher conferences. Current meetings take place on an ongoing basis, formally and informally, through planned or spontaneous meetings. They are initiated by the teacher or the parent, and take place through face-to-face meetings or by email, telephone, or text messages. These encounters are focused on diverse and often sensitive issues that could create conflict between the teacher and parent. Contemporary parent-teacher encounters present the teacher with a wide repertoire of modes of communication, and therefore require her to be a skilled communicator who is open, flexible, and has the ability to engage parents in their children's education.

Although parent-teacher conference simulations have been found effective and helpful, they are not built into teacher training programs. Moreover, teacher training programs do not provide courses that focus on work with the parents in which a wide range of parent-teacher dialogues can be practiced beyond the traditional parent-teacher conference.

Thus, in recent years there has been growing recognition that in the context of teacher training, emphasis must be placed on training students for structured, diverse, and complex situations that require effective communication with parents. A simulation based on role-playing of parent-teacher dialogue in teacher training programs can serve as an effective tool, one that allows students to practice varied encounters with parents and to expand their ability to plan, train, and reflect on their communication skills in a safe environment. The present study was designed to examine the contribution of simulation based on role-playing in teacher training to enhancing the skills required for effective communication with parents.

METHODOLOGY

The present study was conducted in the framework of the course "Working with Parents in the 21st Century." This course is taught in the fourth year of the Early Childhood Education program (ages 3-8) at Levinsky College of Education in Israel. Participants were 143 female student teachers who took the course in five parallel classes in the first semester of the fourth year, which is their internship year. The methodology was the same in each class.

Data Analysis

A qualitative, thematic analysis (Sabar-Ben Yehoshua, 2016) was carried out on the insights reported by the student teachers following the simulations and subsequent reflections on their communication with parents.

Research Procedure

Five groups were created in each class, with 5-6 student teachers in each group. Each student was asked to record in writing and analyze one episode involving communication between a teacher and parent. Following presentation of these events to the group and discussion, each group was asked to choose one episode and plan it as a simulation. The simulation took place in a dedicated simulation room at the college and was analyzed together with the other student teachers and the lecturer.

The process of selecting the episode: Each student described in writing a social episode that included discourse between the teacher and a parent. The episodes were written in accordance with Harré and Secord's (1972) guidelines. The majority of the written episodes described conflictual situations between parents and a teacher. Each student was asked to analyze the content of the episode, the difficulties that arose, the participants' perspectives (feelings, thoughts, and attitudes), and how the teacher coped with the situation. The student teachers were also asked to propose alternative scenarios for how the teacher could have handled the situation. The different perspectives of the participants in the episode (teacher, parent, child) were analyzed using Tal's (2005) guidelines. Following the students' presentations to the group of the events they had described in writing, each group selected one event for simulation.

The simulations were conducted according to the five stages of the Brockbank and McGill model (1998):

- *The first stage – Simulation planning and presentation (Action phase):* Each group planned and presented a simulation based on the selected episode. The group carefully planned the teacher's behavior during the simulation, while thoroughly considering the thoughts, feelings, and manner of coping of all participants in the episode using Tal's guidelines. The simulations were videotaped to enable the students to reexamine and re-reflect on them.

- *The second stage – Reflection on the simulation (Reflection-in-action phase):* After each simulation, each participant shared with her classmates and the lecturer her thoughts and feelings about the performance of the various characters in the simulation, the motives for her reactions, and the strong and weak points of her performance in the simulation.

- *The third stage – Feedback from classmates and the lecturer (Description of the reflection-in-action):* The classmates and lecturer described their feelings and thoughts about how the participants, particularly the student who took the role of the teacher, coped with the simulated event. The reflective dialogue of the participants, classmates, and lecturer regarding the teacher's functioning in the simulation was conducted using Barak-Shtein's (2011) model to assess the quality of interpersonal interactions. During the reflective group dialogue, the group assisted the student who role-played the teacher to expand her understanding of the parents' perspective, to analyze the strong and weak points of her coping with the situation, and to examine other effective alternatives.

- *The fourth stage – Re-simulating and feedback (reflection on action):* Following the reflective feedback of the classmates and lecturer in the previous stage, each group repeated the simulation, seeking to improve the teacher's performance relative to the previous simulation. At the end of the re-simulation, a reflective discussion was held of all participants and the lecturer about the teacher's functioning in the repeated simulation and whether the feedback was implemented.
- *The fifth stage – Integration and conclusion (Reflection on the reflection-on-action):* A class discussion examined the students' insights about effective communication with parents based on integrating the theoretical models studied in the course, the participation in the simulations, and the reflective process that followed.

At the end of the course, the students were asked to submit the video and transcript of the simulation they presented, an analysis of the individual and group reflective process they experienced, and an account of their insights about parent-teacher communication drawn from the simulations and reflective process. These descriptions were analyzed by the researchers for this study.

Research Ethics

The course lecturers are also the researchers of this study. Thus, as in any similar course, the researchers nurtured relationships with the student teachers who participated in the study. The students also know each other. These may affect the findings, which is an inevitable part of qualitative research. The researchers carefully and sensitively read the students' descriptions of their insights about parent-teacher encounters, and did their best to interpret the data objectively. However, qualitative research cannot and does not purport to prevent biases in the collection and interpretation of data, since this process by nature involves and reflects the researcher's point of view. During the course, the lecturers gave space to all the emotions, attitudes, and perspectives of the students as they arose in the simulations and discussions. The researchers closely monitored the students in the experience of encountering parents and were empathetic toward the students in how they coped in the simulations.

FINDINGS

This study examined the insights of student teachers regarding teachers' communication with parents following 28 simulations based on role playing parent-teacher encounters. All the simulations reflected episodes of conflict or disagreement between teacher and parents. Each of the conversations, whether initiated by the teacher or parent, revolved around the child's difficulties or the teacher's attitude toward the child, rather than the more general work of the teacher (such as how she manages and organizes the class, her professional agenda, etc.). Following the simulations and subsequent process of reflection, five main insights emerged from the students' summarized responses of how to communicate effectively with parents:

Working with Parents Requires an Empathic and Respectful Approach

In 21 out of the 28 simulations analyzed, students reported that the role-playing simulation allowed them to put themselves into the parent's shoes and understand their distress concerning the difficulties experienced by their children in school. The students reported that, as a result of the simulations and feedback, they learned to recognize and respond to the distress that seemed to underlie the parents' resistance to the teacher and had led to a conflictual conversation between them. According to the students, the role-playing simulations and the learning processes engendered by the reflective analyses of the simulations enabled them to identify with the parent's emotional difficulty and understand that, in such situations, an empathic and respectful approach is required for optimal communication.

The following are examples of the student teachers' insights derived from the learning process of the simulation based on role-playing:

"We also learned that the teacher must understand the emotional place the parent is coming from and resolve his distress. She should try to put herself into his shoes and understand him as much as possible, and do so in a pleasant way that will calm him down."

"Another thing we learned…is understanding the mother's side. When the mother hears about her child's difficulty, she's afraid it may [adversely] affect him. . .You have to look from her perspective and try to convey the message to her in the most relaxed way possible."

"We concluded, first and foremost, that we have to be in dialogue with the parents, understanding that dialogue about their child and his challenges and difficulties can shock and dismay the parents."

"We are the professionals and part of our job is to understand the parental aspect, to be inclusive, and see how to reconcile the various desires in order to promote the well-being of the child."

"The teacher must take in the feelings of the parents and understand where they are coming from. She needs to show empathy and sensitivity toward the parents and to encourage them to express their feelings. In this way, the parents can feel that the teacher is attentive to them and that it's important for her to hear them out."

"It's important for the teacher to try to put herself into the parents' shoes and understand their point of view."

"It's important to try to imagine how the parent is feeling, how we would feel [in his place], and to maintain communication that is inclusive, centered, and professional, and to remember that the goal is to promote the welfare of the child."

"The conclusions and insights we received from the audience were… [about] how important empathy is and most important to be inclusive of the other side."

"We must try to put ourselves in the parent's shoes and try to understand their position first and then act. We must assume that ultimately there is a common goal – the best interest of the child."

"We learned from the reflection…to constantly try to put ourselves into the parent's shoes and to understand how he thinks, even though it does not necessarily coincide with our path or perceptions."

"In our opinion, it's important that the teacher put herself into the parents' shoes and understand their point of view."

Working with Parents Requires an Approach That Inspires Trust and Confidence in the Teacher

In 23 of the 28 simulations analyzed, the students noted that the role-playing simulation underscored the importance of building trust and confidence with the parents, especially in discussions with them about their child's difficulties.

The following are examples of the student teachers' insights derived from the learning process of the simulation based on role-playing:

"As a result of the reflection and feedback from the audience, we learned that listening to parents is very important, and we must give them a sense of comfort and security."

"We understood the importance of warm communication with parents and creating trust between the education staff and the parents in order to promote and nurture the child."

"We saw that it's important to provide a safe, relaxed environment for someone who is under pressure and fearful."

"We understood that we had to start the conversation with a question for the mother, to understand how she coped with the situation, to ask her what difficulties she encounters and how they manifest themselves.

Through questions like this, we allow the mother to open up, to share, and to feel at ease. . . [We] provide a listening ear for her."

"We identified with the teacher who was very understanding and inclusive. Even when the mother was upset, she was calm."

"It's very important to create trust between the parent and teacher; for this to happen, the teacher should give several examples of what she is describing about how the child relates to herself or to others."

"We have learned that conversations with parents, especially about sensitive subjects, are a great challenge. We must remain calm and relaxed throughout the conversation, create a pleasant atmosphere for the parents, and carefully choose the words we use."

"We realized from the audience feedback that a pleasant atmosphere should be instilled among the participants from the very beginning of the conversation, even starting with brief small talk that encourages openness and instills a sense of security among parents."

"Participating in the simulation and getting the feedback demonstrated the great importance of listening and maintaining calm discourse and their influence on how the other side responds. Often, in the heat of the moment, we don't notice how we speak and what words we choose to use."

Presenting Examples and Documentation of the Child's Functioning Is Important in the Teacher-Parent Dialogue

In 22 of the 28 simulations analyzed, the students cited the importance of detailed planning by the teacher prior to meeting with the parents, including setting the goals of the meeting, preparing documentation of the child's performance, inviting other professionals to the meeting if required, and preparing them in advance for the conversation. Meticulous planning is designed to ensure effective and well-founded dialogue with the parents, and provides a comprehensive, professional response to the issue discussed.

The following are examples of the student teachers' insights derived from the learning process of the simulation based on role-playing:

"Another important thing we learned from the feedback of the audience is that when we explain the child's difficulties to the parents, we must provide extensive examples reflecting the difficulties and challenges, both from the teacher's observation of the child's classroom behavior and from the perspective of other professionals, substitute teachers, and assistants. We have to provide parents with multiple examples of the child's difficulties in a number of situations and places. Another important insight...is that it is necessary to plan the discourse in advance, to plan different ways of coping with the parents' possible responses, and several possible solutions to the problem on the assumption that the parents will agree to at least one of them."

"After the feedback from the audience, we learned the importance of giving a detailed explanation to the parents. It is essential to explain clearly the difficulty we observed in the child, where it is visible, what we have done about it, and of course to bring concrete examples of it. This gives parents a different perspective about what we are describing with visible proofs, and then parents can easily understand what we are talking about."

"We learned that it is important to focus on the subject under discussion with the parents and analyze it in the greatest detail and provide them with evidence... The evidence should be credible and persuasive."

"the teacher came with observation tools and detailed examples of the child's functioning, indicating how the teacher monitored the child's development."

"The simulation and feedback reinforced our feelings that it is essential to hold the discussion with the parents using written notes arranged in categories, so as not to forget anything in the conversation. Especially as we begin our teaching careers, meeting with parents is a very exciting and even stressful experience."

"We have learned that we will not always, and even rarely, get the immediate cooperation of parents when we discuss sensitive issues about their children or the class. Therefore, we should prepare for this in advance and plan different responses and ways of dealing with the parents' reactions and their opposition to what is said."

"The teacher must be consistent and professional. She must enter the conversation with full confidence in her words, present her claims, and back them up by observations and examples."

"Before the date of the conversation with the parents, the teacher must coordinate expectations with all the education staff who will be present at the meeting. They will thereby prepare themselves best for the discussion and know the purpose of it. When the teaching staff held the discussion after preliminary planning had been carried out, they knew exactly what to tell the parents and the division of roles between them. Each staff member knew his role and when he was to speak during the conversation. In addition, the teaching staff will be prepared for any scenario and resistance from the parents. The teacher must clarify to the parents the aim of the conversation... It is important that the entire education staff be in agreement about the information concerning the child, his background, and his educational and personal history from previous years."

Working with Parents Requires Understanding and Addressing the Perspectives That Arise in the Discussion

In 13 out of the 28 simulations analyzed, students noted that it was important for the teacher to understand the perspective of the parents and the other professionals in the discussion, and to address and reference these perspectives during the conversation. The students stressed the importance of a non-judgmental approach of the teacher toward the parents, which allows the parents to feel secure and understood, opens them to the perspective presented by the teacher, and establishes a partnership between them that will promote the child's interests.

The following are examples of the student teachers' insights derived from the learning process of the simulation based on role-playing:

"As a result of the feedback from the audience, we realized that it's impossible to judge anyone in this kind of situation. Everyone has his opinion, how he thinks about things, his character. .Many factors influence our views."

"We learned that some things are hidden, we are not aware of them, and therefore we must be attentive and not judgmental."

"We learned to understand the other side of the story, that of the parent. We understood that we have to think about what the parent is feeling and thinking about the child's situation. A parent entrusts us with what is most precious to him, and expects us to treat the child in the best and most pleasant way. . .It was very strange to be on this side, suddenly to be on the side of the parent and understand him. Suddenly your eyes open to different points of view – maybe the child's interpretation is different, maybe he understands things differently – and to suddenly understand what the parent really feels. . .It was challenging and hard for me, and because I am not yet a mother, it was even stranger to be on this side...inventing myself as a parent for the simulation, especially when I am not there yet."

Working with Parents Requires Assertiveness and Boundary-Setting

In 12 of the 28 simulations analyzed, students cited the importance of the teacher taking an assertive approach and setting limits on the parents if necessary. The students emphasized the teacher's responsibility to remain respectful with the parents and assertively set limits on them if their responses are inappropriate.

The following are examples of the student teachers' insights derived from the learning process of the simulation based on role-playing:

"We learned that the teacher must uphold her honor and position, and remain assertive toward both the parent and child. If a teacher knows she acted correctly, she must stand up for herself and for the correctness of her action."

"We have to set boundaries unequivocally for parents at the very beginning, that is, at the parent-teacher class conference."

"Following the reflection, we learned a lot about the importance of setting boundaries and rules for the parents, and what happens if we trespass the boundaries even once."

"On the one hand, to be sensitive to parents, but, on the other hand, to understand when to stop, when the contact or conversation crosses the line, and to always maintain professional distance to prevent becoming hurt or overly attached."

"The teacher must set very clear boundaries for the relationship between her and the parents and their involvement in her work. Each teacher has her own red lines. . . [The teacher] should set limits and state when there is something she does not accept. One way to set boundaries is the format of the meeting with the parent. . . [The teacher] can place a table between herself and the parents to mark clear boundaries."

"The teacher should set red lines that parents need to understand that they must not cross."

"We learned that when we talk with parents, we have to be assertive and set limits, but also be empathic and understand their pain and the motive for their action. It is important to clarify to the parent that the school system has procedures and we don't take the law into our own hands."

"It's not enough to be a good teacher, one must also function as a classroom manager and face parents, set limits, know how to deal with them."

"We believe that the boundaries set by the teacher at the beginning of the year are very important, as well as how the teacher speaks to both pupils and parents."

DISCUSSION

The current study was focused on simulation based on role-playing during the training of student teachers as a significant learning tool for enhancing effective communication skills with parents. During the course, diverse communication episodes with parents were simulated and analyzed in class. The learning process included meticulous planning of simulations, role-playing diverse communication modes with parents, self- and group-reflection on the simulated teacher functioning, and a repeated simulation in which the individual and group reflections were implemented. Content analysis revealed five main insights regarding the teacher's communication with the parents that were raised by the student teachers in the wake of the simulation:

The Importance of Approaching Parents with Empathy and Respect, Especially When Discussing Their Child's Difficulties

The first insight that emerged from this learning process was that in conflictual situations with parents concerning their children's difficulties in school, the teacher needs to maintain an empathic and respectful approach toward the parents. Empathy is defined by Kohut (1981) as the ability to know specifically and precisely the complex, subjective point of view of another, and to express it in a way that the other feels understood. Kohut discusses empathy in the context of a therapeutic relationship, and regards it as the main tool of the therapist, enabling change in the patient's healing process.

The student teachers' understanding that the teacher should show an empathic and respectful approach toward the parents in conflictual situations emerged from the students' enactment of various roles in the simulations, enabling them to step into the parent's shoes and understand the distress over their child's difficulty in class.

Parents often react with resistance, anger, or aggression in discussing their children's difficulties with the teacher. Theoretical approaches that perceive parenthood as a dynamic developmental process based, inter alia, on the unconscious wish of the parent for self-correction through childrearing, suggest that parental resistance and anger may be related to their distress as a result of identifying with the child's difficulties (Offerman-Zuckerberg, 1992). According to theorists holding this view, the "self" functions of the parent are affected, among other factors, by the disparity between the actual and the desired functioning of the child in various developmental domains. Manzano, Palacio Espasa, and Zilkha (1999) argue that the parent's distress relates to his or her own personal development characteristics – the more fragile the parent's "self," the greater distress or emotional pain caused by the disparities.

Based on these assumptions, one can surmise that a child's difficulty in school may be experienced by some parents as stressful. When parents find it hard to cope with or process their own distress, it can lead to resistance and conflict with the teachers who are called upon to discuss these difficulties and recruit the parents for efforts to resolve them.

During the course, which was based on multiple role-playing simulations, the student teachers learn that the parents' resistance might reflect their distress due to identifying with their child's difficulty, and that it is important for the teacher to step into the parents' shoes and understand their anguish. This skill is critical to winning the parents' cooperation for measures proposed by the teacher on behalf of the child. In such situations, noted the students, if a teacher's responses are not inclusive of the parents and do not relate to their emotional plight (e.g., if they challenge the parents' perception of their child's difficulties, deny the difficulties, defend the parents' claims, etc.), parental resistance may be exacerbated, leading to a parent-teacher conflict that thwarts the cooperation required.

Simulations based on role-playing in the course were an efficient tool for increasing the student teachers' listening skills and learning the importance of an empathic and respectful approach toward the parents in order to promote effective, professional dialogue with them. The use of simulations to train student teachers to work with parents is especially significant at this stage of teacher training, as it enables the students to practice an empathic approach in conflict situations, and improve their ability to establish effective communication with parents for the benefit of the child.

The Importance of Inspiring Trust and Confidence While Conversing with Parents

Hoy and Tschannen-Moran defined the sense of trust as "an individual's or group's willingness to be vulnerable to another party, based on the confidence that the latter party is benevolent, reliable, competent, honest and open" (Hoy & Tschannen-Moran, 1999). Lack of trust means the absence or the opposite of at least one of these elements. For example, even if one perceives another as competent and reliable, but does not believe the other has the good will to perform the tasks, one will be distrustful and unwilling to entrust these tasks to him. Distrust of the other is accompanied by stress and sometimes anxiety about being harmed by the other, and this situation tends to persist. To dissipate the distrust, one must perform activities designed to create and maintain trust (Hoy & Tschannen-Moran, 1999). According to Goddard, Tschannen-Moran, and Hoy (2001), trust among partners in the school system plays a key role in the success of educational processes. The sense of trust depends on the cooperation of all stakeholders in promoting education (Bryk & Schneider, 2003).

Past research has shown that a parent's sense of trust and confidence is one of the most important elements of teacher-parent communication (Adams & Christenson, 2000). Bryk and Schneider (2003) found that teachers who do not have the trust of parents are forced to spend a great deal of time dealing with parental monitoring of them, and a student who does not gain trust from teachers will often justify this lack of trust behaviorally. In a series of studies conducted by Adams and Christenson (2000), positive relationships were found between parents' trust of teachers and measures of school performance, such as parental collaboration and involvement. Tschannen-Moran (2001) also found a significant correlation between teacher-parent trust and the perception of greater cooperation. In another study published together with Hoy, the parents' higher level of trust in teachers was significantly correlated with a greater sense of efficacy of the teachers, enabling them to work better with the children and teach more effectively (Tschannen-Moran & Hoy, 2001).

These studies stress the importance of parental trust and confidence in the teachers, and the contribution of mutual trust to their collaboration and to greater teacher motivation and efficacy. Participating in simulations in the course demonstrated to the student teachers the importance of creating a bond of trust and confidence in their communication with the parents for the sake of the child.

The Importance of Meticulous Advance Planning and Preparation of Detailed Documentation about the Child's Functioning

Another finding of this study concerns the student teachers' understanding of the importance of preparing for the dialogue with the parents. The students noted that the simulations helped them recognize the need for the teacher to formulate the goal of the meeting and to prepare for it meticulously. Plans include the collection of data and documentation about the student's performance, preparing for the participation of other professionals, anticipating the parents' perspective in the conversation, envisioning possible solutions to the problems raised, and planning follow-up meetings with the parents if necessary.

Many of the role-playing simulations in the course were focused on parent-teacher communication regarding a child's difficulties at school. In these simulations, parents often expressed disagreement with or resistance to the teacher's perspective about the child's behavior. The student teachers learned from their experience in the simulations that if a teacher responds defensively, provides partial answers to the parents, has few if any supporting examples, or denies the view of the parents or of other professionals, she is perceived by the parents as unprofessional, making it difficult to recruit them for dialogue about how to help the child. On the other hand, if a teacher comes prepared with documentation and examples in support of her position and is coordinated with the other participating professionals, she is perceived by the parents as reliable, professional, and concerned about helping their child.

The insight of the student teachers regarding their professional responsibility to thoroughly prepare for the discussion with the parents relates to their understanding that such preparation will contribute to the parents' perception of them as professionals, and allow them to accept the perspective presented by the teacher. This finding is consistent with the literature on parent-teacher communication, which observes that parents are interested in hearing detailed descriptions from the teachers about their child's performance in order to understand the child's strengths and challenges, and to help the child accordingly. Freytag (2001), for example, found that parents want to participate in decision-making and problem-solving related to their child's functioning in the school. Parents expressed a desire to receive ongoing feedback from the teacher about their child's functioning, backed up by specific examples, and to feel that the teacher knows their child in depth – personally and individually. Similarly, Symeou, Roussounidou, and Michaelides (2012) found that student teachers who were trained to prepare in advance and in detail for a dialogue with parents were more aware of effective communication modes with parents and had greater professional confidence during the encounter.

Role-playing simulations that took place in the course of teacher training have clearly deepened the students' understanding of the importance of professionally preparing for meetings with the parents. Thorough preparation was perceived by the students as contributing to the parents' respectful attitude toward the teacher and increasing parental motivation to work together with the teacher on behalf of the child's well-being.

The Importance of Understanding and Relating to Perspectives Expressed by the Parents

Another finding concerns the importance of the teacher understanding the diverse perspectives of the parents and other participants in the discourse. The students noted that their experience during the simulations in the roles of teacher and parent gave them greater familiarity with these perspectives and more understanding of their thoughts, feelings, and the complexity that each brings to the discourse. These insights helped the students be more receptive to the parents' viewpoints and understand when they were negative or defiant toward the teacher. In turn, the teacher's willingness to understand and relate to the parents' perspective helped the parents be more open to the teacher and more motivated to work together on solutions to the issues raised.

The simulations enhanced the openness of the student teachers to the different perspectives of the participants. This was made possible by the cognitive and emotional processes of mentalization and active listening (Crozier, 2007; Lasky & Moore, 2000). In designing the simulations, the students were asked to mentalize and plan the approaches of the parents and professionals to the subject to be discussed, a process that required reference to the participants' diverse perspectives and an analysis of their feelings and attitudes. During the simulations, the students had to develop and engage in active listening to the overt and covert messages of the participants, their body language, perceptions, and feelings. The teacher's active listening to the parents enabled her to empathize with their needs and perceptions, and allowed the parents to feel that the teacher was sincerely interested in their viewpoint.

The contribution of simulation based on role-playing to sharpen the teacher's skill at listening to the perspectives of the other participants in the discourse is consistent with the findings of other studies in this field. Professional training that included role playing dialogue between professionals and customers was found to have contributed to the discourse between the professional and the client at both the information and motivational levels (Duhamel & Talbot, 2004; Mansfield, 1991; Paukert, Stagner, and Hope, 2004). Specifically, Symeou et al. (2012) found that students' active listening to parental perspectives as part of their teacher training contributed to the students' positive assessment of their ability to create optimal communication with parents. Thus, simulation based on role-playing as part of teacher training appears to significantly contribute to a teacher's ability to understand and relate to the parent's perspective and promotes better communication between them.

The Importance of an Assertive Approach and Boundary Setting in Conversations with Parents

Discussion of sensitive or conflictual issues is quite common in parent-teacher dialogue, and likely to create a tense, aggressive, threatening, or defensive dialogue that does not serve their common goal. Friedman (2010) notes five parental attitudes to the school that can result from a combination of different levels of parental identification with the educational goals and awareness of what takes place at school: alienation, avoidance, moderate involvement, over-involvement, and involvement lacking identification. According to Friedman, parents who do not identify with or who oppose the school's values and educational approach, who are indifferent to or alienated from it, or who impose their own perspectives on the teachers may engage in destructive dialogue with the teacher and impair their ability to work together.

Katzenelson (2014) cites various factors that may create a negative attitude of parents toward teachers: a parent's negative memories of the education system they experienced, projection of their experiences on their child's performance at school, over-identification with the child's difficulties, questioning the teacher's ability to respond appropriately to the child's needs, discrepancies between the perceptions of the parents and the school regarding requirements and procedures, the parents' fear of criticism of their child because they perceive it as criticism of their parental ability, parental guilt over their child's difficulties and projecting that guilt and responsibility onto the teacher, treating the teacher as a service provider who can be criticized by parents based on their satisfaction with her, parental perception of the teacher as competing in education decisions about their child, a permissive or authoritarian approach by the parent that is incompatible with the school's approach, or linguistic and cultural gaps between parents and teachers that hinder productive dialogue. The teacher's perception of the parents as passive non-contributors, as mere service-providers to the teacher for classroom activities, or as an aggressive, hostile, and threatening agent (Gur and Zalmanson-Levy, 2005) can undermine the teacher's communication with parents, as they may create a partial, tense, or hostile dialogue.

Teachers who encounter an aggressive, disdainful, or defiant attitude on the part of the parents, especially at the beginning of their teaching careers, may feel helpless and vulnerable, and may respond defensively or aggressively in dialogue with the parents. Similarly, the lack of information or failure to coordinate expectations with parents about effective modes of communication with them may cause parents to behave disrespectfully in the discourse. Therefore, it is important that students in teacher training learn to recognize their professional abilities and authority, and develop skills of fruitful dialogue with parents conducted within appropriate and respectful boundaries.

Indeed, the openness of teachers to communication with the parents, combined with boundary setting and dialogue that respects the teacher's authority and professionalism, can enable healthy parental involvement that promotes the child's well-being (Friedman 2010).

In this study, the simulations based on role playing were focused on conflictual discourse between the teacher and parents. In some cases, the role play had parents acting aggressively, challenging the teacher's authority or discretion, or showing disdain for the teacher's views. The student teachers reported that the simulations helped them understand that to be effective in communicating with the parents, they must combine an attentive and respectful attitude with an assertive approach that sets boundaries. They noted that the simulations prepared them well, allowing them to convey their message in a clear, professional manner. They reported that anticipating and preparing for potential pitfalls in the simulated conversation and the planning of responses to parental distress and opposition while remaining respectful and assertive gave them greater confidence in their professional stance vis-à-vis the parents. Thus, it is clear that simulation based on role-playing in teacher training enhances teacher-parent communication as well as the teacher's confidence in her ability to conduct a professional, empathic dialogue that promotes the well-being of the child.

CONCLUSION

Simulation based on role-playing is the main learning tool in the course "Work with Parents in the 21st Century" conducted in the framework of teacher training. The student teachers' thorough and repeated practice of these simulations deepened their intra-personal and interpersonal reflective dialogue in their work with parents. The meticulous preparation of the students for the parent-teacher dialogue simulations, their training in a range of conflictual contexts within a safe environment, the multi-perspective feedback they received from colleagues and the lecturer, and the reflective process they experienced all enhanced their skill set for teacher-parent communication. The role-playing and subsequent reflective analysis deepened their awareness of the motives, attitudes, thoughts, feelings, and skills regarding communication with parents, and helped them become more open, empathic, and respectful in discourse, and more confident in their professional authority and ability to set boundaries during dialogue.

The student teachers' insights about the importance of an empathic, respectful, trust-fostering approach to the parents, combined with an assertiveness in setting appropriate boundaries during communication with them, benefited from a combination of theoretical models studied and meticulous planning, preparation, and repeated training in complex simulations of dialogue, enhanced by their personal and inter-personal reflections. The simulations thereby sharpened the students' insights about the skills required of them for effective communication with parents that promote the best interests of the child.

Thus, simulation based on role-playing as part of teacher training, which includes a thorough implementation of all phases of Brockbank and McGill's (1998) reflective learning model, was found to be an effective and instructive tool for training student teachers to engage in effective communication with parents.

It is advisable for teacher training institutions to undertake a thorough and integrative approach to the teaching of optimal communication skills of teachers with parents. This should include both *theory* – learning the mutual perceptions and expectations of parents, teachers, and the education system; how to deepen parental involvement in the school and its implications for student performance; and the study of theoretical models for creating optimal dialogue with parents – and *practical experience* in the form of discussions and simulations based on role-playing, which train the students in a wide variety of dialogue styles and content with parents. This intensive learning can significantly improve the openness, willingness, and confidence of the student teachers in their ability to engage in fruitful communication with the parents that promotes the child's welfare and helps develop teachers' dialogue skills such as empathy, openness, trust creation, effective planning of discourse, and maintaining its boundaries. Effective communication between the teacher and the parents can contribute to increased involvement of the parents in the classroom and school, and enhanced educational and social adjustment of the child within the education framework.

REFERENCES

Abdullah, N. L., Hanafiah, M. H., & Hashim, N. A. (2013). Developing creative teaching module: Business simulation in teaching strategic management. *International Education Studies*, *6*(6), 95.

Adams, K. S., & Christenson, S. L. (2000). Trust and the family-school relationship examination of parent-teacher differences in elementary and secondary grades. *Journal of School Psychology*, *38*(5), 477-497.

Agboola Sogunro, O. (2004). Efficacy of role-playing pedagogy in training leaders: Some reflections. *Journal of Management Development*, *23*(4), 355-371.

Alkin, M. C., & Christie, C. A. (2002). The use of role-play in teaching evaluation. *American Journal of Evaluation*, *23*(2), 209-218.

Auerbach, S. (2012). Conceptualizing leadership for authentic partnerships: A continuum to inspire practice. In S. Auerbach (Ed.), *School leadership for authentic family and community partnerships* (pp. 29-51). New York, NY: Routledge.

Barak-Shtein, H. (2011). *Plan Communication and Continuity (PCC) strategy for parent-teacher communication*. Retrieved from https://www.hebpsy.net/me_article.asp?id=93&article=2589 [Hebrew].

Beidatsch, C., & Broomhall, S. (2010). Is this the past? The place of role-play exercises in undergraduate history teaching. *Journal of University Teaching and Learning Practice*, *7*(1), 6.

Bender, T. (2005). Role playing in online education: A teaching tool to enhance student engagement and sustained learning. *Innovate: Journal of Online Education*, *1*(4).

Bosse, H. M., Nickel, M., Huwendiek, S., Jünger, J., Schultz, J. H., & Nikendei, C. (2010). Peer role-play and standardized patients in communication training: A comparative study on the student perspective on acceptability, realism, and perceived effect. *BMC Medical Education*, *10*(1), 27.

Brockbank, A., & McGill, I. (1998). *Facilitating reflective learning in higher education*. Society for Research into Higher Education, McGraw-Hill Education (UK).

Bryk, A. & Schneider, B. (2003). Trust in schools: A core resource for school reform. *Educational Leadership*, *60*(6), 40-44.

Chan, Z. C. (2012). Role-playing in the problem-based learning class. *Nurse Education in Practice*, *12*(1), 21-27.

Christenson, S. L. (2004). The family-school partnership: An opportunity to promote the learning competence of all students. *School Psychology Review*, *33*(1).

Cobo, A., Conde, O. M., & Quintela, M. (2011). On-line role-play as a teaching method in engineering studies. *Journal of Technology and Science Education*, *1*(1), 49-58.

Colombo, M. W. (2004). Family literacy nights. *Educational Leadership*, *61*(8), 48-51.

Crozier, G., & Davies, J. (2007). Hard to reach parents or hard to reach schools? A discussion of home-school relations, with particular reference to Bangladeshi and Pakistani parents. *British Educational Research Journal*, *33*(3), 295-313.

Daly, A., Grove, S. J., Dorsch, M. J., & Fisk, R. P. (2009). The impact of improvisation training on service employees in a European airline: A case study. *European Journal of Marketing*, *43*(3/4), 459-472.

Dana, N. F., & Westcott, L. (1995). *Creating Opportunities for Prospective Elementary and Early Childhood Teacher Reflection, Simulations, Teaching Cases, Portfolios, and More.* Paper presented at the annual meeting of the Association of Teacher Educators, St. Louis, MO.

Davies, A. (2013). *The impact of simulation-based learning exercises on the development of decision-making skills and professional identity in operational policing* (Doctoral dissertation). Charles Sturt University, Australia.

de Bruïne, E. J., Willemse, T. M., D'Haem, J., Griswold, P., Vloeberghs, L., & Van Eynde, S. (2014). Preparing teacher candidates for family-school partnerships. *European Journal of Teacher Education, 37*(4), 409-425.

DeNeve, K. M., & Heppner, M. J. (1997). Role play simulations: The assessment of an active learning technique and comparisons with traditional lectures. *Innovative Higher Education, 21*(3), 231-246.

Dotger, B. H. (2010). "I had no idea": Developing dispositional awareness and sensitivity through a cross-professional pedagogy. *Teaching and Teacher Education, 26*(4), 805-812.

Dotger, B. H., Harris, S., Maher, M., & Hansel, A. (2011). Exploring the emotional geographies of parent-teacher candidate interactions: An emerging signature pedagogy. *The Teacher Educator, 46*(3), 208-230.

Duhamel, F., & Talbot, L. R. (2004). A constructivist evaluation of family systems nursing interventions with families experiencing cardiovascular and cerebrovascular illness. *Journal of Family Nursing, 10*(1), 12-32.

Duveen, J., & Solomon, J. (1994). The great evolution trial: Use of role-play in the classroom. *Journal of Research in Science Teaching, 31*(5), 575-582.

Epstein, J. L. (2018). *School, family, and community partnerships: Preparing educators and improving schools.* New York, NY: Routledge.

Epstein, J. L., & Sanders, M. G. (2006). Prospects for change: Preparing teachers for school, family, and community partnerships. *Peabody Journal of Education, 81*(2), 81-120.

Evans, R. (2004). Talking with parents today. *Independent School, 63*, 96-100.

Finlay, I. G., Stott, N. C. H., & Kinnersky, P. (1995). The assessment of communication skills in palliative medicine: A comparison of the scores of examiners and simulated patients. *Medical Education, 29*(6), 424-429.

Flaitz, J. (1986). *A review of simulation in teacher education training.* Paper presented at the annual meeting of the Mid-South Educational Research Association, Memphis, TN.

Freytag, C. E. (2001). *Teacher-parent communication: Starting the year off right.* Paper presented at the *43rd Biennial Convocation of the Kappa Delta Pi International Honor Society in Education*, Orlando, FL.

Friedman, I. (2010). *School-parent-community relations in Israel.* Jerusalem: The Initiative for Applied Educational Research, Israel Academy of Sciences and Humanities [Hebrew].

Goddard, R. D., Tschannen-Moran, M., & Hoy, W. K. (2001). Teacher trust in students and parents: A multilevel examination of the distribution and effects of teacher trust in urban elementary schools. *Elementary School Journal, 102*(1), 3-17.

Gough, J. K., Frydenberg, A. R., Donath, S. K., & Marks, M. M. (2009). Simulated parents: Developing paediatric trainees' skills in giving bad news. *Journal of Paediatrics and Child Health, 45*(3), 133-138.

Graham-Gray, S. (2002). Communicating with parents. *The School Community Journal, 15*(1), 117-130.

Grossman, P., Hammerness, K., & McDonald, M. (2009). Redefining teaching, re-imagining teacher education. *Teachers and Teaching: Theory and Practice, 15*(2), 273-289.

Gur, H., & Zalmanson-Levy, G. (2005). *School-parents' relationships from the critical education perspective: Education and its relations.* Tel Aviv: Kibbutzim College [Hebrew].

Harré, R., & Secord, P. F. (1972). *The explanation of social behavior.* Oxford: Basil Blackwell.

Hays, R. T., & Singer, M. J. (2012). *Simulation fidelity in training system design: Bridging the gap between reality and training.* New York: Springer Science & Business Media.

Henderson, A. T. (Ed.). (2007). *Beyond the bake sale: The essential guide to family-school partnerships.* New York: The New Press.

Hoover-Dempsey, K. V., Walker, J. M., Jones, K. P., & Reed, R. P. (2002). Teachers involving parents (TIP): Results of an in-service teacher education program for enhancing parental involvement. *Teaching and Teacher Education, 18*(7), 843-867.

Hoy, W. K., & Tschannen-Moran, M. (1999). Five faces of trust: An empirical confirmation in urban elementary schools. *Journal of School Leadership,* 9, 184-208.

Jeffries, P. R. (2005). A framework for designing, implementing, and evaluating: Simulations used as teaching strategies in nursing. *Nursing Education Perspectives, 26*(2), 96-103.

Katzenelson, E. (2014). The relation between parents and their child's education system. *Journal of Psychoactualia,* Israel Psychological Association, October, 40-45 [Hebrew].

Kilgour, P. W., Reynaud, D., Northcote, M. T., & Shields, M. (2015). Role-playing as a tool to facilitate learning, self-reflection and social awareness in teacher education. *International Journal of Innovative Interdisciplinary Research, 2*(4), 8-20.

Kohut, H. (1981). "On Empathy." In P. Ornstein (Ed.), *The Search of the Self: Selected Writings of Heinz Kohut* (Vol. 4). New York, NY: International Universities Press.

Korthagen, F. A. (1992). Techniques for stimulating reflection in teacher education seminars. *Teaching and Teacher Education, 8*(3), 265-274.

Lake, J. F., & Billingsley, B. S. (2000). An analysis of factors that contribute to parent-school conflict in special education. *Remedial and Special Education, 21*(4), 240-251.

Lasater, K. (2016). Parent-teacher conflict related to student abilities: The impact on students and the family-school partnership. *School Community Journal, 26*(2), 237-262.

Lasky, S., & Moore, S. (2000). *Closing emotional distance: An analysis of parent-teacher interactions in secondary schools.* Paper presented at the annual meeting of the American Educational Research Association, New Orleans, LA.

Lean, J., Moizer, J., Towler, M., & Abbey, C. (2006). Simulations and games: Use and barriers in higher education. *Active Learning in Higher Education, 7*(3), 227–242.

Maddrell, A. (2007). Teaching a contextual and feminist history of geography through role play: Women's membership of the Royal Geographical Society (1892–1893). *Journal of Geography in Higher Education, 31*(3), 393-412.

Magos, K., & Politi, F. (2008). The creative second language lesson: The contribution of the role-play technique to the teaching of a second language in immigrant classes. *RELC Journal, 39*(1), 96-112.

Mansfield, F. (1991). Supervised role-play in the teaching of the process of consultation. *Medical Education, 25*(6), 485-490.

Manzano, J., Palacio Espasa, F., Zilkha, N. (1999). The narcissistic scenarios of parenthood. *International Journal of Psychoanalysis, 80*(3), 465-476.

Mitri, M., Cole, C., & Atkins, L. (2017). Teaching case: A systems analysis role-play exercise and assignment. *Journal of Information Systems Education, 28*(1), 1.

Morris, R., & Thomas, J. (1976). Simulation in training: Part 5. *Industrial Training International, 11*(3), 66-69.

Nestel, D., & Tierney, T. (2007). Role-play for medical students learning about communication: Guidelines for maximizing benefits. *BMC Medical Education, 7*(1), 3.

Offerman-Zuckerberg, J. (1992). The parenting process: A psychoanalytic perspective. *Journal of the American Academy of Psychoanalysis, 20*(2), 205-214.

Osterman, K. F. (1990). Reflective practice: A new agenda for education. *Education and Urban Society*, *22*(2), 133-152.

Ozmen, F., Akuzum, C., Zincirli, M., & Selcuk, G. (2016). The communication barriers between teachers and parents in primary schools. *Eurasian Journal of Educational Research*, *66*, 27-46.

Paukert, A., Stagner, B., & Hope, K. (2004). The assessment of active listening skills in helpline volunteers. *Stress, Trauma, and Crisis*, *7*(1), 61-76.

Rao, D., & Stupans, I. (2012). Exploring the potential of role play in higher education: Development of a typology and teacher guidelines. *Innovations in Education and Teaching International*, *49*(4), 427-436.

Remer, R. (1990). *Psychodramatic family simulation for teaching and research.* Paper presented at the annual meeting of the American Association for Counseling and Development, Cincinnati, OH.

Sabar-Ben Yehoshua, N. (Ed.) (2016). *Traditions and genres in qualitative research: Philosophies, strategies, and advanced tools.* Tel Aviv: Achva Academic College, Tel-Aviv University [Hebrew].

Sandford, C. T., & Bradbury, M. S. (1971). *Case studies in economics: Projects and role playing in the teaching of economics.* London: Macmillan.

Schön, D. A. (1987). *Educating the reflective practitioner.* San Francisco: Jossey-Bass.

Semke, C. A., & Sheridan, S. M. (2012). Family-school connections in rural educational settings: A systematic review of the empirical literature. *School Community Journal*, *22*(1), 21-47.

Sharma, M. (2015). Simulation models for teacher training: Perspectives and prospects. *Journal of Education and Practice*, *6*(4), 11-14.

Shen, Y., Nicholson, J., & Nicholson, D. (2015). Using a group role-play exercise to engage students in learning business processes and ERP. *Journal of Information Systems Education*, *26*(4).

Smyth, J. (1989). Developing and sustaining critical reflection in teacher education. *Journal of Teacher Education*, *40*(2), 2-9.

Symeou, L., Roussounidou, E., & Michaelides, M. (2012). "I feel much more confident now to talk with parents": An evaluation of in-service training on teacher-parent communication. *School Community Journal,* *22*(1), 65-87.

Tabachnick, B. R., & Zeichner, K. M. (Eds.). (1991). *Issues and practices in inquiry-oriented teacher education* (Vol. 3). London: Falmer Press.

Tal, C. (2005). *Emotional intelligence. Theory and implementation.* Tel Aviv and Haifa: Mofet and Ach [Hebrew].

Terek, E., Glušac, D., Nikolic, M., Tasic, I., & Gligorovic, B. (2015). The impact of leadership on the communication satisfaction of primary school teachers in Serbia. *Educational Sciences: Theory and Practice,* *15*(1), 73-84.

Tschannen-Moran, M. (2001). Collaboration and the need for trust. *Journal of Educational Administration,* *39*(4), 308-331.

Tschannen-Moran, M., & Hoy, W. A. (2001). Teacher efficacy: Capturing an elusive construct. *Teaching and Teacher Education,* *17*(7), 783-805.

Van Ments, M. (1999). *The effective use of role play* (2nd ed.). London: Kogan Page.

Walker, J. M., & Legg, A. M. (2018). Parent-teacher conference communication: A guide to integrating family engagement through simulated conversations about student academic progress. *Journal of Education for Teaching,* *44*(3), 366-380.

Wanat, C. L. (2010). Challenges balancing collaboration and independence in home-school relationships: Analysis of parents' perceptions in one district. *School Community Journal* 20(1), 159-186. Retrieved from http://www.schoolcommunitynetwork.org/SCJ.aspx.

Wandersman, A., Motes, P. S., Lindsay, R., Snell-Johns, J., Amaral, D., & Ford, L. (2002). South Carolina parent survey: A review of the literature and survey development. *Institute for Families in Society.* Columbia SC: University of South Carolina.

Ward, P., Williams, A. M., and Hancock, P. A. (2006). Simulation for performance and training. In K. A. Ericsson, N. Charness, P. J. Feltovich, and R. R. Hoffman (Eds.), *Cambridge Handbook of Expertise and Expert Performance* (pp. 243-262). Cambridge UK: Cambridge University Press.

Wayne, D. B., Butter, J., Siddall, V. J., Fudala, M. J., Linquist, L. A., Feinglass, J., Wade, L. D., & McGaghie, W. C. (2005). Simulation-based training of internal medicine residents in advanced cardiac life support protocols: A randomized trial. *Teaching and Learning in Medicine, 17*(3), 202-208.

Westrup, U., & Planander, A. (2013). Role-play as a pedagogical method to prepare students for practice: The students' voice. *Högre utbildning, 3*(3), 199-210.

Zamboanga, B. L., Ham, L. S., Tomaso, C. C., Audley, S., & Pole, N. (2016). "Try walking in our shoes": Teaching acculturation and related cultural adjustment processes through role-play. *Teaching of Psychology, 43*(3), 243-249.

Zieger, L. B., & Tan, J. (2012). Improving parent involvement in secondary schools through communication technology. *Journal of Literacy and Technology, 13* (2), 30-54.

In: Teacher Training
Editor: Paula E. McDermott

ISBN: 978-1-53615-633-1
© 2019 Nova Science Publishers, Inc.

Chapter 5

THE DIFFICULTIES AND CHALLENGES FACING INTERNS OF EARLY CHILDHOOD EDUCATION REGARDING THEIR WORKING RELATIONS WITH PARENTS: TOWARDS A NEW MODEL OF FAMILY-SCHOOL RELATIONS IN A CULTURALLY DIVERSE AND CHANGING SOCIETY

Alona Peleg[*], Naomi Perchik, Orly Licht Weinish, Iris Levy, Einat Sequerra Ater, Yael Shlesinger, Pninat Tal and Clodie Tal
Levinsky College of Education, Tel Aviv, Israel

---

[*] Corresponding Author's E-mail: peleg.alona@gmail.com.

ABSTRACT

Communication with parents is a central aspect of the teaching profession. Significant changes in the social reality have reshaped home-school relations, requiring of the educational staff a deep understanding of the complexity of relations with parents in a diverse and changing reality, as well as effective skills and strategies for communicating with parents. However, most teacher education institutions fail to help their students develop the knowledge and tools necessary for working with parents in the 21st century. The present study examines how interns of early childhood education interpreted communication with parents, and what difficulties and challenges faced them. The study participants comprised 143 student teachers in the course "Working with Parents in the 21st Century," in the Early Childhood Education program at Levinsky College of Education. All of the student teachers, in their fourth and final year of studies, worked as practicing teachers at kindergartens and elementary schools, as part of their internship. They were asked to write accounts of social episodes describing a significant and authentic event with regard to relations with parents. The accounts of the social episodes were analyzed and coded according to qualitative, content analysis, combined with several quantitative analyses. Data analysis yielded six central themes regarding family-school relations, as reflected in the interns' social episodes. Most of the themes described difficulties, conflicts and challenges in working with parents, centering around two complementary core dimensions: (1) building trust and cultivating close and caring relations with parents; (2) setting boundaries and limits for parental behavior. In addition, two super-categories were revealed to be significant axes, expressed in all of the central themes: (1) cultural diversity and power relations between parents and teachers; (2) the parent's gender: the involvement of fathers and the communication patterns of the educational staff with fathers, in comparison to mothers. These findings show that in a reality of cultural diversity and rapid changes, the meaning and expressions of *cultivating close and caring relations with parents* have changed, requiring of the teachers new skills and strategies, such as cultural sensitivity, skills for working with minority group parents and strengthening the educational partnership with fathers. Indeed, these findings indicate an urgent need for a new model for working with parents in a culturally diverse and changing society. This model is based on a shift from "*the child at the center*" approach, to that of "*the child and his family at the center.*" Hence, school-family relations should be reformulated so that the educational system is committed to the child *and* to the parents, while redefining minority families as *families coping with special needs.* Teacher education institutions may use these insights and recommendations, as expressed in

The Difficulties and Challenges Facing Interns ... 185

the principles of the suggested new model, to provide their student teachers with vital and relevant knowledge, skills and strategies for leading a change in school-family relations, and developing a significant partnership with parents in the 21st century.

Keywords: early childhood education, family - school relations, cultural sensitivity, cultural competence, teacher education

INTRODUCTION

Parents and teachers play an important role in children's developmental and educational processes. Parental support and involvement in their children's education contribute both to the children's social adjustment and to their academic achievements (Neal, 2012; Walker & Dotger, 2012). The quality of the teacher-parent relations also affects the children's academic motivation, and their emotional, social and behavioral adjustment (Fan & Chen, 2001; Henderson & Mapp, 2002; Hughes & Kwok, 2007). In fact, even from early childhood, the influence of effective communication between teachers and parents contributes to the children's development, influencing their later academic achievements in school (McWayne, Hampton, Fantuzzo, Cohen & Sekino, 2004). Moreover, it has been established that efficient teacher-parent communication promotes a positive school climate (Epstein, 2011).

Although parents and teachers alike are committed to the children's progress and are both interested in contributing to their wellbeing, the relationship between them tends to be complex and multidimensional (Lang, Tolbert, Schoppe- Sullivan & Bonomi, 2016; Lang, Mouzourou, Jeon & Buettner, 2017). Contradictory expectations and gaps between the parties might create tension and conflict, which in turn impinge upon the emotional and social development of the children and their academic achievements (Greenbaum & Fried, 2011; Lake & Billingsley, 2000).

Far-reaching social changes that have occurred over the last few decades in Western countries, including Israel, have reshaped the relationship between parents and teachers, making them particularly challenging. These changes include the use of advanced communication technology; immigration from many different countries and cultures; new structuring of family units; changes in the realm of employment; and innovative educational reforms that support the integration of special-needs children within the mainstream educational system. Thus, it is not surprising that many teachers report their feelings of stress and anxiety while communicating with parents, and feel that they lack the appropriate knowledge and skills to deal with the difficulties they experience in resolving conflicts (Addi-Raccah & Arviv- Elyashiv, 2008; Friedman, 2010; Greenbaum & Fried, 2011; Shimoni & Baxter, 1996).

Due to these changes, it is vital that teachers achieve a deep understanding of the complexity of family-school communication, and that they assimilate new knowledge and strategies. However, most teacher education programs are not geared toward helping student teachers develop the knowledge, skills and strategies that are relevant for working with parents in the 21st century. In their curricula, many teacher education institutions do not include courses that can develop working skills with parents. When courses of this nature do exist, they tend to make use of traditional methods of teaching, and do not necessarily provide updated knowledge and relevant strategies for working with parents in a changing and diversified society (Epstein, 2018; Epstein & Sanders, 2006; Lasater, 2016; Meehan & Meehan, 2018, Walker & Dotger, 2012). In a survey of 60 teacher education programs across 22 countries, it was found that only 23% required that the students communicate with families during fieldwork or student teaching. Furthermore, when family-school relations were addressed, those programs employed teaching methods based on reading and lectures (rather than on simulations and case studies), and did not necessarily help to promote meaningful learning (Shartrand, Weiss, Kreider and Lopez, 1997). In a different study which examined student teachers' readiness to communicate with families, findings revealed that the student teachers had high self-efficacy for communicating with parents, but generated a small number of strategies for dealing with various situations and resolving conflicts (Walker & Dotger, 2012).

The Levinsky Education College, a longstanding Israeli college for teacher education, has conducted a compulsory course for many years, dealing with working relations with parents in the 21st century. During the 2017-2018 school year, the team of lecturers instructing the course's groups built a joint syllabus for the training of 4th year student teachers on working with parents. This syllabus included episode analysis and simulations of situations presented in these episodes. All of the student teachers, in their fourth and final year, worked as practicing teachers at kindergartens and elementary schools, as part of their internship. During the course, the interns were asked to write about a social episode related to working with parents. The social episodes were analyzed and coded by categorical content analysis (Ayalon & Sabar Ben-Yehoshua, 2010, Corbin & Strauss, 2008) in the framework of a qualitative study (Shkedi, 2003). Several quantitative analyses were added, in order to expand and deepen our understanding of the findings of the qualitative analysis.

The aim of the current study was to examine how early childhood education interns interpreted communication with parents, and what difficulties and challenges preoccupied them. The identification of the central difficulties and challenges with which teachers are concerned, in all aspects of their working relations with parents, may contribute significantly to the knowledge of family-school relations in a diverse and changing society, both at the theoretical and the practical level. Teacher education institutions will be able to use this new knowledge in order to provide student teachers with skills and strategies that are relevant for work with parents in the 21st century. The knowledge and strategies acquired will help raise student teachers' self-efficacy, reducing their anxiety and stress, and allowing them to construct significant and effective relations with parents.

Family-School Relations

According to Bronfenbrenner's ecological-developmental theory (1986), the child's environment has a crucial influence on his development.

The environment consists of inter-related systems which affect one another. The child's central environments are the family and the educational framework. As the systems surrounding the child interact with greater coordination, the chances of positive development increase. Situations of non-coordination or conflict between the various systems, even if each system operates well on its own, might lead to negative consequences in terms of the child's development (Greenbaum &Fried, 2011).

In the theoretical and research literature, it is customary to use the concept *'parental involvement'* to refer to the general actions that parents implement to advance their children (at home, at school and in other frameworks), as well as actions implemented by teachers to establish contact with parents and integrate them into the educational framework (Fan & Chen, 2001). Based on extensive research, Epstein (1992, 2002) suggested a framework of six types of parental involvement in school-related activities:

1) *parenting*, focuses on an appropriate home environment in order for children to become successful students;
2) *communicating*, stresses effective school-home communications regarding school programs and children's progress;
3) *volunteering*, recruits and organizes parent volunteers at school;
4) *learning at home*, educates families to help children with homework and other curriculum-related activities;
5) *decision making*, encourages parents to participate in school decisions as parent leaders and representatives;
6) *collaborating with the community*, calls for integrating community resources and services to create stronger school programs, family practices, and student learning and development.

Similarly, Mapp (2003) offers four central categories of parental involvement:

1) *parental presence* - strategies and approaches that help parents feel welcome in the educational framework;
2) *parental participation* - teachers and veteran parents offer new families specific activities that may lead to greater involvement;
3) *parents as partners* - schools encourage direct involvement of parents in teaching and learning processes at school;
4) *empowered parents* - parents operating in leadership roles, initiating and activating projects at school.

To conclude, various models mentioned in the literature describe different types and levels of parental involvement. An increase at the level of parental involvement is usually expressed in an increase at the level of partnership and mutuality, i.e., activities initiated both by teachers and parents in order to influence the goals and structure of the schools (Shechtman & Busherian, 2015).

The Nature of Parent-Teacher Relationship

How may we characterize the relationship between families and schools? According to Lang and her colleagues (Lang, Tolbert, Schoppe - Sullivan & Bonomi, 2016), this relationship may be described along three main features: (1) *communication* - the ways parents and teachers exchange information; intentional offering of information; communication strategies and communication topics; (2) *support versus undermining* - the ways in which parents and teachers endorse and encourage each other's actions versus the ways in which they criticize, contradict or subvert each other's practices, in their role as caregivers; 3) *childrearing agreement versus disagreement* - the extent to which partners concur with regard to their morals, values and beliefs about how to raise children. Thus, family-school communication gains significance and effectivity the more the two parties - parents and teachers - intentionally share relevant information with each other, express trust and support, and agree upon educational goals and practices. Moreover, relations of trust and support between parents and teachers tend to increase parents' self-efficacy, and this in turn strengthens parental involvement in the educational system (Green, Walker, Hoover- Dempsey & Sandler, 2007).

The responsibility for effective home-school communication rests upon the professional person - in this case, the school teacher or kindergarten teacher. The teacher needs to establish frequent communication with the parents, and encourage them to be involved both in educational activities and in the children's learning processes (Shechtman & Busherian, 2015). The motivation of parents to be involved in the educational framework is highly influenced by opportunities for involvement created by the educational system, as well as the social norms of the educational system regarding parental involvement. In fact, it was found that suitable efforts made by the educational system to involve parents may succeed even with parents of diverse cultures, and parents who were not initially motivated to be involved (Mapp & Hong, 2010).

Tension and Conflict between Parents and Teachers

Although schools understand the importance of effective communication with parents and the need for them to be involved in the educational system, they do not rush to establish a relationship with parents, nor do the parents seek it (Green, Walker, Hoover- Dempsey & Sandler, 2007). Moreover, there is mutual suspicion and even hostility between teachers and parents (Addi-Raccah & Arviv- Elyashiv, 2008; Greenbaum & Fried, 2011; Friedman, 2010). Kindergarten teachers as well, report that they feel anxiety in their relation with parents and difficulty in resolving conflicts (Shimoni & Baxter, 1996).

How may one explain the mutual tension, suspicion and hostility between teachers and parents? One of the main sources of conflicts between teachers and parents is contradictory expectations. For example, the school may expect appreciation of the teacher's efforts while the parents want the school to answer their child's specific needs (Auerbach, 2012; Wanat, 2010). Lake and Billingsley (2000) identified eight

The Difficulties and Challenges Facing Interns ...   191

categories of factors that escalate parent-school conflict: discrepant views of a child or a child's needs, knowledge, service delivery, reciprocal power, constraints, valuation, communication, and trust.

Finally, Christenson (2004) points to three types of possible barriers for family-school relationship:

1) *Family-related barriers:* economic, emotional and time constraints; low sense of self efficacy; linguistic and cultural differences; adopting a passive role by leaving education to schools; suspicion about treatment from teachers; perceived lack of responsiveness to parental needs.

2) *Teacher-related barriers:* lack of training for teachers on how to create and sustain partnerships with families; ambiguous commitment to working with parents as partners; use of stereotypes about families; doubts about the abilities of families to address schooling concerns; wary of interacting with families or fear of conflict.

3) *Barriers regarding parent-teacher relations:* communication primarily during crises; lack of a routine communication system; limited use of perspective taking or empathizing with the other person; failure to view differences as strengths.

Family-School Relations in a Culturally Diverse and Changing Society

Over the last decades, the Western countries, including Israel, have seen significant social changes. These changes are manifested in various ways: (1) flooding of knowledge, changes in the hierarchical structure of information sources and in access to information, and accelerated technological development; (2) immigration from a variety of countries, and cultural diversity; (3) the development of new family structures; (4) changes in the realm of employment, and a new role division between parents and teachers; (5) innovative educational reforms that promote the integration of special needs children into mainstream education. These changes affect the teacher parent relations, as will be elaborated in detail below.

Flooding of Knowledge, Changes in the Hierarchical Structure of Information Sources and in Access to Information, and Accelerated Technological Development

Nowadays, parents are more highly educated and opinionated in comparison to the past (Noy, 1999). Due to the flooding of knowledge and changes in the hierarchical structure of information sources and in access to information, the teacher's status is blurred as an exclusive source of information and as an expert in matters of education and learning. This might cause parents to more easily undermine the teacher's professional authority. It might also cause the teacher to feel anxiety when encountering the parents, and provide grounds for power play and conflict. Thus, teachers perceive parental involvement as positive only when the parents are considered to be partners rather than threatening entities (Addi - Raccah, & Ainhoren, 2009).

Moreover, the use of innovative means of technology by teachers and parents, such as computers and mobile phones, dictates a 'norm of accessibility', obliging the teachers to be available to the parents at any time and place. This creates a burden of communication and blurring of boundaries between work and private life. The 'norm of accessibility' might impinge upon the efficiency of the communication, and the teachers' ability to withstand expectations of parents (Ho & Chen, 2013; Shechtman & Busherian, 2015).

Immigration and Cultural Heterogeneity

In many Western countries, such as the USA, Britain, Australia and Canada, there are various population groups living side by side, differing from one another in terms of religion, nationality, ethnicity, political inclination and culture. Israel as well is a culturally heterogeneous society. The groups in Israel include Jews and non Jews (Muslims and Christians), religious and secular, veterans and newcomers, European originated and immigrants from Arab countries, politically affiliated liberals or conservatives, and residents of the center of the country or the periphery. According to Banks (2010), these countries are characterized by a shared core culture (*macroculture*) as well as many subcultures (*microcultures*). The values, norms and characteristics of the macroculture are often mediated by, as well as interpreted and expressed differently, within various microcultures. These differences often lead to cultural misunderstandings, conflicts and institutionalized discrimination.

All of the social groups recognize the importance of school-family relations. However, there are differences in patterns of parental involvement amongst various ethnic and class groups. For instance, families from ethnic minorities and a low socio-economic class tend to be involved in their children's education at home to the same extent as do families from dominant groups (Cousins & Mickelson, 2011), while they tend to be less involved at school, in comparison to parents of dominant groups (Henderson & Mapp, 2002; Hill, 2011; Robinson & Harris, 2014).

According to Shechtman and Busherian (2015), the low level of parental involvement among families from ethnic minorities and the low socio-economic class may be due to several reasons: (1) lack of economic resources, transportation and time (especially among the low income groups); (2) difficulties in efficient and fluent communication due to language differences and parental difficulty in speaking the language prevalent in society; (3) a prominent cultural gap between the school culture, which represents the values and beliefs of society's dominant groups, and the unique culture of the family. In cases of significant cultural gaps, when parents do not manage to find a common denominator with the school, they encounter lack of communication and understanding on behalf of the school educational team, and they even sense seclusion (Bicer, Capraro & Capraro, 2013; Hill, 2011). Discrimination, lack of appreciation and mistrust make it difficult for them to be involved in the school (Lee & Bowen, 2006).

While the involvement of middle class parents in educational frameworks contributes to their children's welfare and progress, it also constitutes a means of preserving power relations between parents and teachers. Studies show that relations between schools and upper- or middle-class parents may be accompanied by considerable tension, criticism towards school, and parental supervision of the teachers' work. These parents may also use social connections to influence processes at school (Baquedano-López, Alexander, & Hernandez, 2013).

Accordingly, many policymakers and researchers emphasize the need for cultural sensitivity and cultural competence in working with minority parents. *Cultural sensitivity* is the knowledge, awareness, and acceptance of other cultures. Educational or therapeutic interventions that are sensitive to the cultural background of their participants are therefore called *culture-sensitive interventions*. *Cultural competence* includes the behaviors, attitudes, and policies that come together in agencies or among professionals and enable them to work effectively in cross-cultural situations. (Cross, Bazron, Dennis & Isaacs, 1989; Ror - Strier, 2010).

The Development of New Family Structures

The disintegration of the traditional family unit, the social struggles of women, gender and sexual minorities for equal rights, and advanced fertility technology have brought about the development of alternative family structures such as single parent families, single parents by choice, LGBTQ families, adoptive families, foster families, etc.

According to Goodcar (2009), when teachers encounter alternative families, their own personal emotions and attitudes are evoked and this might affect their interaction with the parents. In order to achieve effective and significant educational partnership between the teachers and the 'new families', it is vital that the teachers suspend judgment and reflect on their own perceptions and attitudes. Moreover, it is necessary that teachers expend time and resources in becoming acquainted with the features and arrangements of the 'new family', examining their needs and coordinating expectations.

Changes in the Realm of Employment, and a New Role Division between Parents and Teachers

Changes in the employment market, such as women going out to work, have increased parental dependence on the educational system as the parents constantly juggle between family and career. Moreover, parents are confused and anxiety-ridden about their role in childrearing and education, due to the abundance of models and approaches concerning child education, leading to their constant search for the right model (Plotnik, 2007).

The troubled parents look for help from the educational system, expecting the teachers to contain their distress and hardships and to be partners in the developmental process of their child. However, the educational system very often does not see itself as committed to the parents. Rather, it places the child at the center and sees the parent as an entity committed to the child's needs, thereby ignoring the parent's needs or even judging their parental competence and functioning. This attitude weakens the parents, increasing their anxiety and feelings of guilt, and may lead to tension and clashes between parents and the educational system.

Plotnik (2007) claims that this situation requires the teacher to acknowledge and listen to the *parental voice*, showing empathy to the parents' difficulties, supporting them and strengthening their parental efficacy. Listening to the *parental voice* and rendering responses to the parents' emotional needs are vital to establishing effective and significant communication with parents, in the reality of the 21st century.

The Integration of Special Needs Children into Mainstream Education

Since the 1990s, advanced legislation and educational reforms in the Western world and in Israel, in the spirit of the social-ecological paradigm and the inclusion movement, have led a revolution in the perception and work methods concerning special needs children. This paradigm emphasizes society's responsibility towards diversity, viewing variance as an advantage rather than a restriction, and encouraging inclusion rather than separation. Hence, more and more children with special and complex needs (such as ADHD, learning disabilities, behavioral difficulties, limited mental development, sensory disabilities, motor handicaps, various illnesses and syndromes, and autism) receive special services while attending special education classes or integrated classes within mainstream schools (Ainscow, Booth, & Dyson, 2006; Devarakonda, 2013; Timor, 2013).

Integrating children with special needs into mainstream education is not simple. It requires the training of the entire system in order to absorb the integrated children. This includes the choosing of teachers with suitable approaches and motivation to cope with the integration, preparing the students and parents of the integrated and regular classes, and therapeutic work with the integrated children and their parents (Wigle & Wilcox, 1996). The parents of the integrated child expect their child to receive the special treatment he is entitled to, and often feel protective of him. The gap between the parents' expectations and the teachers' difficulties creates great tension and conflicts (Shechtman and Busherian, 2015).

The Aim of the Study

Although this subject is important and is addressed repeatedly by teachers, school advisors and principals, the concept of working with parents has not yet taken a central place in the process of educating student teachers at various levels and of various professions. Most teacher education programs do not provide relevant knowledge and efficient strategies for working with parents in the 21st century. Even when teachers participate in enrichment courses, only a small and marginal place is dedicated to family involvement (Epstein, 2018; Epstein & Sanders, 2006; Meehan& Meehan, 2018; Shartrand, Weiss, Kreider and Lopez, 1997; Walker & Dotger, 2012).

Far-reaching changes in the social reality and their impact on family-school relations, as described above, raise many questions regarding the nature and essence of the appropriate education for student teachers on the subject of working with parents in the 21st century. For example: What are the unique challenges that teachers face in the present century, in all aspects related to communicating with parents? In view of these challenges, what innovative perceptions, skills and strategies are required in order to nurture significant and effective relations with parents?

In view of these questions, we conducted a study aimed at examining how interns of early childhood education understood and interpreted communication with parents, and what difficulties and challenges preoccupied them. The identification of the central difficulties and challenges with which teachers are concerned, with regard to communication with parents, may contribute significantly to the knowledge of family- school relations in a diverse and dynamic society, both at the theoretical and the practical level. Teacher education institutions will be able to use this new knowledge in order to provide student teachers with suitable perceptions, skills and strategies that are relevant for work with parents in the 21st century.

METHODS

Participants

The present study was conducted in the framework of the course "Working with Parents in the 21st Century." This course is taught in the fourth year of the Early Childhood Education program (ages 3-8) at Levinsky College of Education in Israel. Participants were 143 female student teachers, in their fourth year of studies towards their BA in Education, and Early Education Teaching Certificate. They took the course in five parallel classes in the first semester of 2017-2018. The research procedure was identical in all of the classes.

All of the student teachers, in their fourth and final year of studies, worked as practicing teachers at kindergartens and elementary schools, as part of their internship. Specifically, most of the students (85%) did their internship as student kindergarten teachers in kindergartens (ages 3-6). The rest (15%) did their internship as student teachers in the lower grades of elementary school (ages 6-8). All of the student teachers had previously undergone fieldwork during their first three years of studies, with a kindergarten teacher mentor or a school teacher mentor.

Research Methodology

This study is mainly qualitative, combined with quantitative analyses (Alpert, 2010; Tashakkori & Teddlie, 2003). It was based on categorical content analysis of social episodes written by interns of early childhood education, regarding work with parents (Ayalon & Sabar Ben-Yehoshua, 2010, Corbin & Strauss, 2008). According to the qualitative approach (Shkedi, 2003), people organize their worldviews through stories that they construct and tell. These human narratives structure the experience, and through them, people understand the world around them. Hence, we chose the qualitative methodology in order to examine how interns of early childhood education understood and interpreted communication with parents. We paid special attention to the central difficulties and challenges with which they were concerned.

In addition to the qualitative analysis, we used quantitative analyses (examining the frequency of the various themes and categories that arose from the qualitative analysis), in order to expand and deepen our understanding of the qualitative analysis findings. In fact, the quantitative analysis added information that could not have been derived solely from qualitative analysis, as will be detailed further on.

Research Tools

The research tools were written accounts of social episodes. Each student in the course was asked to write about a social episode depicting a significant and authentic educational experience, involving parents of children aged 3-8. The episode could be taken from their work as practicing teachers at kindergartens and elementary schools during the intern year, or from their fieldwork as student teachers with a mentoring school or kindergarten teacher throughout their training years.

The precise instructions for episode-writing were as follows:

- Think of a significant event that is connected to the relations between the educational framework and the children's parents. It may be an event from your work as a practicing school or kindergarten teacher during the intern year, or from your fieldwork with a mentoring school or kindergarten teacher during your three training years.
- Write out an account of the event using as many details as possible, relating to the context of a kindergarten/class (children's age, town, kindergarten composite, etc.), as well as unique characteristics of the family presented in the event (country of origin, family structure, socio-economic conditions, etc.).
- Give a title to the event.

Ultimately, there were 150 written accounts of social episodes regarding communication with parents, corresponding to the number of students in the course's classes. We used 143 accounts, as 7 students did not give their permission to be part of the study. All of the school and kindergarten teachers described in the accounts were the interns themselves working as practicing school and kindergarten teachers during their internship, or the mentoring school or kindergarten teachers with whom they practiced during their three training years.

Data Analysis

The written accounts of social episodes were analyzed and coded by categorical content analysis, according to the principles of grounded theory (Ayalon & Sabar Ben-Yehoshua, 2010; Corbin & Strauss, 2008). Three stages of data coding were conducted: *open coding, axial coding, and selective coding.* A line-by-line reading of each written account led to the creation of initial codes (open coding). The initial codes that were most frequent and/or significant were mapped into categories and subcategories (axial coding), e.g., "instances of parents' resistance or impatience in all aspects of integrating children from various cultural and religious groups, or special-needs children." The generation of subcategories involved an examination of the variations within each category and between other categories (e.g., comparing between responses of the kindergarten teachers in each of the cases). This coding scheme was applied to the data, and then revised and reapplied, thereby allowing for the identification of central core themes (selective coding), such as "essential disputes between parents and teachers, with regard to educational worldview and child-rearing techniques." Data analysis ended when the coding scheme and resulting themes accurately reflected the study data.

The qualitative analysis extracted six central themes regarding school-family relations. In addition, two super-categories were revealed to be significant axes crossing all of the themes, i.e., expressed at various degrees and forms in all of them. These super-categories are: (1) cultural diversity and power relations between parents and teachers; (2) parent's gender (i.e., the involvement of fathers in the educational framework and the communication patterns of the educational staff with fathers, in comparison to mothers).

In addition to the qualitative analysis of data, we used quantitative analyses. The quantitative analyses included frequency examination of each central theme. We also examined the frequency of sub-topics (sub-categories) in each theme. Finally, we examined the frequency of each of the super-categories (axes) in the central themes.

The quantitative analyses helped us expand and deepen our understanding of the findings of the qualitative analysis. Moreover, the quantitative analyses added information that we could not have derived solely from the qualitative data. For example, the frequency examination of the super-category (axis) "the parent's gender" in the various themes, revealed differences in the involvement of fathers and in the communication patterns of the educational staff with fathers, in comparison to mothers.

Ethical Aspects of the Research

At the beginning of the course, we told the students about the study and asked their permission to use educational events that they would write about, for the purpose of the research, maintaining anonymity and secrecy. We emphasized to the students that participation in the study was not part of the course requirements, and that the data analysis would be conducted only after the students had been given their final course grade. Hence, there would be no connection between participation in the study and the course grade. Students that were interested in participating in the study signed a form confirming their voluntary participation. Of the 150 course students, 7 did not sign the study participation form. Hence, we related solely to the accounts submitted by 143 students.

Accordingly, the findings' analysis was conducted only after the students had received their final grade for the course. When writing the findings, we omitted names and blurred identifying details, in order to maintain anonymity and secrecy regarding the participants.

Despite the precautionary measures taken, the researchers of this study are also the course lecturers. Quite naturally, they have formed close relations with the study's participants (the students), as in any course of a similar nature. These relations could expose the researchers to various forms of bias when analyzing the data. Therefore, to ensure the reliability of the analysis of the research findings, the following strategies were used (see Creswell, 1998):

1) *Disclosure and transparency*: the research produced was open and candid concerning method, procedure, and analysis, as was described above.
2) *Thick description*: interpretations and commentary that were offered were accompanied by rich and detailed descriptions from the participants' accounts, allowing readers to assess the analysis.
3) *Peer review*: The data were analyzed by the researchers/course lecturers. This analysis was shown - at various meetings throughout the year - to two experienced researchers in the field of

education who did not teach that course. These researchers contributed valuable feedback to the discussion of the research findings, conclusions and recommendations.

FINDINGS

In this chapter, we will present six themes of difficulties and challenges in parents-teachers relations, as seen in the social episodes written by interns of early childhood education. We will then describe two super-categories revealed as significant axes, in the context of home-school communication: (1) cultural diversity and power relations between parents and teachers; (2) the parent's gender - differences in the involvement of fathers and in the communication patterns of the educational staff with fathers, in comparison to mothers. These axes were manifested at various degrees and forms in all of the themes, as will be elaborated below.

Central Difficulties and Challenges in Family-School Relations

Content analysis of the data revealed six central themes that preoccupied interns of early childhood education, as reflected in the social episodes they had written in connection to work with parents. Most of the themes referred to various difficulties and challenges that arose in the interaction between school- and kindergarten teachers and parents. As detailed in the methods chapter, in many cases the interns chose to describe interactions with parents that occurred during their practice as kindergarten teachers or as teachers of the lower grades at elementary school, as part of their internship. In other words, in most cases, the kindergarten teachers or school teachers described in the social episodes were the interns themselves. In other cases, the social episodes that the interns described regarding work with parents, related to kindergarten teachers or teachers of the lower grades at elementary school who had mentored the students during their fieldwork earlier on in their BA studies (first through third year). Table 1 shows the distribution of the themes according to their frequency. Following is the list of themes:

1) Teachers' difficulties in informing parents of their children's problems and/or enlisting their cooperation (24% of all events);
2) Difficulties in building trust and close relations with parents (22% of all events);
3) Teachers' difficulties in placing boundaries for parental behavior that is inappropriate, disrespectful or violent (21% of all events);
4) Essential disputes between parents and teachers, with regard to educational worldview and child-rearing techniques (15% of all events);
5) Coping with parental complaints about the ongoing functioning of the educational staff (14% of all events);
6) Teachers' indecisions regarding parental requests for aid and guidance (4% of all events).

Table 1. Distribution of difficulties and challenges preoccupying interns of early childhood education with regard to working relations with parents, according to frequency (N= 143)

Theme	Number of events	Frequency in %
Teachers' difficulties in informing parents of their children's problems and/or enlisting their cooperation	35	24%
Difficulties in building trust and close relations with parents	32	22%
Teachers' difficulties in placing boundaries for parental behavior	30	21%
Essential disputes between parents and teachers, with regard to educational worldview and child-rearing techniques	21	15%
Coping with parental complaints about the ongoing functioning of the educational staff	20	14%
Teachers' indecisions regarding parental requests for aid and guidance	5	4%
Total	143	100%

The following sections will depict the central themes that preoccupied interns of early childhood education regarding working relations with parents, as reflected in their described episodes. Each central theme will be described in detail, including its sub-themes and relevant examples.

Teachers' Difficulties in Informing Parents of Their Children's Problems and/or Enlisting Their Cooperation (24% of All Events)

Of all the issues preoccupying interns of early childhood education, the most prominent theme dealt with teachers' difficulties in informing parents of their children's problems and/or enlisting their cooperation. Specifically, nearly a quarter of all of the events (35 out of the 143 events - 24%) dealt with this theme. The main difficulty encountered by teachers in informing parents of their children's problems and/or enlisting their cooperation centered on developmental problems and significant gaps in cognitive, linguistic, social and communicative functioning of the child in comparison to other children (20 events out of 35 - 57%). These problems could indicate that the child was coping with special needs, and could raise questions regarding the suitability of the educational framework and the nature of the educational services which the child would require, and which would be most appropriate (integration within a mainstream kindergarten or class; an integrated kindergarten/class, composed of regular and special needs children; or referral to a special education kindergarten/school).

For example, in one of the events, the kindergarten teacher invited the parents of a girl to discuss her cognitive, linguistic and communicative difficulties. She showed them the findings of observations and evaluations that she and the kindergarten psychologist had conducted with the child, together with the psychologist's recommendation to refer the girl to a special education framework. The parents expressed complete refusal. In another conversation, the parents' attitude even became vehement, and they demanded that observations of their daughter cease.

Another type of problem evoking difficulties in informing parents of their children's problems, and/or enlisting their cooperation, concerned behavioral issues of various degrees (15 events - 43%). In a certain event, for instance, a first grade homeroom teacher asked a mother to come meet her, in view of her son's repeated bullying and violent behavior. The mother did not come to the meeting. One day, the boy was again involved in a violent act in the classroom, and the teacher called the mother and asked her to come take her son home. The mother replied that she was at work and that it wasn't her problem if the teacher could not place boundaries. In another case, a kindergarten teacher told parents about their son's difficulties in self-regulation and his bouts of rage. She wanted their permission to ask the school counselor to build an educational-treatment program for the child. The parents refused, saying that he was just being naughty like all of the boys.

Difficulties in Building Trust and Close Relations with Parents (22% of All Events)

Following the subject of difficulties of teachers in informing parents of their children's problems and/or enlisting their cooperation, the interns were preoccupied with the issue of difficulties in building trust and close relations with parents. Specifically, 32 of the 143 events (22% of all events) dealt with this issue.

A mapping of sub-themes showed that almost half of the events (46%) of this issue dealt with difficulties in communicating with parents. For example, in one of the cases, the mother and grandmother arrived at the kindergarten earlier than usual to take the child to a family event. The kindergarten teacher was very surprised, and wouldn't let the girl out earlier. The mother and grandmother claimed that they had informed the assistant, however the assistant said that she didn't remember that. The mother and grandmother were very angry and told the kindergarten teacher off. The girl burst out crying. The mother and grandmother took the child forcefully and claimed they would see the supervisor for kindergartens about the occurrence.

Nearly one third (27%) of the events of this issue related to the difficulty in establishing trusting relationships with parents and maintaining them over a period of time. For example, in one of the events, the kindergarten teacher played a game with the children called "What's missing in the storage room?" The next day a group of angry parents waited for the kindergarten teacher, since one of the mothers had told the other parents that the kindergarten teacher had locked the children in the storage room. The kindergarten teacher was doubly insulted. First, due to the parents' actually believing that she would lock their children in the storage room. Second, from the way that mother had chosen to act upon the (mistaken) information. Instead of talking to the teacher to find out what had happened, she told the other parents and riled them up.

Nearly another third of the events (27%) related to lack of information, or the concealing of information, by either the parents or the kindergarten teacher. Occasionally, it was the parents who did not share vital information, which was later on revealed. For example, in one case at the beginning of the year, the head of the kindergarten asked all of the parents to update her about allergies. A particular mother did not do so. The information was revealed by chance when the little girl told the kindergarten teacher at one of the breaks that she was allergic to broad beans. The kindergarten teacher didn't believe her. This event created tension and an exchange of accusations between the kindergarten teacher and the mother. The mother accused the kindergarten teacher of thinking that her daughter was a liar, while the kindergarten teacher was angry with the mother for hiding sensitive and important information. Only after everyone had relaxed, did the parties involved agree that the child could bring food from home. In another event, a girl told the kindergarten teacher that her father was ill with "a sleeping disease" and that he was getting medicine and sleeping all day. The kindergarten teacher suspected that the father might be coping with depression. She tried to meet with the mother several times, but the mother avoided her with various excuses.

In other cases, it was the kindergarten teachers who did not give vital or important information to the parents, thereby creating confusion and uncertainty. For example, in one of the kindergartens, there was a high turnover of staff members over a short period of time. The parents were not updated and received no explanation. Several parents tried to understand from the kindergarten teacher what was happening. In another case, in an elementary school, first graders were divided into groups according to tests provided by the Ministry of Education, with no prior notice. The parents were angry, since they didn't understand the meaning of the division, and they were afraid it would affect their children's achievements.

Teachers' Difficulties in Placing Boundaries for Parental Behavior That Is Inappropriate, Disrespectful or Violent (21% of All Events)

An additional issue preoccupying the interns was connected to difficulties of teachers in placing boundaries for parental behavior that is inappropriate, disrespectful or violent. Specifically, 30 of the 143 events, i.e., 21% were related to this issue.

Mapping of sub-themes showed that more than half of the difficulties in placing boundaries (53% of the events) centered on parents' belittling and ignoring instructions, procedures and regulations determined by the educational staff according to the policy of the Ministry of Education. This behavior of the parents was expressed in numerous contexts and circumstances: arrival times at the kindergarten; opening the gates to the latecomers; the time allowed for parents to stay with the child; pick up times; who is allowed to pick up from the kindergarten and who is not; appropriate nutrition; and rules regarding parties and celebrations. For example, in a particular kindergarten there was a procedure concerning the length of time that parents are allowed to stay with the child in the morning, in order to make the parting easier. One of the fathers used to ignore the bell ring indicating that it was time to leave, as well as the teacher's request for him to do so. He used to chat with the assistant and make himself coffee. This behavior repeated itself several times, and only stopped after the teacher had a private conversation with him.

Additional difficulties in placing boundaries touched upon threats of violence or aggressive behavior of parents towards the educational staff (27% of the events). For example, in one of the schools, one of the fathers verbally assaulted the homeroom teacher, accusing her of his daughter's behavioral problems, and threatened that he would come over to her house. In another case, a mother complained to the kindergarten teacher that twin boys were hitting her daughter. After this case repeated itself, the mother called the kindergarten teacher furiously and threatened her: "If those fat twins lift their hands on my daughter again, I'll throw your whole kindergarten in the air."

In other cases (13%), the educational staff had to cope with parents' attempts to doubt their professionalism or to influence decisions they had taken. Thus, for example, in one of the cases, a child didn't want to go back to kindergarten after a long vacation. The mother verbally assaulted the kindergarten teacher in a series of questions and accusations, questioning her professionalism: "How long have you been a kindergarten teacher?"; "What are you doing here that makes the kids not want to come back to kindergarten?"

In the rest of the cases (7%), the kindergarten teacher's challenge was to set boundaries for parents in cases of blurred lines between professional and personal relationships. Thus for example, in one case, a kindergarten teacher avoided the offer of one of the mothers to meet with her for coffee during the weekend. In another case, the kindergarten teacher was surprised to find out that one of the mothers had set a trip for the children of the kindergarten without consulting or coordinating with the teacher.

Essential Disputes between Parents and Teachers, with Regard to Educational Worldview and Child-Rearing Techniques (15% of All Events)

Another issue that preoccupied the interns was connected to disputes between parents and teachers regarding educational worldview and child-rearing techniques. Specifically, 21 of the 143 events (15%) related to this issue.

The mapping of the sub-themes showed that more than half of the disputes (57%) were connected to management of the kindergarten, lifestyles, and educational climate: adaptability, weaning, nutrition, watching television during kindergarten hours, tidying up toys, birthday celebrations, teaching non-violent communication, etc. For example, during a parents' meeting at the kindergarten, it was decided that birthday children would share the birthday cake during celebrations. One father opposed this decision, claiming that it could cause his child emotional distress, and demanded that his son have a separate birthday cake. The kindergarten teacher refused. He then provided articles supporting his position, and even spoke to the supervisor of kindergartens, who agreed with him. Following the supervisor's intervention, the child celebrated with a separate cake. In another case, a mother who believed in the "eye for an eye" policy, taught her son to react violently to any aggression he experienced. The homeroom teacher tried to explain the school's policy to her, which educates the children to non-violent communication, restraint and discourse, but to no avail.

Nearly a third of the disputes (29%) concerned acts of opposition or intolerance of parents in anything connected to the integration of children from other cultural or religious groups, or special needs children. Detailed examples of this sub-theme can be found below in the section: *Cultural diversity and power relations between parents and teachers,* under the title: *Teachers demonstrated varying degrees of cultural sensitivity and cultural competence in their communication with parents.*

Another 14% of the disputes were expressed in clashes between, on the one hand, parents' non-conventional educational approaches (democratic education, a secular approach devoid of religion, kibbutz kindergarten, etc.), and on the other, conservative and traditional approaches of the educational staff. Thus, for example, a kindergarten teacher at a non-religious kindergarten invited Habad people (i.e., representatives of a religious organization) to explain about Jewish customs of the High Holidays. Some of the parents opposed having a religious factor enter into the kindergarten. The teacher insisted, so the opposing parents did not send their children to kindergarten on that day. During the year as well, there was great tension between the kindergarten teacher and the parents around holidays and ceremonies with a religious nature. In another case, parents at a kibbutz kindergarten (namely, a kindergarten in a collective settlement) complained to the supervisor about the young kindergarten teacher's functionality, as she had run a city kindergarten for a short while before. They claimed that kibbutz education was different from city education, and that the new kindergarten teacher could not apply their worldview.

Coping with Parental Complaints About the Ongoing Functioning of the Educational Team (14% of All Events)

Out of the 143 educational events accounted by the interns, 20 events (14%) were connected to educational staffs having to cope with parental complaints regarding their ongoing functionality. The mapping analysis indicated that most of the complaints (40%) dealt with the ways that the educational staff treated specific cases of violence between children. Thus, for example, a mother complained to a kindergarten teacher that during recess one of the children had strangled her son until he vomited. The mother was not satisfied with the kindergarten teacher's answers, and decided to involve the head of the kindergarten. In another case, a mother called the homeroom teacher on her day off and told her, very emotionally, that her son had come home bruised and battered, and no one called to tell her what had happened. It turned out that certain teachers had witnessed the event, but no one updated the mother or the homeroom teacher.

A quarter of the events (25%) dealt with complaints regarding lack of personal attention, caring and concern over the children. For example, a mother was angry with the kindergarten teacher for not calling to ask about her daughter who was ill at home. During the conversation, it turned out that the kindergarten teacher herself was ill that day. In a different event, a mother wrote an angry email to the homeroom teacher, saying that her son sat the whole day on his school bag instead of on a chair. According to the mother, the boy had asked two different teachers to help him find a chair, which was only found for him during the last hour. The homeroom teacher updated the staff.

15% of the events related to complaints regarding supervision, security and safety. For example, at the end of a school day in kindergarten, a girl took string out of her coat and tied it around her neck, while she was waiting for her mother. The terrified mother rushed to the child, removed the string, and shouted at the staff that they were negligent. In the rest of the cases (20%), the complaints dealt with various subjects such as cleanliness, unhealthy nutrition, etc.

Parental Requests for Aid and Guidance from the Kindergarten Teacher (4% of All Events)

Parental requests for aid and guidance from the kindergarten teacher was another issue that preoccupied early childhood education interns. Of the 143 events, 5 dealt with this issue (4%).

The mapping analysis of the events of this issue showed that in most of the cases (60%), the parents asked the teachers for aid and guidance due to their difficulty in behaving assertively and placing boundaries to their children. For example, in one kindergarten, a mother was late bringing her son, and he was only wearing his underwear. The mother told the kindergarten teacher that she couldn't handle him and asked for her help. The assistant quickly dressed him. The kindergarten teacher set a meeting with the mother the next day. In another case, a mother asked a kindergarten teacher for help in dealing with the issue of her son biting.

In 20% of the events, the parents were motivated to ask for help from the kindergarten teacher due to their difficulty in parting with the child, and an additional 20% were due to their desire for the kindergarten teacher to help their child become socially integrated in the kindergarten.

Cultural Diversity and Power Relations between Parents and Teachers

An in-depth analysis of the data revealed that the axis of *cultural diversity and parent-teacher power relations* was a significant factor, in the context of working relations with parents. It was present at varying degrees and ways in all of the themes that were raised by early childhood education interns. This axis was highly prevalent in the following themes: difficulties of teachers in informing parents of their children's problems and/or enlisting their cooperation (74%); essential disputes between parents and teachers, with regard to educational worldview and child-rearing techniques (67%); and difficulties in building trust and close relations with parents (40%). It was present to a lesser degree with the other themes: difficulties of teachers in placing boundaries for parental behavior (20%); parental requests for aid and guidance (20%); and coping with parental complaints about the ongoing functioning of the educational staff (15%). Table 2 shows the distribution of the axis *cultural diversity and parent-teacher power relations*, across the various themes, according to frequency.

Table 2. The distribution of *cultural diversity and parent-teacher power relations*, across the various themes, according to frequency (N= 143)

Theme	Number of events dealing with this axis	Total events in this theme	Frequency in %
Teachers' difficulties in informing parents of their children's problems and/or enlisting their cooperation	26	35	74%
Essential disputes between parents and teachers, with regard to educational worldview and child-rearing techniques	14	21	67%
Difficulties in building trust and close relations with parents	13	32	40%
Teachers' difficulties in placing boundaries for parental behavior	6	30	20%
Teachers' indecisions regarding parental requests for aid and guidance	1	5	20%
Coping with parental complaints about the ongoing functioning of the educational staff	3	20	15%

The axis of cultural diversity and parent-teacher power relations, which was found through analysis of the interns' social episodes regarding working relationships with parents, was expressed in the varying themes in three main ways, as will be described below:

1) There was a significant representation of cultural diversity with regard to the families with whom the teachers came into contact;
2) Teachers demonstrated varying degrees of cultural sensitivity and cultural competence in their communication with parents;
3) Power relations between parents and teachers shaped family-school relations and influenced them.

There Was a Significant Representation of Cultural Diversity with Regard to the Families with Whom the Teachers Came into Contact

The social episodes described by the early childhood education interns indicated that the teachers interact with parents who belong to a diverse range of cultural groups, communities and families. Specifically, the interns described difficulties and challenges in working relations with parents from the following groups: parents of an ethnic/religious/cultural minority background (for example, the Arab sector, and Jews of Ethiopian origins), parents of a low social class, parents with non-traditional family compositions (for example, single parent families, same sex families, and single mothers by choice), as well as parents of special needs children.

Another group of parents - revealed through the interns' descriptions, and constituting a significant challenge for teachers - included those dealing with a challenging parenthood. This group included families where one of the parents was dealing with a mental health issue, or where parents were caring for siblings with special needs. This is a group which does not get sufficient attention in both theoretical literature and in fieldwork, but there is definitely a need to account for it. For example, in one of the events, a mother who suffered from a mental disorder called the kindergarten teacher and said that her daughter was suffering from worms because the kindergarten was dirty and neglected. The kindergarten teacher told the mother that the assistants tidy up and clean the kindergarten on a daily basis. The mother was not convinced. The following morning, the mother arrived at the kindergarten, took cleaning supplies, and cleaned the basins, ceramics, taps, toilets and doorknobs in the premises. In another event, a father coping with psychological problems used to disturb the educational staff with numerous phone calls throughout the day, using a different excuse each time.

Of all the groups and communities, the population of parents of special needs children was the most challenging for kindergarten teachers and school teachers. This population stood out in the number of events where it was represented in the varying themes and in the complexity of events (for example, 57% of the events in theme 1 focused on parents of special needs children). The main difficulty for the teachers revolved around informing parents of their children's problems and/or enlisting their cooperation. For many parents, it was the first time they had heard that their child was dealing with a significant difficulty or limitation, in comparison to children of the same age. The parents found it difficult to deal with the "discovery shock," and preferred to be defensive or to blame the teacher. Thus, kindergarten teachers and teachers in the lower grades of elementary schools had to show a high level of sensitivity and professionalism when working with parents of special needs children, in order to get the parents to acknowledge their children's issue and enlist their cooperation. This work included numerous meetings with parents, using a range of assessment tools to determine the child's functionality, and constantly sharing information and advice with the counseling staff at the kindergarten. For example, in one of the events, the parents disagreed with the kindergarten teacher's claim that the child was showing significant gaps in verbal and cognitive functionality. The father shouted at the kindergarten teacher, saying she didn't know what she was doing, and refused to take the child for evaluation or for treatment. Only after repeated conversations throughout the year with the kindergarten teacher, as well as the kindergarten psychologist, was the father convinced, and subsequently took the child for private evaluation. The following year, the child transferred to special needs education.

Teachers Demonstrated Varying Degrees of Cultural Sensitivity and Cultural Competence in Their Communication with Parents

The aspect of cultural diversity and power relations was also expressed in the social episodes written by early childhood education interns, through various teachers who demonstrated varying degrees of cultural sensitivity and cultural competence when working with parents. In some of the cases, the teachers showed a low level of cultural sensitivity and cultural competence. For example, in one of the events, a kindergarten teacher invited parents for a meeting to discuss their son's behavioral issues - the parents were older people of Ethiopian origin, and without strong command of the Hebrew language. The parents were quiet and pleasant throughout the meeting, and the kindergarten teacher took that as a sign that they were happy to cooperate with her. After a few days, the child misbehaved again, and the kindergarten teacher called the father. The father arrived at the kindergarten to take his son and declared he would never bring him back to this kindergarten again, and indeed that was the case. Even though the kindergarten teacher got the supervisor, as well as a regular visitation officer involved, the child never returned to that specific kindergarten. This sequence of events indicates cultural gaps which were not properly mediated. First of all, it is unclear how much of what the kindergarten teacher said was actually understood by the parents, and how much they were able to communicate their thoughts and feelings in a language with which they were not familiar. Second, if the kindergarten teacher were to research information about the Ethiopian community, she would learn that parents of an Ethiopian origin, as well as parents from other ethnic minority backgrounds, are not quick to express disagreements, complaints or dissatisfaction in front of authoritative figures, as that is not acceptable in their society (Bar – Yosef, 2001; Rattenborg, MacPhee, Kleisner Walker & Miller- Heyl, 2018; Smith, Strern & Shatronova, 2008).

What actions could the kindergarten teacher have taken in order to prevent this harsh sequence of events? Obviously, if the kindergarten teacher had invited an interpreter or mediator from the Ethiopian community to join the meeting, that would have eliminated all of the language and communication difficulties. A cultural mediator would have also been able to decipher the parents' behavioral codes and "read" the objections, or the dissatisfaction, which were hidden under the pleasant façade. Moreover, using actions which help create trust, such as making home visits, instead of actions for control and supervision (such as involving the supervisor and the regular visitation officer), could have contributed to more close and caring relations between the kindergarten teacher and the parents, and perhaps would have made the father change his mind.

In a different event, a mother would regularly arrive late with her son at the kindergarten, and would have to wait for quite a while each time, until the next opening of the kindergarten gates. On one of the occasions, the mother told the kindergarten teacher that she was caring for another child with special needs, and therefore found it difficult to arrive on time. The mother asked the kindergarten teacher to show her special consideration and to open the gates for her before the set time, so that she wouldn't be late to work. The kindergarten teacher refused and returned to the kindergarten. The mother was insulted and angrily left the place crying. There is no doubt that the kindergarten teacher did not show cultural sensitivity towards a mother who is dealing with a challenging parenthood. Obviously, there should have been an attempt to invite the parents for a meeting after the incident, to try to understand what difficulties and challenges the family was dealing with, what their sources of support were, and to arrive at a mutual solution (for example, the father or the grandmother could bring the child to kindergarten on time).

In other cases, the kindergarten teachers showed sensitivity and goodwill, but lacked information and tools, and did not always know what to do. For example, a kindergarten teacher spoke to a mother to find out why her daughter was often late or missing school. The kindergarten teacher also wondered why the mother often picked up her daughter in the middle of the day. The mother, who had just moved from the United States to Israel, said that she herself was educated through the democratic education system and that she stood by those principles. And so, she allowed her daughter to choose when to arrive and for how long. The kindergarten teacher did not know what to do. In another event, the mother of a girl afflicted with Celiac (Gluten sensitivity) asked the kindergarten teacher to take her daughter's condition into account. During a conversation between the mother, the kindergarten teacher and the supervisor, it was decided that they would not bake Hallot (i.e., special bread used on Sabbath and festivals) at the kindergarten. However, the other parents objected to it at a parent meeting and demanded that the kindergarten teacher change the decision. The kindergarten teacher gave up and agreed to the parents' demand.

In other cases, the kindergarten teachers demonstrated high degrees of cultural sensitivity and cultural competence when they bravely fought against prejudice and intolerance shown by parents of dominant groups, and arranged relevant explanation activities. For example, in one of the kindergartens at the beginning of the year, a group of parents expressed reservation at letting six children of Ethiopian origin into the kindergarten. They said they were not interested in their children attending a "mixed" kindergarten. During the first parent meeting, the kindergarten teacher put on the song "Equals," and said that all children from all cultures and groups are equal and worthy in her kindergarten. The parents understood the message and did not raise the issue again. In a similar event, a mother tried to turn parents against a child from the Arab sector attending the kindergarten, and have him expelled. The kindergarten teacher held a special parents evening and invited a lecturer to speak about prejudice. Following the activity, the mother who had initiated the opposition changed her position and apologized.

In another case, a father did not agree for his son to study in an integrated class (a class in which mainstream children study with special needs children). According to the father, the integration of special needs children harms the class climate and his son's academic achievements. He met with the homeroom teacher and the school principal and demanded that his son be moved to a mainstream class. The teacher and the principal expressed sympathy towards the father's feelings, but detailed the actions they were taking in order to make sure the level of studies would not be harmed, and emphasized the advantages of the integration for all of the pupils. The father calmed down and his son remained in the integrated class.

Power Relations between Teachers and Parents Shaped Family-School Relations and Influenced Them

The aspect of cultural diversity and power relations was also manifested in the social episodes reported by early childhood education interns, in the manner with which power relations between parents and teachers have shaped and influenced the family-school relations. In certain cases, the teachers' desire to maintain a good relationship with upper class parents, and the fear of confronting them, prevented them from telling parents about their children's various issues. For example, one kindergarten teacher said that when an upper class mother tried to understand what her son was doing in the kindergarten kitchen during recess, she answered that he sat to have a meal with her. The truth was that he was in time out for violent behavior. According to the kindergarten teacher, she refused to tell the mother about her son's behavioral issues for fear of a confrontation with her. In another event, a kindergarten teacher described a child in her kindergarten who was coping with cognitive and social difficulties, and whose parents worked in high profile professions and had good standing in the community. The kindergarten teacher admitted that she kept postponing the conversation with his parents for fear of their reaction.

In other cases, the teachers had to show professional strength when standing up to upper class parents, or parents from dominant groups, who tried to get extra rights for their children, influence decisions made by the educational staff, remove children of non-dominant groups from the kindergarten or school, or doubt the professionalism of teachers from minority backgrounds. For example, in one event, parents from a high socio-economical class set a meeting with the school principal, counsellor and homeroom teacher, demanding that they change decisions regarding the division of their kids into first grade classes. They threatened the principal that if they were turned down, they would use their connections in the municipality and the media against the school. The principal did not give in to their demands.

In another event, a father from a high socio-economical class met with the kindergarten teacher and stated that his daughter would not pick up and tidy the toys in the kindergarten the way all the children do. He said he was willing to bring in a worker to pick up the toys for her. The kindergarten teacher had a long and harsh argument with the father, during which she explained the kindergarten's regulations and how tidying up the kindergarten contributes to the child's development. At the end of the argument, the father agreed with the teacher and gave up his demand. In another event, an Israeli-born mother was angry about the way the teacher was dealing with her son's behavioral issues. However, through the questions and complaints she made to the school principal regarding the homeroom teacher, it was clear that she was displeased with the teacher's origin - a newcomer from the former Soviet Union - and that she had doubts as to her professionalism. Eventually, the mother apologized to the teacher.

Finally, in the extreme events such as the ones described above, parents from dominant groups tried to influence the educational staff regarding the removal of children from the kindergarten or class who were from weaker social groups in Israeli society (children from the Arab sector, Ethiopian origin, special needs). The teachers had to arrange intense explanation activities in order to battle these occurrences.

The Parent's Gender - Differences in the Involvement of Fathers, and in the Communication Patterns of the Educational Staff (Mostly Women) with Fathers, in Comparison to Mothers

An in-depth analysis of the data revealed another axis, *the parent's gender*, as a significantly influencing factor, with regard to the level of the involvement of fathers in the educational framework, and to the communication patterns of the educational staff with fathers, in comparison to mothers. Generally speaking, the fathers' involvement in kindergarten life was significantly low, when compared to the mothers' level of involvement. However, it was possible to see differences in the fathers' levels of involvement in accordance with the various themes. Specifically, the fathers' levels of involvement were relatively high in connection to two themes: difficulties of teachers in informing parents of their children's problems and/or enlisting their cooperation (fathers were involved in 68% of the events); and essential disputes between teachers and parents regarding educational worldview and child-rearing techniques (fathers were involved in 62% of the events). However, the fathers' involvement was exceptionally low in the rest of the themes: difficulties in building trust and close relations with parents (fathers were involved in 31% of the events); teachers' difficulties in placing boundaries for parental behavior (fathers were involved in 27% of the events); coping with parental complaints about the ongoing functioning of the educational team (fathers were involved in 20% of the events); and teachers' indecisions regarding parental requests for aid and guidance (fathers were involved in 0% of the events). Table 3 shows the distribution of *father involvement* across the various themes, according to frequency.

Table 3. The distribution of *father involvement* across the various themes, according to frequency (N= 143)

Theme	Number of events involving fathers (initiation of the staff or the father)	Total events in this theme	Frequency in %
Teachers' difficulties in informing parents of their children's problems and/or enlisting their cooperation	24	35	68%
Essential disputes between parents and teachers, with regard to educational worldview and child-rearing techniques	13	21	62%
Difficulties in building trust and close relations with parents	10	32	31%
Teachers' difficulties in placing boundaries for parental behavior	8	30	27%
Coping with parental complaints about the ongoing functioning of the educational staff	4	20	20%
Teachers' indecisions regarding parental requests for aid and guidance	0	5	0%

These findings show that the educational staff (mostly women) tended to invite the fathers, and/or the fathers tended to increase their involvement in the educational framework, with regard to two specific connections: (1) when discovering that the child is dealing with a developmental issue which could indicate special needs or a significant behavioral issue; (2) when coming across significant differences in opinion and world perceptions between parents and the educational staff. However, with events that dealt with everyday life and ongoing communication, the staff tended not to invite the fathers, or the fathers themselves did not show much interest and involvement in the educational framework. Moreover, in all of the cases described, it was the mother who turned to the educational staff (mostly women) looking for help and guidance. The father was not the one asking for guidance in any of the events.

CONCLUSION

Far-reaching changes in the social reality of Western countries, including Israel, have reshaped parent-teacher interaction and affected it. These changes raise many questions and speculations about the nature and essence of the appropriate training for student teachers, on the subject of working with parents in the 21st century. Accordingly, our goal was to examine how interns of early childhood education interpreted communication with parents, and what difficulties and challenges preoccupied them. The responses to this question helped us re-examine the characteristics of parent-teacher communication in the present era, and reformulate the perceptions, skills and strategies relevant to present-day work with parents.

In this chapter, we will present the central difficulties and challenges that teachers encounter in communication with parents, as found in the present study. We will suggest two efficient strategies which complement each other, and which may help teachers cope with these difficulties and challenges. We will then discuss the implications of two central axes, which were seen to be highly influential in family-school relations: (1) cultural diversity and power relations between parents and teachers; (2) differences in the involvement of fathers and in the communication of the educational staff (consisting mainly of women) with fathers, in comparison to mothers. Finally, we will offer several basic principles, as the basis of a new model of family-school relations in a diverse and changing society. Teacher education institutions will be able to use this model in order to build updated and relevant courses that may provide the appropriate response to the challenges of teachers in their work with parents in the 21st century.

What Are the Central Challenges of Teachers in Their Relations with Parents in the Present Era, and What Strategies Are Required for Coping with Them?

Analysis of social episodes from work at kindergartens and elementary schools, as reported by interns of early childhood education, yielded six central themes, in the context of working relations between teachers and parents. These are: (1) teachers' difficulties in informing parents of their children's problems and/or enlisting their cooperation (35 out of 143 events, 24%); (2) difficulties in building trust and close relations with parents (22%); (3) teachers' difficulties in setting boundaries for parental behavior that is inappropriate, disrespectful or violent (21%); (4) essential disputes between parents and teachers, with regard to educational worldview and child-rearing techniques (15%); (5) coping with parental complaints about the ongoing functioning of the educational staff (14%); (6) teachers' indecisions regarding parental requests for aid and guidance (4%).

The findings of the current study show that interns of early childhood education interpreted communication with parents as a complex and multidimensional task, and formulated family-school relations in terms of difficulties, conflictual situations and challenges. Specifically, it can be seen that the main challenges, facing teachers in their work with parents in the present era, center around two complementary core dimensions: (1) building trust and cultivating close and caring relations with parents; (2) setting boundaries and limits for parental behavior, that is inappropriate, disrespectful or violent.

Walker & Dotger (2012) distinguished between two seemingly contradictory strategies of effective communication with parents: responsiveness and structuring. *Responsiveness* refers to the teacher's ability to respond to the unique needs of the parent, while *structuring* refers to the teacher's maintaining of professional standards and practices. Our findings indicate that teachers need to implement both of these strategies at the same time, in order to communicate effectively with parents in a diverse and changing society. Employing the responsiveness strategy will help them cope with the challenge of building trust and cultivating close and caring relations with parents, while the maintaining of professional standards and practices (the structuring strategy) will help them cope with the challenge of setting boundaries for parental behavior.

In fact, our findings correspond considerably to Plotnik's claim (2007) that teachers of the 21st century cannot limit the help that they render parents solely to the fields of disciplinary knowledge and child development. Rather, they must be able to listen to the *parental voice*, i.e., - to identify the parents' needs (often expressed through accusations, resistance and controversy, or conversely - through avoidance and evasion), and to respond accordingly. Hence, teacher education institutions should expand the knowledge and skills of student teachers; specifically, programs should include knowledge and tools from the fields of psychology and educational consultation, such as empathic listening, non-violent communication and advisory skills (Rosenberg & Chopra, 2015).

Cultural Sensitivity and Aspiring to Equal Power Relations as Key Factors in the Nurturing of Close and Caring Relations with Parents, in a Culturally Diverse and Changing Society

In-depth analysis has revealed that the axis of *cultural diversity and power relations between parents and teachers* is a powerful factor, as far as family-school relations are concerned, in the context of the present era. The axis of cultural diversity and power relations between parents and teachers was present at various levels and forms in all of the themes. Its presence was particularly prominent in the following themes: teachers' difficulties in informing parents of their children's problems and/or enlisting their cooperation (72%); essential disputes between teachers and parents, with regard to educational worldview and child-rearing techniques (67%); difficulties in building trust and close relations with parents (40%).

How were cultural diversity and power relations manifested in the various themes?

They were expressed in three major ways:

1) There was a significant representation of cultural diversity with regard to the families with whom the teachers came into contact;
2) Teachers demonstrated varying levels of cultural sensitivity and competence in their communication with parents;
3) Power relations between parents and teachers shaped the family-school relations and influenced them.

The significant influence of cultural diversity and power relations between parents and teachers on family-school communication indicates an urgent need to nurture cultural sensitivity and cultural competence among student teachers. This is vital for the building of meaningful and effective communication with parents in general, and with parents of non-dominant groups, in particular. These groups include parents of ethnic-cultural minorities; parents of a low social class; parents of non-traditional family structures; parents of special needs children. Our findings revealed an additional group which should be included in this category, and which is rarely mentioned in this context in the research literature and in the field of education. This group consists of parents coping with a challenging parenthood (where one of the parents is coping with a disease or any limitation; parents taking care of special-needs siblings, etc.).

Indeed, one may say that cultural sensitivity and the desire to establish equal power relations between parents of differing social classes and cultural groups constitute key factors for the building of trust and cultivating close and caring relations with parents, in the reality of a diverse and changing society. To a large extent, nurturing close and caring relations with parents in such a reality requires a shift from the approach of the *'child at the center'* to that of *'the child and his family at the center'*. This shift recognizes the fact that, similarly to the reality of special needs children, there are also *families with special needs*. This constitutes a revolution in the perception of family-school relations, reformulating the relational contract between parents and teachers. Until recently, the educational system was committed solely to the child, perceiving the parents as an entity committed to the child's needs, while ignoring the parents' needs, and often criticizing their parental functioning (Plotnik,

2007). However, in the culturally diverse reality of the 21st century, the educational system must be committed both to the child *and* to the parents. It must be able to respond to the unique needs of the parents, to contain them, and provide them with support and protectiveness, thereby strengthening their sense of parental efficacy.

These claims are corroborated by Shechter and Busherian (2015), who contend that the integration of special needs children into the mainstream educational system has invalidated the clear and rigid division between the education and welfare systems, whereby the teacher is committed to the child and welfare is committed to the family. How can teachers build trust and establish close and caring relations with parents of minority groups, including parents of special-needs children? The following are suggestions of efficient strategies, at the individual level as well as the systemic level (Ainscow, Booth & Dyson, 2006; Banks, 2010; Deverakonda, 2013; Greenbaum & Fried, 2011; Shechter and Busherian, 2015):

At the Level of the Individual

1) Teachers must suspend judgment and reflect on their own perceptions and attitudes, biases and stereotypes, with regard to families;
2) Allot time and resources in order to become acquainted with the family's characteristics, arrangements and needs, as well as coordinating expectations;
3) Show flexibility in time and place of meetings;
4) Use the services of an interpreter or community mediator, according to need;
5) Conduct home visits.

At the Level of the System

1) Teachers from minority groups should be included in the educational and management staff;

2) Celebrate events, holidays and parties with parents, adopting a multi-cultural view;
3) Include minority parents in decision-making forums of the educational institute, thereby developing authentic leadership;
4) Invite community organizations, community members or parents to serve as mediators between the school and families;
5) Expand the interventions given to parents within the school framework, to include interventions in which the parents are at the center;
6) In cases of parents of special needs children: appointing a case manager - a designated professional who will instruct the teachers and parents in the integration process, and serve as the school representative for communication with parents;
7) Increase school partnership with welfare and other aiding bodies of the community, to build responses appropriate to the parents.

Breaking Gender Stereotypes and Shifting the Fathers from the Periphery of the Educational Partnership to Its Center

An additional axis expressed in all of the themes and seen to be highly influential in teacher-parent relations deals with the parent's gender, as reflected in the differences in the involvement of fathers, and in the communication of the educational staff with fathers, in comparison to mothers. Generally, the level of involvement of fathers in kindergartens was significantly lower, compared to that of mothers. However, the level of father involvement varied according to the different themes. Specifically, father involvement was relatively high, in the context of two themes: difficulties of teachers in informing parents of their children's problems and/or enlisting their cooperation (fathers were involved in 68% of the events), and essential disputes between parents and teachers, with regard to educational worldview and child-rearing techniques (fathers were involved in 62% of the events). In all of the other themes, father involvement was low (fathers were involved in 31% of the events or less).

The findings of the present study show that the educational staff (consisting mainly of women) tended to invite fathers, and/or fathers tended to increase their involvement in the educational framework, in two specific contexts: (1) when a child was seen to be coping with a developmental problem that could indicate special needs, or behavioral problems affecting his academic progress or social adjustment in the kindergarten or at school (in these cases, both parents must confirm the suitable educational framework, or the required educational services or treatment program); (2) when there was a strong disagreement between the parents and the teachers, with regard to educational approaches and child-rearing practices. Conversely, in current communication and everyday events, the educational staff tended not to invite the fathers, or the fathers showed no interest and involvement in the kindergarten or school activities. Moreover, in all of the cases, it was the mother who turned to the educational staff (consisting mainly of women) to receive help and guidance in coping with the child. In no case did the father initiate a request for guidance.

This split shows that gender stereotypes still shape the perceptions of the educational staff (consisting mainly of women) and of the parents themselves, regarding the division of roles between mothers and fathers in childrearing and education. In other words, the mothers still see themselves - and are seen by the educational staff - as the chief caretaker of the children, so that the partnership and communication are conducted mostly with them. These findings are corroborated by Deverakonda's studies (2013), indicating that mothers receive more opportunities to get information about their children, while fathers are often ignored by the kindergarten teachers.

How can we break the barrier of stereotypical thinking among school and kindergarten teachers, regarding the division of roles between mothers and fathers? Teacher education institutions should raise student teachers' awareness of these gender stereotypes, and encourage them to involve fathers in the educational frameworks. Kahn (2006) offers 4 important complementary models, for the encouraging of father involvement in the educational framework:

1) *Inclusive Communication* - focuses on the importance of considering all aspects of communication to ensure that the setting's communication with mothers and fathers is gender neutral, and that fathers additionally know that they are included and invited to settings' activities;
2) The *Father Directed Activities model* - encourages settings to focus on developing and organizing activities that are adapted to the needs, skills and preferences of parents of both genders;
3) The *Gender Talk model* - focuses on the importance of settings introducing talk about gender and challenging gender roles;
4) The *Leaflet Only* model - gives general ideas and practical tips for involving fathers, inviting settings to address any aspect of fathers' involvement that they choose.

Conclusions and Recommendations - Towards a New Model of Family-School Relations in a Diverse and Changing Society

The findings of the present study emphasize the importance of teaching the subject of *school-family relations in a diverse and changing society*, at teacher education institutions. In fact, it is vital to define *working relations with parents* as *core practice* and the relevant skills required for it as *core competencies*, in all programs of teacher training for all ages and levels. The aim of the practice is to help student teachers understand the complexity of relations with parents in a heterogeneous and dynamic society, developing strategies of responsiveness together with the observance of professional standards and boundaries.

Mapping of the difficulties and challenges facing teachers in their interaction with parents, as reflected in the analysis of the social episodes presented by interns of early childhood education, points to several important principles that must be emphasized when teaching this subject. These principles may serve as the basis of a new model of family-school relations in a diverse and changing society. Although the findings of this study pertain to interns of early childhood education, we believe that these principles are relevant to the training of student teachers for all ages and levels.

The following are the principles that may serve as the basis of a new model of family-school relations in a diverse and changing society:

1) Communication between the school and the parents is the responsibility of the educational staff (and not the parents); it is a systemic, methodical and ongoing effort;

2) The main challenges facing teachers in their work with parents in the present era center around two complementary core dimensions: (1) building trust and cultivating close and caring relations with parents; (2) setting boundaries for parental behavior. Hence, teachers should implement two complementary strategies in order to communicate efficiently with parents: responding to the unique needs of parents, on the one hand, while building professional standards and maintaining boundaries, on the other hand.

3) In a reality of cultural diversity and rapid changes, the meaning and expressions of *cultivating close and caring relations with parents* have changed, requiring of the teachers new skills and strategies, such as cultural sensitivity and working skills with minority group parents.

4) Gender stereotypes affect the communication of the educational staff with fathers (compared to mothers). Hence, it is important to raise awareness of these stereotypes, shifting fathers from the periphery of the educational partnership to the center (together with the mothers), and to encourage their involvement in various ways.

5) To conclude, significant changes in the social reality reshape parent-teacher relations and require a shift from the approach of *'the child at the center'* to the approach of *'the child and his family at the center'*. Accordingly, the relational contract between parents and teachers should be reformulated so that the educational system is committed to the child *and* to the parents, while acknowledging minority families as *families coping with special needs.*

Undoubtedly, this new model of family-school relations should be backed up and supported by the Ministry of Education. It is necessary that the Ministry of Education delineate a clear policy regarding all aspects of parent-teacher relations in a diverse and changing reality, including protocols that will detail working modes with families of various cultural groups. A clear policy of the Ministry of Education, together with protocols, will obligate school and kindergarten teachers to work according to clear guidelines and professional standards, rather than leaving each case to the discretion of the educational staff. Moreover, the policy and protocols will serve as an anchor, compass and guide for the school and kindergarten teachers in their dilemmas and debates.

We hope that the heads of teacher education institutions will adopt the conclusions and recommendations of this study, and that they will include the subject of working with parents in a diverse and changing society as a core subject in their teacher education programs, for all ages and levels. Lecturers in teacher education colleges and pedagogic instructors may use the guiding principles of the new model, as offered in this chapter, to build updated courses providing relevant responses to the challenges of teachers working with parents in the 21st century. Policymakers and education professionals may be assisted by the principles of this model in turning kindergartens and schools into an inclusive educational arena, and thereby leading a significant change in the relations with parents in general, and with parents of non-dominant groups, in particular.

Recommendations for New Research Directions

The research population sample consisted of interns of early childhood education. Although one may draw conclusions from this sample pertaining to the general body of education professionals, it would be interesting to conduct an in-depth study of the specific issues raised by student teachers working with higher ages (elementary school, high school), student teachers of special education, or those specializing in additional roles such as educational counselling, instruction, management, etc.

One of the study's most interesting findings focused on the differences of involvement of fathers, and the communication of the educational staff (consisting mainly of women) with fathers, in comparison to mothers. The kindergarten teachers did not involve fathers, nor did the fathers become involved in the kindergartens, unless the issue arose of a significant developmental problem regarding their child, or basic controversies with the educational staff. In this context, it would be interesting to examine whether father involvement increases as the ages rise in the educational system, and how communication of the educational staff with fathers is characterized at the higher ages.

In addition, the impact of technological changes on parent-teacher relations did not emerge in the events described by interns of early childhood education as a significant source of tension and conflicts between kindergarten teachers and parents. One explanation may be that since one is speaking of early childhood, the kindergarten teachers had internalized the 'norm of accessibility' and tried to be highly accessible to parents, so that there were no conflicts on this account. It would be interesting to examine to what extent technological changes and the 'norm of accessibility' shape parent-teacher relations when the children in question are older (elementary school, high school), and what the challenges are in this respect.

Finally, previous studies (Epstein & Sanders, 2006; Meehan &Meehan, 2018) have doubted the efficiency of traditional modes of instruction (lectures, reading articles), in promoting meaningful learning. Hence, it would be important to explore the efficiency of more advanced pedagogies (simulations, case study, etc.) in constructing a deep understanding of the complexity of home-school communication, and in developing relevant and effective skills and strategies that would meet teachers' challenges with regard to working with parents, in a diverse and changing society.

REFERENCES

Addi-Raccah, A., & Ainhoren, R. (2009). School governance and teachers' attitudes to parents' involvement in schools. *Teaching and Teacher Education, 25,* 805-813.

Addi-Raccah, A., & Arviv-Elyashiv, R. (2008). Parent empowerment and teacher professionalism: Teachers' perspective. *Urban Education, 43,* 394-415.

Ainscow, M., Booth, T., & Dyson, A. (2006). *Improving Schools, Developing Inclusion.* London: Routledge, https://doi.org/10.4324/9780203967157.

Alpert, B. (2010). Combining quantitative data analysis in qualitative research. In L. Kacen & M. Krumer-Nevo (Eds.), *Data analysis in qualitative research* (pp.333-356). Be'er-Sheva: Ben-Gurion University Publications. [Hebrew].

Auerbach, S. (2012). Conceptualizing leadership for authentic partnerships: A continuum to inspire practice. In S. Auerbach (Ed.), *School leadership for authentic family and community partnerships* (pp. 29–51). New York, NY: Routledge.

Ayalon, Y. & Sabar Ben-Yehoshua, N. (2010). The process of content analysis in grounded theory. In L. Kacen & M. Krumer-Nevo (Eds.), *Data analysis in qualitative research* (pp.359-382). Be'er-Sheva: Ben-Gurion University Publications. [Hebrew].

Banks, J.A. (2010). Multicultural education: Characteristics and goals. In: J. A. Banks & C. A. McGee Banks (Eds.) *Multicultural education: Issues and perspectives* (pp. 2- 23). U.S.A: John Wiley & Sons.

Baquedano-López, P., Alexander, R. A., & Hernandez, S. J. (2013). Equity issues in parental and community involvement in schools: What teacher educators need to know. *Review of Research in Education, 37(1),* 149-182.

Bar-Yosef, R. W. (2001). Children of two cultures: Immigrant children from Ethiopia in Israel. *Journal of Comparative Family Studies,* 231-246.

Bicer A., Capraro M. & Capraro, R. (2013). The effects of parent's SES and education level on students' mathematics achievement: Examining the mediation effects of parental expectations and parental communication, *The Online Journal of New Horizons in Education 3 (4)*, 89-97.

Bronfenbrenner, U. (1986). Ecology of the family as a context for human development: Research perspectives. *Developmental Psychology, 22*, 723-742.

Christenson, S. L. (2004). The family-school partnership: An opportunity to promote the learning competence of all students. *School Psychology Review, 33*(1), 83-104.

Corbin, J. & Strauss, A. (2008). *Basics of qualitative research: Techniques and procedures for developing grounded theory (3rd edition)*. Los Angeles, CA: Sage.

Cousins, L. & Mickelson, R. (2011). Making success in education: What Black parents believe about participation in their children's education. *Current Issues in Education, 14 (3)*, 1-15.

Creswell, W.J. (1998). *Qualitative inquiry and research design: Choosing among five traditions*. Thousand Oaks, CA: Sage Publications.

Cross, T., Bazron, B., Dennis, K., & Isaacs, M. (1989). *Towards a culturally competent system of care*, Vol. 1. Washington, DC: Georgetown.

Devarakonda, C. (2013). *Diversity and inclusion in early childhood: An introduction*. London: Sage.

Epstein, J. (1992). School and family partnerships. In M. Aiken (Ed.). *Encyclopedia of educational research, 6th edition*. New York: MacMillan. 1139-1151.

Epstein, J. (2002). *School, family and community partnerships: Your handbook for action (2nd edition)*. Thousand Oaks, CA.: Corwin.

Epstein, J. L. (2011). *School, family, and community partnerships: Preparing educators and improving schools*. Boulder, CO: Westview.

Epstein, J. L. (2018). School, family, and community partnerships in teachers' professional work. *Journal of Education for Teaching, 44*(3), 397-406. doi: 10.1080/02607476.2018.1465669.

Epstein, J. L., & Sanders, M. G. (2006). Preparing educators for school-family–community partnerships: Results of a national survey of colleges and universities. *Peabody Journal of Education, 81(2)*, 81–120.

Fan, X., & M. Chen. (2001). Parental Involvement in Students' Academic Achievement: A Meta-analysis. *Educational Psychology Review, 13*, 1-22.

Friedman, Y. (2010). *School-parents' relationships in Israel*. The Initiative for Applied Education Research: Background information. http://education.academy.ac.il. [Hebrew].

Goodcar, O. (2009). *'New families' from a psychological perspective- part A*. [Hebrew]. Retrieved from: https://www.hebpsy.net/articlesasp?id=2101.

Green, C. L., Walker, J. M. T., Hoover-Dempsey, K. V., & Sandler, H. M. (2007). Parents' motivations for involvement in children's education: An empirical test of a theoretical model of parental involvement. *Journal of Educational Psychology, 99*(3), 532–544. doi:10.1037/0022-0663.99.3.532.

Greenbaum, C., & Fried, D. (Eds.) (2011). *Relations between the Family and the Early Childhood Education System (Preschool to Grade 3): Status Report and Recommendations of the Committee for the Study of the Relations between the Family and the Early Childhood Education System (Preschool to Grade 3) and their Association with the Child's Development and Achievement in the Education System*. Israel Academy of Sciences and Humanities.

Henderson, A. T., & Mapp, K. L. (2002). *A new wave of evidence: The impact of school, family, and community connections on student achievement*. Austin, TX: SEDL.

Hill, N. E. (2011). Undermining partnerships between African-American families and schools: Legacies of discrimination and inequalities. In N. E. Hill, T. L. Mann, & H. E., Fitzgerald (Eds.), *African American Children's Mental Health: Development and Context, Vol. 1* (pp. 199-230). Santa Barbara, CA: Praeger.

Ho, L., Hung, C. & Chen, H. (2013). Using theoretical models to examine the acceptance behavior of mobile phone messaging to enhance parent teacher interactions. *Computers & Education*, 61, 105-114.

Hughes, J., & Kwok, O. (2007). Influence of student–teacher and parent–teacher relationships on lower achieving readers' engagement and achievement in the primary grades. *Journal of Educational Psychology, 99(1)*, 39-51.

Kahn, T. (2006). *Involving fathers in early year's settings: Evaluating four models for effective practice development.* London: Pre-School Learning Alliance.

Lake, J. F., & Billingsley, B. S. (2000). An analysis of factors that contribute to parent–school conflict in special education. *Remedial and Special Education, 21*(4), 240–251.

Lang, S., Mouzourou, C., Jeon, L., Buettner, C., & Hur, E. (2017). Preschool teachers' professional training, observational feedback, child-centered beliefs and motivation: Direct and indirect associations with social and emotional responsiveness. *Child and Youth Care Forum, 46* (1), 69-90. doi:10.1007/s10566-016-9369-7.

Lang, S. N., Tolbert, A. R., Schoppe-Sullivan, S. J., & Bonomi, A. E. (2016). A cocaring framework for infants and toddlers: Applying a model of coparenting to parent–teacher relationships. *Early Childhood Research Quarterly, 34*, 40-52. doi: 10.1016/j.ecresq.2015.08.004.

Lasater, K. (2016). Parent-teacher conflict related to student abilities: The impact on students and the family-school partnership. *School Community Journal, 26*(2), 237-262.

Lee, J. S., & Bowen, N. K. (2006). Parent involvement, cultural capital, and the achievement gap among elementary school children. *American Educational Research Journal, 43*(2), 193-218.

Mapp, K. L. (2003). Having their say: Parents describe why and how they are engaged in their children's learning. *School Community Journal, 13*, 35-64.

Mapp, K. L., & Hong, S. (2010). Debunking the myth of the hard-to-reach parent. In S. L. Christenson & A. L. Reschly (Eds.), *Handbook of school-family partnerships,* (pp. 345-361). New York: Routledge.

McWayne, C., Hampton, V., Fantuzzo, J., Cohen, H. L., & Sekino, Y. (2004). A multivariate examination of parent involvement and the social and academic competencies of urban kindergarten children. *Psychology in the Schools, 41*(3), 363-377. doi: 10.1002/pits.10163.

Meehan, C., & Meehan, P. J. (2018) Trainee teachers' perceptions about parent partnerships: Are parents partners? *Early Child Development and Care, 188(12),* 1750-1763. doi: 10.1080/03004430.2017.1286334.

Neal, R. B. (2012). Checking in or checking out? Investigating the parent involvement reactive hypothesis. *The Journal of Educational Research, 105,* 79-89.

Noy, B. (1999). School, home and what is between them. In A. Paldi (Ed.), *The Israeli Educational System Jubilee, Vol. 2.* Ministry of Education and Culture. [Hebrew].

Plotnick, R. (2007). 'Parents' voice'- Parenting as a developmental-emotional process. In E. Cohen (Ed.), *The experience of parenting: Relations, coping and development* (pp. 333-362). Jerusalem: Ach Ltd. and the School of Education of the Hebrew University. [Hebrew].

Rattenborg, K., MacPhee, D., Kleisner Walker, A., & Miller-Heyl, J. (2018). Pathways to parental engagement: Contributions of parents, teachers, and schools in cultural context. *Early Education and Development.* doi: 10.1080/10409289.2018.1526577.

Robinson, K., & Harris, A. L. (2014). *The broken compass: Parental involvement with children's education.* Cambridge, MA: Harvard Education Press.

Roer-Strier, D. (2010). *Family- educational framework relations from a multicultural view.* The Initiative for Applied Education Research: Background information. http://education.academy.ac.il. [Hebrew].

Rosenberg, M., & Chopra, D. (2015). *Nonviolent communication: A language of life-changing tools for healthy relationships.* Puddledancer Press.

Shartrand, A. M., Weiss, H. B., Kreider, H. M., & Lopez, M. E. (1997). *New skills for new schools: Preparing teachers in family involvement.* Cambridge, MA: Harvard Family Research Project.

Schechtman, Z., & Busharian, O. (Eds.) (2015). *Parent-Teacher Relations in Secondary Education*. Jerusalem: The Initiative for Applied Education Research, Israel Academy of Sciences and Humanities. [Hebrew].

Shimoni, R., & Baxter, J. M. (1996). *Working with families: Perspectives for early childhood professionals*. Don Mills, Ont.: Addison-Wesley Publishers Limited.

Shkedi, A. (2003).*Words of meaning: Qualitative research- Theory and practice*. Tel-Aviv: Ramot. (pp. 23-36). [Hebrew].

Smith, J., Stern, K., & Shatrova, Z. (2008). Factors inhibiting Hispanic parents' school involvement. *Rural Educator, 29 (2)*, 8-13.

Tashakkori, A., & Teddlie, C. (2003). *Handbook of mixed methods in social behavioral research.* Sage Publications.

Timor, T. (2013). The concept of "the different other" in the mirror of inclusion in Israeli society and education: Is it a "significant other"? *Dvarim - Academic Journal,* Oranim College. [Hebrew].

Walker, J. M., & Dotger, B. H. (2012). Because wisdom can't be told: Using comparison of simulated parent–teacher conferences to assess teacher candidates' readiness for family-school partnership. *Journal of Teacher Education, 63*(1), 62-75.

Wanat, C. L. (2010). Challenges balancing collaboration and independence in home-school relationships: Analysis of parents' perceptions in one district. *School Community Journal, 20*(1), 159- 186. Retrieved from http://www.schoolcommunitynetwork.org/SCJ.aspx.

Wigle, S. E., & Wilcox, D. (1996). Inclusion: Criteria for the preparation of education personnel. *Remedial and Special Education, 17*, 323-328.

In: Teacher Training
Editor: Paula E. McDermott

ISBN: 978-1-53615-633-1
© 2019 Nova Science Publishers, Inc.

Chapter 6

"WALKING ON EGGSHELLS" – PATTERNS OF CHANGE AND DEVELOPMENT IN STUDENT TEACHERS' PERCEPTIONS OF PARENT-TEACHER RELATIONSHIPS IN THE FRAMEWORK OF A 'WORKING WITH PARENTS' COURSE

Iris Levy, Yael Shlesinger, Alona Peleg,
Einat Sequerra Ater, Naomi Perchik, Orly Licht Weinish,
Pninat Tal and Clodie Tal
Levinsky College of Education, Tel Aviv, Israel

ABSTRACT

The importance of parent-teacher relationship has been widely recognized by parents, teachers, early childhood specialists, and special education professionals. It is also acknowledged that this relationship can be perceived as challenging by both sides (Addi-Raccah, 2008; Friedman,

2010; Friedman & Fisher, 2009). Research has shown that parents' involvement in school benefits not only the child, but also the parents and teachers. Research further indicates that student teachers express concerns about parents' involvement and their ability to form a positive and effective partnership with them. Therefore, student teachers must continue to develop and expand their skills in order to maximize effective communication with parents.

This study provides a careful investigation into the effects of a course on the parent-teacher relationship on student teachers' and interns' perceptions.

The rationale for this study was derived out of the wish to prepare student teachers to cope effectively with the complex relationship with parents. The general approach, which the rationale of this study is based on, sees parents as partners and emphasizes fostering qualifications and strategies for working with parents during training. Psychological, sociological, and organizational perspectives were integrated throughout the course when discussing the teacher's role.

INTRODUCTION

This chapter presents a study that aimed to examine the process of change in the perceptions of student teachers studying in an early childhood education program regarding the parent-teacher relationship, and the trend of their changing perceptions following a "Working with Parents" course. This course was given in Levinsky College of Education's early childhood education program for student teachers in their first or second year of the academic conversion program (student teachers who own a BA in a different area and attend a two year program to receive a BA in education), and to fourth year student teachers. The study examined student teachers' and interns' perceptions at the beginning (Time 1) and end (Time 2) of the course, via a textual and graphic description, which reveals their professional perceptions, thoughts, and emotions on this topic. The importance of this study stems from its contribution to fostering a more inclusive and professional teacher, who acts as a leader with both parents and children, and who is able to develop an effective partnership with parents.

In this section we review the theoretical background that serves as the basis for the study. The first section explains the historical development of the relationship between parents and the education system in Israel. The second section focuses on the complexity of the partnership between parents and teachers and the difficulties that stem from this complexity. In the third section, we examine the training process and the way it prepares them to manage professional interpersonal communication, particularly with parents. In the fourth section, we explore the processes that lead to the integration of perceptions among student teachers on the one hand, and the causes that lead to a change in the perceptions on the other hand. This is with the purpose of understanding the change processes that the student teachers undergo from the beginning of the course until the end. In the last section, we discuss the meaning of the metaphor and its uniqueness as a tool for reflection and clarification of perception among education students in relation to the change that they underwent during the "Working with Parents" course.

HISTORICAL RELATIONSHIP BETWEEN PARENTS AND THE EDUCATION SYSTEM IN ISRAEL

The relationship between parents and the education system has undergone a gradual process of increasing involvement. In the 1990's the heads of the municipal systems understood the electoral strength of parents' involvement in educational processes and drafted parents as a resource to increase their strength. In this way, they also began looking for ways to answer parent's unique needs. This trend provided parents with influential ability and greater involvement in their children's education. At the same time, the last years of the 20th century were characterized by ambiguity and confusion in relation to the definition of involvement on both sides, which led to friction between them (Friedman, 1990).

The early years of the 21st century were characterized by a strengthening of the customer-service approach following the influence of concepts from the world of management on the educational discourse. This process weakened the teachers' status, negatively influenced their image in the eyes of parents and their children, and encouraged the perception of educators who work in a technical manner (Hursh, 2007). The approach of the customer (parent) always being right and the teacher as the service provider, created an expectation that teachers will focus on the fact that the customer (parent) should always be satisfied and they should not argue with the parent regarding educational issues, even at the expense of the child's needs (Tal & Bar, 2010).

The 2000's have been characterized by parental pressure for measurable achievements at any price, even while damaging teaching methods and reducing deep learning that emphasizes internalization and considerations of heterogeneity. This process is particularly problematic given that in the 1990's the heterogeneity of the student population in Israel increased significantly due to the immigration from the USSR and Ethiopia (Bar Shalom, 2004).

PARTNERSHIP AS PART OF CLASSROOM MANAGEMENT AND ITS COMPLEXITY

Establishing good relationships and continuous communication between educators and their families, which has been central to the discourse in the United States at the beginning of the 21st century, has also influenced the educational discourse in Israel. The purpose of this trend was the promotion and advancement of children's learning abilities (Henderson, Mapp, Johnson, & Davies, 2007). In 2003, the U.S. decided to institute equality for all in teaching in the decision titled, "No Child Left Behind" (U.S. Department of Education, 2006). In this document, parents are perceived as full partners in the learning process that will lead their children to success.

This approach is also apparent in the research literature of this period, which emphasized the necessary and essential contribution of those involved in the parent-educator-child triangle in the promotion of the child's learning process (Hiatt-Michael, 2010; Voorhis, 2011). As part of the basis for the connection between the preschool teacher and the parent body, (Tal and Bar,2010) recommend establishing the process of selecting the parent committee and ensuring representation for all the preschoolers, arranging the payments for projects in an equal manner, and formulating principles that guarantee equal opportunities for all groups and segments of the population.

Part of the difficulty in forming trust and cooperation between parents and teachers stems from the meaningful differences between the educational environment and the home environment, and the differences between the perceptions of those in responsibility in each environment and their primary source of responsibility. A parent's primary responsibility is her particular child's welfare and her desire that all of the child's needs will be met. In contrast, the educator's primary responsibility is to create a learning environment that will allow all the children in the preschool to operate with emotional and physical freedom and safety, and with a sense of belonging (Plotnik, 2009).

The meeting between these various points of responsibility occurs many times when the parents and the preschool teacher discuss educational issues that arise from the child's behavior. Although many parents aim to serve as agents of change for their child, they sometimes reveal vulnerability when examining aspects relating to their parenting. Often, discussing education difficulties between the parents and teacher is viewed as hinting at parents' failures. The moral, social, and emotional implications of these difficulties raise parents' feelings of guilt, anxiety, and defensive reactions of anger and rejection (Cohen, 2006).

Noy (2014) claims that the preschool softens the transition from the home to the school, and suggests a number of ways to promote and strengthen the relations between the preschool teacher and parents: strengthen the respectful relation to the parent as a central figure in the child's life; formal meetings with the parents alongside the spontaneous ones, inviting the parents to the preschool, home visits, and celebrations where the parents are partners; and, exposing parents to the preschool curriculum and its content to include the parents in the preschools' learning goals.

Cooperation between the sides can help create an optimal environment in the preschool, a reduction of incidents of extremism and violence, and a deeper understanding of the students and their various life contexts. In situations where cooperation does not exist, it can create a "disconnect," where information does not pass between the primary partners in the child's life. These situations can undermine the authority of both sides and negatively impact upon the educational process (Omer, 2002).

Greenbaum and Fried (2011) also wrote recommendations that relate to the parent-teacher relationship. The main recommendation is to recognize the importance of the relationship and the parents' right to be involved in what happens to their child. This can be accomplished in a number of ways: a clear definition by the Ministry of Education of the parents' roles and the areas of their authority, training education staff and enabling the acquisition of tools for managing the parent-teacher relationship, acquisition of a work model for cooperation between the sides, adjusting expectations and defining formal times for communication with parents, creating a support system for parents and education staff, and emphasizing the unique characteristics of families from other cultures and with other needs. All of these can be accomplished through legislation, the establishment of a committee for relations between the education system and the family, and the writing of an official document that obligates the parties.

One of the factors that shapes preschool teachers' perceptions towards parents is the teacher-training process. It is therefore important to examine this process in the context of the relations with parents.

Student Teacher Training

The training for becoming a teacher is a challenging and lengthy process, during which students build their educational belief system and the pedagogical foundations upon which they will base their teaching methods (Borg, 1998). These are formed on the basis of meaningful fieldwork encounters (Denzin, 1999). Establishing student teacher perception is considered an important goal during training, and it includes constant interaction between three aspects -- personal, professional, and ecological (Vonk, 1993). Teaching focuses on the learner, his self-realization, development of a connection with his inherent potential, and the assumption of responsibility for learning. These take root in shaping one's image as a teacher (Lam, 1973; Rogers, 1969).

Dvir and Shatz Oppenheimer (2011) emphasize that a teacher's first year is considered a unique stage that stands between the training and the internship, where the teacher designs her identity and professionalism, examines the knowledge that was acquired during training, and tests it with her functioning in the educational and classroom framework. The teacher seeks ways to become part of the professional community and develops relationships with colleagues, students, parents, and others. According to the authors, this stage is characterized by hiding the distress sometimes experienced by student-teachers trying to meet the demands of the system, which results in deep emotional difficulties, and intense feelings of helplessness, loneliness, alienation, insecurity, and ambiguity, which can lead them to feelings of stagnation.

At the training stage, student teachers have trouble in actively practicing the implementation of the parent-teacher relationship, as this relationship is under the authority and responsibility of the preschool teacher, who often does not allow the student teacher to practice this aspect. This is because of the possible implications that may result from the student teacher's lack of success and the effect this may have on the relationship with parents. Moreover, student teachers are exposed to negative messages about parental involvement, in the form of "watch out for them," (Dayan, 2004). Consequently, at the second stage, the stage of entry into teaching, interns initially experience the complexity of the relationship with parents. This difficulty led the American National Association for the Education of Young Children (NAEYC) to publish a document in 2003 that includes five principles for training early childhood professionals (Hyson, 2003). The second principle on this list relates to creating connections with families. That is, deeper training for education students should be emphasized in managing their relations with parents.

Student teachers report not having enough preparation and training in the area of parent-teacher relationships (McBride, 2003). According to Brouwer and Korthagen (2005), student teachers are more interested in acquiring concrete skills and techniques and they value rules, directions, and explicit instructions (Heath 1998; Jensen et al. 1999).

Greenbaum and Fried (2011) reviewed the courses for student teachers that relate to parent-teacher relations and that are given in schools of education in Israel and the United States. They note that the existing courses for early education in Israel emphasize the acquisition of effective communication strategies with parents as a central aim alongside the complexity of the preschool teacher's place vis-à-vis the parents. The courses focus on contending with difficulties that arise from the relations and not in preventing them. Most of these courses in Israel are given in the early education or special education programs and most are given in education colleges and not universities. In addition, most of these are accompanied by practical work. The authors recommend relating to training of student teachers and connecting with parents from an ecological viewpoint, similar to models that exist in the U.S., as well as viewing the population of children and their families through a multicultural lens, understanding the individual (parent and child), and acquiring skills and strategies to create optimal relations with families and their surrounding communities.

In the current study, we use metaphors to highlight the change in student teachers' perceptions of parents. As such, we review metaphors and their meaning in research regarding educators' meaningful perceptions of their experiences.

The Metaphor and Its Significance

Elbow (1986) claims that, "every metaphor casts a different shadow on the illuminated object that we wouldn't have seen had we not illuminated it from different angles" (p. 7). Gardner (1995) notes that we meet metaphors in conversation with children, as well as at the peak of a creation, presentation of a scientific theory, or description of a mood. Zur, Gordon, Eisenberg, and Guttweiser (2005) define metaphor as a connection between two areas. They argue that it is a complicated framework from different parts. Each of these definitions noed relates to metaphors as a reflective tool that connects between different areas, which add and enhance one's examination of one's self, beliefs, and perceptions, and provides a new perspective. Kupferberg (2016) emphasizes that the metaphor is a cognitive structure stored in the brain, which is influenced by one's physical experiences and socio-cultural and historical context. Researching the metaphor requires identifying original elements from the text being studied.

Metaphors can be visual or verbal. The use of metaphors as an artistic, allegorical, metaphorical representation can reliably convey the essence of complex and layered ideas (Rosen Davidi, 2016). A metaphor connects between two phrases and enlarges the connotative and associative loads that are carried forward. Relations are formed between the two that expand their meaning and deepen and enhance them. Additionally, metaphors are a living, dynamic picture that make an abstract picture more precise. Listening to metaphors influences our thoughts and can inspire new classification, awaken life and deep thought (Rosen, 2016). Lakoff and Johnson (1980) point out that new metaphors have the strength to construct a new reality and Gibbs (1994) emphasizes that metaphors are a strong and rich tool that express a person's emotional perspectives.

Zur and colleagues (2005) believe that the use of metaphors can give those who teach teachers, educators, and student-teachers an interesting and fertile tool, with which it is possible to think about the personal world that they bring to work. They can use metaphors to describe in a rich and dynamic way their personal-practical knowledge in the framework of a professional, cooperative, open, and non-judgmental discourse. Kupferberg and Gilat (2002) note that the discourse reveals hidden aspects and serves as a source for constructing new knowledge. Zur et al. (2005) claim that results of studies) show that metaphors are a strong tool that teachers can use to non-verbally express the full meaning of their complex and multi-faceted work. The figurative language exists in the reflective discourse of teachers and others in a spontaneous manner and without guidance, and it clarifies hidden aspects of their thinking (Kupferberg, 2016).

In sum, the use of metaphors in this study will enhance the way we look at education students' feelings regarding their relations with parent, and enable additional was of expressing this. In light of ever-increasing parental involvement in the education system, and the limited experience that education students have with direct communication with parents, there is a need to study the impact of courses that address these areas. This study asks whether and how the course "Working with Parents" influences the shaping of the students' perceptions of the parent-teacher relationship. The study aims to examine whether training in parent teacher communication fosters understanding in this field and provides students with practical tools that increase their sense of ability in this area.

METHODOLOGY

Participants

The study was conducted during the semester course titled "Working with Parents," which is designated for students studying early education. The course is designed to provide theoretical knowledge and practical tools for managing communication that fosters trust and cooperation with parents. Data was collected during two courses that were administered by the chapter's authors. In 2013, 33 students studying education in the academic conversion program at Levinsky College of Education participated in the course. This is a two-year program that combines theoretical studies with practical teaching experience. All of the participants are in the training stage, designed to help beginning teachers develop a professional identity (Feiman-Nemser, 2001; Vonk, 1993). They do not yet work as preschool teachers in the education system, and only a small percentage of the students are in the qualification stage, where they develop an appropriate repertoire of teaching behaviors and beginning teaching skills and work as regular preschool teachers in the education system (Feiman-Nemser, 2001; Vonk, 1993). Two of the student teachers did not provide data in the beginning (Time 1) or end (Time 2) of the course and were therefore not included in the data analysis.

In 2016, 27 students participated in the course. These students are in their internship year, and most actively teach preschool at the pre-service stage. They are at the pre-professional stage, which is designed for developing initial teaching skills (Feiman-Nemser, 2001; Vonk, 1993). Of these students, 18 (67%) participated in the study by completing tasks at Times 1 and 2, the others were missing one time point or did not submit the assignment.

In total, 49 students successfully completed the assignments at both time points. This data and its analysis are presented herein.

Course Structure

The "Working with Parents" course is a single-semester course and includes a theoretical section that focuses on the following: deep understanding of the family system; the nature of parents' roles, the preschool staff's roles and the relationship between them; and, ways to effectively work with parents. Teaching methods include frontal lectures, discussions, and analysis of events. The assignments include reading and analysis of articles, presentations, and a final written assignment.

Procedure

At the beginning (Time 1) and end (Time 2) of the course, the student teachers received the following instructions: "Draw your perception of the parent-teacher relationship, and explain your choice and perception of these relations." At Time 2, the students received their Time 1 responses for comparison purposes. Their drawings and textual explanations were collected and analyzed in order to evaluate the change process from the beginning (Time 1) to the end (Time 2) of the course.

Data Analysis

The researchers organized the data into categories that arose from the textual and graphic assignments. This was done using a multi-step inductive process to identify themes and categories as they arose from the data. This research approach is based on grounded theory, which itself is based on content analysis in stages (Bryant & Charmaz, 2007; Corbin & Strauss, 1984). First, the researchers jointly conducted an open content analysis based on the textual and graphic data, which were deciphered, and categories and themes emerged (Lieblich, Tuval Mashiach, & Zilber, 2010). Thereafter, the researchers identified patterns of change from time 1 to time 2 based on content analysis.

FINDINGS

Analysis of the findings that arose from the study yielded six primary patterns of change between Time 1 and Time 2. Table 1 presents the division of the patterns in descending order according to the number of participants in each pattern.

Table 1. Patterns of Change from Time 1 to Time 2 (N = 49)

Pattern of Change	Number of Participants	Frequency in %
From cooperation to complexity	16	32.7
From suspicion to trust	10	20.5
From distance to closeness	8	16.3
From superiority and compartmentalization to equality and cooperation	6	12.2
No change	6	12.2
From optimism to pessimism	3	6.1
Total	49	100

From Cooperation to Complexity (n = 16)

At Time 1, 32.7% of the student teachers expressed an approach of trust and cooperation, without relating to concerns of difficulties along the way. The visual images included arrows, overlapping circles, hands, and more. In contrast, at Time 2 at the end of the course, these students related to the complexity in the preschool teacher's status, who wants to promote cooperation and reciprocity and to be empathetic to parents' emotions, but without blurring the boundaries between the teacher's position and the parents' position. Table 2 presents examples of students' views at Time 1 and Time 2 (beginning and end of course, respectively), which illustrate their change in perception from cooperation to complexity.

Table 2. From Cooperation to Complexity: Examples of Students' Views

	Time 1	Time 2
Sylvia	Preschool teachers and parents have the joint purpose of promoting the child's success according to his abilities (drew aims and arrows).	I would add a hand shaking a hand to the picture of the target with the purpose. The importance of reciprocity, listening to each other while the teacher has an important task of listening empathically (Drew crossed hands)
Maya	I'm a partner. As much as that sounds banal, for the child's benefit the parents and the teacher have to be united, coordinated (Drew hands barely touching each other)	The hand is always on the pulse. I would emphasize that we are here together concerned with out growth. We are all in the same boat and that is how we will win (hands coming out from the frame of a window and meeting to shake).
Dina	A preschool teacher, who shares and reflects the child's performance to his parents, can foster empowerment, cooperation, and involvement in the parents. She creates a positive relationship between all those involved, and empowers the child's development. (Drew a large and a small heart connected by a curled line)	There are parents with whom the connection is positive smooth. There are others, who may come with different ideas or experiences, and the connection with them is more complicated with more ups and downs, it depends on the situation. (Drew a large heart with 3 coils coming of it, one is connected to the smaller heart)
Mai	There is a give-and-take relationship here for one main reason – the child. (Drew a parent and teacher with the child in the center	I learned that there are different kinds of parents and that directly impacts the relations between the parents and the teacher. (Drew parent, teacher with the child at the center, more detailed)

For example, Ava uses the two graphical images with arrows to describe the reciprocity in the relationship. At the beginning of the course, Ava sees the reciprocity and the joint purpose of the two sides: "The parent-teacher relationships is comprised of a connection that is based on trust and joint purpose for the child's benefit, by thinking about the child's needs, abilities, and those of the environment" (see Figure 1). At the end of the course Ava related to understanding the complexity of the relations, and the need to adapt them to the characters in the relationship:

Figure 1. Ava, Time1.

Figure 2. Ava, Time 2.

"The difference between the two perspectives is expressed primarily in the method of integrating between these relations and not in the belief itself. Compared to my ideas in the past, today I understand that we are not talking about a triangle relationship, but relationships that are integrated one with another and intertwined in all their parts and goals, when the child is the center of these relations"(see Figure 2).

In other words, Ava notes the need to navigate the relations and crack their complexity in order to support the child.

From Suspicion to Trust (n = 10)

About 20.5% of the student teachers demonstrated a pattern of change in their attitudes from suspicion to cooperation between Times 1 and 2. At Time 1, the emphasis was on the experience of threat, examination, and criticism, as well as suspicion and caution. In relating to this pattern, at Time 1, the students describe feelings of difficulty approaching parents, despite wanting to, because of the suspicion that coming closer to the parents will make it harder to set clear boundaries, and the concern that situations of closeness will blur the boundaries and will be used against them in various ways (see Table 3). The students employ the metaphor of eyes, walking on eggs, and other symbols to represent this feeling. In contrast, at Time 2, they talk about recognizing the importance of cooperation with parents, while emphasizing the child's benefit, and using the metaphors of hands, arrows (as symbols for direction), circles, and more.

At Time 1, Sharon described an eye that is proportionally much larger than usual. Sharon's description of the illustration can be interpreted in line with the iconographic explanation of an eye as representing the eye of the Egyptian god Ra, to whom the ability of control is attributed. In addition, the god-eye represents the all-seeing god, who watches and examines each person for good and for bad (Potts, 1982), as can be seen from Sharon's description of the parents' eyes as examining and evaluating the teacher's professionalism.

This description teaches about her suspicion of the parents' "eyes" that see and examine, as she explained (see Figure 3): "Relations that are based on examining eyes." At Time 2, the pattern of change in Sharon's approach is evident, as is her desire to form a partnering relationship with parents:

Table 3. From Suspicion to Trust: Examples of Students' Views

	Time 1	Time 2
Sarah	I chose to draw an eye and a hand on a hand, through writing the sentence, "respect him and suspect him, or hand shaking hands." (Drew an eye and a hand)	I chose to draw a hand shaking a hand, such that the connection between them creates the whole. In other words, the moment that the teacher and the parents work together cooperatively, they provide a certain kind of wholeness to the child. (Drew a hand shaking hand)
Donna	The picture that represents the relations between the teacher and the parent is of two hands, each one reaching to shake hands. There is a question mark that characterizes the teacher's uncertainty – will the parents cooperate, who and what are they. The parents also have questions about the teacher – who is she? Will she be good for my child? What educational approach does she have? And other questions that raise some amount of suspicion and tension for both the teacher and the parents.	This kind of gesture expresses closeness, security and belief in the person whom you are holding like a spouse. There is something in this way of holding that expresses strength and partnership, because essentially, as the year progresses, the communication between the teachers and the parents tightens and becomes a kind of partner relation with a joint purpose – the success and positive development of the child. (Drew hands holding one another)
Ella	My approach is influenced by a meaningful personal experience: My daughter's preschool teacher (last year) underwent a series of criticisms and humiliations by some of the parents. (Drew a triangle with a red question mark inside)	We are on the same side and everyone has the same goal – the child's progress. In times of disagreement, even if it seems that there is a (mental) fence dividing the teacher and the parents, at the end of the day, with effective communication between the sides, you see that the fence isn't really there. (Drew a person jumping over a fence)
Deborah	Relations at the beginning of the year are like a conch shell – closed and it's not so clear what's inside. What information the parents will choose to reveal, what the parents expect from the teacher, do they rely on her, do they check on her, the hidden is greater than what's apparent. (Drew a whirlpool that looks like a conch)	I drew a preschool teacher and a parent and I wrote 'win-win,' a give-and-take situation. A child who is in the center between the parens and teacher. It is the common denominator and the main factor and the parent and teacher are two factors that act for the child, for his benefit and raising him from an emotional, physical, social, and cognitive perspective. Both sides have to be united and help one another to see the child. (Drew a parent and teacher clasping hands)
Rebecca	Relations between teacher and parents: It's like walking on eggshells; you need to be very careful with what you say and how you behave with them. (Drew feet walking on eggs and one egg broken).	With parents you need to be open and of course the parents...when one of the sides isn't open with the other, then the other side starts to be offended and this hurts the child. (Drew an open window)

"At the beginning of the year, I saw the relations between teacher and parent as negative and threatening since the parents examine the teacher, criticize her, confront her, make demands on her, and usually tend to protect their children." She adds, "the teacher has to forge a relationship of involvement and respect between the parents and the preschool, that are characterized by cooperation and communication." At Time 2, Sharon drew a pair of hands forming an initial connection that reveals the change in her perception of the parent-teacher relationship (Figure 4).

Figure 3. Sharon, Time 1.

Figure 4. Sharon, Time 2.

256 *Iris Levy, Yael Shlesinger, Alona Peleg et al.*

From Distance to Closeness (n = 8)

About 16.3% of the students showed this pattern, where at the beginning of the course they used many phrases that represent a perception of separation, difference, and absence of common language. They incorporated various graphic images to express the separation, such as a stormy sea, barrier, door, and physical separation between the images as a visual expression of the distance between the characters. At the end of the course (Time 2), the expressions represent greater cooperation and closeness, the images are closer to each other, and there are arrows between them or they are in some sort of common space, such as a circle or heart (see Table 4).

Table 4. From Distance to Closeness: Examples of Students' Views

	Time 1	Time 2
Tammy	Tammy drew the characters far away from each other and explained it: The teacher is in one place and the parent is in another, there is no step taken together or for the other.	The teacher and parent are close to each other, there is cooperation and reciprocity for the child. The relationship is closer, but there is no touching. (Drew the parent and teacher close to each other)
Naomi	Naomi drew two puzzle pieces with distance between them: There has to be communication between the teacher and the parent from a place of cooperation and a two-way street. (Drew puzzle pieces far apart)	I think there is a place to connect the pieces of the puzzle, which expresses the importance of the optimal communication. (Drew a puzzle with the pieces connected)
Alex	There is distance between the parent and teacher, and sometimes there are arguments and disagreements about what is best for the child. (Drew parent and teacher far apart)	I drew them closer together physical, and even holding hands (cooperating). (Drew the parent and teacher closer together)
Emily	Each one is in a different place and they do not communicate with each other.	The preschool staff has to build open channels of communication to include the parents for the whole years with an atmosphere of welcoming, based on mutual trust. (Drew parent and teacher holding hands)

Leah, for example, drew the parent and the teacher with a stormy see separating them (Figure 5). From the researchers' analysis of this visual representation, the stormy sea can be explained as a symbol of the distance and loneliness that the teacher feels in her relationship with the parents. She describes herself as separate from the parents, who appear as a pair. All the characters are drawn without a body and on an angle, which expresses the emotional storm in Leah's perception of the relationship. This is made clear in her explanation of the illustration: "It describes relationships that include a lot of noise in the communication. Parent-teacher interactions are limited (short, not continuous, not always frontal, don't always include complete information), it creates imprecise explanations for what each side is doing for the child." Leah emphasizes the distance, lack of communication, and gaps in her explanation of the two sides in the relationship.

Figure 5. Leah, Time 1.

Figure 6. Leah, Time 2.

At the end of the course, Leah's perception is more layered and positive. It includes less noise and greater closeness between the sides. She draws a heart with two parents (again, no body or facial features), and next to them are other heads (child and teacher), that are represented as a triple composition. Between the three sections (parents, teacher, child) are double-sided arrows, which represent the relationships and interaction between the two (see Figure 6). All around the description is a heart, representing the emotional section, as Leah explains, and around that is a circle, representing the rational-professional side (Time 2, Leah). Leah describes her illustration:

> There are limits to the interactions between the parent and teacher, and there is still an emotional layer in the relations. Negative feedback from the parent can impact on the teacher's motivation, and thereby influence the quality of her work with the children. Nonetheless, in this picture, I chose to relate to the fact that around the emotional layer that surrounds the factors – parent, teacher, child, is the rational-professional layer that we related to during the course. This layer includes professional understanding of the parents' behaviors, and understanding that can allow the teacher to have relationships that include the personal needs of each of the factors.

At the end of the course, Leah translates the noise of the "emotional layer" that she has to overcome using the tools that she acquired in the course.

From Superiority and Compartmentalization to Equality and Cooperation (n = 6)

About 12.2% of the students portrayed this pattern, where at the beginning of the course (Time 1), they emphasize the teacher's status, her responsibility, and her professional superiority. They focus on the respect and appreciation expected from the parents towards the teacher. Some of the students place the teacher's image above that of the parents. Others didn't necessarily represent the metaphor hierarchically, but their written description highlight that the teacher "sets the tone" or that "her professional approach is important." In contrast, at the end of the course (Time 2), there is an emphasis on cooperation and creating a joint vision relating to the joint purpose. Their pictures highlight this with the help of images of hands, joint circles, closer characters, etc.

Table 5. From Superiority and Compartmentalization to Equality and Cooperation: Examples of Students' Views

	Time 1	Time 2
Lydia	The preschool teacher gives her opinion to the parents, what she thinks is right, because she studied and works according to her profession. If something occurs between the teacher and the parents, the teacher's view is central. (Drew the teacher higher up and the parent diagonally lower)	The teacher and the parents are together, at the same eye-level. By cooperating they are able to promote the child. (Drew the parent and teacher at the same level, but the teacher is slightly larger).
Avigail	One needs to accept the parents and include them but set clear boundaries. The teacher is the one who runs the preschool – creating tough communication at times. She needs to explain the educational approach to the parents, but also set the tone. Not to let the parents run the preschool. (Drew two inseparable circles)	Integration and cooperation. I feel that everything I said was sharpened to one more-focused sentence. I got more confidence. (Drew two inseparable circles)

For example, Anna highlights the difficulty in facing parents' criticisms: "There is criticism from the parents, the feeling is that they are against the preschool teacher," Anna asks the parents to recognize the teacher's authority: "The parents have to respect the teacher's status and to integrate in the preschool where the teacher allows." Anna thinks that the parent needs to abide by the rules that the teacher set using her authority and not disagree with her. At the end of the course, Anna strives towards cooperation between the sides: "We will continue to join hands with the aim of cooperating, as two who embark on an educational journey for the child that is important for both. Since there are hurdles along the road, we need to work together and keep an open dialogue and an empathic approach between us for the entire journey." Anna's perception of the more complex relationship is expressed in her drawing (see Figure 8), which adds details that demonstrate her deeper understanding of the nature of the relations with parents.

Figure 7. Anna, Time 1.

Figure 8. Anna, Time 2.

From Optimism to Pessimism (n = 3)

About 6% of the students revealed the pattern where they had a more optimistic approach at the beginning of the semester and related to cooperation and reciprocity, but at the end, described suspicion and fear of the relationship.

For example, at Time 2, Nina describes the change in her perception from an optimistic one, "A continuous arrow that symbolizes flow," (see Figure 9) to one of suspicion and fear represented by a broken arrow (see Figure 10). She explains the change in her perception:

> In the category of the parent-teacher relationship, the similarity is the existence of the connecting arrow, the relationship between the two and its importance cannot be eliminated in favor of the child. In the first

drawing, there is a continuous arrow symbolizing flow, partnership, and reciprocity, while in the second drawing, it is broken and symbolizes a charged relationship accompanied by fear, doubt, and lack of co-operation. The relationships can improve when the two sides can be open to each other, understand the common goal, behave with mutual respect, discuss the things that distance them and resolve everything via discussion. In the first drawing, sharing and understanding occur automatically, and in the second, more realistic picture, the situation is possible and will occur as soon as both sides put the ego aside and cooperate (Nina, Time 2).

Table 6. From Optimism to Pessimism: Examples of Students' Views

	Time 1	Time 2
Eli	Two adults, equal in what they bring to the relationship. The teacher is larger, in terms of knowledge and professionalism, the parent absorbs, receives knowledge from the teacher who is the sources of authority and knowledge. (Drew the parent and teacher in three situations, each time one of the characters is larger than the other).	With respect to the parent and teacher…I felt very small next to the parents. (Drew parent, teacher and child holding hands. The parent is taller than the teacher)
Kim	I believe that only with cooperation and full backing from the parents towards the teacher can they promote the child at home and in the preschool. (Drew a peace symbol)	I was more optimistic and naïve at the beginning of the course…I came to realize that not all the parents cooperate with the teacher, they may create difficulties and oppose the teacher. (Drew feet walking on eggshells)

Figure 9. Nina, Time 1.

Figure 10. Nina, Time 2.

At Time 2, Nina can point out the difficulty, but also note ways of solving and dealing with it.

DISCUSSION AND CONCLUSION

The current study focused on patterns of change and development in early childhood education students' perceptions of parent-teacher relations in the framework of a "Working with Parents" course. This change and development was examined as expressed by the students via text and drawing at the beginning and end of the course. Processes of change in the educational perception serve as part of the developmental and professionalization process that education students undergo during training. Our study joins others that attempt to understand these processes (Feiman-Nemser, 2001; Vonk, 1995), by empowering discourse and reflective discussion amongst students in order to enable them to cope with their attitudes, perceptions, and feelings regarding the complex relationship between the teacher and the parents (Borg, 1998).

From the analysis of the data, it appears that the students' starting point was defensive. Most are fearful of meeting the parents. Although most of them have not yet encountered direct meetings with parents, they did experience these meetings indirectly as part of their internship – watching the kindergarten teachers, as support staff, and managers, without having acquired the tools to cope with the challenging situations that the parent-teacher encounters may invite (Dvir & Shatz Oppenheimer, 2011). The defensive attitude is expressed by suspicion (from suspicion to trust), distance (from distance to closeness), by maintaining boundaries (from hierarchy to trust), and a limited perception of the relationship (from cooperation to complexity).

At Time 1, the students used a variety of metaphors to express their fear: distance between characters, suspicious eye, walking on eggshells, sea, walls, and fences. These expressed the distance that they fear vis-à-vis parents on the one hand, and their desire for protection in the relationship with parents on the other hand.

At Time 2, there was a change in the metaphors that described the connection between preschool teacher and parent: There was an increase in the description of hands trying to connect, touch, desire to foster relations; the characters were closer to one another; description of details, facial features, and body parts were added that also reflect the desire for closeness and cooperation. It is evident that participation in the course in 2013 and 2016 led to a reduction in the defensive attitude and contributed to a positive change in the students' attitudes towards the parent-teacher relationship. Even though not all the perceptions became more positive, they became more layered and complex. The reflective discourse during the course raised the students' awareness of the complex position of the preschool teacher vis-à-vis the parents, and the empathy towards them (Plotnik, 2009). The course provided the students with models for managing communication from a more secure and relaxed position. This process allowed them to free themselves from the defensive position and perceive the relationship with parents as one that is based more on closeness and cooperation.

By the end of the course, a majority of the education students emphasized the importance of communication as a central factor in normalizing the relationship for the child's benefit. They focused on the professional side of the relationship and highlighted their authority as the possessors of professional and pedagogic knowledge relating to promoting the child in cooperation with the parents, while recognizing the importance of the parents' role and recruitment to the educational process.

The students' use of a metaphor and a text at the beginning and end of the course broadened and refined their reflective view of their perceptions of the parent-teacher relationship. The graphic and textual descriptions and their analysis provided them with tools for a deep introspection. In places where words did not successfully express the emotional and professional difficulty, the metaphor expanded and clarified the student's ability to express herself in a meaningful manner (Gibbs, 1994).

Additionally, the theories, the reflective discourse, and the tools given during the course created an empathic and more encompassing view towards parents and an understanding of their role as leaders and agents of change. This empathic view combined with the tools that were acquired contributed to the change in the students' views of the parent-teacher relations, led to a reduction in the level of suspicion between the sides, and contributed to positive changes in the students' perceptions.

This study provides research evidence for early education students' views of the parent-teacher relationship. Similarly, it contributes to the improvement in the professional and emotional training in the framework of education programs and the process of specialization in the theoretical and practical aspects of the "Working with Parents" course. On the theoretical level, it seems that it is possible to create a positive change in the education students' perceptions of the relations by building empirical and theoretical knowledge relating to parent-teacher relations. On the practical level, it seems possible to ease the construction of the connection between teachers and parents using the guidance of lecturers, pedagogical counselors, and internship counselors.

While learning in the course "Working with Parents" increased the students' awareness of their personal views and perceptions regarding parent-teacher relations, not all the students changed their viewpoints. It may be that a year-long course, like other courses that relate to preschool teachers' communication with professionals and others, will enrich the students with tools and knowledge and lead to even greater results.

REFERENCES

Addi-Raccah, A., & Arviv-Elyashi, R. (2008). Parent empowerment and teacher professionalism: Teachers' perspective. *Urban Education, 43*(3), 394-415.

Bar-Shalom, Y. (2004). *Idea of tikkun: Educational initiative in a multicultural society.* Bnei Brak, Israel: United Kibbutz. [Hebrew].

Borg, S. (1998). Teachers, pedagogical systems and grammar teaching: A qualitative study. *TESOL Quarterly, 5,* 9-32.

Brouwer, N., & F. Korthagen. (2005). Can teacher education make a difference? *American Educational Research Journal, 42*(1), 153–224.

Bryant, A., & Charmaz, K. (2007). Grounded theory in historical perspective: An Epistemological account. In A. Bryant & K. Charmaz (Eds.), *The Sage handbook of grounded theory.* London: Sage. pp. 31-56.

Cohen, J. (2006). Social, emotional, ethical and academic education: Creating a climate for learning, participation in democracy and well-being. *Harvard Educational Review, 76*(2), 201-237.

Corbin, J., & Strauss, A. L. (1984). Collaboration: Couples working together to manage chronic illness. *Image, 4,* 109–115.

Dayan, Y. (2004). It's a heavy bag: Seven kindergarten teachers relate their relations with parents. *Echoes of Kindergarten, 4,* 4-19. [Hebrew].

Denzin, N. K. (1999). Biographical research methods. In J. P. Keeves & G. Lakomski (Eds). *Issues in educational research* (pp. 92-102). Amsterdam: Pergamon.

Dvir, N., & Shatz-Oppenheimer, A. (2006). *Looking in the mirror: The process of constructing a professional identity of beginning teachers as evident from their stories.* Jerusalem: Ministry of Education. [Hebrew].

Elbow, P. (1986). *Embracing contraries.* New York: Oxford University Press.

Ezer, H. Gilat, I., & Sagee, R. (2010). Perception of teacher education and professional identity among novice teachers. *European Journal of Teacher Education, 33*(4), 391-404.

Feiman-Nemser, S. (2001). From preparation to practice: Designing a continuum to Strengthen and sustain. *Teacher College Record.* V. 103. N. 6: 1013-1055.

Friedman, I. (1984). *School, home, and community: Alienation and openness in the educational space.* Jerusalem: Henrietta Szold Institute. [Hebrew].

Friedman, I. (1990). *Community school: Theory & practice.* Jerusalem: Hebrew University, Magnes & Szold Publishing. [Hebrew].

Friedman, I. (2010). *Relations between school, parents, & community.* Retrieved from http://.education.academy.ac.il.

Friedman, I., & Fisher, Y. (2009). Parents and schools: Trust and involvement. *Dapim, 47*, 11-37. [Hebrew].

Friedman, I. & Kas, A. (2001). Teacher efficacy: Task-relationship model. *Megamot, 41*(3), 322-348. [Hebrew].

Gardener, H. (1995). *Thinking and creative brain.* Tel Aviv: Poalim Library. [Hebrew].

Gibbs, R. W. (1994). *The poetics of mind: Figurative thought, language, and understanding.* Cambridge: Cambridge University Press.

Greenbaum, C. W., & Fried, D. (2011). *Relations between the family and the early childhood education system: Status report and recommendations by The Committee for Relations between the Family and the ECE System.* Jerusalem: Israel Academy of Sciences and Humanities. [Hebrew].

Hiatt-Michael, D. B. (2010). Home-school communication. In: D. B. Hiatt-Michael (Ed), *Promising practices for family involvement in schools,* Greenwich, Connecticut: Lap Information Age Publishing, pp. 39-58.

Hursh, D. (2007). Assessing No Child Left Behind and the rise of neoliberal education policies. *American Educational Research Journal, 44*(3), 493–518.

Hyson, M. (2003). *Preparing early childhood professionals. NAEYC's standards for programs.* Washington, DC: National Association for the Education of Young Children. *Teachers College Record, 103*(6), 1013-1055.

Kupferberg, A. (2016). *To touch the sky: Research of text and discourse that integrates figurative language.* Tel-Aviv: MOFET Institute.

Kupferberg, A. & Olstein, A. (2005). *Discourse in education: Educational events as field study.* Tel Aviv: MOFET Institute.

Lakoff, G., & Johnson, M. (1980). *Metaphors we live by.* Chicago: the University Press.

Lam, T. (1973). *Images of teaching, study of ideological opinions, and views of teaching candidates.* Jerusalem University: Ministry of Education. [Hebrew].

Lieblich, A. Tuval Mashiach, R., & Zilber, T. (2010). Between the whole and its parts, between content and form. In L. Kassan & M. Kromer-Nevo (Eds.), *Methods for analyzing qualitative data,* (pp. 21-420). Beer Sheva: Ben-Gurion University. [Hebrew].

McBride, B. A., Bae, J., & Blatchford, K. (2003). Family-school-community partnerships in rural Pre-K at-risk programs. *Journal of Early Childhood Research, 1*(1), 49 – 72.

Milstein, A. & Olstein, A. (2005). Changes in English teachers' beliefs in the framework of an innovative, growing school. In A. Kupferberg & A. Olstein (Eds). *Discourse in education: Educational events as field study* (pp. 132-155). MOFET Institute: Israel. [Hebrew].

Noy, B. (1984). *Teachers and parents as partners in the educational process.* Ministry of Education, Culture, & Sport: School for Senior Teaching Staff.

Noy, B. (1999). School, home, and the relations between them. In A. Peled (Ed). *Jubilee for the education system in Israel* (pp. 815-834). Jerusalem: Ministry of Education, Culture, & Sport.

Omer, S. (2002). Parents and educators: The necessary covenant. *Panim, 19,* [Hebrew].

Pianta, R. C., Mashburn, A. J., Downer, J. T., Hamre, B. K., & Justice, L. (2008). Effect of web-mediated professional development resources on teacher-child interactions in pre-kindergarten classrooms. *Early Childhood Research Quarterly, 23*(4), 431-451.

Pianta, R. C. (2006). Standardized observation and professional development: A focus on individualized implementation and practices.

In M. J. Zaslow & I. Martinez-Beck (Eds.), *Critical issues in early childhood professional development* (pp. 231-254). Baltimore, MD: Brooker.

Plotnik, R. (2008). *To grow up different: The social-emotional word of children with ADHD.* Holon: Yesod. [Hebrew]

Plotnik, R. (2009). 'Parents' Voices': Parenting as a mental-developmental process. In A. Cohen (Ed.), *Parenting experience: Relations, coping, and development* (pp. 333-362). Ach Publishers: Kiryat Bialik.

Provonzo, F., McCloskey, E., Gray, N., Kottkamp, R. B., & Cohen, D. K. (1989).

Metaphor and meaning in the language of teachers. *Teachers College Record, 90* (4), 531-537.

Richardson, V. (1994). *Teacher change and staff development processes.* New York, NY: Teachers College Press.

Rogers, K. (1969). *Seeking to learn.* Rehavia: Workers' Library. [Hebrew].

Rosen Davidi, Y. (2016). Please draw me a picture: Teachers not farmers, not potters. *Echoes of Education, 91*, 106-107. [Hebrew].

Tal, K., & Bar, T. (2010). Relations between the family and the education system in early Childhood from a historical perspective. Background material for the initiative http://education.academy.ac.il/Search/ Advanced.aspx?q=prhsni&nodeId=26.

U.S. Department of Education. (2006). *Remarks by Secretary Spellings at No Child Left Behind summit.* Retrieved May 5, 2006, from http://www.ed.gov.new.

Vonk, J. H. C. (1993). Mentoring beginning teachers: Mentor knowledge and skills. *Mentoring, 1,* 31-41.

Vonk, J. H. C. (1995). *Conceptualizing novice teachers' professional development: A base for supervisory interventions.* Paper presented at the Annual Meeting of the American Educational Research Association, San Francisco, CA.

Voorhis, F. L. V. (2011). Costs and benefits of family involvement in homework. *Journal of Advanced Academics, 22*(2), 220-49.

Zur, A., Gidrom, A., Eisenberg, M., & Gottweiser, I. (2006). *Invitation to metaphorical dance: Integrating imagination and metaphor in teacher training.* Tel-Aviv: MOFET Institute. [Hebrew].

In: Teacher Training
Editor: Paula E. McDermott

ISBN: 978-1-53615-633-1
© 2019 Nova Science Publishers, Inc.

Chapter 7

THE USE OF REPEATED NARRATIVE WRITING BY TEACHERS TO COPE WITH EMOTIONALLY LOADED INCIDENTS IN THE CLASSROOM

Clodie Tal[1], Aalya Kabia[2,†], Margalit Cohen[3,‡] and Rivka Hillel Lavian[4,§]*
Levinsky College of Education, Tel Aviv, Israel

ABSTRACT

The study presented in this chapter examined teachers' use of repeated narrative writing (RNW) based on Pennebaker's (Pennebaker & Evans, 2014) expressive writing method to cope with emotionally loaded incidents related to behavior problems in the preschool classroom. An analysis of sixty narratives written by two Israeli teachers revealed that RNW helped them overcome helplessness, regulate negative feelings

---

* Corresponding Author's E-mail: clodietal@gmail.com.
† Email: alia30@walla.co.il.
‡ Email: margalit1212@walla.co.il.
§ Email: Rivkah@levinsky.ac.il.

towards people and situations involved in the incidents, and develop self-efficacy and self-determination, as well as improve their classroom management competencies. This was manifested in more proactive leadership, a more ecological perspective of the class, improved self-regulation skills, and improved relations with children, staff, and parents.

Keywords: repeated narrative writing, expressive writing, coping with behavior problems, self-regulation, self-determination, classroom management

INTRODUCTION

Behavior problems, roughly defined as "any repeated pattern of behavior, or perception of behavior, that interferes with or is at risk of interfering with optimal learning or engagement in pro-social interactions with peers and adults" (Smith & Fox, 2003, p. 5), are relatively prevalent at preschool age and, when untreated, are likely to correlate with poor academic, emotional, and socially detrimental outcomes (Campbell et al., 2006; Korpershoek, Harms, de Boer, van Kuijk, & Doolaard, 2016). Nevertheless, it is difficult to determine the actual prevalence of behavior problems due to the lack of uniformity of the definitions used in the different studies. Another difficulty in assessing the prevalence of behavior problems stems from their expression on a continuum of severity rather than as a dichotomous phenomenon (Campbell, 2006). Finally, assessing the prevalence of behavior problems in early childhood education is even more complicated as developmental factors impact their definition (Dunlap et al., 2006). What is considered a behavior problem in elementary school children (for example, a temper tantrum) is considered developmentally normative for toddlers and preschool children as self-regulation of attention, emotion, and behavior is strongly affected by developmental factors.

In educational environments, the child's interactions and relationship with the teacher are among the most important factors that can either moderate the child's defiant behavior or contribute to its escalation

(Evertson & Weinstein, 2006; Hamre & Pianta, 2005; Howes & Ritchie, 2002; Kaiser & Rasminsky, 2017). The teachers' relationships with children are just one component of overall classroom management and affected by the teacher's and the child's characteristics as well as environmental factors that impact the relationship directly and indirectly (Evertson & Weinstein, 2006).

Classroom Management (CM)

Classroom management is defined by Evertson and Weinstein as "the actions teachers take to create an environment that supports and facilitates both academic and social-emotional learning" (2006, p. 4). Tal suggests that "effective management of the classroom *is a cyclical process that includes advance planning, implementation, assessment during the implementation, and a final evaluation that takes into account factors related to the children and their environment, intended to bring about progress in the activities carried out for the emotional well-being of the children in the class*" (2016, p. 7). Thus, self-regulation is seen as a foundational component of the teacher's ability to lead a class.

Teachers are perceived as the leaders of their classrooms. To lead classrooms, teachers need conceptual tools to help clarify how classrooms work, create a commitment to the welfare and learning of the children, and provide skills to apply these insights and commitment. The quality of planning and relationships formed with children depend to a great extent on the teachers' overall management of the class. In spite of its importance and complexity, CM seems to suffer from a bad reputation among scholars, and is not given enough focused attention in teacher training (Evertson & Weinstein, 2006; Emmer & Stough, 2001; Stough & Montague, 2015). Indeed, CM is frequently perceived by the teachers themselves as a list of recommended tricks (Landau, 2009) that can "fix" any difficulty that comes up in the intense life of classrooms. As opposed to this perception, Tal (2010, 2016) suggests that classroom management is a teacher's evolving meta-competency, which includes both cognitive mindsets (such as proactive and ecological perceptions of the class) and competencies (such as relations with children, staff, and parents) all directed by moral leadership (regarded as both an approach and a competency). Moral leadership is defined as "the ability to influence children, staff, and parents to maximize everyone's efforts towards ensuring the well-being, sense of belonging, and suitable learning conditions for individuals, groups, and the entire class" (Tal, 2016, p. 8).

Research shows that children's behavior problems are a major issue in CM, and a source of major stress for both novice and experienced teachers (Carlson, Tiret, Bender, & Benson, 2011; Giallo & Little, 2003). Early childhood teachers report that disruptive behavior is one of the greatest challenges they face, and they identify learning the skill for dealing with disruptive behavior as their most significant training need (Griffin, 2010; Gettinger & Fischer, 2015). The question is, what processes can help teachers cope with the stress related to behavior problems in their classrooms?

Self-Determination, Self-Efficacy, and Self-Regulation

Teachers as classroom managers and moral leaders need to find sources to motivate themselves, to act in ways that enhance the children's well-being even in emotionally loaded situations that undermine their self-confidence (Tal, 2014). Moral values that guide teachers' actions must be fully internalized in the teachers' consciousness (Ryan & Deci, 2000, 2017) to enable them to overcome daily obstacles. This internalized motivation is needed in the process of self-regulation – including control over negative emotions toward children displaying behavior problems, the ability to plan and implement actions on behalf of the children, to evaluate the effectiveness of these actions, and to modify them when encountering difficulties. Indeed, Zimmerman (2000), drawing on the work of Bandura (1986, 1997), defines self-regulation as self-generated thoughts, feelings, and actions that are planned and cyclically adapted to environmental variables to bring about the attainment of goals defined by the individual.

At the core of the self-regulation approach is the relationship among cognitive processes, learning strategies, and emotional dynamics, on the one hand, and motivation and meta-cognition or reflection, on the other. Repeated self-regulation efforts that successfully ameliorate the children's behavior problems are likely to promote teachers' perceived competence or sense of self-efficacy, defined as the belief in one's ability to influence events that affect one's life (Bandura, 1994). Self-efficacy beliefs determine how people think, motivate themselves, and behave – and they tend to be situation specific. Thus, a teacher can feel efficacy about teaching subject matter, but unconfident of her ability to cope with behavior problems. Bandura claimed that one of the main sources of self-efficacy is mastery experiences, i.e., the more teachers successfully cope with behavior problems, the more confident they become in their ability to do so in the future. Self-efficacy beliefs, in turn, fuel internal, self-determined motivation to cope with the children's challenging behavior problems and help teachers self-regulate themselves in dealing with these problems and their consequences.

Repeated Narrative Writing (RNW) as a Tool for Coping with Behavior Problems

In this study, we explore the use of RNW by teachers to cope with emotionally loaded incidents related to the behavior problems of young children. We theorize that the recursive use of RNW is likely to support the activation of self-regulation-self-determination-self-efficacy chains for teachers employing the method.

Tal (2005) suggested that RNW of emotionally loaded incidents as a tool for coping with challenging behavior and its impact on the class might lead to the teacher's emotional self-regulation, her better understanding of the context of the problematic behavior, and finally the emergence of practical ways to improve the children's behavior. This is based on Pennebaker's observation of the healing effects of expressive writing (Pennebaker & Evans, 2014; Pennebaker & Chung, 2011; Smyth and

Pennebaker (1999). Pennebaker and his associates showed how repeated narrative writing of emotionally loaded episodes in one's life helps adults better "organize the emotional effects of an experience as well as the experience itself" (Smyth & Pennebaker, 1999, p. 82). "The beauty of a narrative is that it allows us to tie all of the changes in our life into a broad comprehensive story" (p. 83). And as the story is written and rewritten, it becomes shorter, leaving out small and unimportant details. Furthermore, Smyth and Pennebaker show evidence that physical measures such as blood pressure and the general mental health of study participants improved in association with the repeated writing of an emotionally loaded experience. The effects on the participants' health and well-being were equivalent to participation in psychotherapy (Murray, Lamnin, & Carver, 1989). Tal (2005) showed that a teacher who used RNW for stressful episodes related to a boy's challenging behavior elicited – in her fifth and last writing – practical possibilities for coping with his behavior – actions that had not come up in her initial writing about the episode. This emerged in addition to improved measures cited by Smyth and Pennebaker – an increased number of causal, insightful, and positive emotion words versus a decreased number of negative emotion words (Pennebaker & Francis, 1996).

In Pennebaker's studies, RNW entailed writing freely for 10-20 minutes on four consecutive days, disregarding grammar or spelling, about a traumatic experience in clinical and non-clinical samples of adults, including college students. Adult participants were invited "to let go and explore [in their writing] their very deepest emotions and feelings...relationships with others..." (p. 71). It was reported that participants were engaged in the writing and intuitively knew how to organize these events, turning them into coherent narratives (Smyth & Pennebaker, 1999).

The suggestion to "import" expressive writing from therapy to teacher education is consistent with practices of collecting and analyzing critical incidents (Angelides, 2001; Francis, 1997; Griffin, 2003) and journal writing (Moon, 2006; Walker, 2006) as strategies of developing reflective practice by novice teachers. Both repeated narrative writing as well as journal- and critical-incident writing are based on the assumption that expressive writing about meaningful and often traumatic personal experiences help in understanding feelings and situations, regulating feelings, and freeing the mind to better grasp how personal perspectives shape one's understanding of the learning context. All these tools may be perceived as "mirrors of the mind" as they find language to express the writers' or learners' deepest feelings and perceptions (Bowman & Richard, 1983). RNW could be also perceived as recursive writing of critical incidents. Finally, critical incidents as well as repeated narrative writing are often included in the ongoing writing of learning journals. Expressive writing as prescribed by Pennebaker and translated into RNW by Tal guides the individual to write recursively about a traumatic or critical episode in more structured ways in terms of the number of writings, the time spent writing, and the intervals between acts of writing, as compared to journal writing and critical-incident writing. Instructions about expressive writing drawn from Pennebaker's research encourage writers to tell their story freely, without paying attention to grammar, spelling, or punctuation, but impose structure on their mode of writing: about 15 minutes of writing each consecutive day, including at least four or five attempts to formulate and reformulate the personal story of a specific event. Journal writing and the writing of critical incidents do not follow these structural rules. Furthermore, RNW based on Pennebaker's expressive writing method is an unsupervised and self -implemented tool as opposed to the use of critical incidents and journal writing in teacher education, which are usually performed in the context of interactions with mentors and supervisors. It is suggested that the teacher is her own researcher and "therapist" in using RNW.

Coping with Behavior Problems: Recommendations versus Implementation

Although children displaying behavior problems are a source of disruption of classwork, it has been found that they tend to respond well to interventions (Belsky, 2013). There is agreement within the educational and academic communities as to the main principles of effective intervention related to young children's challenging behavior. It is agreed, for example, that teachers need to adhere to a multi-tiered approach including prevention, enhancement of social competencies and detection of difficulties in this area, and finally individualized intervention plans when needed based on positive approaches including praise for pro-social behavior and efforts by the children to regulate their behavior; emphasizing the child's interests and strengths rather than the frequent use of punishment and expulsion (Fox, Dunlap & Powell, 2002; Gettinger & Fischer, 2015).

Research shows, however, that teachers frequently implement prescribed strategies inaccurately, despite the availability of numerous intervention programs for coping with young children's behavior problems (see Gettinger and Fischer, 2015 for a review of the programs). What is likely to prevent accurate implementation of these strategies is the teachers' negative feelings and appraisals of the children's behavior and its implications for the class functioning (McCarthy, Lineback & Reiser, 2015). RNW is proposed here as a tool that enables teachers at different stages in their professional development to work through the negative emotions related to children's behavior and therefore give more clear-headed consideration to the interventions required.

Hence, the research question of this study is, *what was the impact of the teachers' employment of RNW for dealing with emotionally loaded incidents related to children's behavior problems, as reported by them?*

METHODOLOGY AND METHODS

Research Design

A multiple case study approach was adopted to capture the richness and depth of narrative writing related to coping with behavior problems. Clandinin and Connelly (2000) refer to narrative inquiry as a research method enabling researchers to understand the teachers' experience and enhance their abilities.

A case study is defined by Yin (2009, p. 18) as "an empirical inquiry that investigates a contemporary phenomenon in depth and within its real-life context." Furthermore, case studies stress "developmental factors, meaning that a case typically evolves in time" (Flyvbjerg 2011, p. 301). In this study, an effort was made to track the development of the educators writing the narratives for several months. A multiple case study methodology enables the researcher to explore similarities and differences between cases as well as variations within each case.

Participants

Participants in the study were two experienced preschool teachers enrolled in M.Ed. studies (who are co-authors of this paper) and indirectly the children, children's parents, and staff.

Case 1

Aalya is the head teacher of a preschool in a Bedouin village in the north of Israel. At the time of the study, she had 19 years of teaching experience and was enrolled in an M.Ed program in Early Childhood Education. The socioeconomic status of the families in the preschool and the village is low to average and there is a tradition of marriage between relatives, apparently leading to relatively frequent disabilities in the local children. Aalya's class had numerous incidents of problem behavior including aggression in children with diagnosed and undiagnosed learning disabilities, Aalya initiated the RNW program to help herself develop ways to deal with the stressful situation in her class as she felt she did not get enough support from community agencies. The regular staff in the class included Aalya, a full-time assistant, and another assistant who worked several hours a week with one of the boys with behavior problems. The main perpetrators in Aalya's preschool were three children (two boys and a girl).

Case 2

Margalit is the head teacher of a preschool in a town in the center of Israel. She had 24 years of experience and was also enrolled in an MEd program at the time. Children in the preschool are 4-5 years old and were all reported to live in two-parent households. The socioeconomic status of the families was mostly low to average. Most families in this preschool are Jewish and religious. The regular staff included Margalit the head teacher, an assistant, and a volunteer. Four boys were the perpetrators of the incidents reported by Margalit.

Procedures and Data Analysis

The data included 60 narratives of episodes (35 in Case 1 and 25 in Case 2). Case 1 included 7 cycles of RNW with 5 narratives in each cycle (a total of 35 narratives) written from December 2013 until May 2014. Case 2 included 5 cycles of five writings (a total of 25 narratives) written from January to April 2015. Teachers were instructed (see Appendix) to write and rewrite at least four times each story of an emotionally loaded incident related to a behavior problem in their class. The choice of the time of writing was theirs, as long as no more than a week passed between re-writing in the same cycle. Teachers were instructed to write at least five cycles of RNW, i.e., writing related to five different episodes.

The teachers reported that they typically wrote the initial narrative in each cycle at school soon after occurrence of the stressful incident, and subsequent writings were performed at different hours, usually at home.

The data were analyzed in two waves: The first wave took place subsequent to the completion of the narrative writings (in Case 1 in the summer and fall of 2014, and in Case 2 in the summer and fall of 2015). The second wave of analysis was performed in the fall and winter of 2016-17.

First Wave Analysis

Analysis of data in the first wave entailed counting the types of words and expressions cited in the teachers' narratives in categories suggested by

Smyth and Pennebaker: *insight words* (e.g., "I realized," "it dawned on me," "I understood"); *causal statements* (e.g., relating the boy's behavior to inadequate attention at home); *words expressing negative feelings* (e.g., "I feel angry," "I'm exhausted," "the boy was furious"); and *words expressing positive emotions* (e.g., "I'm glad," "I feel satisfied," "the boy smiled"). The second, third, and fourth authors also performed a content analysis of the narratives and drew conclusions about processes that helped them develop coping strategies for the children's behavior problems.

Second Wave Analysis

All data in the first wave analysis were reexamined. This additional analysis had two main foci:

- Examination of changes in the use of expressions representing *helplessness* ("I feel helpless," "I can't see any solution") versus *self-determination* ("I/we decided," "I want," "I discovered") from the first to the last episode in each case), due to our observation that helplessness was repeatedly mentioned in the writings of the first episode in each case.
- Evidence of enactment of mindsets and competencies included in the moral classroom management meta-competency as conceptualized by Tal (2010, 2016) throughout the narratives in the seven episodes of case 1 and five episodes of case 2: (1) *Proactive mindset*: a deliberate form of thinking that anticipates possible scenarios based on knowing the class dynamics and the characteristics of individual students, as well as alternative coping mechanisms. A proactive mindset is distinguished from a reactive response to events by the lack of prior consideration of possible courses of action and pitfalls; (2) *Ecological mindset*: the understanding among teachers that the direct relationship between the teacher and the child, relationships among the children themselves, and relationships between parents of the children and staff members (in addition to factors related to the physical environment, time management, etc.) have an impact on the

functioning of each child and CM in general. (3) *Moral leadership*: The ability to influence children, staff, and parents to maximize everyone's efforts to ensure the well-being, sense of belonging, and suitable learning conditions for individuals, groups, and the entire class. Moral leadership is reflected in decisions and plans, and their implementation. (4) *A social-moral plan as an underlying curriculum of classroom management*: extended curriculum for the whole class, plans for small-group learning, as well as plans for individual children who need special attention, either because of temporary environmental hardships or social, emotional, behavioral, or learning difficulties. A "good" social-moral plan – for the entire class or the individual child – needs to be based on ecological and proactive understanding of situations. (5) *Self-regulation*: A competency including self-generated thoughts, feelings, and actions that are planned and cyclically adapted to environmental variables to bring about the attainment of goals defined by the individual. Self-regulation is frequently referred to in teacher education as reflection. Reflection can be described as an intentional and/or a complex, deliberate process of thinking about and interpreting experience in order to learn from it (Atkins & Murphy, 1995; Russo & Ford, 2006), or as a systematic inquiry into one's own practice (Dinkelman, 2003); (6) *Interpersonal relations*: quality interpersonal relations both with and among the children, as well as with families and staff for attaining school goals – emotional well-being as well as significant learning and high scholastic achievement. Respectful relations based on trust with children, staff and families are perceived as a foundation of CM.

Ethical Considerations

The teachers who wrote and rewrote the narratives are coauthors of this article and gave permission to disclose quotes. The names of the children, their parents, and preschool staff have been changed and the localities are not named.

RESULTS

Findings address the research question, "What was the impact of the teachers' employment of RNW for dealing with emotionally loaded incidents related to children's behavior problems, as reported by them?" The findings are presented in the following order:

1. *Changes in frequency of emotional and cognitive measures* from the first to the last writing within each cycle and from the first to the last cycle in each case; these data are presented in keeping with Smyth and Pennebaker's benchmarks for improved well-being;
2. *Evidence of enhanced self-determination* in both teachers following a content analysis of the narratives and a comparison of first and subsequent writings within each cycle and writings from cycle to cycle;
3. *Evidence of enhanced classroom management competencies*, including organized and ecological action plans;

Changes in Frequencies of Emotional and Cognitive Measures

Pennebaker and Francis (1996) found that a decrease in the use of negative emotional words combined with an increase in positive emotional words, causality, and insight expressions were related to the participants' psychological and physical well-being. In the present study, each case included a number of cycles of rewriting, each cycle focused on a different stressful incident related to children's behavior, rather than a single cycle as reported by Smyth and Pennebaker (1999).

Table 1 presents the mean frequencies of positive and negative emotional words and of combined cognitive words (insight and causality) for the first and final writings of narratives included in all cycles (Case 1 – 7 cycles; Case 2 – 5 cycles).

Table 1. Mean frequencies of cognitive and emotional words in the first versus the final writing of each cycle

	Case 1 (7 cycles)			Case 2 (5 cycles)		
Criterion	M	SD	t	M	SD	t
Negative feelings, first writing	4.57	2.70	2.77	11.8	3.11	7.90
Negative feelings, final writing	1.67	2.14	P < .05	0.40	0.89	P < .0001
Positive feelings, first writing	1.14	1.07	1.91	1.60	1.14	1.11
Positive feelings, final writing	2.86	2.12	P < .10	2.40	1.14	n/s
Cognitive expressions (insight + causality), first writing	0.29	0.49	1.72 p < .10	0.40	0.55	5.30 P < .001
Cognitive expressions (insight + causality), final writing	1.57	1.72		3.40	1.14	

The data in Table 1 reveal a dramatic decrease in the frequency of negative words from the first to the final writing across cycles, in both cases. An increased trend of positive emotional words that does not reach statistical significance was found in both cases. Finally, we found a significant increase in the number of cognitive expressions in Case 2, and a trend of increased cognitive expressions in Case 1. It is also important to note that more expressions of negative feelings were found in the first writings of Case 2 compared to Case 1. In addition, more cognitive expressions were found in the final writings of Case 2 compared to Case 1. Interestingly, the teacher in Case 1 seemed to need seven cycles of writing to reach the calmness and cognitive organization needed to form a mega-plan for coping with behavior problems in her preschool, whereas the teacher in Case 2 seemed to need only five cycles to regulate her feelings and build plans for coping with the children's behavior. Yet, in both cases, as we show in the next two sections, cognitive expressions seemed to help teachers understand the sources of the pressure and the negative feelings they experienced – an understanding that led to actions that were adopted in the preschools. The very low use of cognitive words in the first writings, in both cases, is noticeable and could be indicative of the overwhelming impact of the incidents on the teachers and their initial inability to process the information. This suggestion is strengthened by the content of the first writings, which show that coping with extreme incidents, including children's aggression towards other children and staff, was very stressful. The data thus show common trends in both cases (in alignment with the findings of Pennebaker and others (Pennebaker & Evans, 2014; Pennebaker and Francis, 1996), with individual differences reflected in the number of negative feelings, cognitive expressions, and how many cycles were needed by the teacher to feel in control of the situation and know what to do. In this study, the increase of positive emotions appears to be less meaningful than the decrease of negative emotions for the emergence of effective strategies to cope with behavior problems.

We will present the development of the teachers' plans of action and their activation in section 3 below, which deals with the emergence of classroom management competencies, as plans of action are a matter of elaboration and coherence rather than quantity.

Evidence of Enhanced Self-Determination

Among the negative feelings that emerged in the initial narrative writings (anger toward the perpetrator, the assistant [in Case 1], and a parent; fear of criticism [in Case 1] or that something bad will happen to one of the children due to the behavior problems, loneliness, guilt, or fatigue), what stood out was the sense of helplessness described by the teachers writing the narratives. In the second wave of data analysis, expressions of helplessness were examined in greater depth, and we found that a sense of helplessness was cited in the repeated writings in all cycles of Case 1 and in the first cycle of Case 2. Typically, acknowledgement of helplessness did not occur before the second writing in any cycle. The first writings contained expressions of anger, fatigue, exhaustion, and loneliness, followed in both cases by straightforward acknowledgement of helplessness. Helplessness and loneliness tended to co-occur in the narratives.

Initially, Feelings of Helplessness and Loneliness

Case 1

The *first episode*, third writing focused on coping with Omar's aggression and bullying of other children. The special assistant accompanied him and patiently tried to make him comply, but he seemed to always be on the move, doing harm. Aalya wrote, "I have a hard time. I don't want to cope *alone...* I'm feeling *helpless* – as if *there's no solution* – not now and not in the near future" (11 November 2013).

Case 2

The *first episode,* second writing focused on coping with Amir's extreme lack of compliance culminating in his throwing a cup of water at the psychologist who visited the preschool to help Margalit find a way to cope with his misbehavior. She wrote, "I'm angry and feel *helpless* – I feel *alone* and that the solution is far away, but I keep thinking about how to make things easier for Amir" (9 January 2015).

Emergence of Self-Determination

Following the repeated writings, the teachers gradually freed themselves from the grip of helplessness and fear, and became more aware of their commitment to the children – the perpetrators, victims, and other classmates – a commitment that led to the determination to proactively think of ways to cope with the challenging behavior. In more advanced writings in each cycle, we found in both cases expressions of self-determination (e.g., "I decided," "I want," and so on). Nevertheless, in Case 1, momentary feelings of helplessness recurred in several re-writings in conjunction with the determination to act on behalf of the children involved.

Analysis of the last episodes showed that both teachers reached an elaborated, coherent formulation of the contribution of RNW to their growing self-efficacy and self-determination in coping with children's behavior problems. These clearly appear in their final reports:

Case 1

One of the advantages of RNW is the emergence of solutions for the educator-writer's negative feelings *without relying on an external counselor.* Through the use of repeated narrative writing, *I discovered* various solutions for coping with stressful situations that I experienced in my preschool: using internet sites and professional books, etc. (November 2014).

Case 2

Intervention plans emerged from the analysis of my actions and not from external counseling. I tend to *create* more and more professional ways of my own to cope with behavior problems. RNW is a tool that helps me regulate myself and contributes to improvement in my thinking and to the *creation of more elaborate interventions* [compared to actions adopted not in the context of repeated narrative writing]. Although the [school] psychologist is likely to suggest interventions, she does not, however, possess magic solutions. Although I need help, I am the head of the preschool; *I understand who I have* to recruit and what extra help is needed. How to find extra resources that could be really helpful to me. Such as asking for young national service girls [volunteers] to work in the preschool (November 2015).

The teachers' summaries above show that the emergence of self-determination through the course of the re-writings of the episodes led to the emergence of intervention plans focused on the challenges posed by the children's behavior. In the next section we analyze expressions of moral classroom management stemming from self-determination, which appear throughout the re-writings.

EVIDENCE OF ENHANCED CLASSROOM MANAGEMENT MINDSETS AND COMPETENCIES

Analysis of the narratives showed that both teachers moved *from being reactive* and overwhelmed by incidents to attempting to understand them more ecologically and *assuming leadership guided by proactive thinking.* Furthermore, there is evidence of having moved from a sense of isolation, loneliness, and threat (by children's parents, staff, or both) to *forming collaborative relations* with staff and the children's parents. At the heart of the transformations undergone by the teachers seem to be *self-regulatory processes fueled by and reinforcing self-determination.* All these were finally expressed in a gradual construction of socio-moral interventions described in the teachers' narratives.

Case 1

At the beginning of her narrative writing (November 2013 – January 2014), Aalya showed anxiety about the criticism from parents and municipal officials who had been approached by the victims' parents. The parents' involvement and Aalya's anxiety had the initial effect of paying greatest attention to the victims and directing the assistant's attention to the victims at all times:

> The reactions of parents to their young children being affected by other children's outbursts of challenging behavior places lots of pressure and anger on the staff, and makes me fearful that a mega-behavior problem will erupt in my class – all these make me feel disappointed with

the children's parents. I feel anxious about some of the extreme reactions of a few parents and sometimes some of the parents' reactions make me feel more frustrated than the event itself (January 2014)!

As she continued to write, Aalya gradually reached the conclusion that the perpetrators needed attention and care as well, and she developed a deep commitment to them as the foundation of good relationships with children who display behavior problems in spite of the "trouble" they cause. Her assistant's comment that the parents' approach was responsible for the child's misbehavior (12 March 2014, sixth episode, fourth re-writing) became engraved in Aalya's mind and was apparently a source of much contemplation about the possible correctness of this claim and its meaning. A claim like this could have led to disengagement from the perpetrator. However, in thinking about the hard life of Mahmud, the perpetrator, Aalya became *more and more concerned about his well-being and the quality of his preparation for first grade.* Following an incident in which Mahmud repeatedly threw sand on other children (5 March, sixth episode, first writing), Aalya was successful in having a "real talk" with the boy, one of the very few interactions that exposed the boy's vulnerability rather than his violence and defiance. Aalya spoke to the boy calmly and patiently, asking him to sit next to her and watch the other children play, as he did not stop throwing sand after she had repeatedly demanded this of him. She said to him, "You're a big boy and next year you'll be in first grade. In first grade, the children don't play with sand...Why don't you take the time this year to enjoy playing with the sand? In first grade, you'll have less free time; you'll sit with your mom and do homework. You'll write and you'll read." To this, the boy answered sadly, "But my mom is always working. Who will help me? I don't know how to write and read." This seemed to have had a dramatic impact on the teacher, reflected in the re-writings of the sixth and seventh episode. And indeed, the second writing of the sixth episode is devoted to thoughts about this boy's fate and how to help him. She worries about the "hard life he would have in the future." She writes that she feels she has to be attentive to this boy, but, she notes, he rejects her attempts to be nice to him; he does not comply with her requests, he runs away, and gets furious all the time. In this writing, Aalya is caught in an internal struggle: Although she wants to pay more attention to and take care of the boy, on the other hand, she expresses a desire to liberate herself from responsibility for him, both because of the mother's lack of cooperation, her refusal to take the boy to occupational therapy, and his own resistant behavior. Nevertheless, Aalya decides to help him. She goes to the college library and reads Haim Omer's book *The Struggle against Children's Violence*, which claims that violence is a symptom, and that one should find and address the roots of the violence in each case and not the symptom. Aalya writes that she deeply agrees with this claim. In the fifth record of the same episode, she writes:

> I think that our job is to educate the children and help them out when they don't succeed...Tomorrow I will call the superintendent and ask for help for Mahmud. I want to help him learn as much as possible before first grade so that it will be easier for him when he starts school. For two days I have been surfing the internet and found interesting articles...and I want to reinforce Mahmud's good traits, and what he is good at. I'll give him a responsible role; I'll make him responsible for the doctor's center in the preschool.

The repeated writings helped Aalya *regulate her negative feelings* towards perpetrators, their parents, and staff, and helped her understand the perpetrators' behavior more *ecologically*. She understood both how the boy's relationships with his parents contributed to his behavior and how interactions in her preschool with and among parents and staff affected her ability to act on behalf of these children. Discussions with the perpetrators helped form *caring relationships* with them. The repeated writings and reflections generated by this process helped her assume *leadership* that generated *proactive* coping with the children's misbehavior and finally generated an elaborated plan of action focused on all "problematic children." Furthermore, the plan includes both a learning and a behavioral agenda – compatible with the perspective of classroom management in striving to create conditions of security, learning, and a sense of belonging for all the children, as opposed to perceiving classroom management as a way to impose order in the classroom. Furthermore, her plan of action is reflective and focused as will be shown in the last section of the results, on goals related to ways to regulate her thoughts and feelings as well as on actions focused on assuring educational support for the children.

At the end of the fourth recording of the seventh and last episode, Aalya writes in a matter of fact way (no expressions of feelings can be found in this narrative (28 April 2014):

> We have two more months until the end of the school year. I decided that I have to help the "problematic children" in my preschool advance/learn as much as I can until the end of the school year so that they are as ready as possible for school.
>
> CONCLUSIONS [capital letters in the original]

1. Be less pressured by discontent parents, by children's interference, by assistants who will always find something to gossip about; I am the director of my preschool and I have to be a leader of the children and the staff;
2. I must strengthen myself in this area. I am the preschool teacher and it is my responsibility not only to focus on the consequences of children falling, hitting someone, or pulling someone's hair. I am responsible for their education/learning.
3. I insisted and I am going to get extra help for the children who have shown learning difficulties in my class. Two kinds of extra help – math and occupational therapy. In addition, I started to give responsibility for all sorts of tasks to the problematic children.

Case 2

The narratives written by Margalit show that in each cycle of writing, she initially felt frightened by the intensity of the children's anger and aggression; in all cases, however, she adopted actions to stop the aggressor and prevent further damage. In all the episodes from the very first, Margalit seems to pay attention both to the perpetrator and the victim as well as the burden on the assistant due to her direct handling of the aggressive behavior. *Moral leadership* is thus present in her coping with children's challenging behavior from the very beginning.

The repeated writings contributed to the gradual emergence of *ecological* intervention plans that took into account the child, his/her parents, the other staff, and the community resources needed to help each child overcome the difficulties that gave rise to the behavioral problems. *Proactive thinking* based on an ecological perception of the class emerged gradually. At first, proactive thinking is focused on actions to be undertaken to stop aggression; it then focuses on attempts to facilitate good relations among children frequently in conflict. Ways to cooperate with the staff are the focus of additional contemplation. Interestingly, in all cases Margalit assumes leadership and copes by herself with the children's severe outbursts while assuring her assistant's support in taking care of the other children.

In the first episode, for example, Margalit's thinking while at home gradually led her to formulate a plan of action that was eventually implemented. She testified that she could not stop thinking about Amir, a boy who displayed aggressive and non-compliant behavior, disrupting the class by destroying children's block constructions and spilling water everywhere, culminating in throwing a glass of water at the psychologist who came to give Margalit counseling.

> I decided to think about ways [of intervention]. [About] actions, what I do in order to be more available for Amir. How will I get closer to Amir's mother and get her more interested in what is going on in the preschool. And, of course, how do I continue to set limits on Amir's behavior in a consistent way – for his own sake and the sake of all the children? However, I am also aware of the assistant's distress as she has to cope with all the children [while Margalit is coping with Amir]. It's very hard to decide what to do: take care of the extra burden put on the assistant or take care of Amir as I sense that he needs my support. I am also worried about the other children and thinking about them all the time...

The Use of Repeated Narrative Writing by Teachers ...		293

Next Margalit contemplates how to achieve parental cooperation even in hard cases, such as that in the first episode in which the mother seemed to deny the boy's problems or in the fifth episode focused on Ofir, whose parents had a hard time setting limits on their child's behavior. Proactive thinking, based on an ecological understanding of the situation and the preschool, leads Margalit to formulate the children's problems in broad terms (such as seeing relationships between the child's behavior problem, his learning disabilities, and the resources available for dealing with his difficulties in state agencies in the community). In all cases, after analyzing the difficulties directly related to the functioning of the perpetrators and their indirect impact on the management of the preschool, Margalit asks for additional help, either as counsel (for example, to discuss Yigal's terrible anger outbursts with the psychologist and decide together what to do on his behalf as she suspects that the learning disability contributes to the boys challenging behavior), or in the form of national service volunteers in the preschool (in the first episode), or professional treatment for the children (speech or educational therapy, art therapy in episodes 1, 2 and 5), as seen in Margalit's third narrative of the second episode.

Margalit's proactive thinking and planning helped her find an opportunity to act on behalf of Amir and the other children as shown in the fourth re-writing of the first episode (11 January 2015):

> On Friday morning when Amir's mother brought him to the preschool, I asked her to tell us [the whole class] about her workplace – the fire station. The children were very attentive and I asked her to send us pictures of the fire station. On Sunday, Amir's mother sent photos to my mobile phone and I asked Amir to take the phone and show the children the pictures. I felt that Amir was glad about this. He seemed quite pleased that we shared the pictures with all the preschool children. After the talk I had with Amir's mother, she took him for a visit to her workplace.

Margalit's intervention did not end there. In the fifth and last writing of the first episode (12 January 2015), she writes:

> I understand that I have to act more intensively. To get additional help for the preschool, I call the municipal preschool department and ask for extra help [volunteers]. I don't give in. Two days later, I get a joyful message: I will get a volunteer and extra help from an emotion therapist and a speech therapist.

The fifth and last episode focused on Margalit's coping with Ofir's tantrum following her request to have skates returned home by the boy's father, and shows how the teacher acts as a moral leader, making decisions in favor of the child's improved functioning in the preschool. In this case, no signs of helplessness or fatigue appear, even in the first writing of the episode, but rather focused thinking on how to help the child cope better with limits set on his behavior. Repeated observations of Ofir's behavior led Margalit to realize that she had to guide him how to play in preschool and to work collaboratively with his parents on setting limits. An understanding dawned that the boy may also be experiencing learning disabilities. This led her to arrange a meeting with the boy's parents and ask a community agency for professional treatment for him. *The negative feelings experienced by Margalit in the first two writings of the skate episode* (anger toward the boy's uncontrolled behavior) *are transformed into comprehension of the context of his behavior and a suitable treatment plan for him.* In the fifth and last episode, Margalit seemed to handle the situation smoothly, following a pattern that gradually emerged through repeated writings of the previous episodes. Thus, the repeated writings helped Margalit develop classroom management competencies such as ecological and proactive perceptions of the preschool based on the moral leadership she started with the repeated narrative writings. The repeated narrative writings helped her rely on her judgements and ask for professional help she considered necessary for the development of the children.

DISCUSSION

Repeated narrative writing emerged in this study as a potentially useful tool for teachers coping with young children's behavior problems. Findings show (as indicated in Figure 1) that severe incidents, frequently involving aggression related to children's behavior problems, elicit extreme fear, anger, guilt, and helplessness in experienced teachers. These feelings were associated with fragmented perceptions of the situation and reactive conduct adopted by the teachers. The intensive use of RNW for a few incidents triggered *self-regulatory* processes, intensive thinking about the situation that led to the assumption of *leadership*, and *self-determination* to act on behalf of the perpetrators, the victims, and all the children in the class or preschool. As predicted by Self-Determination Theory (Ryan & Decy, 2000 and 2017), repeated narrative writing seems to help teachers liberate themselves and their actions from the control of fear, guilt, helplessness, and despair, allowing them to think of more creative, ecological solutions for coping with the challenging behavior. This self-determination helped teachers organize their thinking about the resources available in the class and community, and contributed to *proactive thinking* of actions to be taken based on an *ecological perception* of the class, including links between children and staff, among children, among staff, and between staff and the children's parents. There is frequent mention in the narratives of a need to establish *good relationships with perpetrators (despite their defiant behavior), victims, children's parents, and staff.* The narratives show that actions taken to implement the plans are subject to further reflection and lead to further action. Thus, all elements in Tal's (2010, 2016) model of moral classroom management emerged from the analysis of narratives (and are represented in Figure 1). Furthermore, as can be seen in the figure and shown in the first section of the results above, the repeated writing of each episode displayed a reduction in negative emotional words from the first to the last writing, and a concomitant increase of positive emotional and cognitive effects (causality and insight words), reflecting the improved organization of thought and self-regulation undergone by the teachers. All these are intended to bring about improved learning and well-being of the children.

The research literature shows that negative emotions can lead teachers to use ineffective classroom management strategies, which in turn can exacerbate children's behavior problems (Sutton, Mudrey-Camino, & Knight, 2009). As noted, RNW appears to be effective in reducing a teacher's negative emotions associated with children's behavior problems.

In both of the cases presented in this study, self-determination replaced helplessness, though feelings of helplessness occasionally recurred when coping with new crises provoked by the children's behavior. The emergence of self-determination appears to require numerous cycles of narrative writings and time. Thus, in both cases, we witnessed throughout the repeated narrative re-writings a transformation from helplessness to a fully formulated, self-determined stance leading to emergence or activation of classroom management mindsets and competencies, culminating in the creation of socio-moral intervention plans for perpetrators, victims, and the class as a whole. Furthermore, in Case 1 we found a real transformation in the perception of intervention as the teacher began to regard the children showing behavior problems as in need for support and help as much as the victims.

Even though the approach of the two teachers toward behavior problems seems to have been transformed from being fragmented and reactive into a proactive, ecological approach committed to the well-being of the children, temporary feelings of helplessness reappear now and then. Thus, it is important to differentiate between temporary feelings of helplessness and "learned helplessness," which could lead to burnout (McCarthy, Lineback & Reiser, 2015). Hence, we suggest further inquiry into the possibility that using RNW for emotionally loaded incidents related to children's behavior problems may be helpful in preventing teacher burnout.

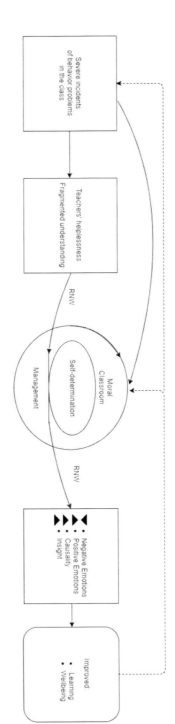

Figure 1. Repeated narrative writing, self-determination, classroom management and children's wellbeing, and improved learning conditions.

A well internalized motivation to benefit the children, to become fully committed to their learning and well-being, is more likely to flourish in the context of feelings of security and relatedness (Ryan & Deci, 2017). Indeed, what initially seemed to jeopardize Aalya's leadership of her preschool and her own well-being was a lack of emotional security and a sense of disconnect with her staff and the children's parents. Her engagement with RNW helped her find sources of emotional support for herself (a friend in her village, her husband and daughters, a teacher colleague). From a more secure, socially connected base, she was prepared to proactively and strategically cope with threats and overcome them for the full benefit of all the children involved. Margalit, feeling initially lonely and overwhelmed, planned and implemented partnerships during the course of the RNW with the children's parents and her staff as part of the effective intervention plans for the children.

What emerged from this study is the understanding that mindsets (moral leadership, proactive and ecological thinking) and competencies (self-regulation and relationships with children' parents and staff) that are part of moral classroom management are activated and improved during the course of the repeated narrative writings. Data analysis led to the conclusion that a teacher's self-determination constitutes the heart of moral classroom management. Moral leadership of children, parents, and staff toward creating the conditions of well-being and learning for all is impossible without a teacher's well-developed self-determination that guides her actions from an internalized sense of commitment to the people involved. Furthermore, self-regulation – required for improving one's functioning in response to conditions and difficulties encountered in the real world – is activated from a stance of self-determination and directly benefits from RNW when applied to the stressful coping with children's behavior problems and their impact on the environment. Analysis of additional cases of RNW is needed to support this conceptualization.

CONCLUSION

Coping with behavior problems as a component of classroom management, needs to be perceived as a core competency in teaching and in teacher education, as an essential component of what Ball and Forzani (2009) call "the work of teaching" – "the core tasks that teachers must execute to help pupils learn" (p. 497). Stough (2006) suggested that classroom management should be integrated as a fundamental component of all teacher preparation programs. Yet, as Stough & Montague (2015) conclude in their review of how novice and experienced teachers learn to be classroom managers, there is a need for more training in this area.

In this small-scale study, we showed how the systematic use and analysis of RNW about emotionally loaded episodes related to children's challenging behaviors helped two experienced teachers regulate their negative feelings towards perpetrators, the perpetrators' parents, or staff and helped them develop coping methods to deal with complex situations posed by the children's behavior and become self-determined moral leaders of preschools. *However, based on the findings of this study, we cannot conclude that this procedure would work for inexperienced teachers.* Nevertheless, the findings of this small-scale study are compatible with Pennebaker's findings based on hundreds of studies (for example, Pennebaker & Chung, 2011) that indicate that expressive recursive writing focused on emotionally loaded episodes was associated with improved wellness and functioning. Implementation of the RNW tool is manageable, inexpensive, and congruent with journal and critical-incident writing that are frequently used tools in teacher education. Therefore, we suggest further research on a larger scale to evaluate the usefulness of RNW in coping with behavior problems both at preparation and professional development levels.

REFERENCES

Angelides, P. (2010). The development of an efficient technique for collecting and analyzing qualitative data: The analysis of critical incidents. *International Journal of Qualitative Studies in Education*, *14*(3), 429-449.

Atkins, S., & Murphy, K. (1995). Reflective practice. *Nursing Standard*, *9*(45), 31-37.

Bandura, A. (1986). *Social foundations of thought and action: A social-cognitive theory*. Englewood Cliffs, NJ: Prentice Hall.

Bandura, A. (1994). Self-efficacy. In V. S. Ramachaudran (Ed.), *Encyclopedia of human behavior* (vol. 4, pp. 71-81). New York: Academic Press.

Bandura, A. (1997). *Self-efficacy and the exercise of control*. New York: Freeman.

Belsky, J. (2013). Differential susceptibility to environmental influences. *International Journal of Child Care and Education Policy*, *7*(2), 15-31.

Bowman. R. F. Jr & Richard, F. (1983) The personal student journal: mirror of the mind. *Contemporary Education*, *55*, 25-27.

Campbell, S. B. (2006). Maladjustment in preschool children: A developmental psychopathology perspective. In K. McCartney, & D. Phillips (Eds.) *Handbook of early childhood development* (pp. 358-377). Malden, MA: Blackwell.

Campbell, S., Spieker, S., Burchinal, M., Poe, M., & National Institute of Child Health and Human Development Early Child Care Research Network (2006). Trajectories of aggression from toddlerhood to age 9 predict academic and social functioning through age 12. *Journal of Child Psychology and Psychiatry*, *47*, 791-800.

Carlson, J. S., Tiret, H. B., Bender, S. L., & Benson, L. (2011). The influence of group training in the incredible years teacher classroom management program on preschool teachers' classroom management strategies. *Journal of Applied School Psychology*, *27*(2), 134-154. doi: 0.1080/15377903.2011.565277.

Clandinin, D. J., & Connelly, F. M. (2000). *Narrative inquiry: Experience and story in qualitative research*. San Francisco: Jossey-Bass.

Dinkelman, T. (2003). Self-study in teacher education: A means and ends tool for promoting reflective teaching. *Journal of Teacher Education, 54*(1), 6-19.

Dunlap, G., Strain, P. S., Fox, L., Carta, J. J., Conroy, M., & Smith, B. (2006). Prevention and intervention with young children's challenging behavior: Perspectives regarding current knowledge. *Behavioral Disorders, 32*, 29-45.

Emmer, E. T, & Stough, L. M. (2001). Classroom management: A critical part of educational psychology. *Educational Psychologist, 36*, 103-112.

Evertson, C. M., & Weinstein, C. S. (2006). Classroom management as a field of inquiry. In C. M. Evertson & C. S. Weinstein (Eds.), *Handbook of classroom management: Research, practice and contemporary issues* (pp. 3-17). Mahwah, NJ: Erlbaum.

Flyvbjerg, B. (2011). Case study. In N. K. Denzin, & Y. S. Lincoln (Eds.), *Sage handbook of qualitative research* (4th ed., pp. 301-316). Thousand Oaks CA: Sage.

Fox, L., Dunlap, G., & Powell, D. (2002). Young children with challenging behavior: Issues and consideration for behavior support. *Journal of Positive Behavior Interventions, 4*, 208-217.

Francis, D. (1997). Critical incident analysis: A strategy for developing reflective practice. *Teachers and Teaching, 3*(2), 169-188.

Gettinger, M., & Fischer, C. (2015). Early childhood education classroom management. In E. T. Emmer, & E. J. Sabornie (Eds.). *Handbook of classroom management* (pp. 141-166). New York and London: Routledge.

Giallo, R., & Little, E. (2003). Classroom behavior problems: The relationship between preparedness, classroom experiences, and self-efficacy in graduate and student teachers. *Australian Journal of Educational and Developmental Psychology, 3*, 21-34.

Griffin, J. A. (2010). Research on the implementation of preschool intervention programs: Learning by doing. *Early Childhood Research Quarterly, 25*, 267-269.

Griffin, M. L. (2003). Using critical incidents to promote and assess reflective thinking in preservice teachers. *Reflective Practice, 4*(2), 207-220.

Hamre, B. K., & Pianta, R. C. (2005). Can instructional and emotional support in the first-grade classroom make a difference for children at risk of school failure. *Child Development, 76*, 949-967.

Howes, C., & Ritchie, S. (2002). *A matter of trust: Connecting teachers and learners in the early childhood classroom.* New York: Teachers College Press.

Kaiser, B., & Rasminsky, J. S. (2017). *Challenging behavior in young children* (4th edition). Boston: Pearson.

Korpershoek, H., Harms, T., de Boer, H., van Kuijk, M., & Doolaard, S. (2016). A meta-analysis of the effects of classroom management strategies and classroom management programs on students' academic, behavioral, emotional, and motivational outcomes. *Review of Educational Research, 86*(3), 643–680. doi: 10.3102/ 003465431 5626799.

Landau, B. (2009). Classroom management. In L. J. Saha & A. J. Dworkin (Eds.), *International handbook of research on teachers and teaching* (pp. 739-755). New York: Springer.

McCarthy, C. J., Lineback, S., & Reiser, J. (2015). Teacher stress, emotion, and classroom management. In E. T. Emmer, & E. J. Sabornie (Eds.). *Handbook of classroom management* (pp. 301-321). New York and London: Routledge.

Moon, J. (2006). Learning journals. *A handbook for reflective practice and professional development.* London: Routledge.

Murray, E. J., Lamnin, A. D., & Carver, C. S. (1989). Emotional expression in written essays and psychotherapy. *Journal of Social and Clinical Psychology, 8*, 414-429.

Pennebaker, J. W. & Francis, M. E. (1996). Cognitive, emotional, and language processes in disclosure. *Cognition and Emotion, 10*, 601-626.

The Use of Repeated Narrative Writing by Teachers ... 303

Pennebaker, J. W., & Chung, C. K. (2011). Expressive writing and its links to mental and physical health. In H. S. Friedman (Ed.), *Oxford handbook of health psychology* (pp. 263-284). New York: Oxford University Press.

Pennebaker, J. W., & Evans, F. (2014). *Expressive writing: Words that heal*. Idyll Arbor, Incorporated.

Russo, T. C., & Ford, D. J. (2006). Teachers' reflection on reflective practice. *Journal of Cognitive Affective Learning*, 2(2), 1-12.

Ryan, R. M. & Deci, E. L. (2000). Self-determination theory and the facilitation of intrinsic motivation, social development, and well-being. *American Psychologist*, 55(1) 68-78.

Ryan, R. M. & Deci, E. L. (2017). *Self-determination theory: Basic psychological needs in motivation development and wellness*. New York: Guilford Press.

Smith, B., & Fox, L. (2003). *Systems of service delivery: A synthesis of evidence relevant to young children at risk of or who have challenging behavior*. Tampa: Center for Evidence-Based Practice: Young Children with Challenging Behavior, University of South Florida.

Smyth, J. M., & Pennebaker, J. W. (1999). Sharing one's story: Translating emotional experiences into words as a coping tool. In C. R. Snyder (Ed.). *Coping: The psychology of what works* (pp. 70-89). New York: Oxford University Press.

Stough, L. M. (2006). The place of classroom management and standards in teacher education. In C. M. Evertson & C. S. Weinstein (Eds.), *Handbook of classroom management: Research, practice and contemporary issues* (pp. 909-923). Mahwah, NJ: Erlbaum.

Stough, L. M., & Montague, M. L. (2015). How teachers learn to be classroom managers. In E. T. Emmer & E. J. Sabornie (Eds.). *Handbook of classroom management* (pp. 446-458). New York and London: Routledge.

Sutton, R. E., Mudrey-Camino, R. & Knight, C. C. (2009). Teachers' emotion regulation and classroom management. *Theory into Practice*, 48(2) 130-137.

Tal, C. (2005). *Emotional intelligence*. Tel Aviv and Haifa: Mofet Institute and Ach Publishing House [Hebrew].

Tal, C. (2010). Moral classroom management. In S. B. Thompson (Ed.). *Kindergartens: Programs, functions, and outcomes* (pp. 115-132). New York, NY: Nova Science Publishers.

Tal, C. (2014). Self-transcendence values, relationships, and participatory practice in early childhood education. *Education Research International, 2014*, Article ID 371831. doi:10.1155/2014/371831.

Tal, C. (2016). *Moral classroom management in early childhood education*. New York: Nova Science books.

Yin, R. K. (2009). *Case study research: Design and methods* (4th ed.). Thousand Oaks, CA: Sage.

Zimmerman, B. J. (2000). Attaining self-regulation: A social-cognitive perspective. In M. Boekaerts, P. R. Pintrich, & M. Zeidner (Eds.), *Handbook of self-regulation* (pp. 13-39). San Diego, CA: Academic Press.

APPENDIX

Guidelines to teachers for repeated narrative writing related to behavior problems:

Below are guidelines to teachers for repeated narrative writing related to behavior problems (based on Smyth & Pennebaker, 1999; adapted by Tal, 2005).

Over the next four or five days, please write a personal story about a stressful, difficult, or traumatic event in which you participated related to a child displaying behavioral problems in your class. Please write your deepest thoughts and feelings about this particular event. I invite you to feel free to learn about your thoughts and feelings. You might link the topic to your relations with others; you might link it to your past, present, or future, or to who you have been, who you would like to be, or who you are now. You may write about the same issue or experience every day of your writing, or you may write about different stressful events each day.

In: Teacher Training
Editor: Paula E. McDermott

ISBN: 978-1-53615-633-1
© 2019 Nova Science Publishers, Inc.

Chapter 8

PRACTICAL ARGUMENTS: MAKING TEACHERS' REFLECTIONS ON TEACHING PRACTICES VISIBLE

Lea Lund[*]
Centre for Teaching Development and Digital Media, Aarhus,
Aarhus University, Denmark

ABSTRACT

This chapter demonstrates an approach to elicit and make visible teachers' ideas of teaching and their reflections on teaching practices. Inspired by the approach of constructing a *practical argument* allows for analysis of teachers' thinking in combination with their actions in the classroom. This approach can be viewed as a vehicle for encouraging the growth of teacher development. Drawing on an eight-month study of teachers – novice and experienced teachers – in Adult Education in Denmark this novel research approach provides the opportunity to support, stimulate and nurture critical reflection by the teachers of their own practices.

---

[*] Corresponding Author's E-mail: Lealund@tdm.au.dk

Keywords: teacher beliefs, teacher reflection, critical friend, teacher vocabulary, practical arguments

INTRODUCTION

Learning through Experience

Teachers gain reflections of teaching through a teacher education and professional development programs. However, the time they spend in the classroom is central to the development of their repertoire of good practices. It is therefore surprising that there is little focus in the educational literature on how and what teachers learn through their classroom practices. This chapter suggest that teachers may benefit from critical pedagogical reflection that exposes the hidden aspects of their everyday teaching. The research on teacher thinking points to a strong connection between teachers' beliefs and their actions in the classroom. It is therefore important to focus on that perspective when investigating the practice of teachers. The chapter illustrates a dialogical approach where pedagogical questions are generated to support reflection that encourages the development of a pedagogical vocabulary, eliciting and making visible teachers' reflections on classroom practice. For teachers' professional development, this approach is important when considering how to foster teachers' pedagogical and educational awareness about their everyday practices in the classroom.

The research was initiated through curiosity about a deep understanding of 'learning in practice', the processes of informal learning and on the job learning. Following an ethnographic approach, the concern was to acknowledge and capture teachers' everyday work, their up and downs, their success and struggles and their voices and experiences. These aspects are of great importance to teacher-training colleges as well as student teachers, who enter the teaching profession with beliefs and experiences which are also worth investigating. The study combined class observations, teacher's written reflection journals and two collections of

Practical Arguments 307

semi-structured interviews, the first grounded in their reflection journal, and the second following directly after the in-class observation. As the study progressed, I became aware of the changes in the way in which teachers both reflected on their practices and on the language, they used to describe and present arguments for what they were doing.

The aim and the outcome of this chapter is to demonstrate and propose a method to elicit and make visible teachers' reflections on teaching practices while acknowledging the voices of teachers. The approach may therefore have three distinct advantages. *First*, it may benefit educational research by analysing the way in which teachers think and act in the classroom. *Second*, it may help student teachers to reflect on the experiences they gain during teacher training. And *third*, it may support the in-school professional development of teachers. The last two benefits could potentially provide the opportunity to stimulate and nurture critical reflection of the teachers' own practices.

The Composition of the Chapter

This chapter proceeds by first providing a brief description from literature on learning through experience, teacher thinking using the perspective understood by Erling L. Dale's terms (1998). In the following sections the research design is presented while findings from this study are presented in other work (Lund 2015; Lund 2016; Lund & Robinson 2017). Finally follows an illustration of the approach of how the data were analyzed with illustrative examples from the study (Lund 2015; Lund 2016). In conclusion, I consider the contribution and the possible application of this method to teacher education in the future.

The Background of the Chapter

In this chapter, I share with you a murky phenomenon and shed some light on the Schön-like 'swampy lowland' (1983) where teachers must be able to articulate and justify the choices they make as leaders of learning. His metaphor of teachers walking in a muddy, murky and swampy classroom highlights the situation where teachers do not necessarily "make effective use of research-based theory and technique" but, as leaders of learning, they articulate and justify their choices through "trial and error, intuition, and muddling through" situations that are often "confusing 'messes'" (Schön 1983, p.42). The study had to embrace this 'muddling' through practice and thus became an investigation of how and to what extent teachers' reflective processes inform their professional development.

Even though humans recognize that they have learned things through experience they do not necessarily remember how or when (Eraut 2009, p.2). Since we know that humans find it difficult to establish a verbal connection between what has been learned and what has been learned from, it is a difficult task to gain insight into the phenomenon of learning through experience. If it was possible to investigate the teachers' professional growth by viewing the processes of reflection as a part of their potential learning by experience we would learn much about internal and invisible mechanisms that affect their professional lives and those of the learners they interact with. But as Michael Eraut states it not that simple: "One of its best established findings… is that people *do not know what they know"* (Eraut's underline 1994, p.15). As teachers spend most of their career actually teaching it is reasonable to assume that a great deal of their competency and skills develop on the spot and in the heat of the moment – during the classroom activities. Therefore, we must assume that teachers also acquire knowledge about teaching through their teaching experiences (Darling-hammond 1999; Richardson 1996). The research into adult learning suggests that teacher knowledge is constantly in the process of development (Merriam et al. 2007). It is well known that teachers, like other professions, continually learn on the job because their work involves engagement in a succession of cases or problems which they have to learn about as they experience them. But, in contrast to learning in formal settings, there is only weak evidence of how the phenomenon of learning through experience develops (Eraut 1994).

Practical Arguments

309

The aim of the study was not only to get insight to their processes of learning in practice by assessing their ability to articulate their thoughts (as van Manen's levels of reflection: 1977, p.226) but also to be able to say something about teachers' thinking processes from their perspective too. It was important to find a way to establish a technique that was credible and trustworthy to both the research society and the teachers themselves. The starting point was to both acknowledge and capture the teachers' everyday work, by giving them a voice (Elbaz 1983; Clandinin 1995; Connelly & Clandinin 1990) at all times during their practice, when things went well and when they did not. It is often in the bumpy moments (Romano 2006), the critical incidents (Tripp 1994; Angelides 2001) the disjuncture of routines (Jarvis 2002) that humans learn and change habits and minds and thereby have learned and developed professionally, which go back to John Dewey (1933). By sharing these kinds of expcriences, we become witness to some of the most valuable in a teachers' career.

LITERATURE REVIEW

Teacher Thinking – Acknowledging Beliefs as Predictors of Actions

The research on teacher thinking points to a strong connection between teachers' beliefs and their actions (Kompf & O'Connell Rust 2013; Richardson 1996; Pajares 1992; Donahue 2000; Orton 1996). Much of this research acknowledges that beliefs are the foundation of action and a key determinant of behavior. But we also know that teachers' beliefs are hard to change (Hoekstra et al. 2009). As Yerrick and colleagues (1997) proves in their study teachers assimilate new ideas into their existing belief systems and use new language to describe their teaching but without adjusting their underlying beliefs. And as Donahue (2000) concludes in his study on preservice teachers' service learning beliefs, experiences and context is of great important therefore he argues for "implementing a new pedagogy to thoughtful reflection on the value-laden act of teaching" (p.

429). The teachers' beliefs have a huge impact on the teacher's perspective on teaching, schooling and curriculum therefore they are of great importance to teacher development.

By studying the beliefs that inform teachers' thinking (Priestley et al. 2015; Nespor 1987; Meirink et al. 2009; Orton 1996) educational researchers are in a better position to understand the processes that guide teachers with respect to behavior, judgment, decision-making, and planning. The importance of the complexity of the construct 'belief' is important as it has entangled connotations to the construct 'knowledge' (Referring mainly to: Pajares 1992; Richardson 1996; Nespor 1987). Knowledge is seen as facts whereas beliefs are regarded as opinions. Knowledge is often viewed as something that changes while beliefs are more static. Beliefs are stronger predictors of behavior and far more influential than knowledge in determining how individuals organize and define tasks and problems (Nespor 1987; Further discussed by: Brinkmann 2007; Orton 1996).

In the area of research on Mathematic instruction and teaching there is currently a huge interest into the connection between beliefs and the selection of tasks (Furinghetti & Morselli 2011; de Araujo 2017) and warranting the mathematic teachers' pedagogical considerations (Nardi et al. 2012; Leatham 2006). The interest in the construct 'belief' in educational settings originates with scholars such as Kagan (1992; Kagan & Tippins 1991) and Pajares (1992). When we study thinking processes it leads to an understanding of the processes that guide teacher behaviour, judgment, decision-making and planning (Ibid.; Priestley et al. 2015). Teachers lean towards their prior 'implicit theories' and beliefs and experiences when learning to teach (Clark & Yinger 1977, p.295). Even when teachers accept information from others "they filter it through their own personal belief system, translating and absorbing it into their own unique pedagogies" (Kagan 1992, p.75). Research shows that experiences and reflection on action may lead to changes in and/or additions to beliefs as the beliefs and actions are regarded as interactive (Mansour 2009).

Dale's perspective provides a framework for capturing the teachers' reflection on practice. Dale's (1998; 1999) research on teacher's

Practical Arguments

professional practices distinguishes between three levels of competence. These levels are (1998, p.256): C1) the carrying out of teaching (teaching activities), C2) the construction of teaching programs, curriculum, and lesson planning and C3) the communication and construction of a theory of teaching plans, the act of teaching, and pupils' learning process. At the final level C3, Dale (ibid, p. 256) articulates the importance of collaborative peer reflection and underlines the synergy between the *why* (theory of education, the subjects, the curriculum) and *how* (method and approach) in teaching. Furthermore, when all three competencies coexist, Dale proposes that the teacher and school have achieved an 'educational rationality' (1998, p. 256), a kind of communicative act of teaching that gives "priority to goal-setting, planning, and evaluation".

Dale argues that the synergy between the three competences shapes a professional school and teachers must have the opportunity to handle educational responsibility by incorporating C3, reflection and dialogue. It may be easier to achieve levels C1 and C2, which are about technical performance, but since teaching is not merely a technical act, teachers must also be able to achieve C3. A focus on all three levels reminds us not to let the *how* dominate – not seeing teaching as merely a technique and the teachers as minions – but regard teachers as reflective agents and co-developers of teaching and education. Furthermore, by giving priority to all three levels reminds us not to focus solely on teaching concepts as the solution achieving learning goals or only measure learning in terms of student outcome. The perspective of educational rationality and thereby the incorporation of the third level (C3) of meta-discussions and thinking helps shed a light on the attitude and beliefs held by the teachers. By focusing on C3 teachers are able to devote time to the *why* in teaching, which is unpredictable and open to constant negotiation. See also Biesta (2009) and Klafki (2000) and Westbury (2000).

Therefore, the incorporation and the constant synergy with the third level is important, but understanding how mechanisms for reflection on practices can be initiated and supported, are equally as important. Educational rationality encompasses the reflective process of thinking and arguing and giving good reasons for what one does or says.

It is important to stress that by using this approach suggested in this chapter one is not investigating the teachers' ability to argue and reflect and give good reasons during their teaching act. That is what Michael Eraut illustrated as the busy kitchen scenario when serving a hot menu (2002). In that position, one cannot argue verbally but must just act rapidly as these – 'hot moments' – in class are often tacit and an unspoken way of knowing. The reflective part I investigate, does of course relate to moments of serving a hot menu, that concerns immediate/urgent actions and habits and events taking place at C1, but the dialogue and teachers writing occurs at C2+C3. The research design described below demonstrates how it is possible to capture all levels of practice as described above.

RESEARCH DESIGN

The research design was structured initially to help answer the following: How can teachers' experiences of practice become visible? How and what do teachers learn through reflection? How can meta-reflection, or analysis, be supported? Data collection took place in the Adult Education Centres in Denmark over a period of eight months (Lund 2016; Lund 2015). Ten teachers of adult learners (7 females and 3 males) volunteered to participate in this study. Participants' teaching experience ranged between 1-27 years. Their head teacher characterized participants as eager to investigate and question their own teaching. See appendix A for details on teacher participants, subjects, age and gender, hours of observation, hours of recording, verbatim transcribed, and teachers' journal. The number of informants (N=10) from the key study (Lund 2015; Lund 2016) prohibits me from making statistical generalisations but align with others in the field such as Elbaz (1983; 2015), Conelley and Cladinin (Clandinin & Connelly 1987; Connelly & Clandinin 1990) and Biesta et al. (2017) and Vásquez-Levy (1993). Figure 1 below describes the methodological triangulation. The data sources define the four elements described in Figure 1 following Figure 2. The numbers in Figure 1 indicate the timeline for the data collection.

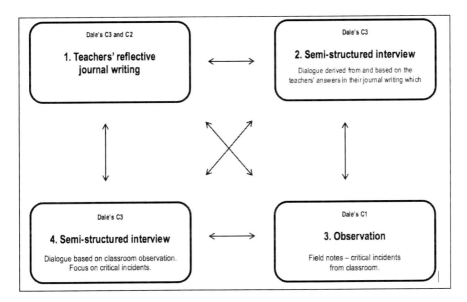

Figure 1. Research Design for Capturing teacher reflection.

The arrows in Figure 1 illustrate the workflow between reflective writing (#1 see also appendix B) and dialogue (#2) combined with observation (#3) and immediately dialogue again (#4). The focus on the teachers' practice and beliefs becomes holistic and dynamic. The arrows that cross each other in the middle symbolize the interaction between the data sources during the analysis process. The different sources combined to generate a thickness in themes emerged.

This approach strives to give the teacher a voice. I have worked specifically on the thickness and density of emerging themes to comply with the scientific standard of qualitative research. In line with this, triangulation supports the validity of the analysis in depth (Gibbs 2007, p.86) and the trustworthiness (illustrated in: Lund 2015; Lund 2016; Lund & Robinson 2017). All the data has been analyzed in an open coding process – a data-driven process (Miles & Hubermann 1994) – starting with hundreds of open themes end ending with 61 emerged themes in the entire data material. The work was done in Nvivo to ensure transparency (findings revealed in: Lund & Robinson 2017; Lund 2015; Lund 2016). Capturing all three levels of competencies, following Dale (1998, 1999), the research design can be summed up as follows:

- Capturing the teachers' experiences (C1: in class) and thoughts out of class (C2, C3): by talking and elaborating on their vocabulary during reflection journals (#1) and interviews (#2).
- Capturing the teachers' actions in class and preparing the lessons (C1, C2) by observation (#3), by talking (#4) and all together elaborating on their vocabulary used during reflection journals and interviews.

How to Make Teachers' Reflections on Teaching Practices Visible

The interview process follows the basic idea from Brinkmann's epistemic interview technique (2007), where the informant - the teacher - is seen as a responsible citizen, able to argue and give reasons more than just telling about feelings and experiences as in phenomenological approaches which search only for lived experiences (discussed in: Brinkmann 2007; Pendlebury 1990). As Brinkmann states:

"Plato's dialogues were precisely designed as ways of testing whether the conversation partners have knowledge, that is, whether they are capable of adequately justifying their beliefs, and, if they cannot (which is normally the case), if their beliefs are unwarranted, the dialogues unfold as dialectical processes of refining their beliefs – their doxa – in light of good reasons, to approach episteme." (Brinkmann 2007, p. 1124)

And in the perspective of epistemic interviews the researcher becomes a critical friend (Baskerville et al. 2009; Kiewkor et al. 2014; Gibbs &

Angelides 2008) provoking the teacher to take a stand and argue for and against (at C3) as in an Socratic dialogue demonstrated by Plato's examples (Brinkmann 2007, p. 1124).

In order to understand the teachers' process of reflection on the *why* and *how* in education, and relating to the first person perspective (following: Giorgi 1985), the approach strives to combine the tacit aspects of teachers' often unspoken beliefs (Kompf & O'Connell Rust 2013; Richardson 1996; Calderhead 1996) with their actual actions/performances (C1) and their way of thinking before, during and after teaching related to all three competence levels (C1, C2, C3). The research design connects the three competence levels illustrated in Figure 2 below:

First: Focussing on teacher's experiences related to specific situations (captured by teacher's journal writing) an approach that enables the researcher to combine both the teacher's thoughts (C2+C3) elaborated outside the hot moments and the teacher's experienced actions/events (C1).

Second: Collecting a first round of semi structured interview with the teacher using her/his answers written in the reflection journal as an interview guide (connecting the hot moments at C1 to their thoughts/beliefs)

Third: Collecting classroom observations (hot moments at C1) during the dialogues following the initial observations the researcher is able to elicit more of the beliefs that might drive the teacher's way of working with the students.

Fourth: Conducting a second round of semi-structured interview having a dialogue about the classroom observation (connecting the hot moments at C1 to their thoughts/beliefs)

Figure 2. Data Collecting Process Connecting the Three C's.

Interaction between the teachers' practice (C1 and C2) was constructed through open-ended questions in the teachers' reflection journals (inspired by: Kaplan et al. 2007; Surbeck 1994, see Appendix B) and the teacher's beliefs (C3) inspired by Fenstermacher and Richardson (1993) and Vásquez-Levy (1993). I sought to unfold the teacher's beliefs, working with the premises for construction of a 'practical argument' and an approach was developed to initiate C3 – the highest level of reflection. This approach was sensitive to the value of hot moments (labelled as hot actions by: Eraut 1985, p. 128; Eraut 1994, p. 53) existing during the present action at C1. Further I was inspired by Tripp (1994; Tripp 1993) and Angelides (2001) who focus on observation of 'critical incidents' followed immediately by a dialogue, where the researcher comes close to the situation being sensitive to the field and not just as an outside observer (Hammersley & Atkinson 1995). Through the combination of the design elements, in giving the teachers time and support into the articulation of reflection on action, the teachers in the study became able to articulate what and why he/she was doing and following the guidelines the teachers were able to rationalize as in Dale's ideal. Only by combining and nurturing the process of reflection did the educational rationality occur. It became evident that the saturation did not occur when only using a single method. Accordingly, the combination nurtured the reflective process.

The intention was to create the synergy between the teacher's practice (in C1 and C2) and her beliefs at C3 (often not articulated) and to make sure not to undermine the tacit and often unarticulated way of knowing about what and why one is doing. This approach involved structured discussions between teacher and researcher to examine the teachers' 'practical reasoning' to develop a 'practical argument' called 'elicitation' and 'reconstruction' (following the six premisses described in: Fenstermacher & Richardson 1993; examplefied by: Vásquez-Levy 1993; discussed in: Pendlebury 1990; Fenstermacher 1987a; Fenstermacher 1987b; Orton 1996). The process evolves through three essential phases (Vásquez-Levy 1993, p. 126) described in Figure 3 below:

Phase 1. The elicitation and reasoning phase
The elicitation of the teachers' beliefs about approaches to teaching, theories of content and theories of student learning. The teacher is evolving his/her practical reasoning on educational issues.

Phase 2. The elicitation and construction phase
The appraisal of teacher beliefs by using strict standards for examining premises and engaging in ongoing dialogue to advance, support and modify claims and advance competing/alternative premises that are grounded in evidence and truth while excluding those that do not meet this criterion.

Phase 3. The reconstruction phase
The reconstruction of teacher's chain of premises that normalises his/her practical argument – his/her logical chain of reasoning. The reconstruction is as a practical argument.

Figure 3. Three Essential Phases when Working on Practical Arguments.

Practical Arguments 317

These three phases in Figure 3 involve six premises 1) value, 2) stipulative, 3) empirical, 4) situational 5) logic and 6) intent to act (Fenstermacher & Richardson 1993; Vásquez-Levy 1993). All six premises, outlined in Appendix C, are explored through the semi-structured interviews and the teachers' written reflection journals. This approach is a process where the researcher (or it could be a teacher educator or teacher colleague) gently provokes elicitation of beliefs on teaching. First, the teacher is asked to express an opinion on an exemplified teaching experience and, after scrutiny of these responses, a value-driven claim/reasoning is elicited (see in Appendix B). When the teacher has a value-driven statement, the semi-structured interview explores the next premise.

When the teacher engages in discussion away from the actual actions in the classroom it helps her to explain and learn from her reflections which leads to articulation of reasoning and thereby developing a practical argument. During the semi-structured interview, she is forced to reflect – using her pedagogic vocabulary – on her everyday practice and distance herself from her common beliefs and to give good reasons for her actions and choices of content and method as Dale stresses as 'educational rationality' (Dale, 1998, p. 256).

Following the three phases described in Figure 3 and the six premises outlined in appendix C, one can start the work of elicitation and reconstruction of a practical argument. The phases and the premises should be supported by questions such as: Why do you find that group work in your class is the best way of learning for your students? If one parent asked for your justification for your actions, what would your answer be? The first question opens up to practical reasoning (in line with beliefs) described in phase 1, and the second helps the elicitation and reconstruction of a practical argument (reflection on beliefs and actions) described as phase 2 and 3.

The process involves structured dialogues inspired by Brinkmann's epistemic approach (2007) relating to Socratic dialogues. As mentioned above this approach consists of a dialogue between researcher and teacher to examine the teachers' 'practical reasoning', to develop (elicitation and reconstruction) a 'practical argument' inspired by (Fenstermacher & Richardson 1993; Vásquez-Levy 1993). I combine the six premises of constructing and reconstructing a practical argument with Stephen Toulmin's method of argumentation (described in: Horner 1988). Toulmin's model is a basic method of reasoning. It simply involves the *fact, claim,* and *warrant* see Appendix 4A. Below in Figure 4 my method of investigation is illustrated.

- *The claim or conclusion* is what you are proving with the fact.
  It is often the teachers' first beliefs and immediate reasoning when working on elicitation of a practical reason
  Implies: Premises 1 + 2: value + stipulative / phase 1.

- *The fact* is the evidence used to prove the claim.
  It is often the teachers' examples from her classroom experiences or it could be facts that are not just experience driven but also theoretical/research/data driven
  Implies: Premises 3 + 4: empirical + situational/ phase 2.

- *The warrant* is the principle or assumption that connects the fact to the claim.
  When having a dialouge about the elements in the arguments the teacher who poses the claim and in the process of constructing a practical argument, is the one who tries to convince the interlocutor
  Implies: Premise 5: Logical/ phase 2 + 3.

Figure 4. Approach to Make Teachers' Reflections on Teaching Practice Visible.

One must remember that a conversation seldom occurs in this chronological process above in Figure 4. The approach should be seen as a part of the investigation process both during the data collecting and during the process of analyzing. The three elements of an argument, *claim, fact* and *warrant,* are all regarded as necessary to support a good argument (Horner, 1988), and help the researcher in the dialogue with the teacher and in the analysis of her written reflection journal. The researcher constantly refers to how the teacher reasons and states *claim, fact and warrant* every time she talks about one of the six premises for articulating

Practical Arguments and constructing a practical argument[1]. Teacher's reasoning becomes a topic for inquiry only after the teacher has acted and, relating it to Dale's concept of educational rationality (C1, C2, C3), the action-minded stage of discussion on the intention to act (premise 6) is fulfilling Dale's ideal of the developmental idea in the synergy between all three levels of competencies.

EXAMPLES FROM PRACTICE

Teachers' Reflections on Teaching Practices

In the following section an example of how the data formats establish, build and illustrate the levels of competence and reflection, are presented. The example is from Sue, a language teacher (Lund 2015).

(Question 4) Please describe an unsuccessful teaching situation you have had.

"The students had read a text which they thought was very difficult. In order to accommodate their regret [a sadness or disappointment over previous school experiences], I set them up to work with the introductory page - read and understand in pairs. Then I reviewed the rest of the text for them. The situation was controlled solely by me. Along the way, I noticed the keen click on a pair of keyboards [some kind of computer game going on] on the back row, asking them to close the screen, which one did while the other continued unpredictably. Then I asked her to close it in somewhat sharper tone, which she also did. With all signs of being deeply offended [could be translated: mortally offended]" (Journal writing, Sue's written reflections).

---

[1] Premise 6 is not a part of Figure 4. In a teacher developmental perspective, the sixth premise: 'An action or intention to act' is a part of the process of a practical argument but might not engage the elements of Toulmin and therefore is not a part of Figure 4.

320
Lea Lund

(Question 5) Please describe why this specific situation was unsuccessful in your opinion.

> "I hate to scold; it makes me feel inadequate. And quite honestly, I think I feel powerless in relation to this class. I think only a few students learned something this lesson – in fact not much English was spoken at all.
>
> I think it was unsuccessful - professionally it was a failure because I don't think they really learned anything but also pedagogically because I do not like to ask people to close computers, put mobile phones away and that kind of thing. Without really being able to put my finger on why I have not found the right way to say these things, so I often feel annoyed" (Journal writing, Sue's written reflections)

Sue's description of an unsuccessful teaching experience comes from her reflective journal and is central to guide the semi-structured interview. Both quotes relate to 'premise 4: situational', capturing the hot moments at level C1 and, in addition, relate this experience to the teacher's thinking at level C3. This basic information provides a situational foundation for the dialogue.

Initial analysis of the two quotes above demonstrate the teacher's beginning reasoning which the researcher – a dialogical partner – extends by asking *why*, through the semi-structured interview following as illustrated below. The researcher is sensitive when eliciting argumentation to make sure the situational aspect is understood. There is a danger that the teacher may want to please the researcher and therefore warranted facts are not openly sought although the teacher is expected to articulate her reasoning.

Interviewer:

> "What do you experience in that moment you describe as a failure? Why do you think you reacted that way and tell her to stop what she was doing?"

Practical Arguments 321

Sue, a language teacher:

> "I don't think that my class is just a 'place to hang out' and that they could just do as they please and did not want to do what was asked and just ignored everything else. I found that really provoked me; the clicking on the laptops and playing their computer games. I really feel that I am bad at handling those kinds of situations"

As the teacher continues to recount her emotions from the situation and the researcher seeks to guide construction of reasoning and to elaborate on experience on why it is not alright to scold at an adult (student) even when the student obviously is disturbing the teaching and showing lack of respect to the teacher. Here the teacher's reasoning (beliefs) about good teaching are touched upon and connected with what a good learning environment is in the teacher's opinion. Therefore, it is necessary to play the role of the critical friend, in a Socratic way, and ask questions as in an epistemic interview approach (Brinkmann 2007). In the next phase, the researcher seeks to make the teacher articulate her *claim, warrant and fact* and in relation to her lived experience from the classroom.

Interviewer:

> "Would you consider removing the student from the next session/class? You could for example, come up with some sanctions like asking her to stay outside the door of the classroom, or could you simply ignore her tapping on the laptop? I mean have you considered other options than scolding her for her behaviour, or do you just want her to stop but still have her in class?"

Teacher Sue:

> "I feel bad about such confrontations, so I do not know why that is, I do not know. I think she (the student) in some ways also seems to be fragile."

Interviewer:

"Yes, but why do you feel it is wrong to scold?"
[Claim/conclusion: the teacher should not scold/reprimand]

Teacher Sue:

"Because it upsets people"
[underlying warrant: people who are hurt/sad are not capable of learning]

Interviewer:

"And that's not a good thing?"

Teacher Sue:

"No, sometimes it's really alright to scold some people but I sometimes feel that some students are vulnerable and then I do not like to hurt them. With respect to this student I do not think it is a problem that I asked her to shut down her computer. It is a problem for her that she feels hurt and opts out of the class in the way she does. Sometimes I feel that there are just some students that need something that no one really gives them but scolding is not the right answer."
[underlying warrant: When vulnerable students feel upset because of the teacher's reprimands the learning environment becomes negative which hinders learning. As exemplified by Sue in her description of the situation that nobody learned much English during that lesson. Therefore, the teacher should not scold because it could hurt the students' feelings and create a bad learning environment. Here we see that the fifth premise: 'An action or intention to act' a part of a practical argument is articulated in practical argument as she navigates in relation to the diverse needs of the students in the class].

Practical Arguments 323

To sum up Sue's elaboration on practical argument provides insights to her way of thinking and, at the same time, gives her the opportunity to articulate an event she feels frustrated about. It could be reported thus:

> *Claim:* The teacher should not scold/reprimand.
>
> *Fact:* Many of the students at this institution are vulnerable.
>
> *Warrant:* People who are vulnerable are at higher risk of being hurt and will not be not capable of learning (unspoken warrant: while being in a process of learning, one needs to feel safe/secure).
>
> *Underlying warrant:* When vulnerable students feel upset because of the teacher's reprimands, there is a negative learning environment which results in hindering learning (unarticulated warrant: a positive leaning environment is the goal of the teacher).

Earlier in the interview, Sue elaborated on creating a positive learning environment after having described a successful teaching experience. The same approach was used to elicit her reasoning but here the researcher employed an explicitly critical method. As the experience was positive, it was easier to act more in line with the epistemic interview approach and explicitly state that warranted statements were being sought. Here are some examples.

Interviewer:

> "You just used the word 'fun', why does the teaching situation have to be fun?"
>
> [asking for her fact and warrant underlying her claim about that teaching needs to be fun].

Teacher Sue:

> "Because in the moment when something is fun, it is positive right? It makes more people interested. So, if you as a teacher tell to the students 'you have to learn something' they will say okay, 'well fine' but when you say 'we are going to have fun', they will say 'yes we would like to'. So, that's the same as when they feel comfortable in the classroom and they need to get a feeling that they can relax, and you can say that

humour and that kind of stuff plays a big part. It's not like I play the circus clown but just that I like to create a setting in the classroom where it's okay to ask strange or inquisitive questions. I try to act curious instead of being the expert."

Given this statement, the researcher interrogates Sue's warrant by inquiring about this perspective. The teacher recounts her own learning experiences as a student as well as her own teacher training. She remembers these moments of being in a comfort zone and feeling safe as being positive for her learning. These comments were made without telling her that her rationale and reasoning is right or wrong. Following this phase, she is explicitly asked for her rationale – to give a reasonable argument as a lawyer in the court room would. It quickly became evident that this provocation awakens something very important to her – the students and her obligation as a teacher in this institution – and relates to premise one: 'value' and premise four: 'the situational' aspect. In the interview below the researcher plays the devil's advocate, asking for warranted facts.

Interviewer:

"I'm not asking you to relate to some sort of educational theory. But I would like to try to play the devil's advocate. Try to think of all those sports practitioners, though I know it's not sport when you're teaching in class. Or try to think of people who have accomplished a lot even though it was tough and maybe not fun. For example, a man like, Steve Jobs, he was as I recall orphaned and was in an orphanage, or raised by foster parents. Those people in our society or in the world who really had to struggle and did well any way."

Sue starts afterwards to construct an argument articulating the fact behind her claim about why teaching needs to be fun, which relates to the fact that the positive classroom environment fosters good learning experiences and that is what her students need because most are struggling finishing their college degree for the second time. Many dropped out of high school and know what failure feels like. Sue responded:

Practical Arguments 325

Teacher Sue:

"I get your point and I have an answer to that...I experience that there are many students who have a lot of all kinds of failures, due to their backgrounds and negative experiences. And that means that they all have something in their backgrounds that leaves enormously long shadows. What I might be afraid of that is that if we start pushing them – and I get into the answer to that now – if we start pushing them and setting them up against each other then they break down even before they enter the classroom.

So, the classroom environment needs to be good and not only for me as a teacher. But there is only so much I can do to create the classroom environment that makes them want to continue to learn. In fact, they themselves are really, really, important because by showing each other recognition and respect they also experience self-recognition and respect. That is the only way they will survive really. So instead of feeling bad about yourself and feeling that you do not fit in and so on, there will be a positive environment where you feel accepted for what you are even though you are different"

[Claim: The teaching situation needs to be fun, the students need to feel safe and the teacher should not push too hard]

[Fact: Because the students at this institution bring all kinds of prior failure into the learning experiences, they struggle a lot]

[Underlying warrant: People who are struggling with prior failure from schooling are vulnerable and should not to be pushed too hard and experience even more defeats or to be pushed into any sort of competition if they are to be able to learn]

This approach has demonstrated that the whole process is of benefit to the teacher, as we saw in the dialogue when Sue constructed a practical argument elaborating on the reasoning in her claim: The teacher should not scold/reprimand. Likewise a quote from Fie, a geography teacher below, who states that she would like to incorporate this form of reflection (elaborating on her attitudes, beliefs and reasoning) on her practice into her daily routine, underlines the credibility of the approach. Fie states:

Fie, a geography teacher:

"... It is nice to be able to sit down quietly and go through point-by-point and then just write a little because I am not accustomed to it ... It was especially the last question 'what will you do?' or the coaching-style question 'what will you do differently next time?"

As a part of the dialogical interview process, Fie added that the journal writing exercise changed her perspective on her classroom and made her more aware of her actions. This awareness of her way of doing and thinking allowed her to make successful changes that addressed previously challenging situations with the students. Likewise, Sue the language teacher, stated that her experience of being a part of a research process, having her assumptions questioned, gave her a novel view on her way of thinking about teaching situations:

Sue, a language teacher:

"When I've been writing this [reflection journal] it was amazing how much it's about myself ... You could suddenly see some things. Yes, some patterns emerge and the moment you see them, then you start – you might be able to work a little with them ... Maybe something that has been developing gradually.... the moment you suddenly see that then things have a certain colour and then thinking, well, it's there, I have to work on it. So, in this way there will be a move in a new direction ... [like using] Litmus paper! [teacher's outbreak]"

The teacher's new vocabulary and ability to articulate (at C3) their teaching experiences (at C1) was helpful in guiding them to be able to tackle and meet students' needs more effectively.

As we have seen above, reflective journal writing combined with dialogue generates discussion and leads to the investigation of teachers' beliefs on teaching and learning in terms of their practice and actions in the classroom. In other words, it is possible to investigate practice at level C1 after teaching has been completed by asking questions regarding the teachers' experience of successful and unsuccessful teaching situations.

Practical Arguments 327

The quotes below are taken from a dialogue during observations of a teacher called Ann, and demonstrate the importance of relating such observations to events in the classroom concerned. They also illustrate a synergy between Dale's three levels of competence.

Interviewer's observation notes (extract):

> The lesson has started, and a young student (Timothy) turns up five minutes late, with another young student (Molly) turning up ten minutes later. All the other students are older than these two (in their mid-fifties or mid-sixties). The teacher asks all the students questions about the weather while asking Timothy (in a rather firm voice) to get all his books out. Timothy answers 'yes'. Later Ann asks Molly to remove her legs from the table in a very demanding tone of voice. Ann does not adopt a strict tone when talking to the older students.

In the interview following the observation, the interviewer asks Ann about the episodes in which she spoke strictly to the two young students, Timothy and Molly. Ann replies that Molly is not well integrated into Danish norms and culture because she is a foreigner who arrived in Denmark a couple of years ago. Ann also says that she has to use the same tone of voice when talking to Timothy because he has a mild Asperger diagnosis, even though he is part of a class of regular students. She says that Molly and Timothy need help in order to function suitably in class. The rest of the class do not know about Timothy's diagnosis.

She tells the interviewer that she feels responsible for bringing up the young students – her role as a teacher includes making sure that they know how to behave. She elaborates on her claim that Timothy needs her to be strict:

Teacher Ann (6 years of teaching experience teaching English as a second language):

> "This student needs to be given orders – it's no good beating around the bush with him. He likes everything to be in boxes, and he doesn't like change. And he didn't ask any questions today, but he's the type of student who can go on asking about the difference between 'do' and

328   *Lea Lund*

'does', what do they mean and how should they be used? And he can go on asking, again and again."

The interviewer asked Ann how she coped when Molly and Timothy paid no attention in class, and how she insisted that they needed to do their homework.

Interviewer asks Ann:

"You walk over to Molly's desk and touch her on the arm and smile, but what you say is 'You really need to practice'. If she's read something aloud and not done very well language-wise, you tell her twice that she needs to practice, and you tell her in Danish that she'll have to work harder and you say to them both: Please practice next week when the school's closed. You must practice... (..)... Can you explain this to me – you might not treat the more mature members of the class in the same way as you treat the two young people. It's all about the way you deal with the situation. What goes through your mind when you tell them they will have to do some work at home?"

[Interviewer is asking for Ann's reasoning and justifications in connection with the actions and claims stated above]:

Here is a quote in which Ann explains her reasons and the practical arguments that justify her strict approach to the two young students:

"I just think that it's important for them (working with the material, reading and doing their homework) – it's important for their own sake. If they want to get on in life. Otherwise they'll just end up hanging around the school. They just have to pull themselves together and do something about it. Laziness never helped anyone get anywhere, and they need to learn this and that's all there is to it in my view. It's no good them imagining that things will just land in their laps or that they can skip a week and just go on next week, because they'll fall behind in the textbook. Molly has been off sick and Timothy has been absent a lot of the time. I had words with him in the corridor on Tuesday because he should have been here on Tuesday morning from 8 to 10, but he didn't turn up (not for the first time), and then I saw him in the corridor about

Practical Arguments 329

11, so I asked him where he'd been. So, I took him by the arm and he's walking alongside me, and I just don't care, and he said he'd overslept and I said that was hopeless and simply not good enough."

[Claim: if the students are to make any educational progress, they need to make an effort and it is the role of the teacher to force them to be aware of that fact]

The interviewer wants Ann to justify her claim even further:

"And you do this because?"

Teacher Ann:

"I tell Timothy he's been absent a lot and that he needs to come to the lessons and keep up with the teaching. He said he was aware of this and promised to improve, and he said that he'd been at school on Thursday. But on Thursday the teaching was cancelled and this had been announced on the school's intranet and we've talked about this many times before, but he was absent so he hadn't heard it, and he hadn't checked the intranet. So I said he must have been told about it in the office, and it's true that he had been in the office and they had said it and fortunately I had written in the book that the lessons were cancelled and the same thing was announced on the intranet so bad luck, but I said that I thought for his own sake that he should start attending class and I wrote to the student counsellor that we needed to keep an eye on Timothy because I think these young people really need to finish this course, that it's important for their future."

[Fact: if the students are to make any educational progress, they need to make an effort and it is the role of the teacher to force them to be aware of that fact]

The interviewer wants Ann to justify her claim even more:

"And you think that if you keep a close eye on them ...?"

Teacher Ann:

"Yes, we've got to keep an eye on them, and I know a bit about Timothy's background (his Asperger diagnosis), and my actions are based on everything I know about him, and that's why I wrote to the student counsellor. And she called him straightaway yesterday, she simply picked up the phone, and he solemnly promised to come to school and you heard him too, it was the last thing he said today."

[Warrant: students who are vulnerable like Timothy and Molly need someone to act like a parent towards them because they are not able to take responsibility for their own lives. The teacher does this by being strict and demanding]

Interviewer replies:

"Yes, he said that to you today [after the observation in class], I heard that in the canteen. It works for him."

Teacher Ann:

"Yes, he said: I promise to come for the rest of the course, and even though we had to get strict with him to make him come to class, I definitely think it's worth doing."

If we go back to the beginning of the situation with Ann: the interviewer who observed the teacher was wondering why the teacher was so strict with the two young students and asked for the teacher's reasoning, which can be summed up as follows:

Claim: The young vulnerable students like Molly and Timothy need a strict teacher (that's why Ann acted as she did).

Fact: If the students are to make any educational progress, they need to make an effort and it is the role of the teacher to force them to be aware of that fact.

Warrant: Students who are vulnerable like Timothy and Molly need a parental role model because they are unable to take responsibility for their own lives. The teacher assumes this parental role by being strict and demanding, as if these students were young children.

Underlying warrant: The teacher did not obviously base her actions on any research or data from the field of educational theory, or any research into Asperger's syndrome. It would perhaps have been interesting to ask the teacher to investigate alternative approaches and consider the research into Asperger's syndrome as well as other new teaching methods of which she was unaware.

As we have just seen in the example of dialogue with Ann, in which this investigative approach is employed, such an approach does not necessarily mean that the interviewer asks direct or explicit questions about the teacher's claims and warrants when constructing practical arguments. Instead, an inquiry-based approach is adopted, which is more epistemic and which implicitly asks questions which encourage the teacher to respond in terms of justifications and explanatory arguments. And it is this epistemic approach that gives researchers insight into the practical world of teachers. An inquiry-based approach gives us insights which we could not have gained by simply observing Ann in her teaching. As an observer, I felt that Ann's teaching was rather strict, and that she distinguished between the mature and young students. But the epistemic, inquiry-based approach reveals that Ann's actions were actually rooted in sound pedagogical considerations, and that she could construct a practical argument to describe her actions in class in relation to the two young students.

DISCUSSION

The findings from the key study (Lund 2015; Lund 2016) is in line with Vásquez-Levy (1993, pp.135, 138) showing trustworthiness within the teachers own experiences of the process. Furthermore, a number of teachers commented on incorporating this form of reflection on practice (elaborating on beliefs and reasoning) into their daily routine. The teachers found the guide questions to the journal writing helpful to change their perspective on the classroom and to heighten awareness of their actions and make changes to previously problematic situations. It was these comments that brought awareness of the possible contribution this design might make towards teacher education and professional development. These experiences – by new and experienced teachers alike – could be applied to teacher education as Ball and Cohen (Ball & Cohen 1999, p. 13) advocate: "Thus, the pedagogy of professional education would in considerable part be a 'pedagogy of investigation' " (p. 13). Teacher training should include investigation, with teachers engaging in real inquiries into practice which emphasizes the importance of observations in real classroom settings. Such investigations would help teachers to refine and improve their teaching. This approach supports the incorporation of a combination of these research methods as a tool to support the professional development of teachers and teacher training in general. During the second interview, some teachers were able to meta-reflect on the reflection process to a level where they were able to analyse and pin-point moments in their practices that were pivotal. Through this analysis they were then able to apply new practices in situations that arose.

What is evident to the teachers is the visibility of their own actions, previously invisible to them. They are able to articulate an educational rationality (construct by Dale, 1998, 1999), giving substance to thought, providing argument, qualifying judgment and rationale. These practical implications give us the notion of internal trustworthiness by the teachers themselves. And furthermore, school leaders report (in a Danish handbook for teachers: Lund 2017) that the arguments the teachers are obliged to provide on their practices is beneficial to their way of talking and articulating their knowledge of teaching and learning. The framework described in this chapter has the potential to make a contribution to professional learning communities (Stoll et al. 2006) in whatever context they find themselves and ultimately to school-wide improvement.

CONCLUSION

This chapter demonstrates how to achieve insights into teachers' practice. The chapter illustrates a method to elicit and make visible teachers' reflections on teaching practices. The construction of the practical argument can be viewed as a vehicle for encouraging the growth of curriculum development. Using this approach allows for analysis of teachers' thinking in combination with their actions in the classroom. This novel research approach provides the opportunity to support, stimulate and nurture critical reflection by the teachers of their own practices. The teachers' curriculum development is more likely to evolve if their beliefs are talked about and criticized.

The approach draws on teachers' professional work described by Dale (1998; 1999). Dale differentiates between three levels of competency (C) in a school setting and claims that when all three coexists then 'educational rationality', which is a kind of communicative act of teaching that gives "priority to goal-setting, planning, and evaluation" (Dale, 1998, p. 256), is achieved. This resonates with Schön's (1983; 1987) well-known piece on reflective practitioners where the rationale is on the evaluation of one's habits, one's routines and one's way of acting when teaching.

Dale's construct of 'educational rationality' is meant as an ideal for the teaching profession. Education and the pedagogy that the teachers perform can never be unintended; education is a medium for carrying a message. To nurture and support pedagogies in practice in the classroom, a research design was formulated that incorporated journal writing, semi-structured interviews with different purposes and classroom observations. While the data gathered in this process was extremely interesting the process of gathering data also became of interest. The process elicited awareness about otherwise invisible practices and demonstrated that teacher reflection when structured in this way resulted in a range of reflection competences and modes that equipped teachers to reflect on their classroom practices and to be able to change practices in the future.

The question is how such approaches can support the professional development and training of teachers. In relation to supporting the professional development of teachers, they could be used as an element in teachers' everyday practices, requiring the time and space to reflect on their practices and actions. Extracting these experiences of practice from the actual situation and discussing and analysing them will enable us (to some extent) to gain insight into teachers' practice-in-action, thereby bringing their reflections out into the open. In relation to supporting the training of teachers, it might be beneficial if student teachers learned how to act as 'the Other' in a critical dialogue with a peer, and to ask critical and epistemic questions about the actions and convictions of teachers. This would enable them to use the premises that are implicit in the approach to construct practical arguments, asking questions that explore teachers' ideas about teaching and learning. I have presented these ideas in handbooks for teachers and student teachers (Lund 2017; Lund 2019) – including exercises which also occur in this chapter, likewise I use this approach when educating school leaders and teachers to enable them to have a dialogue centered around pedagogic (Lund 2018a; Lund & Boie 2017; Lund 2018b).

This approach to exercises in critical reflection in relation to teaching practice has been tested to find out how it can ensure that teachers function as critical friends for each other in a dialogue about teaching (N=400 teachers at five different high schools during the spring and autumn of 2016). The same approach is also being used currently by a Danish - programme[2] of supplementary education for teachers of upper-secondary students, including 48 teachers from five different high schools, with ten managers and eight educational consultants also being trained to use the approach at the five schools concerned. In yet another school development project[3] – educational leadership in high schools is in focus – and the approach is being used as the framework for educating the school leaders to be able to have pedagogical dialogues with their staff. The project participants are working with the teaching practices of teachers in the light

---

[2] See the website for the teacher training programme KLEO: https://open-tdm.au.dk/blogs/kleo/.
[3] See the website for the teacher training programme FPL: https://open-tdm.au.dk/blogs/fpl/

Practical Arguments

335

of their convictions and attitudes. These measures, and the interest which this approach has attracted, demonstrate that people are prepared to listen to teachers' voices and pay attention to their actions, with teachers being recognised as both authentic and important.

REFERENCES

Angelides, P., 2001. The development of an efficient technique for collecting and analyzing qualitative data: The analysis of critical incidents. *International Journal of Qualitative Studies in Education*, 14(3), pp.429–442. Available at: http://www.tandfonline.com/doi/abs/10.1080/09518390110029058 [Accessed January 14, 2012].

de Araujo, Z., 2017. Connections between secondary mathematics teachers' beliefs and their selection of tasks for English language learners. *Curriculum Inquiry*, 47(4), pp.363–389.

Ball, D. L. & Cohen, D. K., 1999. Developing practice, developing practitioners: Toward a practice-based theory of professional education. In G. Sykes & L. Darling-hammond, eds. *Teaching as the learning profession: Handbook of policy and practice*. San Francisco, CA: Jossey-Bass., pp. 3–32.

Baskerville, D., Goldblatt, H. & Ccje, F., 2009. Learning to be a critical friend: from professional indifference through challenge to unguarded conversations. *Cambridge Journal of Education*, 39(2), pp.205–221. Available at: http://www.informaworld.com.

Biesta, G., 2009. Good education in an age of measurement: On the need to reconnect with the question of purpose in education. *Educational Assessment, Evaluation and Accountability*, 21(1), pp.33–46.

Biesta, G., Priestley, M. & Robinson, S., 2017. Talking about education: exploring the significance of teachers' talk for teacher agency. *Journal of Curriculum Studies*, 49(1), pp.38–54. Available at: https://www.tandfonline.com/doi/full/10.1080/00220272.2016.1205143.

Brinkmann, S., 2007. Could Interviews Be Epistemic?: An Alternative to Qualitative Opinion Polling. *Qualitative Inquiry*, 13(8), pp.1116–1138.

Calderhead, J., 1996. Teachers: Beliefs and Knowledge. In D. Berliner & R. Calfee, eds. *Handbook of educational psychology*. Macmillan Library references USA, pp. 709–725.

Clandinin, D. J., 1995. Personal Study of Images Practical Teachers' Knowledge : A Classroom. *Curriculum Inquiry*, 15(4), pp.361–385.

Clandinin, D. J. & Connelly, F. M., 1987. Teachers' personal knowledge: What counts as "personal" in studies of the personal. *Journal of Curriculum Studies*, 19(6), pp.487–500.

Clark, C. M. & Yinger, R. J., 1977. Research on Teacher Thinking. *Curriculum Inquiry*, 7(4), pp.279–304.

Connelly, F. M. & Clandinin, D. J., 1990. Stories of Experience and Narrative Inquiry. *Educational Researcher*, 19(5), pp.2–14.

Dale, E. L., 1999. *Pædagogik og professionalitet* 1. udg. 2., Århus: Forlaget Klim. [*Education and professionalism*]

Dale, E. L., 1998. The essence of teaching. In B. B. Gundem & S. Hopmann, eds. *Didaktik and/or Curriculum, an international dialogue*. Peter Lang Publishing - American University studies:ser. 14 vol. 41.

Darling-Hammond, L., 1999. Teacher Quality and Student Achievement : A Review of State Policy Evidence by Center for the Study of Teaching and Policy Center for the Study of Teaching and Policy. *Center for the Study of Teaching and Policy A National Research Consortium*, 1999(December), p.45.

Day, C., 1999. *Developing Teachers: The Challenge of Lifelong Learning*, London and NY.: Rutledge Falmer. Taylor & Francis Group.

Day, C., 1993. The Importance of Learning Biography in Supporting Teacher Development: An Empirical Study. In C. Day, J. Calderhead, & P. Denicolo, eds. *Research on Teacher Thinking: Understanding Professional Development*. pp. 221–232.

Dewey, J., 1933. *How we think: A Restatement of the Relation of Reflective Thinking to the Educative Process*, Boston, NY, Chicago: D.C. Heath & Co. publishers.

Donahue, D. M., 2000. Charity basket or revolution: Beliefs, experiences, and context in preservice teachers' service learning. *Curriculum Inquiry*, 30(4), pp.429–450.

Elbaz-Luwisch, F. & Orland-Barak, L., 2015. Chapter 5 From Teacher Knowledge to Teacher Learning in Community: Transformations of Theory and Practice. *Teacher Thinking to Teachers and Teaching: The Evolution of a Research Community Advances in Research on Teaching,*, 19, pp.97–113.

Elbaz, F., 1983. *Teacher thinking: a study of practical knowledge*, London; New Tork, Croom Helm, Nichols Pub. Co.

Eraut, M., 1994. *Developing Professional Knowledge And Competence*, The Falmer Press.

Eraut, M., 2009. How Professionals Learn through Work. In N. Jackson, ed. *Learning to be Professional through a Higher Education*. e-book, pp. 1–28. Available at: http://learningtobeprofessional.pbworks.com/How-professionals-learn-through-work.

Eraut, M., 1985. Knowledge creation and knowledge use in professioal contexts. *Studies in Higher Education*, 10(2), pp.117–133.

Eraut, M., 2002. Menus for Choosy Diners. *Teachers and Teaching*, 8(3), pp.371–379.

Fenstermacher, G. D., 1987a. A Reply to My Critics. *Educational Theory*, 37(4), pp.413–421.

Fenstermacher, G. D., 1987b. Prologue to My Critics. *Educational Theory*, 37(4), pp.357–360.

Fenstermacher, G. D. & Richardson, V., 1993. The elicitation and reconstruction of practical arguments in teaching. *Journal of curriculum studies*, 25(2), pp.101–114.

Furinghetti, F. & Morselli, F., 2011. Beliefs and beyond: Hows and whys in the teaching of proof. *ZDM - International Journal on Mathematics Education*, 43(4), pp.587–599.

Gibbs, G. R., 2007. Comparative analysis. In *Analyzing qualitative data*. Sage Publications.

Gibbs, P. & Angelides, P., 2008. Understanding friendship between critical friends. *Improving Schools*, 11(3), pp.213–225. Available at: http://imp.sagepub.com/cgi/doi/10.1177/1365480208097002.

Giorgi, A., 1985. Sketch of a phenomenological Method. In *Phenomenology and Psychological Research*. Pittsburg. Duquesne University Press, pp. 8–22.

Hammersley, M. & Atkinson, P., 1995. Field relations. In M. Hammersley & P. Atkinson, eds. *Ethnography. Principles in practice*. London and NY.: Routhledge.

Hoekstra, A. et al., 2009. Experienced teachers' informal learning: Learning activities and changes in behavior and cognition. *Teaching and Teacher Education*, 25(5), pp.663–673.

Horner, W. B., 1988. *Rhetoric in the Classical Tradition*, New York: St. Martins: Palgrave Macmillan.

Jarvis, P., 2002. *Paradoxes of Learning, on Becoming an Individual in Society* S. Francisco, ed., Jossey-Bass Publishers.

Kagan, D. M., 1992. Implication of Research on Teacher Belief. *Educational psychologist*, 27(1), pp.65–90.

Kagan, D. M. & Tippins, D. J., 1991. How Teachers' Classroom Cases Express Their Pedagogical Beliefs. *Journal of Teacher Education*, 42(4), pp.281–291.

Kaplan, D., Rupley, W. & Sparks, J., 2007. Comparing traditional journal writing with journal writing shared over e-mail list serves as tools for facilitating reflective thinking: A study of preservice teachers. *Journal of Literacy*, 39(3), pp.357–387.

Kiewkor, S., Wongwanich, S. & Piromsombat, C., 2014. Empowerment of Teachers through Critical Friend Learning to Encourage Teaching Concepts. *Procedia - Social and Behavioral Sciences*, 116, pp.4626–4631. Available at: http://linkinghub.elsevier.com/retrieve/pii/S18770 42814010143.

Klafki, W., 2000. The Significance of Classical Theories of Buildung for a Contemporary Concept of Allgemeinbildung. In I. Westbury, S. Hopmann, & K. Riquarts, eds. *Teaching and reflective practice. The German Didatik Tradition*. Mahway, New Jersey, London.

Kompf, M. & O'Connell Rust, F., 2013. Chapter 1: The International Study Association on Teachers and Teaching (ISATT): Seeing Tracks and Making More. *From Teacher Thinking to Teachers and Teaching: The Evolution of a Research Community*, 19, pp.3–38.

Leatham, K. R., 2006. Viewing mathematics teachers' beliefs as sensible systems. *Journal of Mathematics Teacher Education*, 9(1), pp.91–102.

Lund, L., 2019. Lærerens didaktiske vokabular – at skabe sammenhæng mellem undervisningens intention og udførsel. In A. Qvortrup, ed. *Formålsdrevet undervisning* [*Teacher's educational vocabulary - coherence between intention and performance*] In A. Qvortrup, ed. Purposeful teaching. Frederikshavn: Dafolo.

Lund, L., 2018a. *Juni - Tegn på lærerudvikling – Rapport 1. En evaluering af KLEO-projektets første runde juni 2018 [Signs of teacher development - Report 1. Evaluation of the KLEO project's first round - June 2018]*, Aarhus: CUDIM, AU.

Lund, L., 2018b. When school-based, in-service teacher training sharpens pedagogical awareness. *Improving Schools*, p.online-1-15.

Lund, L., 2017. *Didaktisk refleksion - når lærere sætter ord på egen praksis [Educational reflections - when teachers articulate their doing]*, Frederikshavn: Dafolo.

Lund, L., 2016. How teachers reflect on their pedagogy: Learning from teachers' pedagogical vocabulary. *International Society for Teacher Education (JISTE-journal)*, 20(2), pp.22–35.

Lund, L., 2015. *Lærerens verden - almendidaktiske refleksioner over klasserumserfaringer [The teacher's world - pedagogical reflections on classroom experiences]*. Doctoral dissertation., Aarhus: Aarhus universitet.

Lund, L. & Boie, M. a. k., 2017. *Baggrundsrapport september 2017: Relationskompetence og Klasseledelse i gymnasiet - et aktionsforskningsprojekt [Background report September 2017, Teachers' Interpersonal Competence and Classroom management in High school - action research]*, Aarhus: CUDIM, AU.

Lund, L. & Robinson, S., 2017. Teachers' vocabulary developing educational awareness. *Presented at: ECER/EERA, 22.-25. August 2017*. Copenhagen.

van Manen, M., 1977. Linking ways of knowing with ways of being practical. *Curriculum inquiry*, 6(3), pp.205–228.

Mansour, N., 2009. Science Teachers' Beliefs and Practices: Issues, Implications and Research Agenda. *International Journal of Environmental & Science Education*, 4(1), pp. 25–48.

Meirink, J. A. et al., 2009. Understanding teacher learning in secondary education: The relations of teacher activities to changed beliefs about teaching and learning. *Teaching and Teacher Education*, 25(1), pp.89–100.

Merriam, S. B., Caffarella, R. S. & Baumgartner, L. M., 2007. *Learning in Adulthood. A Comprehensive Guide* 3. edition., San Francisco: Jossey-Bass.

Miles, M.. & Hubermann, A.., 1994. *An expanded sourcebook. Qualitative Data Analysis*, Sage Publications.

Nardi, E., Biza, I. & Zachariades, T., 2012. "Warrant" revisited: Integrating mathematics teachers' pedagogical and epistemological considerations into Toulmin's model for argumentation. *Educational Studies in Mathematics*, 79(2), pp.157–173.

Nespor, J., 1987. The role of beliefs in the practice of teaching. *Journal of curriculum studies*, 19(4), pp.317–328.

Orton, R. E., 1996. How Can Teacher Beliefs about Student Learning Be Justified? *Curriculum Inquiry*, 26(2), pp.133–146.

Pajares, 1992. Teachers' beliefs and educational research: Cleaning up a messy construct. *Review of Education Research*, 62(3), pp.307–332.

Pendlebury, S., 1990. Practical Arguments and Situational Appreciation in Teaching. *Educational Theory*, 40(2), pp.171–179.

Priestley, M., Biesta, G. & Robinson, S., 2015. The role of beliefs in teacher agency. *Teachers and Teaching: theory and practice*, 21(6), pp.624–640.

Richardson, V., 1996. The role of attitudes and beliefs in learning to teach. In J. Siluka, T. J. Buttery, & E. Guyton, eds. *Handbook of research on teacher education: A project of the Association of teacher Educators*. New York: Macmillan Library references, pp. 102–119.

Romano, M. E., 2006. "'Bumpy moments'" in teaching : Reflections from practicing teachers. *Teaching and Teacher Education*, 22(8), pp.973–985. Available at: http://www.sciencedirect.com/science/chapter/pii/S0742051X06000643 [Accessed January 14, 2012].

Schön, D. A., 1987. *Educating the Reflective Practitioner: Toward a New Design for Teaching and Learning in the Professions*, Jossey-Bass; 1 edition.

Schön, D. A., 1983. *The Reflective Practitioner: How Professionals Think in Action*, Farnham, Surrey: England: Ashgate Publishing.

Smyth, J., 1989. Developing and Sustaining Critical Reflection in Teacher Education. *Journal of Teacher Education*, 40(2), pp.2–9.

Stoll, L. et al., 2006. Professional Learning Communities: A Review of the Literature. *Journal of educational change*, 7, pp.221–258. Available at: http://dx.doi.org/10.1007/s10833-006-0001-8.

Surbeck, E., 1994. Journal writing with preservice teachers. *Journal chapter by Elaine Surbeck; Childhood*.

Tripp, D., 1993. *Critical Incidents in Teaching*, London: Routledge.

Tripp, D., 1994. Teachers lives critical incidents and professioanl practice. *Qualitative Studies in Education*, 7(1), pp.65–76.

Vásquez-Levy, D., 1993. The use of practical arguments in clarifying and changing practical reasoning and classroom practices: two cases'. *Journal of Curriculum Studies*, 25(2), pp.125–143.

Westbury, I., 2000. Teaching as a Reflective Practice: What Might Didaktik Teach Curriculum. In S. Hopmann & K. Riquarts, eds. *Starting a dialogue: a beginning conversation between didaktik and the curriculum tradition*.

Yerrick, R., Parke, H. & Nugent, J., 1997. Struggling to promote deeply rooted change: The "filtering effect" of teachers' beliefs on understanding transformational views of teaching science. *Science Education*, 81(2), pp.137–159.

APPENDIX A – DATA OVERVIEW

Data collection took place over a period of eight months during the fall of 2011 and spring of 2012 (Lund 2016; Lund 2015)

Table 1. Data Overview

	John	Sue	Fie	Ivy	Tom	Mia	Max	Ann	Eva	Liz	Text in total*
Length of interview #2: Hours, minutes, seconds	0:40:49	0:43:27	0:42:00	1:32:59	0:19:47	0:53:09	0:36:06	0:39:00	0:42:20	0:29:55	10 interviews Interview #2 = 7 hours of interviews
Interview #2 Date and year	Jan. 10. 2012	March 22. 2012	Jan. 11. 2012	March 21. 2012	Feb. 22.2012	March 28. 2012	Feb. 29. 2012	March 01. 2012	Feb. 24. 2012	Feb. 23. 2012	10 interviews Interview #2 = 7 hours of interviews
Teachers' subject during observation	Social science	Language	Geographic	Language	Social science	English	Language	Language	Language	Social science	7 different subjects/ disciplines
Number of classes	2	1	2	2	1	3	2	2	2	1	18 classes= 13 hours of observation 10 pieces of handwritten field notes from 13 hours of observation during class
Date, year / time of observation	Jan. 10. 2012 / 10:05 -11:45 AM	March 22. 2012 / 02:45-03:30 PM	Jan. 11. 2012 / 08:05-09:45 AM	March 21. 2012 / 10:05-12:45 AM	Feb. 22. 2012 / 08:05-08:55 AM	March 28. 2012 / 08:05-10:55 AM	Feb. 29. 2012 / 12:05- 01:45 PM	March 01. 2012 / 12:05-01:45 PM	Feb. 24. 2012 /11:05-12:50 AM/PM	Feb. 23. 2012 / 01:00-01:45 PM	
Length of the interview #1: Hours, minutes, seconds	1:03:14	1:18:54	1:05:00	1:15:02	0:56:20	1:20:20	1:25:52	1:01:38	1:05:31	1:05:55	
Interview #1: On the basis of the teachers' written reflection journals	Sept. 19. 2011 / 12:30 PM	Oct. 07. 2011 / 10:00 AM	Oct. 06. 2011 / 02:00 PM	Oct. 12. 2011 / 01:00 PM	Sept. 29. 2011 / 08:30 AM	Sept. 06. 2011 / 11:00 AM	Oct. 25. 2011 / 10:00 AM	Sept.12. 2011 / 09:00 AM	Sept. 13. 2011 / 10:00 AM	Sept. 19. 2011 / 02:00 PM	10 interviews Interview #1 = 12 hours of interviews
Date and year of receiving the teachers' reflections journal	Sept. 17. / 2011	Oct. 05. / 2011	Oct. 04. / 2011	Oct. 10. / 2011	Sept. 27. / 2011	Sept. 04. / 2011	Oct. 23. / 2011	Sept. 12. / 2011	Sept. 11. / 2011	Sept. 17. / 2011	10 written reflection journals
Years of experience of teaching	11	7	3	13	1	22	25	6	15	17	
Age	42	40	35	46	30	49	61	48	56	52	
Sex Female or Male	M	F	F	F	M	F	M	F	F	F	
Informant pseudonym	John	Sue	Fie	Ivy	Tom	Mia	Max	Ann	Eva	Liz	Text in total*

*50 pages of transcription per informants' transcriptions in total= 500 pages of text excluding the handwritten field notes contained in Nvivo during the analysis

APPENDIX B – EIGHT QUESTIONS IN REFLECTIVE JOURNAL WRITING

The following questions in the open-ended reflective journal writing serves as the outset for the scrutiny of the teacher's beliefs and thoughts, always relating to the acting/performing, in that way the conversation is about an example from teaching to let the teacher invite the researcher into the classroom:

Table 2. Appendix B - Eight Questions in Reflective Journal Writing

1. Please describe a successful teaching experience you have had.
• Try to think of your teaching within the last couple of days or weeks and try to describe a specific successful situation from the classroom. • If you have a hard time remembering a specific present situation you may think further back in time. • Describe the situation as detailed as possible. • What happened? What did you do?
2. Please describe why this specific situation was successful in your opinion.
• Try to describe what it was about the situation that made it successful from your point of view?
3. Please describe what affected the situation to make it turn out well.
• Try to describe what might have affected the situation in a positive way?
4. Please describe an unsuccessful teaching experience you have had.
• Try to think of your teaching within the last couple of days or weeks and try to describe a specific unsuccessful situation from the classroom. • If you have a hard time remembering a specific present situation you may think further back in time. • Describe the situation as detailed as possible. What happened? What did you do?
5. Please describe why this specific situation was unsuccessful in your opinion.
• Try to describe what it was about the situation that made it unsuccessful in your point of view. • For instance, point to the obstacles.
6. Please describe what caused the situation to not turn out well.
• Try to describe what might have affected the situation in a negative way?
7. Please describe what circumstances could have changed the unsuccessful situation for the better.
• Try to describe what you think might have contributed to the situation being successful • What could, for example, have been done differently? • What could you do differently in a similar situation?
8. Please describe what happened after the unsatisfactory/unsuccessful teaching situation.
• Try to describe what you were thinking or how you acted or reacted just immediately after the failed situation.

344 Lea Lund

I am inspired by the process concerning reflective journal writing described in details in Lund (2015) In the dialogue and the open ended questions in the teachers written reflection journal I am inspired partly by Fenstermacher and Richardson's premises for elicitation and reconstruction of a practical argument (1993) and partly by a Socratic inspired epistemic interview technique (Brinkmann 2007). And regarding the specific opening questions (listed above) pushing forward a process of reflection I am inspired by the questions constructed by: (Smyth 1989; Day 1999; Day 1993).

APPENDIX C – THE SIX PREMISES

Table 3. The Six Premises

1)	**Value premise:** A moral claim about what should or ought to be the case. Describing the values or the goal for the outcome of the action. The premise may be phrased as a declarative statement. 'My goal is to help children become successful human beings' or as an imperative 'Every child must learn to write'.
2)	**Stipulative premise:** A statement that provides individual meaning or perspective. Descriptions that provide meaning or theoretical rationales for the activities under inquiry. Sometimes the premise arises from theory as when teachers attempt to explain their action by calling on some theory of how children learn to write. e.g., writing is being able to construct a sentence and to be able to explain one's thoughts.
3)	**Empirical premise:** A claim that empirical evidence would establish as true or false. Premises that prove the empirical support (if it exists) for the action. A set of statements, subjects to empirical scrutiny, to test. These statements can be confirmed or denied using methods common to science. E.g., students whose parents read a lot to them when they are young will learn how to read faster than students whose parents do not read to them.
4)	**Situational premise**: A statement that provides a description for the context in which the action takes place. Premises that clarify and acknowledge the situational realities that are the context for the action. (Debated and illustrated by Pendlebury (1990)).
5)	**Logic:** The coherence of the chain of premises that forms the argument (Vásquez-Levy's point).
6)	**An action or intention to act**: The conclusion of a practical argument. The reasoning of the teacher becomes a topic for inquiry after the teacher has acted.

To examine the teachers' practical reasoning – using belief interviews – to develop (elicitation and reconstruction) a 'practical argument' I point to the process of six premises (following: Fenstermacher & Richardson 1993, pp.106–110; Vásquez-Levy 1993, p.129). The six premises guide the teacher's dialogical partner and involve a dynamic social interaction relating to the teacher's beliefs of and actions in teaching. The last two points are actually not premises but relate to the first four premises and should be regarded as a part of examining the teachers' practical argument.

ABOUT THE AUTHOR

Lea Lund, PhD, is an Assistant Professor at the Centre for Teaching Development and Digital Media, Faculty of Arts, Aarhus University, Denmark. Lea is an educational researcher whose interests are teacher development in practice, teacher thinking and teacher collaboration. Lea has carried out multiple action research projects with teachers and school leaders in Denmark. She is in the editorial board of a peer reviewed Danish journal (Kognition og pædagogik) cognition and pedagogic. She is a peer reviewer in Danish and international journals. She is a board member of the teacher education for high school teachers in Denmark. She has published and edited books for teacher education in Denmark.

INDEX

#

21st century, x, xi, xii, 69, 76, 96, 143, 144, 152, 153, 171, 184, 186, 187, 195, 196, 197, 221, 223, 225, 230, 241, 242
21st century learning skills, x, 76

A

abilities, 3, 5, 8, 39, 44, 80, 103, 129, 138, 171, 178, 191, 235, 242, 251, 252, 279
academic achievement, 8, 22, 70, 106, 144, 185, 217, 234
academic conversion program, 240, 248
academic learning, 147
academic motivation, 185
academic performance, 22
academic progress, 180, 227
accelerated, 191, 192
accelerated technological development, 191, 192
accessibility, 192, 231
acculturation, 148, 181
acquaintance, 78, 103, 107, 109, 115

acquainted, 3, 10, 12, 22, 37, 77, 103, 104, 109, 122, 194, 225
acquisition, ix, 2, 47, 99, 244, 246
action research, 15, 16, 17, 46, 51, 54, 55, 56, 339, 345
activities, 25, 33, 38, 40, 42, 44, 45, 53, 54, 61, 70, 71, 77, 81, 82, 95, 96, 115, 121, 136, 166, 170, 188, 189, 190, 216, 219, 227, 228, 273, 308, 311, 338, 340, 344
adjustment, 22, 37, 144, 181, 185
adult learning, 308
adult-child interaction, 48, 49
adulthood, 3, 5, 103
adults, vii, viii, 1, 3, 8, 25, 27, 36, 41, 42, 59, 79, 80, 96, 104, 108, 110, 118, 138, 261, 272, 276
advanced, ix, 2, 15, 179, 181, 186, 194, 195, 231, 268, 269, 286
advanced communication technology, 186
age, 5, 8, 24, 81, 131, 199, 214, 272, 300, 312, 335
aggression, 22, 26, 71, 164, 209, 279, 285, 286, 291, 292, 295, 300
aggressive behavior, 16, 17, 207, 292
alienation, 170, 245
alternative families, 194

348 *Index*

alternative family structures, 194
ambiguity, 241, 245
American Educational Research Association, 178, 268
American Psychological Association, 72
anger, 16, 145, 164, 243, 285, 288, 291, 293, 294, 295
anxiety, 20, 166, 186, 187, 190, 192, 195, 243, 288
aspects, 3, 13, 32, 34, 39, 42, 52, 57, 59, 61, 77, 79, 86, 87, 96, 97, 98, 103, 112, 113, 117, 135, 148, 150, 187, 197, 200, 201, 228, 230, 243, 245, 247, 264, 306, 315
assertive, xii, 35, 144, 162, 163, 169, 171
assessment, 19, 24, 45, 70, 88, 104, 111, 149, 169, 175, 176, 179, 214, 273
assessment tools, 214
assignments, 7, 10, 25, 29, 51, 58, 59, 60, 63, 64, 249, 250
atmosphere, 11, 32, 159, 256
attitudes, 14, 24, 30, 31, 32, 64, 72, 106, 132, 148, 149, 154, 156, 169, 172, 194, 225, 232, 253, 262, 263, 325, 335, 341
authentic, xii, 21, 173, 184, 198, 226, 232, 335
authority, 171, 172, 192, 244, 245, 259, 261, 263
awareness, 23, 37, 43, 48, 106, 139, 147, 148, 150, 151, 152, 170, 172, 175, 177, 194, 227, 229, 263, 264, 306, 326, 332, 333, 339
axial coding, 199

B

beginning teachers, 71, 248, 265, 268
behavior problems, viii, xiv, 66, 271, 272, 274, 275, 277, 278, 279, 281, 283, 285, 287, 289, 295, 296, 298, 301, 304
behaviors, 30, 65, 66, 69, 149, 194, 249, 258, 299

belief, 3, 17, 19, 55, 62, 63, 80, 244, 252, 254, 275, 309, 310, 338, 345
belief systems, 309
beliefs, 24, 26, 29, 43, 55, 70, 74, 99, 141, 149, 189, 193, 235, 247, 267, 275, 306, 309, 310, 311, 313, 314, 315, 316, 317, 321, 325, 326, 331, 333, 335, 336, 337, 338, 339, 340, 341, 343, 345
benefit, 8, 12, 165, 251, 252, 253, 254, 263, 298, 306, 307, 325
blogs, 19, 81, 84, 87, 112, 334
boundaries, xiii, 3, 29, 34, 43, 56, 105, 117, 136, 162, 163, 171, 172, 173, 184, 192, 203, 205, 207, 208, 211, 212, 219, 220, 222, 223, 228, 229, 251, 253, 259, 263
brain, 247, 266
building blocks, 43
bullying, 22, 26, 205, 286

C

capacity-based, 3
caregivers, 30, 189
caring, xiii, 3, 17, 18, 103, 184, 210, 213, 215, 222, 223, 224, 225, 229, 290
case studies, vii, x, xi, 26, 54, 56, 76, 80, 102, 112, 146, 147, 186, 279
categorical content analysis, 187, 198, 199
challenges, vii, viii, ix, xi, xii, 2, 19, 56, 61, 76, 80, 95, 143, 149, 157, 160, 168, 184, 187, 197, 198, 202, 203, 213, 216, 221, 222, 228, 229, 230, 231, 274, 288
challenging, ix, xiii, 2, 3, 4, 17, 41, 43, 44, 54, 63, 66, 68, 69, 70, 76, 134, 145, 148, 149, 162, 171, 186, 213, 228, 239, 244, 263, 275, 278, 286, 288, 292, 293, 295, 299, 301, 302, 303, 326
change, vi, xiii, 13, 16, 17, 19, 24, 26, 30, 36, 40, 42, 48, 67, 70, 78, 79, 80, 81, 86, 88, 91, 97, 99, 109, 148, 149, 164, 176, 185, 215, 216, 218, 230, 239, 240, 241,

243, 246, 250, 251, 253, 255, 260, 262, 263, 264, 268, 309, 327, 332, 333, 341

child and his family at the center, xiii, 184, 224, 229

child at the center, xiii, 184, 195, 224, 229, 251

child development, 145, 223

child was coping with special needs, 204

child with special needs, 216

childcare, 138

childhood, vii, viii, x, xii, xiii, 5, 7, 9, 18, 25, 29, 40, 63, 66, 68, 69, 70, 73, 74, 84, 102, 105, 115, 127, 139, 140, 142, 184, 185, 187, 197, 198, 202, 203, 204, 211, 213, 214, 217, 221, 222, 228, 230, 231, 233, 237, 239, 240, 245, 262, 266, 268, 272, 274, 300, 301, 302, 304

childrearing, 164, 189, 195, 227

child-rearing practices, 227

children from other cultural or religious groups, 209

children of non-dominant groups, 218

claim, 5, 10, 17, 39, 47, 50, 214, 223, 247, 289, 317, 318, 321, 322, 323, 324, 325, 327, 329, 330, 344

class, xi, xiv, 10, 13, 15, 16, 19, 21, 30, 31, 33, 38, 43, 46, 52, 55, 56, 72, 105, 106, 144, 147, 150, 153, 155, 156, 160, 162, 163, 164, 174, 193, 194, 199, 204, 217, 218, 219, 272, 273, 275, 278, 279, 280, 281, 288, 291, 292, 293, 295, 296, 304, 306, 312, 314, 317, 320, 321, 322, 324, 327, 328, 329, 330, 331

class observations, 306

classification, 247

classroom, vii, viii, xiv, 1, 3, 6, 7, 18, 30, 38, 39, 52, 53, 54, 55, 56, 57, 62, 64, 65, 67, 68, 69, 70, 71, 72, 73, 78, 99, 160, 163, 170, 173, 175, 205, 245, 271, 272, 273, 274, 281, 283, 285, 288, 290, 294, 295, 296, 297, 298, 299, 300, 301, 302, 303, 304, 305, 306, 307, 308, 317, 321,

323, 324, 325, 326, 332, 333, 339, 341, 343

classroom environment, 324, 325

classroom management, vii, viii, xiv, 1, 3, 6, 30, 39, 44, 46, 52, 53, 54, 55, 56, 57, 58, 62, 64, 67, 68, 71, 72, 73, 78, 272, 273, 281, 283, 285, 288, 290, 294, 295, 296, 297, 298, 299, 300, 301, 302, 303, 304, 339

classroom settings, 332

clinical teacher education, 6

closeness, 250, 253, 254, 256, 258, 263

cognition, 275, 338, 345

cognitive, x, 3, 10, 47, 48, 49, 67, 72, 76, 77, 83, 86, 87, 95, 97, 98, 103, 112, 113, 133, 142, 169, 204, 214, 218, 247, 254, 273, 275, 283, 284, 295, 300, 302, 303, 304

cognitive development, 48, 72, 142

cognitive function, 214

cognitive performance, 48

cognitive perspective, 254, 304

cognitive process, 98, 275

cognitive theory, 300

coherence, 285, 339, 344

collaboration, ix, xi, 2, 8, 31, 45, 46, 56, 62, 63, 64, 72, 96, 102, 115, 142, 166, 180, 237, 265, 345

college students, 276

colleges, 57, 58, 230, 234, 246, 306

communication, viii, ix, xii, xiv, 2, 3, 31, 32, 35, 36, 37, 38, 45, 56, 61, 79, 138, 144, 145, 146, 147, 150, 151, 152, 153, 155, 156, 157, 158, 163, 165, 166, 167, 168, 169, 170, 171, 172, 173, 174, 176, 178, 179, 180, 181, 184, 185, 186, 187, 189, 190, 191, 192, 193, 195, 197, 198, 199, 200, 202, 209, 212, 214, 215, 219, 220, 221, 222, 223, 224, 226, 227, 228, 229, 231, 233, 236, 240, 241, 242, 244, 246, 248, 254, 255, 256, 257, 259, 263, 264, 311

350   *Index*

communication patterns, xiii, 184, 200, 202, 219

communication skills, xii, 144, 146, 147, 150, 151, 153, 163, 172, 176

communication strategies, 189, 246

communication with parents, viii, xii, 32, 36, 61, 144, 146, 153, 156, 158, 169, 170, 172, 184, 187, 195, 197, 198, 199, 209, 212, 221, 222, 224, 226, 244, 248

community, 47, 62, 96, 136, 173, 175, 176, 188, 215, 218, 225, 226, 232, 233, 234, 245, 266, 267, 279, 292, 293, 294, 295

community relations, 176

competence, 22, 23, 24, 25, 26, 27, 49, 59, 65, 66, 69, 70, 74, 106, 174, 194, 195, 214, 224, 233, 275, 311, 315, 319, 327, 337, 339

competencies, v, vii, viii, xiv, 1, 5, 9, 10, 18, 39, 45, 53, 55, 56, 58, 59, 60, 61, 62, 64, 73, 236, 272, 274, 281, 283, 285, 288, 294, 296, 298, 311, 314, 319

competency-based education, 6, 68

complexity, xii, 53, 84, 96, 144, 148, 168, 184, 186, 213, 228, 231, 241, 242, 245, 246, 250, 251, 252, 253, 263, 273, 310

conflict, 8, 25, 72, 80, 145, 149, 152, 156, 165, 177, 178, 185, 188, 190, 191, 192, 235, 292

conflictual situations, 148, 154, 164, 222

confusion, 83, 86, 89, 95, 112, 145, 206, 241

connection, iv, 105, 119, 201, 202, 219, 243, 245, 247, 251, 252, 254, 255, 263, 264, 306, 308, 309, 310, 328

constructing new knowledge, 8, 247

construction, 4, 9, 74, 106, 109, 116, 117, 124, 130, 132, 134, 137, 138, 264, 288, 311, 315, 321, 333

constructivist, x, 76, 78, 83, 84, 86, 89, 90, 91, 95, 96, 98, 109, 110, 114, 175

content analysis, xiii, 11, 163, 184, 187, 198, 199, 202, 232, 250, 281, 283

context, 5, 18, 19, 23, 25, 27, 29, 42, 43, 45, 77, 99, 104, 130, 135, 150, 152, 164, 199, 202, 211, 222, 223, 224, 226, 231, 233, 234, 236, 244, 247, 275, 277, 279, 287, 294, 298, 309, 332, 336, 344

continuity of care, 34

conversations, 72, 79, 109, 111, 148, 156, 159, 180, 214, 335

cooperation, 29, 31, 35, 45, 59, 62, 89, 115, 160, 165, 166, 203, 204, 205, 211, 212, 214, 219, 220, 222, 223, 226, 243, 244, 248, 250, 251, 253, 255, 256, 258, 259, 260, 261, 263, 264, 290, 293

cooperative learning, 7, 68, 70, 72, 90, 97, 139

coping with behavior problems, 272, 278, 284, 299

core competencies, ix, 2, 6, 30, 37, 39, 40, 43, 59, 61, 64, 73, 228

core competency in teaching, 299

core practices, v, vii, viii, 1, 2, 5, 6, 7, 17, 18, 39, 44, 58, 62, 68, 71

core professional competencies, vii, viii, 1

crises, 17, 29, 41, 44, 191, 296

critical episodes, 32, 33, 55, 64

critical friend, 306, 314, 321, 334, 335, 337, 338

critical incidents, 276, 300, 302, 309, 315, 335, 341

critical thinking, 110, 147

criticism, 170, 194, 253, 259, 285, 288

cultural, xiii, 3, 9, 10, 21, 47, 103, 104, 105, 106, 107, 114, 115, 117, 122, 126, 132, 133, 134, 135, 137, 141, 145, 146, 170, 181, 184, 185, 191, 192, 193, 194, 200, 202, 209, 211, 212, 213, 214, 215, 216, 217, 221, 223, 224, 229, 235, 236, 247, 265

cultural background, 3, 107, 134, 135, 194

cultural competence, 185, 194, 209, 212, 214, 216, 224

cultural differences, 191

Index

351

cultural diversity, xiii, 122, 136, 137, 184, 191, 200, 202, 209, 211, 212, 213, 214, 217, 221, 223, 224, 229

cultural heritage, 105, 114, 118

cultural heterogeneity, 192

cultural mediator, 215

cultural sensitivity, xiii, 21, 106, 115, 184, 185, 194, 209, 212, 214, 216, 223, 224, 229

culturally diverse, vi, xiii, 31, 183, 184, 191, 223, 225

culturally diverse and changing society, xiii, 184

culturally diverse reality, 225

culture, xi, 13, 31, 65, 102, 106, 114, 118, 119, 192, 193, 194, 236, 267, 327

culture-sensitive interventions, 194

curricula, 18, 43, 55, 133, 135, 137, 186

curriculum, vii, ix, x, xi, 2, 4, 6, 7, 9, 18, 19, 21, 39, 44, 45, 50, 52, 56, 58, 60, 61, 62, 66, 70, 73, 74, 76, 77, 78, 79, 81, 83, 86, 87, 88, 89, 91, 92, 93, 94, 95, 97, 99, 100, 101, 102, 103, 104, 107, 108, 109, 110, 111, 112, 113, 115, 116, 117, 118, 123, 124, 128, 129, 132, 133, 134, 135, 136, 137, 138, 140, 142, 188, 244, 282, 310, 311, 333, 335, 336, 337, 340, 341

curriculum development, 132, 333

customer-service approach, 241

D

data analysis, 83, 141, 201, 232, 249, 285

data collection, 63, 313

data-driven, 313

dealing with a challenging parenthood, 213

decisions, 53, 54, 64, 80, 145, 170, 188, 208, 218, 282, 294

deficit-based, 3

deliberate, 5, 281

Department of Education, 104, 242, 268

depth, 44, 56, 57, 79, 81, 82, 168, 211, 219, 223, 230, 278, 279, 285, 313

development, vi, ix, xiv, 2, 8, 9, 13, 17, 21, 23, 24, 25, 30, 32, 42, 43, 47, 48, 51, 52, 54, 58, 60, 62, 64, 65, 66, 68, 69, 70, 71, 72, 73, 74, 77, 89, 91, 97, 100, 104, 110, 114, 124, 126, 128, 131, 132, 133, 135, 138, 141, 142, 145, 146, 149, 150, 160, 164, 173,175, 179, 180, 185, 187, 188, 191, 194, 196, 218, 223, 233, 234, 235, 236, 239, 241, 245, 251, 254, 262, 267, 268, 278, 279, 285, 294, 299, 300, 302, 303, 305, 306, 307, 308, 310, 332, 333, 334, 335, 339, 345

developmental factors, 272, 279

developmental process, 164, 195, 268

developmental psychopathology, 300

dialogue, xi, 22, 74, 77, 90, 141, 144, 146, 150, 152, 154, 157, 159, 165, 167, 168, 169, 170, 171, 172, 259, 311, 312, 313, 315, 316, 317, 318, 320, 325, 326, 331, 334, 336, 341, 344

differences, 67, 85, 95, 105, 116, 131, 132, 134, 149, 173, 191, 193, 200, 202, 219, 220, 221, 226, 231, 243, 279, 285

different, xi, 5, 6, 12, 14, 17, 21, 30, 32, 82, 83, 93, 104, 105, 107, 109, 110, 114, 116, 117, 118, 122, 124, 125, 126, 128, 129, 130, 131, 134, 136, 144, 150, 151, 154, 160, 162, 169, 170, 186, 189, 209, 210, 213, 215, 226, 237, 240, 246, 251, 256, 268, 272, 278, 280, 283, 304, 313, 325, 333, 334

difficulties, vi, viii, x, xii, 3, 10, 11, 16, 22, 23, 24, 26, 27, 28, 31, 32, 33, 46, 53, 55, 56, 61, 72, 76, 81, 86, 87, 88, 89, 91, 95, 97, 119, 126, 127, 134, 144, 145, 146, 154, 156, 157, 158, 160, 164, 165, 167, 170, 183, 184, 186, 187, 193, 195, 196, 197, 198, 202, 203, 204, 205, 207, 211, 212, 213, 215, 216, 218, 219, 220, 221, 222, 223, 226, 228, 241, 243, 245, 246,

Index

251, 261, 274, 278, 282, 291, 292, 293, 298

digital blogs, 19

disability, 66, 293

disciplines, 79, 110, 111, 117

discourse, x, xii, 4, 8, 9, 10, 12, 13, 14, 16, 17, 18, 19, 21, 22, 39, 47, 48, 49, 50, 51, 73, 76, 80, 88, 93, 98, 110, 116, 118, 119, 121, 123, 124, 125, 126, 127, 128, 129, 130, 131, 132, 134, 135, 136, 139, 144, 145, 152, 154, 159, 160, 168, 169, 171, 172, 173,209, 242, 247, 262, 263, 264, 267

discrimination, 105, 107, 193, 234

distance, xi, 79, 96, 102, 111, 163, 178, 250, 256, 257, 261, 263, 317

distress, 157, 164, 165, 171, 195, 245, 292

diverse, vii, viii, x, xii, 3, 6, 9, 12, 20, 31, 38, 52, 54, 56, 101, 106, 107, 112, 113, 114, 115, 120, 122, 126, 133, 134, 135, 137, 146, 147, 151, 152, 163, 168, 169, 184, 187, 190, 197, 213, 221, 222, 224, 228, 229, 230, 231, 322

diverse and changing reality, xii, 184, 230

diverse cultures, 107, 115, 126, 190

diverse range of cultural groups, 213

diverse SES, 113

diversified society, 186

diversity, xiii, 3, 14, 20, 22, 82, 102, 105, 107, 108, 116, 122, 131, 132, 135, 137, 139, 184, 191, 195, 200, 202, 209, 211, 212, 214, 217, 221, 223, 224, 229, 233

division of roles between mothers and fathers, 227

documentation, x, 18, 28, 63, 76, 77, 78, 79, 81, 82, 96, 97, 99, 102, 109, 139, 159, 167

documenting, 45, 64, 78, 134

E

early childhood education (ECE), v, vi, vii, viii, x, xi, xii, 1, 2, 4, 7, 8, 9, 11, 15, 17, 18, 19, 22, 23, 24, 29, 31, 40, 57, 58, 59, 60, 61, 62, 63, 66, 68, 70, 72, 73, 74, 75, 76, 77, 78, 79, 80, 82, 91, 95, 98, 100, 101, 102, 103, 104, 107, 109, 110, 111, 112, 115, 117, 132, 133, 135, 139, 140, 142, 143, 153, 183, 184, 185, 187, 197, 198, 202, 203, 204, 211, 213, 214, 217, 221, 222, 228, 230, 231, 234, 240, 262, 266, 272, 279, 301, 304

ECE preparation programme, 78, 102, 110

ECE programme, x, 79, 80, 102, 103, 104, 110, 112

ECE teacher preparation programme, 103

ecological approach, 25, 296

ecological perception of the class, 292, 295

ecological system, 103, 117, 124, 131

ecological viewpoint, 246

ecologies, 136

economic resources, 193

economic status, 113

economics, 147, 179

educational consultation, 223

educational counselling, 231

educational discourse, 242

educational environment, 106, 108, 243, 272

educational exchanges, 109

educational experience, 198

educational institutions, 40

educational practices, 45

educational process, 166, 185, 241, 244, 264, 267

educational psychology, 67, 72, 301, 336

educational rationality, 311, 316, 317, 319, 332, 333

educational research, 138, 141, 233, 265, 307, 310, 340, 345

Index

educational services, 204, 227

educational settings, 179, 310

educational system, xiii, 106, 107, 110, 137, 184, 186, 190, 195, 224, 225, 229, 231, 236

educators, 68, 70, 71, 107, 108, 109, 141, 175, 232, 233, 234, 242, 246, 247, 267, 279

effective, xii, xiv, 42, 52, 53, 55, 63, 144, 146, 148, 151, 152, 155, 159, 163, 165, 168, 171, 172, 173, 180, 184, 185, 187, 188, 190, 194, 195, 197, 222, 224, 231, 235, 240, 246, 254, 273, 278, 285, 296, 298, 308

effective communication, xiv, 144, 146, 151, 152, 155, 163, 165, 168, 172, 173, 185, 190, 222, 224, 240, 246, 254

effective partnership, xiv, 240

elementary school, xii, 6, 9, 29, 52, 176, 177, 184, 187, 197, 198, 202, 206, 214, 222, 230, 231, 235, 272

emergent, v, vii, ix, x, xi, 2, 4, 6, 7, 9, 18, 19, 21, 39, 44, 45, 50, 51, 52, 55, 56, 60, 61, 62, 70, 74, 75, 76, 77, 78, 79, 81, 82, 83, 86, 87, 88, 89, 91, 92, 93, 94, 95, 97, 99, 100, 101, 102, 104, 108, 109, 110, 111, 112, 114, 115, 116, 117, 118, 123, 124, 128, 129, 132, 133, 134, 135, 136, 138, 140, 142

emergent curriculum, v, vii, ix, x, xi, 2, 4, 6, 7, 9, 18, 19, 21, 39, 44, 45, 50, 52, 56, 60, 61, 62, 70, 74, 75, 76, 77, 78, 79, 81, 83, 86, 87, 88, 89, 91, 92, 93, 94, 95, 97, 99, 100, 101, 102, 104, 108, 109, 110, 111, 112, 114, 115, 116, 117, 118, 123, 124, 128, 129, 132, 133, 134, 135, 136, 138, 140, 142

emotion regulation, 303

emotional, x, xi, xii, 5, 10, 25, 26, 27, 28, 29, 37, 45, 49, 52, 53, 59, 61, 66, 68, 69, 70, 71, 74, 76, 79, 83, 86, 87, 95, 96, 97, 102, 110, 112, 113, 133, 144, 152, 157,

164, 165, 169, 175, 178, 180, 185, 191, 195, 208, 235, 236, 243, 245, 247, 254, 257, 258, 264, 265, 268, 272, 273, 275, 282, 283, 284, 295, 298, 302, 303, 304

emotional conflict, 95

emotional distress, 208

emotional experience, 303

emotional problems, 29

emotional processes, 169

emotional security, 298

emotional well-being, 52, 53, 273, 282

emotions, 26, 43, 96, 107, 148, 149, 156, 194, 240, 251, 274, 276, 278, 281, 285, 296, 321

empathetic, 156, 251

empathy, 15, 27, 35, 36, 45, 147, 148, 152, 157, 158, 164, 173, 177, 195, 263

employment, 186, 191, 195, 278, 283

empowered, 134, 189

empowering, xi, xii, 102, 106, 136, 137, 144, 262

empowerment, 11, 15, 232, 251, 265

empowers, 106, 116, 251

encounters, xii, 4, 12, 13, 16, 25, 27, 34, 44, 45, 48, 50, 53, 144, 152, 156, 158, 245, 263

environment, xii, 27, 42, 46, 47, 51, 53, 54, 70, 77, 88, 97, 104, 106, 108, 115, 116, 119, 124, 141, 144, 147, 148, 153, 158, 172, 187, 188, 243, 244, 252, 273, 281, 298, 321, 322, 323, 324, 325

environmental aspects, 86, 87

environmental factors, 87, 273

environmental influences, 65, 300

environmental variables, 274, 282

epistemic interview technique, 314, 344

equal, 94, 105, 107, 108, 115, 117, 129, 134, 135, 137, 194, 217, 223, 224, 243, 261

equal power relations, 223, 224

equality, 139, 242, 250

equally, 118, 124, 136, 311

equity, 3, 68, 106, 115, 116, 117, 119, 122, 132, 135, 136, 139, 232

equity pedagogy, 3, 106, 115, 116, 119, 122, 132, 135, 136

ethnic, 105, 106, 131, 136, 193, 224

ethnic diversity, 131

ethnic minority, 215

ethnicity, 192

evidence, 8, 28, 34, 36, 69, 70, 160, 234, 264, 276, 288, 303, 308, 344

expectations, 23, 30, 31, 37, 38, 41, 43, 45, 145, 146, 161, 171, 172, 185, 190, 192, 194, 196, 225, 233, 244

experience, ix, xii, 2, 4, 5, 12, 18, 19, 20, 44, 46, 47, 48, 50, 51, 53, 55, 61, 62, 64, 66, 67, 70, 84, 93, 95, 97, 105, 108, 114, 115, 133, 144, 148, 151, 152, 156, 160, 167, 168, 172, 186, 198, 236, 245, 248, 253, 254, 262, 268, 276, 279, 280, 282, 301, 304, 306, 307, 308, 312, 317, 320, 321, 323, 325, 326, 327, 336

expression, xi, 43, 45, 55, 78, 80, 102, 110, 119, 127, 129, 132, 135, 136, 256, 272, 302

expressive writing, viii, xiv, 41, 271, 272, 275, 276, 303

external environment, 42

external influences, 43

externalizing problems, 22

extra help, 287, 291, 294

F

fact, 12, 34, 185, 190, 198, 223, 224, 228, 242, 258, 291, 318, 320, 321, 323, 324, 325, 329, 330

families, xi, xiii, 3, 20, 21, 30, 31, 40, 46, 53, 56, 57, 102, 103, 107, 113, 120, 121, 122, 123, 124, 133, 134, 136, 175, 180, 184, 186, 188, 189, 191, 193, 194, 212, 213, 224, 225, 226, 229, 230, 234, 237, 242, 244, 246, 279, 280, 282

families coping with special needs, xiii, 184, 229

families from dominant groups, 193

families from ethnic minorities and a low socio-economic class, 193

families of various cultural groups, 230

families with special needs, 224

family characteristics, 65

family involvement, 196, 236, 266, 269

family members, 127

family system, 175, 249

family units, 186

family-school communication, 186, 189, 224

family-school relations, vi, viii, xiii, 173, 183, 184, 186, 187, 191, 196, 202, 212, 217, 221, 222, 223, 224, 228, 229, 230

father from a high socio-economical class, 218

father involvement, 220, 226, 227, 231

fathers, xiii, 184, 200, 202, 207, 219, 220, 221, 226, 227, 228, 229, 231, 235

fathers tended to increase their involvement, 220, 227

fathers were involved, 219, 226

fear, 86, 88, 95, 145, 170, 191, 217, 260, 261, 263, 285, 286, 295

feedback, xi, 5, 6, 42, 54, 56, 79, 81, 111, 144, 148, 150, 151, 154, 155, 157, 158, 159, 160, 161, 168, 172, 202, 235, 258

feelings, viii, xii, xiv, 3, 16, 17, 26, 29, 32, 41, 43, 44, 45, 49, 50, 78, 80, 86, 96, 115, 144, 145, 148, 149, 150, 151, 154, 157, 160, 168, 169, 172, 186, 195, 215, 217, 243, 245, 248, 253, 262, 271, 274, 276, 277, 278, 281, 282, 284, 285, 286, 287, 290, 291, 294, 295, 296, 298, 299, 304, 322

field journal, 13, 60, 61

Index 355

fieldwork, x, 4, 7, 9, 19, 20, 28, 30, 44, 46, 50, 51, 53, 55, 56, 58, 59, 60, 63, 64, 81, 89, 102, 186, 198, 199, 202, 213, 245

fostering, xiv, 4, 80, 129, 137, 172, 240

fragmented preparation, 59

free expression, 18

frequency, 11, 37, 198, 200, 203, 212, 220, 250, 283, 284

frequency examination, 200

friendship, 20, 337

G

gender, xiii, 8, 20, 31, 56, 105, 106, 135, 184, 194, 200, 202, 219, 226, 227, 228, 229, 312

gender role, 228

gender stereotypes, 226, 227, 229

geography, 147, 178, 325, 326

goal-setting, 311, 333

good reasons, 311, 312, 314, 317

governance, 64, 139, 232

grades, 6, 9, 38, 55, 173, 197, 202, 214, 235

graduate program, 15, 46, 51, 57

graduate students, 15, 57

grounded theory, 199, 232, 233, 250, 265

group, xi, 5, 7, 8, 9, 10, 11, 12, 13, 14, 16, 17, 20, 21, 25, 30, 32, 43, 52, 57, 65, 79, 81, 84, 87, 88, 89, 91, 93, 94, 104, 107, 109, 110, 111, 112, 113, 114, 115, 116, 117, 118, 119, 120, 121, 123, 124, 126, 127, 129, 130, 131, 132, 133, 134, 136, 140, 144, 150, 151, 153, 154, 155, 163, 165, 179, 206, 213, 217, 224, 282, 300, 317, 336

group activities, 81

group discourse, 89, 110, 115, 116, 118, 120, 124, 134, 136

group interactions, 89

group work, 7, 8, 15, 17, 25, 39, 42, 44, 49, 60, 61, 73, 91, 142, 317

growth, xiv, 3, 8, 19, 43, 55, 103, 251, 305, 333

growth mindsets, 3

guidance, x, 5, 8, 9, 10, 25, 64, 76, 117, 203, 211, 212, 220, 221, 222, 227, 248, 264

guidelines, 55, 154, 179, 230, 304, 316

guiding principles, 230

H

health psychology, 303

helplessness, viii, xiv, 86, 145, 245, 271, 281, 285, 286, 294, 295, 296

heterogeneity, 136, 242

heterogeneous, xi, 3, 6, 7, 8, 9, 16, 44, 77, 78, 81, 87, 102, 103, 104, 107, 110, 113, 127, 133, 135, 137, 192, 228

heterogeneous groups, xi, 3, 6, 7, 9, 16, 44, 77, 81, 102, 103, 104, 107, 110, 113, 133, 137

high school, 108, 230, 231, 324, 334, 345

higher education, 65, 69, 174, 178, 179

higher-order thinking, 110

history, 40, 147, 148, 174, 178

home environment, 188, 243

home visits, 215, 225, 243

homes, vii, x, 37, 101, 126, 133

home-school communication, 190, 202, 231, 266

home-school relations, xii, 174, 180, 184, 237

homework, 38, 188, 269, 289, 328

human behavior, 300

human development, 42, 47, 65, 66, 138, 141, 233

human nature, 67

hundred languages, 78, 126, 132, 135, 139

I

identification, viii, 58, 60, 170, 187, 197, 200

identity, 73, 100, 117, 118, 142, 175, 245, 248, 265

immigrants, 107, 113, 193

immigration, 186, 191, 242

implementation, v, vii, x, 1, 6, 8, 11, 17, 19, 21, 23, 26, 28, 29, 33, 34, 44, 52, 56, 57, 58, 59, 60, 61, 62, 63, 73, 77, 78, 87, 88, 95, 101, 108, 110, 122, 138, 172, 180, 245, 267, 273, 277, 278, 282, 299, 302

implications, v, ix, 1, 2, 67, 69, 70, 97, 137, 172, 221, 243, 245, 278, 332, 340

importance, xiii, 9, 12, 19, 23, 29, 34, 35, 47, 54, 57, 59, 63, 80, 90, 96, 103, 104, 107, 114, 119, 126, 137, 146, 151, 158, 159, 160, 161, 162, 164, 165, 166, 167, 168, 169, 172, 190, 193, 228, 239, 240, 244, 251, 253, 256, 260, 263, 273, 306, 310, 311, 327, 332,336

important, 8, 13, 22, 25, 34, 35, 37, 39, 45, 49, 53, 54, 78, 82, 88, 114, 116, 119, 130, 136, 149, 157, 158, 159, 160, 161, 163, 165, 166, 171, 185, 196, 206, 227, 228, 229, 231, 244, 245, 251, 259, 272, 284, 296, 306, 309, 310, 311, 312, 324, 325, 328, 329, 335

inclusion, 11, 15, 17, 24, 49, 56, 64, 108, 110, 115, 132, 135, 195, 232, 233, 237

inclusion movement, 195

inclusive, 3, 11, 13, 62, 99, 102, 110, 115, 122, 135, 142, 157, 158, 159, 165, 228, 230, 240

inclusive educational arena, 230

individual, ix, xi, 2, 3, 4, 8, 16, 17, 27, 30, 31, 36, 38, 44, 45, 46, 47, 53, 60, 70, 76, 77, 78, 79, 102, 103, 104, 114, 115, 116, 119, 136, 137, 142, 149, 155, 163, 165, 225, 246, 274, 277, 281, 285, 338, 344

individual child, ix, xi, 2, 3, 8, 30, 31, 53, 77, 78, 102, 103, 104, 114, 136, 137, 282

individual children, ix, xi, 2, 3, 8, 53, 77, 102, 137, 282

individual differences, 285

individual students, 38, 281

individualized intervention plans, 23, 24, 278

influence, 23, 24, 43, 63, 106, 134, 159, 161, 185, 187, 189, 194, 208, 218, 219, 224, 235, 241, 258, 274, 275, 282, 300

informal learning, 306, 338

innovative means of technology, 192

inquiry, xi, 4, 12, 18, 19, 21, 44, 46, 50, 51, 53, 55, 56, 57, 64, 73, 74, 77, 79, 96, 100, 102, 111, 139, 142, 180, 233, 278, 279, 282, 296, 301, 319, 331, 335, 336, 340, 344

insecurity, 245

insight, 32, 96, 160, 164, 167, 281, 283, 284, 295, 308, 309, 331, 334

institutions, xii, 41, 65, 172, 184, 186, 187, 197, 221, 223, 227, 228, 230

integration, 57, 59, 61, 62, 64, 87, 98, 106, 107, 108, 150, 155, 186, 192, 195, 196, 204, 209, 217, 225, 226, 241, 259

intentionality, 5, 48, 49, 50

interaction, 3, 42, 47, 48, 50, 51, 70, 84, 104, 106, 108, 194, 202, 221, 228, 245, 258, 313, 315, 345

intern year, 199

internalized motivation, 274, 298

internalized problems, 22

internship, xi, xii, 33, 144, 153, 184, 187, 197, 199, 202, 245, 249, 262, 264

interpersonal, 37, 47, 53, 71, 74, 147, 148, 149, 155, 172, 241, 282, 339

interpersonal communication, 37, 147, 241

interpersonal interactions, 155

interpersonal processes, 149

interpersonal relations, 47, 53, 71, 74, 282

interpreter, 215, 225

Index

357

interpreter or community mediator, 225

intervention, 16, 17, 22, 23, 24, 25, 26, 27, 28, 29, 30, 44, 52, 66, 70, 140, 145, 209, 278, 288, 292, 294, 296, 298, 301, 302

intervention plans, 16, 17, 29, 44, 52, 287, 288, 292, 296, 298

intervention programs, 22, 278, 302

intervention strategies, 26

invite fathers, 227

involvement, xiii, 12, 13, 31, 34, 35, 38, 40, 53, 59, 60, 64, 66, 88, 134, 145, 146, 147, 163, 166, 170, 171, 172, 177, 181, 184, 185, 188, 189, 190, 192, 193, 194, 200, 202, 219, 221, 226, 227, 228, 229, 231, 232, 234, 235, 236, 237, 240, 241, 245, 248, 251, 255, 266, 288

involvement of fathers, xiii, 184, 200, 202, 219, 221, 226, 231

issues, 15, 22, 31, 32, 33, 35, 46, 56, 66, 71, 82, 88, 106, 132, 136, 152, 160, 168, 169, 204, 214, 217, 218, 230, 232, 242, 243, 268, 301, 303

J

journal, 41, 65, 68, 69, 70, 71, 72, 73, 74, 99, 137, 139, 140, 142, 173, 174, 175, 176, 177, 178, 179, 180, 181, 232, 233, 234, 235, 236, 237, 265, 266, 267, 269, 276, 299, 300, 301, 302, 303, 307, 312, 318, 319, 320, 326, 332, 333, 335, 336, 337, 338, 339, 340,341, 343, 344, 345

journal writing, 276, 319, 320, 326, 332, 333, 338, 341, 343, 344

K

kindergarten, 15, 35, 38, 70, 71, 73, 130, 138, 190, 197, 199, 200, 202, 204, 205, 206, 207, 208, 209, 210, 211, 213, 214,

215, 216, 217, 218, 219, 227, 230, 231, 236, 262, 265, 267

kindergarten children, 236

knowledge, viii, xi, xii, 4, 5, 6, 8, 9, 14, 18, 19, 24, 26, 32, 37, 45, 47, 50, 76, 79, 80, 83, 84, 85, 89, 90, 95, 96, 98, 102, 103, 104, 106, 107, 108, 110, 112, 115, 116, 117, 118, 124, 125, 126, 130, 132, 134, 136, 137, 138, 145, 148, 149, 151, 184, 186, 187, 191, 192, 194, 196, 197, 223, 245, 247, 248, 261, 263, 264, 268, 301, 308, 310, 314, 332, 336, 337

knowledge construction, 4, 9, 106, 130

L

language development, 74

language impairment, 140

languages, 66, 78, 109, 110, 116, 118, 123, 126, 128, 129, 132, 133, 134, 135, 136, 139, 147

leadership, xiv, 64, 148, 173, 180, 189, 226, 232, 272, 274, 282, 288, 290, 292, 294, 295, 298, 334

learn, 5, 6, 10, 12, 19, 22, 30, 32, 36, 39, 41, 46, 47, 52, 57, 59, 63, 72, 77, 80, 93, 96, 104, 111, 114, 126, 132, 165, 171, 215, 268, 282, 290, 291, 299, 303, 304, 306, 308, 309, 312, 317, 323, 325, 328, 337, 344

learned helplessness, 296

learners, 47, 79, 95, 147, 148, 150, 277, 302, 308, 312, 335

learning difficulties, 22, 282, 291

learning disabilities, 196, 279, 293, 294

learning environment, 43, 51, 70, 77, 88, 138, 148, 243, 321, 322, 323

learning process, vii, x, xi, 19, 22, 76, 77, 78, 79, 80, 81, 82, 83, 84, 85, 86, 87, 88, 89, 90, 91, 93, 94, 95, 96, 97, 98, 102, 112, 114, 118, 119, 122, 123, 124, 126,

129, 132, 133, 134, 135, 137, 145, 147, 150, 157, 158, 159, 161, 162, 163, 164, 189, 190, 242, 243, 311

learning skills, x, 76, 149

learning through experience, 307, 308

learning through experience develops, 308

learning tool, vi, viii, xi, 143, 144, 146, 147, 148, 151, 163, 171

life-world approach, 2, 103

listen, 10, 18, 51, 78, 79, 89, 90, 91, 96, 103, 130, 132, 195, 223, 335

listener, 124, 126, 130, 132

listening, x, 22, 42, 59, 76, 78, 82, 84, 85, 93, 99, 104, 108, 109, 110, 123, 124, 129, 130, 132, 134, 136, 137, 141, 158, 159, 165, 169, 179, 195, 223, 247, 251

listening empathically, 251

listening to children, 78, 124

listening to the children, 108, 109, 123, 132, 134, 135, 136

literacy, 8, 9, 51, 74, 137, 174, 181, 338

loneliness, 245, 257, 285, 288

M

management, vii, viii, xiv, 1, 3, 6, 15, 30, 31, 40, 51, 52, 53, 54, 55, 56, 57, 62, 64, 67, 68, 71, 72, 74, 78, 139, 147, 173, 208, 225, 231, 242, 272, 273, 281, 283, 285, 288, 290, 293, 294, 295, 296, 297, 298, 299, 300, 301, 302, 303, 304, 339

mandatory, 23, 31, 51, 52, 107, 140

mandatory schooling law, 107, 140

mathematics, 8, 51, 65, 148, 233, 335, 339, 340

meanings, 10, 49, 82, 94, 118

mediated learning experiences, vii, viii, 1, 6, 18, 39, 46, 49, 50, 52, 58

mediation, x, 4, 10, 16, 22, 30, 39, 46, 47, 48, 49, 51, 76, 233

mediation of behavior control, 49

mediation of feelings of competence, 49

mediation of meaning, 49

mediator, 47, 215

mediators, 44, 226

medicine, 147, 176, 181, 206

meetings, 38, 59, 61, 63, 81, 87, 89, 109, 112, 113, 152, 167, 168, 201, 214, 225, 243, 262

mental development, 196

mental disorder, 213

mental health, 213, 276

mental processes, 48

mentor, 19, 23, 26, 29, 30, 36, 37, 79, 81, 83, 96, 97, 111, 112, 114, 117, 118, 150, 198

mentoring, 12, 46, 76, 99, 199, 268

mentors, x, xi, 10, 19, 23, 42, 44, 46, 54, 55, 58, 61, 62, 63, 64, 76, 79, 95, 96, 97, 102, 111, 112, 114, 133, 277

mesosystem, 45, 46

meta-competency, 6, 39, 52, 53, 57, 273, 281

metaphor, 110, 241, 246, 247, 253, 259, 264, 269, 308

metaphors, 246, 247, 248, 253, 263, 267

methodology, xi, 3, 102, 112, 153, 198, 279

methods of teaching, 95, 186

microsystem, 42

middle class parents, 194

migrant, 107

Ministry of Education, 33, 60, 141, 207, 230, 236, 244, 265, 267

minorities, 133, 193, 194, 224

minority families, xiii, 184, 229

minority group parents, xiii, 184, 229

minority groups, 225

minority parents, 194, 226

mobile phone, 192, 235, 293, 320

modes of instruction, 231

mother tongue, 116, 126

mother who is dealing with a challenging parenthood, 216

motivation, 54, 166, 168, 190, 196, 235, 258, 274, 298, 303

multicultural, xi, 102, 103, 105, 106, 112, 119, 122, 124, 126, 133, 135, 137, 138, 139, 232, 236, 246

multicultural education, 102, 103, 105, 106, 112, 122, 124, 135, 138, 139, 232

multi-cultural view, 226

multiculturalism, 106, 129, 140

multidimensional, 185, 222

N

narratives, viii, xiv, 72, 198, 271, 276, 279, 280, 281, 282, 283, 284, 285, 288, 291, 295

needs, 11, 13, 17, 19, 35, 36, 38, 39, 46, 47, 50, 60, 77, 78, 81, 97, 103, 104, 108, 109, 110, 112, 114, 119, 129, 133, 134, 136, 145, 146, 157, 164, 169, 170, 190, 191, 194, 195, 196, 214, 217, 222, 223, 224, 225, 228, 229, 241, 242, 243, 244, 252, 258, 259, 282, 292, 299, 303, 322, 323, 324, 325, 326, 327, 328, 329

negative, viii, xiv, 29, 44, 45, 49, 168, 170, 188, 245, 255, 258, 271, 274, 276, 278, 281, 283, 284, 285, 287, 290, 294, 295, 296, 299, 322, 323, 325

negative consequences, 188

negative emotions, 274, 278, 285, 296

new family, 191, 194

new family structures, 191, 194

new role division between parents and teachers, 191

new structuring of family units, 186

No Child Left Behind, 242, 266, 268

non-violent communication, 208, 223

norm of accessibility, 192, 231

nutrition, 207, 208, 210

Nvivo, 314

O

observation, 18, 24, 36, 104, 107, 109, 138, 149, 150, 160, 267, 275, 281, 307, 312, 313, 314, 315, 327, 330

observational, 104, 105, 235

observational learning, 105

observe, 18, 23, 25, 26, 36, 80, 103, 104, 149

open, xi, 11, 12, 77, 81, 86, 87, 88, 90, 102, 104, 108, 112, 115, 124, 127, 129, 131, 134, 136, 146, 152, 159, 162, 165, 168, 172, 199, 201, 216, 247, 250, 254, 256, 259, 261, 311, 313, 315, 334, 343, 344

open coding, 199, 313

open discourse, xi, 90, 102, 104, 108, 124, 131, 134, 136

openness, 78, 93, 109, 148, 152, 159, 169, 171, 173, 266

opinions, 14, 45, 90, 267, 310

opportunities, 48, 54, 59, 87, 91, 105, 109, 134, 136, 190, 227, 243

optimal, 63, 146, 157, 169, 172, 244, 246, 256, 272

organization of the environment, 53

organize, 198, 276, 295, 310

orientation, xi, 3, 102, 103, 137

P

parental attitudes, 170

parental consent, 23

parental involvement, 31, 34, 145, 146, 171, 172, 177, 188, 189, 190, 192, 193, 234, 236, 245, 248

parental participation, 189

parental pressure, 242

parental support, 144

parental voice, 195, 223

parent-child relationship, 40

parent-educator-child, 243

parenthood, 31, 164, 178, 213, 216, 224
parenting, 135, 178, 188, 236, 243
parents coping with a challenging parenthood, 224
parents from dominant groups, 218, 219
parents from other ethnic minority backgrounds,, 215
parents of a low social class, 213, 224
parents of an ethnic/religious/cultural minority background, 213
parents of dominant groups, 193, 216
parents of non-dominant groups, 224, 230
parents of special needs children, 213, 224, 226
parents of special-needs children, 225
parents with non-traditional family compositions, 213
parent-teacher, vi, viii, xiii, xiv, 145, 151, 152, 155, 156, 162, 165, 167, 169, 172, 173, 175, 178, 180, 189, 191, 211, 212, 221, 229, 230, 231, 235, 237, 239, 240, 244, 245, 246, 248, 249, 252, 255, 257, 260, 262, 263, 264
parent-teacher communication, 151, 155, 167, 173, 221
parent-teacher power relations, 211, 212
parent-teacher relations, vi, viii, xiii, xiv, 189, 191, 229, 230, 231, 237, 239, 240, 244, 245, 246, 248, 249, 252, 255, 260, 262, 263, 264
parent-teacher relationships, vi, 239, 246, 252
participants, xi, xii, 8, 9, 50, 80, 83, 110, 129, 144, 147, 148, 150, 154, 155, 159, 168, 169, 184, 194, 201, 248, 250, 276, 283, 312, 334
participation, 8, 11, 13, 15, 16, 17, 38, 43, 45, 94, 107, 129, 132, 135, 138, 147, 152, 155, 167, 189, 201, 233, 263, 265, 276

partners, xiv, 18, 26, 34, 35, 37, 41, 45, 66, 137, 166, 189, 191, 192, 195, 236, 240, 242, 243, 244, 267, 314
pedagogic, xi, 78, 79, 81, 83, 96, 97, 102, 106, 112, 118, 133, 230, 263, 317, 334, 345
pedagogic mentor, 81, 83, 97, 112, 118
pedagogical, x, 3, 15, 40, 43, 76, 77, 79, 80, 91, 95, 96, 97, 98, 102, 103, 109, 110, 111, 112, 114, 123, 146, 181, 244, 264, 265, 306, 310, 331, 334, 338, 339, 340
pedagogical relationships, 3, 77
pedagogy, 3, 19, 64, 73, 99, 100, 106, 109, 115, 116, 119, 122, 132, 135, 136, 141, 142, 173, 175, 309, 332, 333, 339
pedagogy of investigation, 332
peer group, 25, 43
peer relationship, 44
peer review, 345
peers, 4, 8, 11, 13, 14, 15, 16, 18, 20, 21, 22, 25, 27, 30, 40, 42, 47, 59, 96, 104, 105, 115, 122, 132, 135, 136, 151, 272
perception of learning, x, 78, 84, 97, 102, 110
perceptions, vi, vii, viii, ix, xiv, 4, 8, 11, 20, 32, 37, 53, 66, 75, 76, 81, 82, 83, 85, 87, 90, 91, 92, 93, 95, 97, 98, 107, 119, 126, 130, 131, 132, 134, 135, 137, 145, 148, 158, 169, 170, 172, 180, 194, 197, 220, 221, 225, 227, 236, 237, 239, 240, 241, 243, 244,246, 247, 248, 262, 263, 264, 274, 277, 294, 295
permission, iv, 199, 201, 205, 282
perpetrators, 45, 279, 280, 286, 289, 290, 293, 295, 296, 299
personal blogs, 81, 112
personal development, 164
personal goals, 50, 64
personal history, 161
personal learning, 90
personal relations, 208
personal stories, 137

Index

personal views, 264

personality, 71, 114, 130, 133

perspectives, 1, iii, v, vii, x, xi, xiv, 12, 36, 37, 41, 42, 67, 68, 69, 74, 75, 98, 101, 102, 106, 122, 134, 136, 138, 139, 144, 146, 147, 150, 151, 154, 156, 161, 168, 169, 170, 177, 179, 232, 233, 237, 240, 247, 252, 277, 301

photographs, 81, 113, 117, 121, 136

physical, 37, 38, 40, 46, 47, 50, 52, 54, 110, 243, 247, 254, 256, 276, 281, 283, 303

physical environment, 46, 54, 281

physical health, 303

physical well-being, 283

plan, xii, 9, 15, 18, 26, 27, 28, 29, 30, 33, 36, 78, 87, 95, 118, 144, 153, 160, 169, 173, 274, 282, 284, 290, 292, 294

planning, 6, 7, 18, 23, 26, 29, 33, 34, 40, 54, 56, 86, 151, 154, 159, 161, 163, 167, 171, 172, 173, 273, 293, 310, 311, 333

playing, xii, 32, 144, 147, 148, 151, 153, 157, 163, 168, 172, 174, 177, 289, 321

policy, 57, 58, 62, 135, 141, 207, 209, 230, 335

positive approach, 23, 29, 30, 278

positive attitudes, 31

positive emotions, 281, 285

positive reinforcement, 24, 25

positive relationship, 166, 251

power relations, xiii, 184, 194, 200, 202, 209, 211, 212, 214, 217, 221, 223, 224

power relations between parents and teachers, xiii, 184, 194, 200, 202, 209, 212, 217, 221, 223, 224

practical argument, vi, viii, xiv, 305, 306, 315, 316, 317, 318, 319, 322, 323, 325, 328, 331, 333, 334, 337, 340, 341, 344, 345

practical arguments, 306, 328, 331, 334, 337, 341

practical knowledge, 150, 247, 337

practice, vii, viii, x, xii, 1, 3, 4, 6, 7, 9, 11, 12, 15, 19, 24, 30, 34, 37, 45, 46, 50, 54, 55, 56, 57, 58, 60, 61, 62, 63, 68, 71, 72, 76, 78, 79, 81, 98, 102, 109, 111, 112, 122, 135, 138, 139, 144, 147, 148, 150, 152, 165, 172, 173, 174, 176, 179, 180, 181, 199, 202, 228, 232, 235, 237, 245, 266, 276, 282, 301, 302, 303, 304, 306, 308, 309, 310, 312, 313, 315, 316, 317, 318, 319, 325, 326, 328, 331, 333, 334, 335, 337, 338, 340, 341, 345

practice-centered teacher education, 6

pre-determined curriculum, 18

prejudice, 106, 116, 216

preparation, iv, v, ix, x, xi, 2, 4, 7, 9, 10, 17, 23, 28, 30, 31, 34, 39, 40, 41, 45, 51, 52, 53, 54, 55, 56, 57, 58, 59, 60, 61, 62, 63, 64, 67, 75, 76, 78, 98, 101, 102, 110, 151, 167, 168, 172, 237, 246, 266, 289, 299

preparation program, v, ix, x, xi, 2, 4, 7, 9, 23, 31, 40, 45, 51, 52, 59, 63, 75, 76, 102, 299

preprocess, 79

preschool, viii, xiv, 13, 14, 15, 20, 24, 27, 29, 30, 33, 34, 35, 55, 56, 57, 63, 66, 74, 78, 79, 87, 88, 89, 90, 95, 104, 105, 107, 108, 109, 111, 112, 113, 114, 118, 119, 120, 122, 124, 126, 127, 129, 130, 133, 135, 136, 137, 138, 234, 235, 243, 244, 245, 246, 248, 249, 251, 254, 255, 256, 259, 261, 263, 264, 271, 272, 279, 280, 283, 284, 286, 287, 290, 291, 292, 293, 294, 295, 298, 300, 302

preschool children, 13, 14, 66, 272, 293, 300

preschoolers, 72, 243

preservice teachers, 302, 309, 336, 338, 341

primary school, 179, 180

principles, xi, xiii, 53, 58, 86, 87, 95, 97, 102, 104, 110, 112, 114, 123, 129, 133,

134, 136, 150, 185, 199, 216, 221, 228, 229, 230, 243, 245, 278

proactive, xiv, 36, 37, 52, 54, 64, 272, 274, 281, 288, 290, 292, 293, 294, 295, 296, 298

pro-active, 24

proactive thinking, 36, 288, 292, 293, 295

problem behavior, 73, 279

problem solving, 148

problem-based learning, 174

problem-solving, 8, 69, 147, 168

problem-solving skills, 69, 147

professional development, ix, 2, 9, 30, 52, 54, 58, 60, 62, 64, 97, 148, 267, 268, 278, 299, 302, 306, 307, 308, 332, 334, 336

professional development programs, 306

professional development programs., 306

professional identity, 175, 248, 265

professional learning communities, 332, 341

professional literature, 147

professional preparation, ix, 2, 54

professional teacher, 240

professionalism, 52, 171, 208, 214, 218, 219, 232, 245, 253, 261, 265

professionalization, 262

professionals, ix, xiii, 2, 99, 141, 157, 159, 160, 161, 167, 169, 194, 230, 237, 239, 245, 264, 266, 337, 341

project, 9, 15, 16, 20, 21, 56, 123, 236, 334, 339, 341

prosocial behavior, 22, 23, 24

proximal processes, 42, 47

psychological problems, 213

psychological processes, 73

psychological tools, 47, 50

psychologist, 204, 214, 286, 287, 292, 293, 338

psychology, 66, 71, 223, 303

psychotherapy, 147, 276, 302

public education, 112

Q

qualitative, xi, xii, 12, 67, 102, 141, 153, 156, 179, 184, 187, 198, 200, 232, 233, 237, 265, 267, 300, 301, 313, 335, 337, 340, 341

qualitative analysis, 187, 198, 200

qualitative analysis findings, 198

qualitative analysis of data, 200

qualitative approach, 198

qualitative methodology, 198

qualitative research, 67, 156, 179, 232, 233, 237, 301, 313

qualitative study, 187, 265

quality, 10, 30, 41, 47, 53, 54, 60, 62, 66, 68, 110, 114, 127, 133, 139, 155, 185, 258, 273, 282, 289, 336

quantitative analyses, xiii, 184, 187, 198, 200

quantitative analysis, 198

R

racial, 105, 106

rationality, 311, 316, 317, 319, 332, 333

reactive, 24, 46, 54, 59, 236, 281, 288, 295, 296

read-alouds, 9, 12, 14, 15, 73

reading, 4, 10, 12, 13, 14, 20, 57, 73, 74, 93, 94, 116, 120, 122, 126, 127, 130, 138, 139, 140, 186, 199, 231, 249, 328

reality, xii, 54, 105, 138, 139, 177, 184, 195, 224, 229, 230, 247

reasoning, 150, 316, 317, 319, 320, 321, 323, 324, 325, 328, 330, 331, 341, 344, 345

reciprocal interaction, 42

reciprocity, 17, 31, 36, 47, 48, 49, 50, 251, 252, 256, 260, 261

reflect, 17, 32, 41, 44, 55, 77, 78, 79, 85, 96, 109, 111, 112, 119, 127, 153, 154, 165,

194, 225, 263, 307, 312, 317, 332, 333, 334, 339

reflection, x, xiv, 5, 12, 28, 29, 31, 41, 44, 57, 73, 76, 78, 79, 80, 93, 96, 97, 102, 109, 114, 118, 119, 124, 126, 132, 133, 149, 154, 155, 156, 158, 162, 163, 177, 179, 241, 275, 282, 295, 303, 305, 306, 307, 308, 309, 310, 311, 312, 313, 314, 315, 317, 318, 319, 325, 326, 331, 333, 334, 341, 344

reflection journals, 306, 314, 315, 317

reflective, xi, 9, 11, 16, 28, 41, 78, 80, 98, 99, 107, 109, 137, 141, 144, 146, 149, 150, 151, 154, 155, 157, 172, 174, 179, 247, 248, 262, 263, 264, 276, 291, 300, 301, 302, 303, 308, 311, 312, 313, 316, 320, 326, 333, 336, 338, 341, 343, 344

reflective practice, 78, 109, 149, 150, 179, 276, 300, 301, 302, 303, 338, 341

reflective writing, 313

relations with parents, xii, 184, 187, 197, 203, 204, 205, 211, 212, 213, 219, 220, 222, 223, 224, 225, 228, 229, 230, 244, 246, 260, 265

relationship, xiii, xiv, 20, 25, 29, 30, 35, 36, 37, 41, 99, 163, 164, 185, 189, 190, 217, 239, 240, 241, 244, 245, 249, 251, 252, 253, 255, 256, 257, 259, 260, 261, 262, 263, 266, 272, 275, 281, 301

religion, 131, 192, 209

repeated narrative writing, vi, viii, xiv, 271, 272, 275, 276, 287, 294, 295, 297, 298, 304

repeated picture book reading, ix, 1, 6, 7, 9, 12, 16, 73

representation, 117, 146, 147, 212, 213, 224, 243, 247, 257

research design, 233, 278, 307, 312, 313, 314, 315, 333

research-based theory, 308

respect, 13, 35, 49, 123, 146, 164, 171, 231, 254, 255, 258, 259, 261, 310, 321, 322, 325

respectful, xii, 144, 156, 157, 162, 164, 165, 168, 171, 172, 243, 282

responding, 142, 229

response, 4, 38, 39, 48, 118, 134, 140, 150, 159, 221, 281, 298

responsibility, iv, 30, 38, 52, 55, 62, 90, 162, 167, 170, 190, 195, 229, 243, 245, 258, 290, 291, 311, 330

responsibility for learning, 245

responsiveness, 21, 45, 48, 108, 152, 191, 222, 228, 235

responsiveness strategy, 223

role play, 24, 148, 156, 169, 171, 174, 175, 178, 179, 180

role-playing, xii, 144, 147, 148, 151, 152, 156, 157, 158, 159, 161, 162, 163, 165, 167, 169, 171, 172, 173

rules, 27, 32, 33, 35, 36, 39, 45, 53, 56, 147, 162, 207, 246, 259, 277

S

safe, xii, 10, 35, 110, 115, 144, 147, 148, 153, 158, 172, 323, 324, 325

same-gender parenthood, 31

scalable, 11

scholastic achievement, 282

school activities, 227

school advisors, 196

school climate, 144, 185

school culture, 31, 106, 193

school failure, 68, 302

school performance, 166

school success, 105

school work, 8, 18

school-family relations, xiii, 184, 193, 200, 228

schooling, 108, 142, 191, 310, 325

Index

Schooling Law, 107
science, 8, 51, 62, 111, 341, 344
scientific knowledge, 149
scientific theory, 247
second language, 10, 99, 116, 178, 327
secondary education, 340
secondary schools, 178, 181
secondary students, 334
selective coding, 199
self-awareness, xii, 144, 148
self-confidence, 13, 274
self-correction, 54, 164
self-determination, viii, xiv, 272, 274, 275, 281, 283, 285, 286, 287, 288, 295, 296, 297, 298, 303
self-efficacy, viii, xii, xiv, 17, 26, 34, 65, 71, 144, 151, 186, 187, 190, 272, 274, 275, 287, 300, 301
self-esteem, 65, 70
self-expression, 119, 132
self-reflection, x, 29, 76, 96, 114, 133, 177
self-regulation, xiv, 29, 50, 53, 64, 205, 272, 273, 274, 275, 282, 295, 298, 304
semi-structured interviews, 81, 82, 307, 317, 333
sensitivity, xiii, 3, 21, 44, 71, 106, 115, 119, 138, 148, 157, 175, 184, 185, 194, 209, 212, 214, 216, 224, 229
separate, 89, 208, 257
siblings, 30, 42, 213, 224
siblings with special needs, 213
simulation, vi, viii, xi, 32, 143, 146, 147, 148, 149, 151, 152, 153, 154, 155, 156, 157, 158, 159, 160, 161, 162, 163, 169, 171, 172, 173, 175, 176, 177, 178, 179, 180, 181
single-parent families, 31, 57, 113
skills, x, xii, xiv, 5, 8, 12, 16, 18, 24, 25, 39, 69, 70, 73, 76, 78, 86, 96, 105, 106, 108, 110, 115, 123, 124, 136, 137, 144, 146, 147, 149, 150, 151, 153, 163, 165, 171, 172, 175, 176, 179, 184, 186, 187, 197,

221, 223, 228, 229, 231, 236, 240, 246, 249, 268, 272, 273, 308
small, vii, viii, x, 1, 3, 4, 6, 7, 8, 9, 11, 12, 14, 15, 16, 17, 19, 20, 22, 24, 25, 26, 27, 29, 36, 39, 41, 44, 45, 49, 50, 51, 52, 56, 57, 60, 61, 70, 73, 74, 77, 78, 79, 81, 82, 88, 89, 91, 100, 102, 103, 104, 105, 107, 111, 112, 113, 115, 119, 120, 122, 124, 126, 127, 128, 129, 131, 133, 135, 137, 140, 142, 159, 186, 196, 248, 251, 261, 276, 282, 299
small group, ix, 2, 3, 7, 9, 14, 15, 16, 17, 19, 20, 22, 24, 25, 26, 29, 36, 39, 41, 44, 45, 49, 51, 52, 56, 57, 60, 61, 70, 73, 74, 78, 79, 81, 82, 88, 91, 100, 102, 103, 104, 105, 111, 113, 115, 119, 124, 126, 127, 128, 129, 135, 137, 142
small group work, 7, 15, 25, 39, 42, 44, 49, 60, 61, 73, 100, 142
small heterogeneous groups, ix, x, 1, 4, 9, 11, 19, 50, 102, 112, 119, 137
social, ix, x, xii, 2, 3, 4, 5, 6, 7, 9, 10, 11, 12, 16, 17, 20, 21, 22, 23, 24, 25, 26, 27, 28, 30, 39, 41, 43, 44, 46, 47, 50, 52, 58, 60, 65, 66, 67, 68, 69, 70, 71, 72, 73, 74, 76, 77, 78, 94, 98, 102, 103, 104, 105, 106, 108, 109, 110, 113, 115, 117, 119, 122, 123, 124, 132, 133, 136, 137, 138, 140, 141, 144, 152, 154, 173, 177, 184, 185, 187, 190, 191, 193, 194, 195, 196, 198, 199, 202, 204, 212, 213, 214, 217, 221, 222, 224, 227, 228, 229, 235, 236, 237, 243, 254, 265, 268, 272, 273, 278, 282, 300, 302, 303, 304, 338, 345
social adjustment, 173, 185, 227
social behavior, 24, 25, 44, 177, 237, 278
social change, 185, 191
social class, 105, 106, 213, 224
social cognitive approach to learning, 4
social competence, 22, 23, 24, 25, 26, 27, 44, 58, 65, 66, 72
social competencies, 9, 11, 16, 23, 278

Index

social construct, x, 76, 78, 95, 102, 108, 109, 110, 138
social constructivist, x, 76, 78, 95, 102, 108, 109, 110
social constructivist perception, x, 76, 78, 95, 102, 110
social development, 24, 25, 71, 185, 303
social episodes, xii, 6, 24, 25, 41, 60, 184, 187, 198, 199, 202, 212, 213, 214, 217, 222, 228
social exchange, 105, 115, 132
social group, 193, 219
social interaction, 22, 50, 104, 272, 345
social justice, 71, 141
social learning, 17
social life, 105
social norms, 190
social participation, 43
social phenomena, 50
social problems, 23, 26, 29, 30, 60
social reality, xii, 184, 196, 221, 229
social skills, 12, 16, 25, 73, 123, 124, 136, 144
social support, 20, 21, 65
socially, 4, 102, 110, 113, 120, 211, 272, 298
socially diverse, 113, 120
society, viii, xiii, 47, 73, 106, 139, 142, 184, 186, 187, 192, 193, 195, 197, 215, 219, 221, 222, 224, 228, 229, 230, 231, 237, 265, 309, 324
socio-constructivist, 18, 46, 77, 80
sociocultural, 104, 117, 122
sociocultural backgrounds, 122
socio-culturally, 126
socio-economic status (SES), 32, 113, 279, 280
Socratic dialogues, 317
special education, xiii, 108, 140, 177, 196, 204, 230, 235, 237, 239, 246

special needs, 10, 77, 106, 108, 192, 195, 196, 204, 209, 213, 217, 219, 220, 224, 225, 227
special needs children, 10, 77, 192, 195, 204, 209, 213, 217, 224, 225
special needs education, 214
special-needs children, 186, 200
special-needs siblings, 224
speech, 48, 293, 294
spelling, 276, 277
staff, ix, xii, xiv, 2, 15, 19, 27, 28, 29, 37, 38, 39, 40, 42, 45, 52, 54, 57, 59, 60, 61, 62, 63, 64, 66, 88, 106, 158, 161, 184, 200, 202, 203, 206, 207, 208, 209, 210, 212, 213, 214, 218, 219, 220, 221, 222, 225, 226, 227, 229, 230, 231, 244, 249, 256, 262,267, 268, 272, 274, 279, 280, 281, 283, 285, 288, 290, 291, 292, 295, 298, 299, 334
staff development, 268
staff members, ix, 2, 38, 45, 59, 60, 61, 62, 88, 206, 281
staff work, ix, 2, 46, 59
stereotypes, 191, 225, 227, 229
stereotypical thinking, 227
strategic management, 173
strategies, xii, xiv, 7, 8, 22, 23, 26, 54, 57, 95, 99, 115, 177, 179, 184, 186, 187, 189, 196, 197, 201, 221, 222, 225, 228, 229, 231, 240, 246, 275, 276, 278, 281, 285, 296, 300, 302
stress, 22, 71, 86, 88, 95, 112, 166, 186, 187, 274, 279, 302, 312
stressful events, 304
structuring, 186, 222
student achievement, 234
studies, vii, viii, x, xi, xii, 1, 8, 9, 11, 15, 23, 26, 43, 53, 54, 55, 56, 57, 76, 79, 80, 95, 96, 97, 102, 110, 111, 112, 115, 124, 133, 137, 139, 141, 146, 147, 152, 166, 169, 173, 174, 179, 184, 186, 194, 197, 202, 217, 227, 231, 232, 247, 248, 272,

276, 279, 299, 300, 335, 336, 337, 340, 341

studies approach is used to reveal the learning processes, x

supervision, 10, 194, 210, 215

supervisor, 205, 209, 215, 216

support, x, xi, xiv, 16, 17, 20, 21, 22, 24, 25, 26, 30, 31, 35, 43, 50, 52, 56, 59, 60, 61, 62, 63, 65, 67, 68, 69, 74, 76, 79, 80, 88, 96, 97, 102, 103, 110, 111, 112, 118, 144, 167, 181, 185, 186, 189, 216, 225, 244, 253, 262, 275, 279, 291, 292, 296, 298, 301, 302, 305, 306, 307, 316, 318, 332, 333, 334, 344

support staff, 262

support system, x, xi, 76, 79, 96, 102, 110, 111, 112, 118, 244

suspicion, 56, 145, 190, 191, 250, 253, 254, 260, 263, 264

sustainable, 11, 61, 63

sustained, x, 4, 11, 59, 76, 103, 104, 105, 113, 119, 122, 132, 133, 135, 137, 174

sustained group, 105, 122, 132, 135, 137

symbol, 117, 257, 261

T

teacher beliefs, 24, 74, 306, 340

teacher development, xiv, 305, 310, 319, 336, 339, 345

teacher education, v, ix, xii, 1, 2, 5, 6, 7, 9, 31, 39, 46, 55, 58, 59, 61, 62, 64, 65, 67, 68, 71, 72, 73, 99, 144, 175, 176, 177, 179, 180, 184, 185, 186, 187, 196, 197, 221, 223, 227, 228, 230, 232, 237, 265, 276, 282, 299, 301, 303, 306, 307, 332, 338, 339, 340, 341, 345

teacher education colleges, 230

teacher education institutions, xii, 184, 186, 187, 197, 221, 223, 227, 228, 230

teacher education programs, xii, 144, 186, 196, 230

teacher parent relations, 192

teacher preparation, x, 2, 9, 23, 30, 31, 52, 54, 55, 57, 58, 59, 61, 62, 67, 77, 102, 103, 299

teacher preparation programme, 77, 102

teacher reflection, 175, 306, 313, 333

teacher relationships, 235, 246, 252

teacher thinking, 306, 307, 309, 336, 337, 339, 345

teacher training, vii, ix, xi, 2, 4, 54, 73, 143, 146, 149, 151, 152, 165, 168, 169, 171, 172, 179, 228, 269, 273, 307, 324, 332, 334, 339

teacher vocabulary, 306

teacher-child interactions, 30, 43, 267

teacher-parent communication, 166, 171, 172, 176, 180, 185

teacher-parent relations, 30, 31, 42, 185, 226

teacher-parent relationships, 30, 31, 42

teachers from minority backgrounds, 218

teachers from minority groups, 225

teaching evaluation, 173

teaching experience, 248, 279, 308, 312, 317, 320, 323, 326, 327

teaching practices, vi, viii, x, xiv, 5, 78, 102, 305, 307, 319, 333, 334

teaching strategies, 177

teaching-learning processes, x, 76, 81, 87, 90, 91, 97

technological changes, 231

technology, 19, 70, 105, 181, 186, 192, 194

tension, 145, 185, 190, 194, 195, 196, 206, 209, 231, 254

theoretical approach, 84

therapeutic interventions, 194

therapeutic relationship, 164

therapist, 164, 277, 294

therapy, 276, 293

Index

thinking, viii, xiv, 8, 17, 29, 37, 48, 69, 86, 91, 98, 105, 109, 110, 119, 147, 149, 150, 162, 206, 248, 252, 266, 281, 286, 287, 289, 292, 294, 295, 298, 302, 305, 306, 307, 309, 310, 311, 315, 320, 323, 326, 333, 336, 338, 345

thoughts, viii, xii, 3, 18, 26, 41, 43, 45, 74, 78, 79, 89, 90, 91, 93, 95, 96, 109, 110, 115, 123, 126, 132, 136, 137, 142, 144, 148, 149, 150, 151, 154, 168, 172, 215, 240, 247, 274, 282, 289, 291, 304, 309, 314, 343, 344

threat, 253, 288

toddlers, 235, 272

tolerance, 110, 115, 117, 136

traditional, x, 18, 20, 76, 78, 80, 83, 84, 85, 87, 92, 94, 95, 97, 99, 108, 114, 121, 122, 135, 136, 142, 152, 175, 186, 194, 209, 224, 231, 338

traditional-positivist, x, 76, 94

training, x, xii, xiv, 3, 5, 55, 73, 77, 102, 137, 144, 146, 148, 149, 151, 152, 163, 169, 172, 173, 174, 176, 177, 178, 180, 181, 187, 191, 196, 199, 221, 229, 235, 240, 241, 244, 245, 246, 248, 262, 264, 274, 299, 300, 306, 332, 334

training program, 77, 137, 146, 149,

transcendence, 48, 49, 304

transformation, vii, ix, x, 75, 76, 79, 80, 82, 83, 84, 85, 86, 87, 89, 90, 91, 92, 93, 94, 95, 96, 97, 98, 110, 114, 296

transformation processes, 76, 84, 97, 110

transformative learning, 5, 76, 79, 80

treatment, 191, 196, 205, 214, 227, 293, 294

trust, xii, xiii, 31, 35, 36, 144, 145, 158, 159, 165, 166, 172, 173, 174, 176, 177, 180, 184, 189, 191, 203, 205, 211, 212, 215, 219, 220, 222, 223, 224, 225, 229, 243, 248, 250, 251, 252, 253, 254, 256, 263, 266, 282, 302

trusting, 23, 54, 205

U

understanding, iv, xii, 3, 7, 10, 11, 12, 13, 17, 21, 23, 24, 31, 32, 34, 35, 36, 37, 41, 43, 45, 52, 73, 77, 80, 89, 96, 97, 103, 109, 118, 119, 129, 131, 132, 139, 144, 145, 148, 150, 151, 155, 157, 159, 161, 164, 167, 168, 184, 186, 187, 193, 198, 200, 231, 241, 244, 246, 248, 249, 252, 258, 260, 261, 264, 266, 275, 277, 281, 284, 293, 294, 298, 306, 310, 311, 336, 337, 340, 341

universities, 57, 58, 234, 246

upper class mother, 217

upper class parents, 217, 218

upper-secondary students, 334

V

values, 5, 80, 90, 96, 103, 107, 115, 116, 119, 132, 136, 149, 170, 189, 193, 274, 304, 344

victims, 286, 288, 295, 296

videotaped simulations, viii, xi, 32, 33, 144

violence, 73, 207, 210, 244, 289

violent behavior, 205, 218

visual, 78, 82, 109, 247, 251, 256

visual images, 251

vocabulary, 12, 110, 306, 314, 317, 326, 339

vocational training, 147

W

weaker social groups, 219

welfare, 158, 173, 194, 225, 226, 243, 273

welfare system, 225

well-being, 4, 6, 8, 30, 31, 39, 41, 43, 45, 52, 53, 54, 60, 146, 157, 168, 171, 265,

273, 274, 276, 282, 283, 289, 296, 298, 303
work with parents, ix, 2, 31, 33, 34, 36, 37, 56, 165, 172, 187, 197, 198, 202, 221, 222, 229, 249
working with parents, xi, xii, xiv, 35, 37, 39, 46, 57, 143, 184, 186, 187, 191, 196, 214, 221, 230, 231, 240

worldview, 200, 203, 208, 209, 211, 212, 219, 220, 222, 223, 226
written accounts, 32, 33, 34, 198, 199

Y

young people, 328, 329

Related Nova Publications

Research in Education: Teacher Training Issues

Editors: Fernando Córdova Lepe, Ph.D. and Héctor Rojas Castro

Series: Education in a Competitive and Globalizing World

Book Description: This book includes varied research articles associated to the initial training of teachers in a wide range of areas and developed by groups of researchers linked to one of the abovementioned plans in a Chilean university.

Softcover ISBN: 978-1-53614-914-2
Retail Price: $95

Understanding Cultural Diversity in Education: Perceptions, Opportunities and Challenges

Author: Inmaculada González-Falcón

Series: Education in a Competitive and Globalizing World

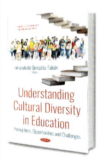

Book Description: *Understanding Cultural Diversity in Education: Perceptions, Opportunities and Challenges* is the result of a collective work by different European, American and Asian experts. The aim is to encourage reflection on cultural diversity in the area of social sciences, particularly in the field of education.

Hardcover ISBN: 978-1-53614-061-3
Retail Price: $195

To see complete list of Nova publications, please visit our website at www.novapublishers.com